WITHDRAWN

THE GREEK ANTHOLOGY
IV

LCL 85

THE GREEK ANTHOLOGY

BOOKS X–XII

WITH AN ENGLISH TRANSLATION BY

W. R. PATON

HARVARD UNIVERSITY PRESS

CAMBRIDGE, MASSACHUSETTS

LONDON, ENGLAND

First published 1918
Revised and reprinted 1971, 1979

LOEB CLASSICAL LIBRARY® is a registered trademark
of the President and Fellows of Harvard College

ISBN 978-0-674-99094-4

Printed on acid-free paper and bound by
The Maple-Vail Book Manufacturing Group

CONTENTS

GREEK ANTHOLOGY

BOOK X

THE HORTATORY AND ADMONITORY EPIGRAMS

THE first seventeen epigrams in this book, some very pretty, are chiefly addresses to harbour gods derived from all three of the main sources of the *Anthology*. We have next, with some epigrams from Agathias' Cycle and some others inserted, a large collection of the epigrams of Palladas of Alexandria, a versifier as to whose merit there is much difference of opinion, but who is at least interesting as the sole poetical representative of his time and surroundings (Nos. 18–99). Then we have (100–103) a short fragment of Philippus' *Stephanus*, and then a miscellany mostly not of epigrams but of verse extracts from literary sources.

ΑΝΘΟΛΟΓΙΑ

I

ΕΠΙΓΡΑΜΜΑΤΑ ΠΡΟΤΡΕΠΤΙΚΑ

1.—ΛΕΩΝΙΔΟΥ

Ὁ πλόος ὡραῖος· καὶ γὰρ λαλαγεῦσα χελιδὼν
ἤδη μέμβλωκεν, χὠ χαρίεις Ζέφυρος·
λειμῶνες δ᾽ ἀνθεῦσι, σεσίγηκεν δὲ θάλασσα
  κύμασι καὶ τρηχεῖ πνεύματι βρασσομένη.
ἀγκύρας ἀνέλοιο, καὶ ἐκλύσαιο γύαια,   5
  ναυτίλε, καὶ πλώοις πᾶσαν ἐφεὶς ὀθόνην.
ταῦθ᾽ ὁ Πρίηπος ἐγὼν ἐπιτέλλομαι ὁ λιμενίτας,
  ὤνθρωφ᾽, ὡς πλώοις πᾶσαν ἐπ᾽ ἐμπορίην.

Goldwin Smith in Wellesley's *Anthologia Polyglotta*, p. 49 ;
J. A. Pott, *Greek Love Songs and Epigrams*, i. p. 32 ; H. C.
Beeching, *In a Garden*, p. 96.

2.—ΑΝΤΙΠΑΤΡΟΥ ΣΙΔΩΝΙΟΥ

Ἀκμαῖος ῥοθίη νηῒ δρόμος, οὐδὲ θάλασσα
  πορφύρει τρομερῇ φρικὶ χαρασσομένη·
ἤδη δὲ πλάσσει μὲν ὑπώροφα γυρὰ χελιδὼν
  οἰκία, λειμώνων δ᾽ ἀβρὰ γελᾷ πέταλα.

2

GREEK ANTHOLOGY

BOOK X

THE HORTATORY AND ADMONITORY EPIGRAMS

1.—LEONIDAS

IT is the season for sailing; already the chattering swallow has come, and the pleasant Zephyr, and the meadows bloom, and the sea with its boiling waves lashed by the rough winds has sunk to silence. Weigh the anchors and loose the hawsers, mariner, and sail with every stitch of canvas set. This, O man, I, Priapus, the god of the harbour, bid thee do that thou mayst sail for all kinds of merchandise.

2.—ANTIPATER OF SIDON

IT is the season for the ship to travel tearing through the waves; no longer does the sea toss, furrowed by dreadful fret. Already the swallow is building her round houses under the roof, and the tender leaves of the meadows smile. Therefore, ye

τοὔνεκα μηρύσασθε διάβροχα πείσματα ναῦται,　5
ἕλκετε δ' ἀγκύρας φωλάδας ἐκ λιμένων·
λαίφεα δ' εὐυφέα προτονίζετε.　ταῦθ' ὁ Πρίηπος
ὕμμιν ἐνορμίτας παῖς ἐνέπω Βρομίου.

3.—ΑΔΗΛΟΝ

Εἰς ἀίδην ἰθεῖα κατήλυσις, εἴτ' ἀπ' Ἀθηνῶν
στείχοις, εἴτε νέκυς νίσεαι ἐκ Μερόης.
μὴ σέ γ' ἀνιάτω πάτρης ἀποτῆλε θανόντα·
πάντοθεν εἷς ὁ φέρων εἰς ἀίδην ἄνεμος.

J. A. Symonds, M.D., *Miscellanies.*

4.—ΜΑΡΚΟΥ ΑΡΓΕΝΤΑΡΙΟΥ

Λῦσον ἀπ' εὐόρμων δολιχὰ πρυμνήσια νηῶν,
εὔτροχα δ' ἐκπετάσας λαίφεα ποντοπόρει,
ἔμπορε· χειμῶνες γὰρ ἀπέδραμον, ἄρτι δὲ κῦμα
γλαυκὸν θηλύνει πρηΰγελως Ζέφυρος·
ἤδη καὶ φιλότεκνος ὑπὸ τραυλοῖσι χελιδὼν　5
χείλεσι καρφίτην πηλοδομεῖ θάλαμον·
ἄνθεα δ' ἀντέλλουσι κατὰ χθόνα· τῷ σὺ Πριήπῳ
πειθόμενος πάσης ἅπτεο ναυτιλίης.

5.—ΘΥΙΛΛΟΥ

Ἤδη πηλοδομεῦσι χελιδόνες, ἤδη ἀν' οἶδμα
κολποῦται μαλακὰς εἰς ὀθόνας Ζέφυρος·
ἤδη καὶ λειμῶνες ὑπὲρ πετάλων ἐχέαντο
ἄνθεα, καὶ τρηχὺς σῖγα μέμυκε πόρος.
σχοίνους μηρύεσθε, ἐφ' ὁλκάδα φορτίζεσθε　5
ἀγκύρας, καὶ πᾶν λαῖφος ἔφεσθε κάλοις.
ταῦτ' ὕμμιν πλώουσιν ἐπ' ἐμπορίην ὁ Πρίηπος
ὁ λιμενορμίτης ναυτιλίην γράφομαι.

4

sailors, coil your wet hawsers and drag the anchors from their nests in the harbour. Haul up your well-woven sails. This is the bidding of me, Priapus of the harbour, the son of Bromius.

3.—ANONYMOUS

THE way down to Hades is straight, whether you start from Athens or whether you betake yourself there, when dead, from Meroe. Let it not vex thee to die far from thy country. One fair wind to Hades blows from all lands.[1]

4.—MARCUS ARGENTARIUS

LOOSE the long hawsers from your well-moored ships, and spreading your easily-hoisted sails set to sea, merchant captain. For the storms have taken flight and tenderly laughing Zephyr now makes the blue wave gentle as a girl. Already the swallow, fond parent, is building with its lisping lips its chamber out of mud and straw, and flowers spring up in the land; therefore listen to Priapus and undertake any kind of navigation.

5.—THYILLUS

ALREADY the swallows build their mud houses, already on the flood Zephyr is bosomed in the soft sails. Already the meadows shed flowers over their green leaves, and the rough strait closes its lips in silence. Wind up your hawsers and stow the anchors on shipboard, and give all your canvas to the sheets. This is the advice that Priapus of the harbour writes for you who sail the seas seeking merchandise.

[1] Probably an epitaph on an Athenian who died at Meroe.

6.—ΣΑΤΥΡΟΥ

Ἤδη μὲν Ζεφύροιο ποητόκου ὑγρὸν ἄημα
  ἠρέμα λειμῶνας πίτνει ἐπ' ἀνθοκόμους·
Κεκροπίδες δ' ἠχεῦσι· γαληναίη δὲ θάλασσα
  μειδιάει, κρυερῶν ἄτρομος ἐξ ἀνέμων.
ἀλλ' ἴτε θαρσαλέοι, πρυμνήσια λύετε, ναῦται,   5
  πίτνατε δὲ πτερύγων λεπταλέας στολίδας.
ὦ ἴτ' ἐπ' ἐμπορίην πίσυνοι χαρίεντι Πριήπῳ,
  ὦ ἴτε δὴ λιμένων δαίμονι πειθόμενοι.

7.—ΑΡΧΙΟΥ

Τοῦδέ με κυμοπλῆγος ἐπὶ σκοπέλοιο Πρίηπον
  ναῦται Θρηϊκίου θέντο πόρου φύλακα,
πολλάκις οἷς ἤϊξα ταχὺς καλέουσιν ἀρωγός,
  ξεῖνε, κατὰ πρύμνης ἡδὺν ἄγων Ζέφυρον.
τοὔνεκεν οὔτ' ἄκνισον, ὅπερ θέμις, οὔτ' ἐπιδευῆ   5
  εἴαρος ἀθρήσεις βωμὸν ἐμὸν στεφάνων,
ἀλλ' αἰεὶ θυόεντα καὶ ἔμπυρον· οὐδ' ἑκατόμβη
  τόσσον ὅσον τιμῇ δαίμοσιν ἁνδάνεται.

8.—ΤΟΥ ΑΥΤΟΥ

Βαιὸς ἰδεῖν ὁ Πρίηπος ἐπαιγιαλίτιδα ναίω
  χηλήν, αἰθυίας οὔποτε †ἀντιβίας,[1]
φοξός, ἄπους, οἷόν κεν ἐρημαίῃσιν ἐπ' ἀκταῖς
  ξέσσειαν μογερῶν υἱέες ἰχθυβόλων.
ἀλλ' ἤν τις γριπεύς με βοηθόον ἢ καλαμευτὴς   5
  φωνήσῃ, πνοιῆς ἵεμαι ὀξύτερος.
λεύσσω καὶ τὰ θέοντα καθ' ὕδατος· ἦ γὰρ ἀπ' ἔργων
  δαίμονες, οὐ μορφᾶς γνωστὸν ἔχουσι τύπον.

---

[1] Perhaps αἰθυίαις συντρόφος ἀμφιβίοις, which I render.

6

6.—SATYRUS

ALREADY the moist breath of Zephyr, who giveth birth to the grass, falls gently on the flowery meads. The daughters of Cecrops[1] call, the becalmed sea smiles, untroubled by the cold winds. Be of good heart, ye sailors, loose your hawsers and spread out the delicate folds of your ships' wings. Go to trade trusting in gracious Priapus, go obedient to the harbour god.

7.—ARCHIAS

STRANGER, I, Priapus, was set up on this sea-beaten rock to guard the Thracian strait,[2] by the sailors, whom I had often rushed to help when they called upon me, bringing from astern the sweet Zephyr. Therefore, as is meet and right, thou shalt never see my altar lacking the fat of beasts or crowns in the spring, but ever smoking with incense and alight. Yet not even a hecatomb is so pleasing to the gods as due honour.

8.—BY THE SAME

LITTLE am I to look on, Priapus, who dwell on this spur by the beach, companion of the gulls, denizens of land and sea, with a peaked head and no feet, just such as the sons of toiling fishermen would carve on the desert shore. But if any netsman or rod-fisher call on me for help, I hie me to him quicker than the wind. I see, too, the creatures that move under the water, and indeed the character of us gods is known rather from our actions than from our shapes.

---

[1] i.e. the swallows.　　[2] The Bosporus.

9.—ΑΔΗΛΟΝ

Τὸν βραχύν, ἰχθυβολῆες, ὑπὸ σχίνῳ με Πρίηπον
στειλάμενοι κώπαις τὰν ὀλίγαν ἄκατον,
(δίκτυ' ἄγ' ἁπλώσασθε,) πολὺν δ' ἁλινηχέα βῶκα
καὶ σκάρον, οὐ θρίσσης νόσφιν, ἀρυσσάμενοι,
γλαυκὸν ἐνιδρυνθέντα νάπῃ σημάντορα θήρης   5
τίετ', ἀπ' οὐκ ὀλίγων βαιὸν ἀπαρχόμενοι.

10.—ΑΡΧΙΟΥ ΝΕΩΤΕΡΟΥ

Πανά με τόνδ' ἱερῆς ἐπὶ λισσάδος, αἰγιαλίτην
Πᾶνα, τὸν εὐόρμων τῇδ' ἔφορον λιμένων,
οἱ γριπῆες ἔθεντο· μέλω δ' ἐγὼ ἄλλοτε κύρτοις,
ἄλλοτε δ' αἰγιαλοῦ τοῦδε σαγηνοβόλοις.
ἀλλὰ παράπλει, ξεῖνε· σέθεν δ' ἐγὼ οὕνεκα ταύτης   5
εὐποιῆς πέμψω πρηῢν ὄπισθε νότον.

11.—ΣΑΤΥΡΟΥ

Εἴτε σύ γ' ὀρνεόφοιτον ὑπὲρ καλαμῖδα παλύνας
ἰξῷ ὀρειβατέεις, εἴτε λαγοκτονέεις,
Πᾶνα κάλει.   κυνὶ Πὰν λασίου ποδὸς ἴχνια φαίνει·
σύνθεσιν ἀκλινέων Πὰν ἀνάγει καλάμων.

12.—ΑΔΕΣΠΟΤΟΝ

Τῇδ' ὑπὸ τὰν ἄρκευθον ἴτ' ἀμπαύοντες, ὁδῖται,
γυῖα παρ' Ἑρμείᾳ σμικρὸν ὁδοῦ φύλακι,

8

9.—ANONYMOUS

YE fishermen, who pulled your little boat ashore here (Go, hang out your nets to dry) having had a haul of many sea-swimming bogue and parrot-wrasse, not without shad, honour me with slender first-fruits of a copious catch, the little Priapus under the lentisc bush, the sea-blue god, the revealer of the fish your prey, established in this grove.

10.—ARCHIAS THE YOUNGER

THE fishermen dedicated me, Pan, here on this holy cliff, Pan of the shore, the guardian of this secure haven. Sometimes I care for the weels, and sometimes for the fishers who draw their seine on this beach. But, stranger, sail past, and in return for this beneficence I will send a gentle south-west wind at thy back.

11.—SATYRUS

WHETHER thou walkest over the hills with bird-lime spread on the reeds to which the birds resort, or whether thou killest hares, call on Pan. Pan shows the hound the track of velvet-paw, and Pan guides higher and higher, unbent, the jointed reeden rod.[1]

12.—ANONYMOUS

COME and rest your limbs awhile, travellers, here under the juniper by Hermes, the guardian of the

[1] There was a means of gradually lengthening the limed rod so as to reach the birds high up in the trees. I suppose it was put together like a fishing-rod.

μὴ φύρδαν, ὅσσοι δὲ βαρεῖ γόνυ κάμνετε μόχθῳ
καὶ δίψᾳ, δολιχὰν οἶμον ἀνυσσάμενοι.
πνοιὴ γὰρ καὶ θῶκος εὔσκιος, ἅ θ' ὑπὸ πέτρᾳ   5
πῖδαξ εὐνήσει γυιοβαρῆ κάματον·
ἔνδιον δὲ φυγόντες ὀπωρινοῦ κυνὸς ἆσθμα,
ὡς θέμις, Ἑρμείην εἰνόδιον τίετε.

13.—ΣΑΤΥΡΟΥ

Ἦ καλὸν αἱ δάφναι, καλὸν δ' ὑπὸ πυθμέσιν ὕδωρ
πιδύει, πυκινὸν δ' ἄλσος ὑποσκιάει
τηλεθάον, ζεφύροισιν ἐπίδρομον, ἄλκαρ ὁδίταις
δίψης καὶ καμάτου καὶ φλογὸς ἠελίου.

14.—ΑΓΑΘΙΟΥ ΣΧΟΛΑΣΤΙΚΟΥ

Εὔδια μὲν πόντος πορφύρεται· οὐ γὰρ ἀήτης
κύματα λευκαίνει φρικὶ χαρασσόμενα·
οὐκέτι δὲ σπιλάδεσσι περικλασθεῖσα θάλασσα
ἔμπαλιν ἀντωπὸς πρὸς βάθος εἰσάγεται.
οἱ ζέφυροι πνείουσιν, ἐπιτρύζει δὲ χελιδὼν   5
κάρφεσι κολλητὸν πηξαμένη θάλαμον.
θάρσει, ναυτιλίης ἐμπείραμε, κἂν παρὰ Σύρτιν,
κἂν παρὰ Σικελικὴν ποντοπορῇς κροκάλην·
μοῦνον ἐνορμίταο παραὶ βωμοῖσι Πριήπου
ἢ σκάρον ἢ βῶκας φλέξον ἐρευθομένους.   10

15.—ΠΑΥΛΟΥ ΣΙΛΕΝΤΙΑΡΙΟΥ

Ἤδη μὲν ζεφύροισι μεμυκότα κόλπον ἀνοίγει
εἴαρος εὐλείμων θελξινόοιο χάρις·
ἄρτι δὲ δουρατέοισιν ἐπωλίσθησε κυλίνδροις
ὁλκὰς ἀπ' ἠϊόνων ἐς βυθὸν ἑλκομένη.

road—not a mixed crowd, but those of you whose knees ache from heavy toil and who thirst after accomplishing a long day's journey. There is a breeze and a shady seat, and the fountain under the rock will still the weariness that weighs on your limbs. Escaping the midday breath of Autumn's dog-star, honour Hermes of the wayside as is meet.

13.—SATYRUS

How lovely are the laurels and the spring that gushes at their feet, while the dense grove gives shade, luxuriant, traversed by Zephyrs, a protection to wayfarers from thirst and toil and the burning sun!

14.—AGATHIAS SCHOLASTICUS

THE deep lies becalmed and blue; for no gale whitens the waves, ruffling them to a ripple, and no longer do the seas break round the rocks, retiring again to be absorbed in the depth. The Zephyrs blow and the swallow twitters round the straw-glued chamber she has built. Take courage, thou sailor of experience, whether thou journeyest to the Syrtis or to the beach of Sicily. Only by the altar of Priapus of the harbour burn a parrot-wrasse or some red bogue-fish.

15.—PAULUS SILENTIARIUS

Now the heart-entrancing spring in all the beauty of her meadows opens the closed folds of her bosom to the Zephyrs; now the ship slides down the wooden rollers, pulled from the beach into the deep. Go

λαίφεα κυρτώσαντες ἀταρβέες ἔξιτε, ναῦται,   5
πρηὺν ἀμοιβαίης φόρτον ἐς ἐμπορίης.
πιστὸς νηυσὶ Πρίηπος, ἐπεὶ Θέτιν εὔχομαι εἶναι
ἡμετέρου πατρὸς ξεινοδόκον Βρομίου.

16.—ΘΕΑΙΤΗΤΟΥ ΣΧΟΛΑΣΤΙΚΟΥ

Ἤδη καλλιπέτηλον ἐπ' εὐκάρποισι λοχείαις
λήϊον ἐκ ῥοδέων ἀνθοφορεῖ καλύκων·
ἤδη ἐπ' ἀκρεμόνεσσιν ἰσοζυγέων κυπαρίσσων
μουσομανὴς τέττιξ θέλγει ἀμαλλοδέτην·
καὶ φιλόπαις ὑπὸ γεῖσα δόμους τεύξασα χελιδὼν   5
ἔκγονα πηλοχύτοις ξεινοδοκεῖ θαλάμοις.
ὑπνώει δὲ θάλασσα, φιλοζεφύροιο γαλήνης
νηοφόροις νώτοις εὔδια πεπταμένης,
οὐκ ἐπὶ πρυμναίοισι καταιγίζουσα κορύμβοις,
οὐκ ἐπὶ ῥηγμίνων ἀφρὸν ἐρευγομένη.   10
ναυτίλε, ποντομέδοντι καὶ ὁρμοδοτῆρι Πριήπῳ
τευθίδος ἢ τρίγλης ἀνθεμόεσσαν ἴτυν,
ἢ σκάρον αὐδήεντα παραὶ βωμοῖσι πυρώσας,
ἄτρομος Ἰονίου τέρμα θαλασσοπόρει.

17.—ΑΝΤΙΦΙΛΟΥ

Ἀρχέλεω, λιμενῖτα, σὺ μέν, μάκαρ, ἠπίῳ αὔρῃ
πέμπε κατὰ σταθερῆς οἰχομένην ὀθόνην
ἄχρις ἐπὶ Τρίτωνα· σὺ δ' ἠόνος ἄκρα λελογχὼς
τὴν ἐπὶ Πυθείου ῥύεο ναυστολίην·
κεῖθεν δ', εἰ Φοίβῳ μεμελήμεθα πάντες ἀοιδοί,   5
πλεύσομαι εὐαεῖ θαρσαλέως Ζεφύρῳ.

forth fearlessly, ye sailors, your sails strutting with the wind, to the gentle task of loading the merchandise ye gain by barter. I, Priapus, am faithful to ships, since I boast that Thetis was the hostess of my father Bromius.[1]

16.—THEAETETUS SCHOLASTICUS

ALREADY the fair-foliaged field, at her fruitful birth-tide, is aflower with roses bursting from their buds; already on the branches of the alleyed cypresses the cicada, mad for music, soothes the sheaf-binder, and the martin, loving parent, has made her house under the eaves and shelters her brood in the mud-plastered chamber. The sea sleeps, the calm dear to the Zephyrs spreads tranquilly over the expanse that bears the ships. No longer do the waters rage against the high-built poops, or belch forth spray on the shore. Mariner, roast first by his altar to Priapus, the lord of the deep and the giver of good havens, a slice of a cuttle-fish or of lustred red mullet, or a vocal parrot-wrasse, and then go fearlessly on thy voyage to the bounds of the Ionian Sea.

17.—ANTIPHILUS

BLEST god of the harbour, accompany with gentle breeze the departing sails of Archelaus through the undisturbed water as far as the open sea, and thou who rulest over the extreme point of the beach,[2] save him on his voyage as far as the Pythian shrine. From thence, if all we singers are dear to Phoebus, I will sail trusting in the fair western gale.

---

[1] Hom. *Il.* v. 135.   [2] Another god.

18.—ΑΡΓΕΝΤΑΡΙΟΥ

Γῶβρυ, Διώνυσός σε καὶ ἡ φιλεράστρια Κύπρις
τέρποι, καὶ γλυκεραὶ γράμμασι Πιερίδες·
ὧν μὲν γὰρ σοφίην ἀποδρέπτεο· τῆς δ᾽ ἐς ἔρωτας
ἔρχεο· τοῦ δὲ φίλας λαβροπότει κύλικας.

19.—ΑΠΟΛΛΩΝΙΔΟΥ

Ἡδὺ παρειάων πρῶτον θέρος ἤματι τούτῳ
κείρεο, καὶ γενύων ἠιθέους ἕλικας,
Γάιε· σὸν δὲ πατὴρ χερὶ δέξεται εὐκτὸν ἴουλον
Λεύκιος, αὐξομένου πουλὺν ἐς ἠέλιον.
δωρεῦνται χρυσέοισιν, ἐγὼ δ᾽ ἱλαροῖς ἐλέγοισιν·   5
οὐ γὰρ δὴ πλούτου Μοῦσα χερειοτέρη.

20.—ΑΔΔΑΙΟΥ

Ἤν τινα καλὸν ἴδῃς, εὐθὺς τὸ πρῆγμα κροτείσθω·
βάζ᾽ ἃ φρονεῖς· ὄρχεων δράσσεο χερσὶν ὅλαις·
ἢν δ᾽ εἴπῃς, "Τίω σε, καὶ ἔσσομαι οἷά τ᾽ ἀδελφός,"
αἰδώς σου κλείσει τὴν ἐπὶ τοὔργον ὁδόν.

21.—ΦΙΛΟΔΗΜΟΥ

Κύπρι γαληναίη, φιλονύμφιε, Κύπρι δικαίων
σύμμαχε, Κύπρι Πόθων μῆτερ ἀελλοπόδων,
Κύπρι, τὸν ἡμίσπαστον ἀπὸ κροκέων ἐμὲ παστῶν,
τὸν χιόσι ψυχὴν Κελτίσι νιφόμενον,
Κύπρι, τὸν ἡσύχιόν με, τὸν οὐδενὶ κοῦφα λαλεῦντα,   5
τὸν σέο πορφυρέῳ κλυζόμενον πελάγει,

18.—MARCUS ARGENTARIUS

Gobrys, let Dionysus and Aphrodite, who loves dalliance, delight thee, and the sweet Muses too with their letters. Their wisdom thou hast plucked ; but enter now on her loves and drain his dear bowls.

19.—APOLLONIDES

Shear on this day, Gaius, the first sweet harvest of thy cheeks and the young curls on thy chin. Thy father Lucius will take in his hand what he had prayed to see, the down of thee who shalt grow to look on many suns. Others give golden presents, but I joyful verses ; for indeed the Muse is not the inferior of wealth.

20.—ADDAEUS

If you see a beauty, strike while the iron is hot. Say what you mean, grab his testicles full-handed. But if you say " I reverence you and will be like a brother," shame will close your road to accomplishment.

21.—PHILODEMUS

Cypris of the Calm, lover of bridegrooms ; Cypris, ally of the just ; Cypris, mother of the tempest-footed Loves ; save me, Cypris, a man but half torn away from my saffron bridal chamber, and chilled now to the soul by the snows of Gaul. Save me, Cypris, thy peaceful servant, who utters no vain words to any, tossed as I am now on thy deep blue

Κύπρι φιλορμιστειρα, φιλόργιε, σῶζέ με, Κύπρι,
Ναϊακοὺς ἤδη, δεσπότι, πρὸς λιμένας.

22.—ΒΙΑΝΟΡΟΣ

Μὴ πόδα γυμνὸν ἔρεσσε δι' ὑλάεσσαν ἀταρπὸν
Αἰγύπτου· χαροπῶν φεῦγε διὲξ ὀφίων,
ἀγρεῦ δουνακοδιφα· τὸν ἐκ χέρσου δὲ φύλαξαι
ἰόν, ὁ τοξεύειν ὄρνιν ἐπειγόμενος.

23.—ΑΥΤΟΜΕΔΟΝΤΟΣ

Νικήτης ὀλίγοις μὲν ἐπὶ προτόνοισιν, ἀήτης
οἱάτε, πρηείης ἄρχεται ἐκ μελέτης·
ἀλλ' ὅταν ἐμπνεύσῃ, κατὰ δ' ἱστία πάντα φέρηται,
λαίφεα πακτώσας, μέσσα θέει πελάγη,
ναῦς ἅτε μυριόφορτος, ἕως ἐπὶ τέρματα μύθων   5
ἔλθῃ ἀκυμάντους †ἔμπροσθεν εἰς λιμένας.

24.—ΚΡΙΝΑΓΟΡΟΥ

Φρὴν ἱερὴ μεγάλου 'Ενοσίχθονος, ἔσσο καὶ ἄλλοις
ἠπίη, Αἰγαίην οἳ διέπουσιν ἅλα·
κἠμοὶ γὰρ Θρήϊκι διωκομένῳ ὑπ' ἀήτῃ
ὤρεξας πρηεῖ' ἀσπασίῳ λιμένας.

25.—ΑΝΤΙΠΑΤΡΟΥ

Φοῖβε, Κεφαλλήνων λιμενοσκόπε, θῖνα Πανόρμου
ναίων, τρηχείης ἀντιπέρην 'Ιθάκης,

---

[1] We may compare Book V. 17, and for Naias see Book V.
107. Although he talks as if she were his wife here, she was,
of course, his mistress. It is a question if the cold of Gaul
and the voyage are literal or metaphorical

sea! Cypris, who lovest to bring ships to port, who lovest the solemn rites of wedlock, save me now, my queen, and bring me to the haven of my Naias.[1]

22.—BIANOR

FOWLER in search of reeds, move not with naked feet in the forest paths of Egypt, but fly far from the grey-eyed snakes; and hastening on thy way to shoot the birds of the air, beware of being poisoned by the earth.

23.—AUTOMEDON

NICETES,[2] like the breeze, when a ship has little sail up, begins with gentle rhetoric, but when he blows strongly and all sails are let out, he stiffens the canvas and races across the middle of the ocean, like a ship of vast burden, till he reaches the end of his discourse in the unruffled harbour.

24.—CRINAGORAS

HOLY spirit of the mighty Earth-shaker, be gracious to others, too, who cross the Ægean brine. For to me, driven swiftly by the Thracian breeze,[3] gently hast thou granted the harbour I was fain to reach.

25.—ANTIPATER OF THESSALONICA

PHOEBUS, guardian of the Cephallenians' harbour, dwelling on the beach of Panormus that faces rough

---

i.e. the eloquence of Nicetes. He was a rhetor of the latter end of the first century A.D.
[3] The north wind, the most favourable in summer.

δός με δι' εὐπλώτοιο πρὸς Ἀσίδα κύματος ἐλθεῖν,
Πείσωνος δολιχῇ νηὶ συνεσπόμενον·
καὶ τὸν ἐμὸν βασιλῆα τὸν ἄλκιμον εὖ μὲν ἐκείνῳ   5
ἵλαον, εὖ δ' ὕμνοις ἄρτισον ἡμετέροις.

26.—ΛΟΥΚΙΑΝΟΥ

Ὡς τεθνηξόμενος τῶν σῶν ἀγαθῶν ἀπόλαυε,
  ὡς δὲ βιωσόμενος φείδεο σῶν κτεάνων.
ἔστι δ' ἀνὴρ σοφὸς οὗτος, ὃς ἄμφω ταῦτα νοήσας
  φειδοῖ καὶ δαπάνῃ μέτρον ἐφηρμόσατο.

27.—ΤΟΥ ΑΥΤΟΥ

Ἀνθρώπους μὲν ἴσως λήσεις ἄτοπόν τι ποιήσας,
  οὐ λήσεις δὲ θεοὺς οὐδὲ λογιζόμενος.

28.—ΤΟΥ ΑΥΤΟΥ

Τοῖσι μὲν εὖ πράττουσιν πᾶς ὁ βίος βραχύς ἐστιν,
  τοῖς δὲ κακῶς μία νὺξ ἄπλετός ἐστι χρόνος.

29.—ΤΟΥ ΑΥΤΟΥ

Οὐχ ὁ Ἔρως ἀδικεῖ μερόπων γένος, ἀλλ' ἀκολάστοις
  ψυχαῖς ἀνθρώπων ἔσθ' ὁ Ἔρως πρόφασις.

30.—ΑΔΗΛΟΝ

Ὠκεῖαι χάριτες γλυκερώτεραι· ἢν δὲ βραδύνῃ,
  πᾶσα χάρις κενεή, μηδὲ λέγοιτο χάρις.

Ithaca, grant that I may sail to the Asian land through favouring waves in the wake of Piso's long ship. And attune my doughty emperor to be kind to him and kind to my verses.[1]

26.—LUCIAN

Enjoy thy possessions as if about to die, and use thy goods sparingly as if about to live. That man is wise who understands both these commandments, and hath applied a measure both to thrift and unthrift.

27.—By the Same

If thou doest any foul thing it may perchance be hidden from men, but from the gods it shall not be hidden, even if thou but thinkest of it.

28.—By the Same

For men who are fortunate all life is short, but for those who fall into misfortune one night is infinite time.

29.—By the Same

It is not Love that wrongs the race of men, but Love is an excuse for the souls of the dissolute.

30.—Anonymous

Swift gratitude is sweetest; if it delays, all gratitude is empty and should not even be called gratitude.

---

[1] For Piso see indices to previous volumes. The date is probably A.D. 11, in which year Piso went to govern Pamphylia.

31.—ΛΟΥΚΙΑΝΟΥ

Θνητὰ τὰ τῶν θνητῶν, καὶ πάντα παρέρχεται ἡμᾶς·
ἢν δὲ μή, ἀλλ' ἡμεῖς αὐτὰ παρερχόμεθα.

32.—[ΠΑΛΛΑΔΑ]

Πολλὰ μεταξὺ πέλει κύλικος, καὶ χείλεος ἄκρου.

33.—ΑΔΗΛΟΝ

Ἐσθλὰ λέγειν αἰεὶ πάντας, καλόν· αἰσχρὰ δέ, δεινόν,
κἂν ὦσιν τούτων ἄξιοι ὧν λέγομεν.

34.—ΠΑΛΛΑΔΑ

Εἰ τὸ μέλειν δύναταί τι, μερίμνα καὶ μελετω σοι·
εἰ δὲ μέλει περὶ σοῦ δαίμονι, σοὶ τί μέλει;
οὔτε μεριμνήσεις δίχα δαίμονος, οὔτ' ἀμελήσεις·
ἀλλ' ἵνα σοί τι μέλῃ, δαίμονι τοῦτο μέλει.

A. J. Butler, *Amaranth and Asphodel*, p. 73.

35.—ΛΟΥΚΙΑΝΟΥ

Εὖ πράττων, φίλος εἶ θνητοῖς, φίλος εἶ μακάρεσσι,
καί σευ ῥηϊδίως ἔκλυον εὐξαμένου·
ἢν πταίσῃς, οὐδεὶς ἔτι σοι φίλος, ἀλλ' ἅμα πάντα
ἐχθρά, Τύχης ῥιπαῖς συμμεταβαλλόμενα.

36.—ΤΟΥ ΑΥΤΟΥ

Οὐδὲν ἐν ἀνθρώποισι Φύσις χαλεπώτερον εὗρεν
ἀνθρώπου καθαρὰν ψευδομένου φιλίην·

31.—LUCIAN

ALL that belongs to mortals is mortal, and all things pass us by; or if not, we pass them by.

32.—[PALLADAS][1]

THERE's many a slip 'twixt the cup and the lip.

33.—ANONYMOUS

IT is good to speak ever well of all; but to speak ill is a shame, even if men merit what we say.

34.—PALLADAS

IF concern avail aught, take thought and let things concern thee; but if God is concerned for thee, what does it concern thee? Without God thou shalt neither take thought nor be unconcerned; but that aught concern thee is the concern of God.

35.—LUCIAN

IF thou art fortunate thou art dear to men and dear to gods, and readily they hear thy prayers; but if thou meetest with ill-fortune thou hast no longer any friend, but everything goes against thee, changing with the gusts of fortune.

36.—BY THE SAME

NOTHING more noxious hath Nature produced among men than the man who simulates pure

[1] A very ancient proverb, by some attributed to Homer.

οὐ γὰρ ἔθ᾽ ὡς ἐχθρὸν προφυλασσόμεθ᾽, ἀλλ᾽ ἀγα-
πῶντες
ὡς φίλον, ἐν τούτῳ πλείονα βλαπτόμεθα.

37.—ΤΟΥ ΑΥΤΟΥ

Ἡ βραδύπους βουλὴ μέγ᾽ ἀμείνων· ἡ δὲ ταχεῖα
αἰὲν ἐφελκομένη τὴν μετάνοιαν ἔχει.

38.—ΔΙΟΝΤΣΙΟΥ

Ὥρη ἐρᾶν, ὥρη δὲ γαμεῖν, ὥρη δὲ πεπαῦσθαι.

39.—ΑΔΗΛΟΝ

Θησαυρὸς μέγας ἔστ᾽ ἀγαθὸς φίλος, Ἡλιόδωρε,
τῷ καὶ τηρῆσαι τοῦτον ἐπισταμένῳ.

40.—ΑΔΗΛΟΝ

Μή ποτε, τὸν παρεόντα παρεὶς φίλον, ἄλλον ἐρεύνα,
δειλῶν ἀνθρώπων ῥήμασι πειθόμενος.

41.—ΛΟΤΚΙΑΝΟΥ

Πλοῦτος ὁ τῆς ψυχῆς πλοῦτος μόνος ἐστὶν ἀληθής·
τἆλλα δ᾽ ἔχει λύπην πλείονα τῶν κτεάνων.
τόνδε πολυκτέανον καὶ πλούσιον ἔστι δίκαιον
κλήζειν, ὃς χρῆσθαι τοῖς ἀγαθοῖς δύναται.
εἰ δέ τις ἐν ψήφοις κατατήκεται, ἄλλον ἐπ᾽ ἄλλῳ   5
σωρεύειν αἰεὶ πλοῦτον ἐπειγόμενος,
οὗτος ὁποῖα μέλισσα πολυτρήτοις ἐνὶ σίμβλοις
μοχθήσει, ἑτέρων δρεπτομένων τὸ μέλι.

---

[1] As a fact said by Timon in speaking of Dionysius of
Heraclea, a Stoic philosopher who deserted to the Epicureans

friendship; for we are no longer on our guard against him as an enemy, but love him as a friend, and thus suffer more injury.

37.—By the Same

Slow-footed counsel is much the best, for swift counsel ever drags repentance behind it.

38.—DIONYSIUS

A time to love, and a time to wed, and a time to rest.[1]

39.—Anonymous

A good friend, Heliodorus, is a great treasure to him who knows also how to keep him.

40.—Anonymous

Never give up the friend you have and seek another, listening to the words of worthless men.

41.—LUCIAN

The wealth of the soul is the only true wealth; the rest has more trouble than the possessions are worth. Him one may rightly call lord of many possessions and wealthy who is able to use his riches. But if a man wears himself out over accounts, ever eager to heap wealth on wealth, his labour shall be like that of the bee in its many-celled honeycomb, for others shall gather the honey.

in his old age. It was preceded by the punning line, ἡνίκ' ἐχρῆν δύνειν, νῦν ἄρχεται ἡδύνεσθαι, "Now when it was time for him to set, he begins to seek pleasure."

42.—ΤΟΥ ΑΥΤΟΥ

Ἀρρήτων ἐπέων γλώσσῃ σφραγὶς ἐπικείσθω·
κρείσσων γὰρ μύθων ἢ κτεάνων φυλακή

43.—ΑΔΗΛΟΝ

Ἐξ ὧραι μόχθοις ἱκανώταται· αἱ δὲ μετ' αὐτὰς
γράμμασι δεικνύμεναι ΖΗΘΙ λέγουσι βροτοῖς.

44.—ΠΑΛΛΑΔΑ

Ἢν ὁ φίλος τι λάβῃ, "Δόμινε φράτερ" εὐθὺς
    ἔγραψεν·
  ἢν δ' αὖ μή τι λάβῃ, τὸ " Φράτερ" εἶπε μόνον·
ὤνια γὰρ καὶ ταῦτα τὰ ῥήματα.   αὐτὰρ ἔγωγε
  οὐκ ἐθέλω Δόμινε, οὐ γὰρ ἔχω δόμεναι.

45.—ΤΟΥ ΑΥΤΟΥ

Ἂν μνήμην, ἄνθρωπε, λάβῃς, ὁ πατήρ σε τί ποιῶν
  ἔσπειρεν, παύσῃ τῆς μεγαλοφροσύνης.
ἀλλ' ὁ Πλάτων σοὶ τῦφον ὀνειρώσσων ἐνέφυσεν,
  ἀθάνατόν σε λέγων καὶ φυτὸν οὐράνιον.
ἐκ πηλοῦ γέγονας· τί φρονεῖς μέγα; τοῦτο μὲν
    οὕτως   5
  εἶπ' ἄν τις, κοσμῶν πλάσματι σεμνοτέρῳ.
εἰ δὲ λόγον ζητεῖς τὸν ἀληθινόν, ἐξ ἀκολάστου
  λαγνείας γέγονας καὶ μιαρᾶς ῥανίδος.

42.—By the Same

Let a seal be set on the tongue concerning words that should not be spoken; for it is better to guard speech than to guard wealth.

43.—Anonymous

Six hours are most suitable for labour, and the four that follow, when set forth in letters,[1] say to men " Live."

44.—PALLADAS

If a friend receives a present he at once writes beginning " Lord brother," but if he gets nothing he only says " Brother." For these words are to be bought and sold. I at least wish no " Lord," for I have nothing to give.[2]

45.—By the Same

If thou rememberest, O man, how thy father sowed thee, thou shalt cease from thy proud thoughts. But dreaming Plato hath engendered pride in thee, calling thee immortal and a "heavenly plant." " Of dust thou art made. Why dost thou think proudly?" So one might speak, clothing the fact in more grandiloquent fiction; but if thou seekest the truth, thou art sprung from incontinent lust and a filthy drop.

[1] The letters of the alphabet were used as figures: ZHΘI (meaning " Live ") is 7, 8, 9, 10.
[2] The pun is on *Domine* (the Latin for "Lord") and *domenai* (the Greek for "to give").

46.—ΤΟΥ ΑΥΤΟΥ

Ἡ μεγάλη παίδευσις ἐν ἀνθρώποισι σιωπή·
μάρτυρα Πυθαγόραν τὸν σοφὸν αὐτὸν ἔχω,
ὅς, λαλέειν εἰδώς, ἑτέρους ἐδίδασκε σιωπᾶν,
φάρμακον ἡσυχίης ἐγκρατὲς εὑρόμενος.

47.—ΤΟΥ ΑΥΤΟΥ

Ἔσθιε, πῖνε, μύσας ἐπὶ πένθεσιν· οὐ γὰρ ἔοικεν
γαστέρι πενθῆσαι νεκρόν· Ὅμηρος ἔφη·
καὶ γὰρ ὁμοῦ θάψασαν ὀλωλότα δώδεκα τέκνα
σίτου μνησαμένην τὴν Νιόβην παράγει.

48.—ΤΟΥ ΑΥΤΟΥ

Μήποτε δουλεύσασα γυνὴ δέσποινα γένοιτο,
ἐστὶ παροιμιακόν. τῷδε δ᾽ ὅμοιον ἐρῶ·
μήτε δίκην δικάσειεν ἀνὴρ γεγονὼς δικολέκτης,
μηδ᾽ ὅταν Ἰσοκράτους ῥητορικώτερος ᾖ.
πῶς γὰρ ὁ μισθαρνεῖν εἰθισμένος οὐδὲν ἑταίρας   5
σεμνότερον, δικάσαι μὴ ῥυπαρῶς δύναται;

49.—ΤΟΥ ΑΥΤΟΥ

Καὶ μύρμηκι χολὴν καὶ σέρφῳ φασὶν ἐνεῖναι·
εἶτα χολὴν μὲν ἔχει ζῷα τὰ φαυλότατα,
ἐκκεῖσθαι δ᾽ ἐμὲ πᾶσι χολὴν μὴ ἔχοντα κελεύεις,
ὡς μηδὲ ψιλοῖς ῥήμασιν ἀνταδικεῖν
τοὺς ἔργοις ἀδικοῦντας; ἀποφράξαντα δεήσει   5
λοιπὸν ὁλοσχοίνῳ τὸ στόμα, μηδὲ πνέειν.

---

¹ Hom. Il. xxiv. 691.

46.—By the Same

SILENCE is men's chief learning. The sage Pythagoras himself is my witness. He, knowing himself how to speak, taught others to be silent, having discovered this potent drug to ensure tranquillity.

47.—By the Same

EAT and drink and keep silence in mourning ; for we should not, as Homer said, mourn the dead with our belly. Yes, and he shows us Niobe, who buried her twelve dead children all together, taking thought for food.[1]

48.—By the Same

IT is a proverb, that no woman who has been a slave should ever become a mistress. I will tell you something similar. " Let no man who has been an advocate ever become a judge, not even if he be a greater orator than Isocrates. For how can a man who has served for hire in a fashion no more respectable than a whore judge a case otherwise than dirtily ? "

49.—By the Same

THEY say that even ants and gnats have bile. So, while the most insignificant beasts have bile, do you bid me have no bile and lie exposed to the attacks of all the world, not even wronging by mere words those who wrong me by deeds ? I have for the rest of my life to stop up my mouth with a rush [2] and not even breathe.

[2] A phrase borrowed from Aeschines, 31, 5, but there it is " to sew up," which is more intelligible.

50.—ΤΟΥ ΑΥΤΟΥ

Τὴν Κίρκην οὔ φημι, καθὼς εἴρηκεν Ὅμηρος,
    ἀντ' ἀνδρῶν ποιεῖν ἢ σύας ἠὲ λύκους
τοὺς αὐτῇ προσιόντας· ἑταίρα δ' οὖσα πανοῦργος,
    τοὺς δελεασθέντας πτωχοτάτους ἐποίει·
τῶν δ' ἀνθρωπείων ἀποσυλήσασα λογισμῶν,   5
    εἶτ' ἀπὸ τῶν ἰδίων μηδὲν ἔχοντας ἔτι
ἔτρεφεν ἔνδον ἔχουσα δίκην ζῴων ἀλογίστων.
    ἔμφρων δ' ὢν Ὀδυσεύς, τὴν νεότητα φυγών,
οὐχ Ἑρμοῦ, φύσεως δ' ἰδίας ἐμφύντα λογισμὸν
    εἶχε γοητείας φάρμακον ἀντίπαλον.   10

51.—ΤΟΥ ΑΥΤΟΥ

Ὁ φθόνος οἰκτιρμοῦ, κατὰ Πίνδαρον, ἐστὶν ἀμείνων·
    οἱ βασκαινόμενοι λαμπρὸν ἔχουσι βίον·
τοὺς δὲ λίαν ἀτυχεῖς οἰκτείρομεν. ἀλλά τις εἴην
    μήτ' ἄγαν εὐδαίμων, μήτ' ἐλεεινὸς ἐγώ.
ἡ μεσότης γὰρ ἄριστον, ἐπεὶ τὰ μὲν ἄκρα πέφυκεν   5
    κινδύνους ἐπάγειν, ἔσχατα δ' ὕβριν ἔχει.

52.—ΤΟΥ ΑΥΤΟΥ

Εὖγε λέγων, τὸν Καιρὸν ἔφης θεόν, εὖγε, Μένανδρε,
    ὡς ἀνὴρ Μουσῶν καὶ Χαρίτων τρόφιμος·
πολλάκι γὰρ τοῦ σφόδρα μεριμνηθέντος ἄμεινον
    προσπεσὸν εὐκαίρως εὗρέ τι ταὐτόματον.

53.—ΤΟΥ ΑΥΤΟΥ

Εἰ τοὺς ἀνδροφόνους εὐδαίμονας ὄντας ὁρῶμεν,
    οὐ πάνυ θαυμάζω· τοῦ Διός ἐστι γέρας.

BOOK X. EPIGRAMS 50–53

50.—By the Same

I deny that Circe, as Homer says, changed those who visited her from men into pigs or wolves. No! she was a cunning courtesan, and made them who took her bait poorest of the poor. Stripping them of their human sense, she now, when they could gain nothing for themselves, reared them in her house like senseless animals. But Ulysses, having his wits about him and avoiding the folly of youth, possessed a counter-charm to enchantment, his own nature, not Hermes,[1] emplanting reason in him.

51.—By the Same

Envy, says Pindar, is better than pity.[2] Those who are envied lead a splendid life, while our pity is for the excessively unfortunate. I would be neither too fortunate nor too badly off; for the mean is best, since the height of fortune is apt to bring danger, while the depth of misery exposes to insult.

52.—By the Same

Well didst thou say it, right well, **Menander,** and like a true nursling of the Muses and Graces, that Opportunity is a god; for often a thought that occurs opportunely of itself finds something better than much reflection.

53.—By the Same

That we see murderers blest by fortune does not surprise me much. It is the gift of Zeus. For he

[1] As in Homer.   [2] *Pyth.* i. 85.

τὸν γὰρ γεννήσαντα μεμισηκὼς καὶ ἐκεῖνος
κτεῖνεν ἄν, εἰ ὁ Κρόνος θνητὸς ἐτύγχανεν ὤν·
ἀντὶ δὲ τοῦ κτεῖναι σὺν τοῖς Τιτῆσι κολάζει,   5
δέσμιον, ὡς λῃστήν, εἰς τὸ βάραθρον ἐνείς.

54.—ΤΟΥ ΑΥΤΟΥ

Οὐ ποιεῖ θάνατον μόνον ἡ φθίσις· ἀλλὰ τὸν αὐτὸν
καὶ πολλὴ παχύτης πολλάκις εἰργάσατο.
τοῦδ' ὁ τυραννήσας Διονύσιος Ἡρακλείας
τῆς ἐν τῷ Πόντῳ μάρτυς, ὁ τοῦτο παθών.

55.—ΤΟΥ ΑΥΤΟΥ

Ἂν πάνυ κομπάζῃς προστάγμασι μὴ ὑπακούειν
τῆς γαμετῆς, ληρεῖς· οὐ γὰρ ἀπὸ δρυὸς εἶ,
οὐδ' ἀπὸ πέτρης, φησίν· ὅ θ' οἱ πολλοὶ κατ' ἀνάγκην
πάσχομεν, ἢ πάντες, καὶ σὺ γυναικοκρατῇ.
εἰ δ', "Οὐ σανδαλίῳ," φής, "τύπτομαι, οὐδ', ἀκολά-
    στου   5
οὔσης μοι γαμετῆς, χρή με μύσαντα φέρειν,"
δουλεύειν σε λέγω μετριώτερον, εἴ γε πέπρασαι
σώφρονι δεσποίνῃ μηδὲ λίαν χαλεπῇ.

56.—ΤΟΥ ΑΥΤΟΥ

Οὐδὲν σωφροσύνης τεκμήριόν ἐστι πρόδηλον·
τοῖς ἐμπαιζομένοις ἀνδράσι ταῦτα λέγω.
οὔτε τὸ δύσμορφον πάντως ἀνύποπτον ὑπάρχει,
οὔτ' ἀκολασταίνειν πᾶσα πέφυκε καλή.
καὶ γάρ τις διὰ τὴν ὥραν τοῖς πολλὰ διδοῦσιν   5
οὐχ ἕπεται· πολλὰς δ' ἐστὶ γυναῖκας ἰδεῖν

would have killed his father, whom he hated, had
Cronos chanced to be mortal. Now, instead of killing
him, he punishes him in the same place as the Titans,
casting him bound like a robber into the pit.

54.—By the Same

CONSUMPTION is not the only cause of death, but
extreme obesity often has the same result. Dio-
nysius, tyrant of the Pontic Heraclea, testifies to
this, for it is what befel him.

55.—By the Same

IF you boast that you don't in any way obey your
wife's orders, you are talking nonsense : for you are
not made of tree or stone, as the saying is,[1] and you
suffer what most or all of us suffer, you are ruled by
a woman. But if you say, " She does not smack me
with her slipper, nor have I an unchaste wife whom
I must put up with and shut my eyes," I say your
servitude is milder than that of others, as you have
sold yourself to a chaste and not very severe mistress.

56.—By the Same

THERE is no manifest sign of chastity : this I tell
husbands who are made fools of. Neither are ill-
looks quite free from suspicion, nor is every pretty
woman naturally vicious. For a woman may refuse
to yield to those who are ready to pay a high price
owing to her beauty, and we see many who are not

[1] Hom. *Od.* xix. 162.

οὐχὶ καλὰς τὴν ὄψιν, ὀπυιομένας ἀκορέστως,
καὶ τοῖς χρησαμένοις πολλὰ χαριζομένας.
οὐκ εἴ τις συνάγει τὰς ὀφρύας, οὐδὲ γελῶσα
φαίνεται, ὀφθῆναί τ' ἀνδράσιν ἐκτρέπεται,   10
σωφροσύνης τρόπος οὗτος ἐχέγγυος· ἀλλά τις εὕροι
μαχλάδα μὲν κρύβδην τὴν πάνυ σεμνοτάτην,
τὰς δ' ἱλαρὰς καὶ πᾶσι φιλανθρώπως προσιούσας
σώφρονας, εἰ σώφρων ἐστὶ γυνή τις ὅλως.
ἡλικίᾳ τοίνυν τάδε κρίνεται; ἀλλ' Ἀφροδίτης   15
οἴστρων εἰρήνην οὐδὲ τὸ γῆρας ἔχει.
ὅρκοις λοιπὸν ἄγει τε πεποίθαμεν· ἀλλὰ μεθ' ὅρκον
ζητεῖν ἐστι θεοὺς δώδεκα και †νερεου.[1]

57.—ΤΟΥ ΑΥΤΟΥ

Γαστέρα μισήσειε θεὸς καὶ βρώματα γαστρός·
εἵνεκα γὰρ τούτων σωφροσύνα λύεται.

58.—ΤΟΥ ΑΥΤΟΥ

Γῆς ἐπέβην γυμνός, γυμνός θ' ὑπὸ γαῖαν ἄπειμι·
καὶ τί μάτην μοχθῶ, γυμνὸν ὁρῶν τὸ τέλος;

W. M. Hardinge, in *The Nineteenth Century*, Nov. 1878, p. 886.

59.—ΤΟΥ ΑΥΤΟΥ

Προσδοκίη θανάτου πολυώδυνός ἐστιν ἀνίη·
τοῦτο δὲ κερδαίνει θνητὸς ἀπολλύμενος.
μὴ τοίνυν κλαύσῃς τὸν ἀπερχόμενον βιότοιο·
οὐδὲν γὰρ θανάτου δεύτερόν ἐστι πάθος.

J. A. Pott, *Greek Love Songs and Epigrams*, i. p. 108.

[1] In line 17 I write ἄγει for αἰεί. I suggest at the end καινοτέρους, and render so. "After swearing by the old

good-looking never satisfied with amorous intercourse, and giving large presents to those who possess them. Nor if a woman is always frowning and is never seen to laugh, and avoids showing herself to men, is this behaviour a pledge of chastity. On the contrary, the most grave of them may turn out to be whores in secret, and the merry ones who are amiable to everyone may be virtuous, if any woman is entirely virtuous. Is age, then, a criterion? But not even old age has peace from the goad of Aphrodite. We trust then to oaths and her religious awe. But after her oath she can go and seek out twelve newer gods.

57.—By the Same

May God look with hatred on the belly and its food : for it is owing to them that chastity breaks down.

58.—By the Same

Naked I alighted on the earth and naked shall I go beneath it. Why do I toil in vain, seeing the end is nakedness?

59.—By the Same

The expectation of death is a trouble full of pain, and a mortal, when he dies, gains freedom from this. Weep not then for him who departs from life, for there is no suffering beyond death.

---

twelve gods, she can get twelve new gods to forgive her for her perjury," *i.c.* she can become a Christian and conciliate the Apostles.

60.—ΤΟΥ ΑΥΤΟΥ

Πλουτεῖς· καὶ τι τὸ λοιπόν; ἀπερχόμενος μετὰ σαυτοῦ
τὸν πλοῦτον σύρεις, εἰς σορὸν ἑλκόμενος;
τὸν πλοῦτον συνάγεις δαπανῶν χρόνον· οὐ δύνασαι δὲ
ζωῆς σωρεῦσαι μέτρα περισσότερα.

J. A. Pott, *Greek Love Songs and Epigrams*, i. p. 109.

61.—ΤΟΥ ΑΥΤΟΥ

Φεύγετε τοὺς πλουτοῦντας, ἀναιδέας, οἰκοτυράννους,
μισοῦντας πενίην μητέρα σωφροσύνας.

62.—ΤΟΥ ΑΥΤΟΥ

Οὐ λόγον, οὐ νόμον οἶδε Τύχη, μερόπων δὲ τυραννεῖ,
τοῖς ἰδίοις ἀλόγως ῥεύμασι συρομένη.
μᾶλλον τοῖς ἀδίκοισι ῥέπει, μισεῖ δὲ δικαίους,
ὡς ἐπιδεικνυμένη τὴν ἄλογον δύναμιν.

63.—ΤΟΥ ΑΥΤΟΥ

Μηδέποτε ζήσας ὁ πένης βροτὸς οὐδ' ἀποθνήσκει·
καὶ ζῆν γὰρ δοκέων, ὡς νέκυς ἦν ὁ τάλας.
οἱ δὲ τύχας μεγάλας καὶ χρήματα πολλὰ λαχόντες,
οὗτοι τὸν θάνατον πτῶσιν ἔχουσι βίου.

64.—ΑΓΑΘΙΟΥ ΣΧΟΛΑΣΤΙΚΟΥ

Ἦ ῥά γε πού τὸ φρύαγμα τὸ τηλίκον; οἱ δὲ περισσοι
πῆ ἔβαν ἐξαίφνης ἀγχίποροι κόλακες;

---

[1] "Pulling them into the coffin" (Mackail); "pulled" in
my rendering would mean "driven in a hearse." If σορός is

60.—By the Same

You are wealthy. And what is the end of it? When you depart do you trail your riches after you as you are being pulled to your tomb?[1] You gather wealth spending time, but you cannot pile up a heavier measure of life.

61.—By the Same

Avoid the rich; they are shameless, domestic tyrants, hating poverty, the mother of temperance.

62.—By the Same

Fortune knows neither reason nor law, but rules men despotically, carried along without reason by her own current. She is rather inclined to favour the wicked, and hates the just, as if making a display of her unreasoning force.

63.—By the Same

A poor man has never lived, and does not even die, for when he seemed to be alive the unfortunate wretch was like a corpse. But for those who enjoy great prosperity and much wealth death is the ruin of life.

64.—AGATHIAS SCHOLASTICUS

On a former Magistrate

Where, I ask, is that vast insolence? And where have they suddenly departed, the crowds of flatterers who used to walk by your side? Now you are gone

a portable coffin and not, as I suppose, a stone one, M. is right.

νῦν γὰρ ἑκὰς πτόλιος φυγὰς ᾤχεο· τοῖς πρότερον δε
οἰκτροῖς τὴν κατὰ σοῦ ψῆφον ἔδωκε Τύχη.
πολλή σοι, κλυτοεργὲ Τύχη, χάρις, οὕνεχ᾽ ὁμοίως   5
πάντας ἀεὶ παίζεις, κεῖσέτι τερπόμεθα.

65.—ΠΑΛΛΑΔΑ

Πλοῦς σφαλερὸς τὸ ζῆν· χειμαζόμενοι γὰρ ἐν αὐτῷ
πολλάκι ναυηγῶν πταίομεν οἰκτρότερα.
τὴν δὲ Τύχην βιότοιο κυβερνήτειραν ἔχοντες,
ὡς ἐπὶ τοῦ πελάγους, ἀμφίβολοι πλέομεν,
οἱ μὲν ἐπ᾽ εὐπλοΐην, οἱ δ᾽ ἔμπαλιν· ἀλλ᾽ ἅμα πάντες   5
εἰς ἕνα τὸν κατὰ γῆς ὅρμον ἀπερχόμεθα.

66.—ΑΓΑΘΙΟΥ ΣΧΟΛΑΣΤΙΚΟΥ

Εὖτέ τις ἐκ πενίης πλούτου τύχοι ἠδὲ καὶ ἀρχῆς,
οὐκέτι γινώσκει, τίς πέλε τὸ πρότερον.
τὴν ποτὲ γὰρ φιλίην ἀπαναίνεται· ἀφρονέων δε
τέρψιν ὀλισθηρῆς οὐ δεδάηκε Τύχη.
ἧς ποτε γὰρ πτωχὸς ταλαπείριος· οὐκ ἐθέλεις δέ,   5
αἰτίζων ἀκόλους, νῦν ἑτέροις παρέχειν.
πάντα, φίλος, μερόπεσσι παρέρχεται· εἰ δ᾽ ἀπιθήσεις,
ἔμπαλιν αἰτίζων μάρτυρα σαυτὸν ἔχοις.

67.—ΜΑΚΗΔΟΝΙΟΥ ΥΠΑΤΟΥ

Μνήμη καὶ Λήθη, μέγα χαίρετον· ἡ μὲν ἐπ᾽ ἔργοις
Μνήμη τοῖς ἀγαθοῖς, ἡ δ᾽, ἐπὶ λευγαλέοις.

R. Bland, in *Collections from the Greek Anthology*, 1813,
p. 114 ; J. A. Pott, *Greek Love Songs and Epigrams*, ii. p. 114.

to exile far from the city, and Fortune has made those whom you formerly pitied judges to condemn you. Great thanks to thee, Fortune, performer of glorious deeds, for that thou ever mockest all alike, and we have that to amuse us.

65.—PALLADAS

LIFE is a perilous voyage; for often we are tempest-tossed in it and are in a worse case than shipwrecked men. With Fortune at Life's helm we sail uncertainly as on the open sea, some on a fair voyage, others the reverse: but all alike reach one harbour under the earth.

66.—AGATHIAS SCHOLASTICUS

WHEN a man rises from poverty to wealth and office, he no longer recognizes what he once was. For he repudiates his former friendships, and in his folly learns not how playful slippery fortune is. You were once a miserable pauper, and now you who used to "beg for a pittance"[1] refuse it to others. My friend, everything that is man's passes away, and if you will not believe it, you will go begging again and testify to it yourself.

67.—MACEDONIUS THE CONSUL

MEMORY and Oblivion, all hail! Memory I say in the case of good things, and Oblivion in the case of evil.

---

[1] The phrase is Homeric (*Od.* xvii. 222).

68.—ΑΓΑΘΙΟΥ

Καλὸν μὲν στυγόδεμνον ἔχειν νόον· εἰ δ' ἄρ' ἀνάγκη,
ἀρσενικὴ φιλότης μή ποτε σε κλονέοι.
θηλυτέρας φιλέειν ὀλίγον κακόν, οὕνεκα κειναις
κυπριδίους ὀάρους πότνα δέδωκε φύσις.
δέρκεο τῶν ἀλόγων ζῴων γένος· ἦ γὰρ ἐκείνων   5
οὐδὲν ἀτιμάζει θέσμια συζυγίης·
ἄρσενι γὰρ θήλεια συνάπτεται· οἱ δ' ἀλεγεινοὶ
ἄνδρες ἐς ἀλλήλους ξεῖνον ἄγουσι γάμον.

69.—ΤΟΥ ΑΥΤΟΥ

Τὸν θάνατον τί φοβεῖσθε, τὸν ἡσυχίης γενετῆρα,
τὸν παύοντα νόσους καὶ πενίης ὀδύνας;
μοῦνον ἅπαξ θνητοῖς παραγίνεται, οὐδέ ποτ' αὐτὸν
εἶδέν τις θνητῶν δεύτερον ἐρχόμενον·
αἱ δὲ νόσοι πολλαὶ καὶ ποικίλαι, ἄλλοτ' ἐπ' ἄλλον   5
ἐρχόμεναι θνητῶν, καὶ μεταβαλλόμεναι.

70.—ΜΑΚΗΔΟΝΙΟΥ ΥΠΑΤΟΥ

Εἰ βίον ἐν μερόπεσσι Τύχης παίζουσιν ἑταῖραι
Ἐλπίδες ἀμβολάδην πάντα χαριζόμεναι,
παίζομαι, εἰ βροτός εἰμι. βροτὸς δ' εὖ οἶδα καὶ αὐτὸς
θνητὸς ἐών· δολιχαῖς δ' ἐλπίσι παιζόμενος,
αὐτὸς ἑκοντὶ γέγηθα πλανώμενος, οὐδὲ γενοίμην   5
ἐς κρίσιν ἡμετέρην πικρὸς Ἀριστοτέλης.
τὴν γὰρ Ἀνακρείοντος ἐνὶ πραπίδεσσι φυλάσσω
παρφασίην, ὅτι δεῖ φροντίδα μὴ κατέχειν.

68.—AGATHIAS

It is good to have a mind that hates sexual intercourse, but if you must, let not the love of males ever disturb you. It is a small evil to love women, for gracious Nature gave them the gift of amorous dalliance. Look at the race of beasts; not one of them dishonours the laws of intercourse, for the female couples with the male. But wretched men introduce a strange union between each other.

69.—By the Same

Why fear death, the mother of rest, death that puts an end to sickness and the pains of poverty? It happens but once to mortals, and no man ever saw it come twice. But diseases are many and various, coming first to this man, then to that, and ever changing.

70.—MACEDONIUS THE CONSUL

If the Hopes, the companions of Fortune, make sport of human life, delaying to grant every favour, I am their plaything if I am human, and being mortal, I well know I am human. But being the sport of long-deferred hopes, I am willing and pleased to be deceived, and would not in judging myself be as severe as Aristotle,[1] for I bear in mind Anacreon's advice [2] that we should not let care abide with us.

---

[1] A Roman would have said "Cato."
[2] The reference is to *Anacreontea* xli.

71.—ΤΟΥ ΑΥΤΟΥ

Πανδώρης ὁρόων γελόω πίθον, οὐδὲ γυναῖκα
 μέμφομαι, ἀλλ᾽ αὐτῶν τὰ πτερὰ τῶν Ἀγαθῶν.
ὡς γὰρ ἐπ᾽ Οὐλύμποιο μετὰ χθονὸς ἤθεα πάσης
 πωτῶνται, πίπτειν καὶ κατὰ γῆν ὄφελον.
ἡ δὲ γυνὴ μετὰ πῶμα κατωχρήσασα παρειὰς   5
 ὤλεσεν ἀγλαΐην ὧν ἔφερεν χαρίτων.
ἀμφοτέρων δ᾽ ἥμαρτεν ὁ νῦν βίος, ὅττι καὶ αὐτὴν
 γηράσκουσαν ἔχει, καὶ πίθος οὐδὲν ἔχει.

72.—ΠΑΛΛΑΔΑ

Σκηνὴ πᾶς ὁ βίος καὶ παίγνιον· ἢ μάθε παίζειν,
 τὴν σπουδὴν μεταθείς, ἢ φέρε τὰς ὀδύνας.

J. H. Merivale, in *Collections from the Greek Anthology*,
1813, p. 110 ; John Hall Stevenson, *Crazy Tales*, title-motto ;
J. A. Pott, *Greek Love Songs and Epigrams*, i. p. 106.

73.—ΤΟΥ ΑΥΤΟΥ

Εἰ τὸ φέρον σε φέρει, φέρε καὶ φέρου· εἰ δ᾽ ἀγανακτεῖς
 καὶ σαυτὸν λυπεῖς, καὶ τὸ φέρον σε φέρει.

J. A. Pott, *Greek Love Songs and Epigrams*, i. p. 105.

74.—ΠΑΥΛΟΥ ΣΙΛΕΝΤΙΑΡΙΟΥ

Μήτε βαθυκτεάνοιο τύχης κουφίζεο ῥοίζῳ,
 μήτε σέο γνάμψῃ φροντὶς ἐλευθερίην.
πᾶς γὰρ ὑπ᾽ ἀσταθέεσσι βίος πελεμίζεται αὔραις,
 τῇ καὶ τῇ θαμινῶς ἀντιμεθελκόμενος.
ἡ δ᾽ ἀρετὴ σταθερόν τι καὶ ἄτροπον, ἧς ἔπι μούνης   5
 κύματα θαρσαλέως ποντοπόρει βιότου.

---

[1] *i.e.* the escape of the Goods of life. In the older and
more usual story it is the Evils of life that were in Pandora's
jar and escaped. Macedonius seems in the last lines to make

71.—BY THE SAME

I SMILE when I look on the picture of Pandora's jar, and do not find it was the woman's fault, but is due to the Goods having wings.[1] For as they flutter to Olympus after visiting every region of the world, they ought to fall on the earth too. The woman after taking off the lid grew pale-faced, and has lost the splendour of her former charm. Our present life has suffered two losses; woman is grown old and the jar has nothing in it.

72.—PALLADAS

ALL life is a stage and a play: either learn to play laying your gravity aside, or bear with life's pains.

73.—BY THE SAME

IF the gale of Fortune bear thee, bear with it and be borne; but if thou rebellest and tormentest thyself, even so the gale bears thee.

74.—PAULUS SILENTIARIUS

NEITHER be lifted up by the strong blast of opulent fortune, nor let care bend thy freedom. For all thy life is shaken by inconstant breezes and is constantly dragged this way and that; but virtue is the steadfast and constant support on which alone thou canst travel boldly over the waves of life.

Pandora symbolise womankind in general. The second couplet seems to mean that Pandora thought the Goods would light on earth, but that, instead, they all flew up to the sky.

41

75.—ΠΑΛΛΑΔΑ

Ἠέρα λεπταλέον μυκτηρόθεν ἀμπνείοντες
ζώομεν, ἠελίου λαμπάδα δερκόμενοι,
πάντες ὅσοι ζῶμεν κατὰ τὸν βίον· ὄργανα δ᾽ ἐσμέν,
αὔραις ζωογόνοις πνεύματα δεχνύμενοι.
εἰ δέ τις οὖν ὀλίγην παλάμῃ σφίγξειεν ἀϋτμήν,   5
ψυχὴν συλήσας εἰς ἀΐδην κατάγει.
οὕτως οὐδὲν ἐόντες, ἀγηνορίῃ τρεφόμεσθα,
πνοιῆς ἐξ ὀλίγης ἠέρα βοσκόμενοι.

76.—ΠΑΥΛΟΥ ΣΙΛΕΝΤΙΑΡΙΟΥ

Οὐ τὸ ζῆν χαρίεσσαν ἔχει φύσιν, ἀλλὰ τὸ ῥῖψαι
φροντίδας ἐκ στέρνων τὰς πολιοκροτάφους.
πλοῦτον ἔχειν ἐθέλω τὸν ἐπάρκιον· ἡ δὲ περισσὴ
θυμὸν ἀεὶ κατέδει χρυσομανὴς μελέτη.
ἔνθεν ἐν ἀνθρώποισιν ἀρείονα πολλάκι δήεις   5
καὶ πενίην πλούτου, καὶ βιότου θάνατον.
ταῦτα σὺ γινώσκων κραδίης ἴθυνε κελεύθους,
εἰς μίαν εἰσορόων ἐλπίδα, τὴν σοφίην.

77.—ΠΑΛΛΑΔΑ

Τίπτε μάτην, ἄνθρωπε, πονεῖς καὶ πάντα ταράσσεις,
κλήρῳ δουλεύων τῷ κατὰ τὴν γένεσιν;
τούτῳ σαυτὸν ἄφες, τῷ δαίμονι μὴ φιλονείκει·
σὴν δὲ τύχην στέργων, ἡσυχίην ἀγάπα·
μᾶλλον ἐπ᾽ εὐφροσύνην δὲ βιάζεο, καὶ παρὰ μοίρην,   5
εἰ δυνατόν, ψυχὴν τερπομένην μετάγειν.

75.—PALLADAS

WE live—all who live as this life is—and gaze on the flame of the sun, breathing through our nostrils delicate air; we are organs which receive health as a gift from the life-creating breezes. But if anyone with his hand presses tightly a little of our breath, he robs us of our life and brings us down to Hades. So being nothing we are fed with vanity, pasturing on air drawn from a breath of wind.

76.—PAULUS SILENTIARIUS

THERE is no natural pleasure in life itself, but in casting off from our mind anxieties that whiten the temples. I wish for sufficient wealth, but mad lust for gold is a superfluous care that ever devours the heart. Therefore among men thou shalt often find poverty better than wealth, and death than life. Knowing this, make straight the ways of thy heart, looking to one hope, even to wisdom.

77.—PALLADAS

WHY dost thou labour in vain, O man, and disturb everything, being, as thou art, the slave of the lot that fell to thee at birth? Resign thyself to this, and struggle not against Fate, but content with thy fortune, love tranquillity. Yet strive thou rather, even against Fate, to lead thy delighted spirit to mirth.

78.—ΤΟΥ ΑΥΤΟΥ

Ῥίπτε γόους, μὴ κάμνε, πόσον χρόνον ἐνθάδε μίμνων,
    ὡς πρὸς ἐκεῖνον ὅλον τὸν μετὰ ταῦτα βίον.
πρὶν τοίνυν σκώληκα βαλεῖν τύμβοις τε ῥιφῆναι,
    μη δαμάσῃς ψυχὴν ζῶν ἔτι κρινομένην.

79.—ΤΟΥ ΑΥΤΟΥ

Νυκτὸς ἀπερχομένης γεννώμεθα ἦμαρ ἐπ' ἦμαρ,
    τοῦ προτέρου βιότου μηδὲν ἔχοντες ἔτι,
ἀλλοτριωθέντες τῆς ἐχθεσινῆς διαγωγῆς,
    τοῦ λοιποῦ δὲ βίου σήμερον ἀρχόμενοι.
μὴ τοίνυν λέγε σαυτὸν ἐτῶν, πρεσβῦτα, περισσῶν·   5
    τῶν γὰρ ἀπελθόντων σήμερον οὐ μετέχεις.

80.—ΤΟΥ ΑΥΤΟΥ

Παίγνιόν ἐστι Τύχης μερόπων βίος, οἰκτρός, ἀλήτης,
    πλούτου καὶ πενίης μεσσόθι ῥεμβόμενος.
καὶ τοὺς μὲν κατάγουσα πάλιν σφαιρηδὸν ἀείρει,
    τοὺς δ' ἀπὸ τῶν νεφελῶν εἰς ἀΐδην κατάγει.

81.—ΤΟΥ ΑΥΤΟΥ

Ὦ τῆς βραχείας ἡδονῆς τῆς τοῦ βίου·
τὴν ὀξύτητα τοῦ χρόνου πενθήσατε.
ἡμεῖς καθεζόμεσθα καὶ κοιμώμεθα,
μοχθοῦντες ἢ τρυφῶντες· ὁ δὲ χρόνος τρέχει,
τρέχει καθ' ἡμῶν τῶν ταλαιπώρων βροτῶν,
φέρων ἑκάστου τῷ βίῳ καταστροφήν.

78.—By the Same

Cast away complaint and be not troubled, for how brief is the time thou dwellest here compared with all the life that follows this! Ere thou breedest worms and art cast into the tomb torment not thy soul, as if it were damned while thou still livest.

79.—By the Same

We are born day by day when night departs, retaining nothing of our former life, estranged from the doings of yesterday and beginning to-day the remainder of our life. Do not then, old man, say thy years are too many, for to-day thou hast no part in those that have gone by.

80.—By the Same

The life of men is the plaything of Fortune, a wretched life and a vagrant, tossed between riches and poverty. Some whom she had cast down she casteth on high again like a ball, and others she brings down from the clouds to Hades.

81.—By the Same

Alas for the brevity of life's pleasure! Mourn the swiftness of time. We sit and we sleep, toiling or taking our delight, and time is advancing, advancing against us wretched men, bringing to each the end of life.

82.—ΤΟΥ ΑΥΤΟΥ

Ἆρα μὴ θανόντες τῷ δοκεῖν ζῶμεν μόνον,
Ἕλληνες ἄνδρες, συμφορᾷ πεπτωκότες
ὄνειρον εἰκάζοντες εἶναι τὸν βίον;
ἢ ζῶμεν ἡμεῖς, τοῦ βίου τεθνηκότος;

83.—ΤΟΥ ΑΥΤΟΥ

Καὶ τὸ φρονεῖν πλουτεῦντι περίστασις, ὄχλος·
ἀνάγκη . . .
†ζώνη ποικίλη καὶ κολάκων ἀνάγκη.

84.—ΤΟΥ ΑΥΤΟΥ

Δακρυχέων γενόμην, καὶ δακρύσας ἀποθνήσκω·
δάκρυσι δ᾽ ἐν πολλοῖς τὸν βίον εὗρον ὅλον.
ὦ γένος ἀνθρώπων πολυδάκρυτον, ἀσθενές, οἰκτρόν,
φαινόμενον [1] κατὰ γῆς, καὶ διαλυόμενον.

85.—ΤΟΥ ΑΥΤΟΥ

Πάντες τῷ θανάτῳ τηρούμεθα, καὶ τρεφόμεσθα
ὡς ἀγέλη χοίρων σφαζομένων ἀλόγως.

86.—ΤΟΥ ΑΥΤΟΥ

Οὐ δαψιλῶς μέν, ἀλλ᾽ ὅμως κἀγὼ τρέφω
παῖδας, γυναῖκα, δοῦλον, ὄρνιθας, κύνα·
κόλαξ γὰρ οὐδεὶς τοὺς ἐμοὺς πατεῖ δόμους.

87.—ΤΟΥ ΑΥΤΟΥ

Ἂν μὴ γελῶμεν τὸν βίον τὸν δραπέτην,
Τύχην τε πόρνην ῥεύμασιν κινουμένην,
ὀδύνην ἑαυτοῖς προξενοῦμεν πάντοτε,
ἀναξίους ὁρῶντες εὐτυχεστέρους.

[1] φερόμενον MS.: corr. Boissonade.

82.—By the Same

Is it not true that we are dead and only seem to live, we Greeks,[1] fallen into misfortune, fancying that a dream is life? Or are we alive and is life dead?[2]

83.—By the Same

Even wisdom to the wealthy is a difficulty, a trouble, a necessity . . .

84.—By the Same

In tears I was born and after tears I die, finding the whole of life a place of many tears. O race of men tearful, weak, pitiful, scarce seen on earth and straight dissolved!

85.—By the Same

We are all kept and fed for death, like a herd of swine to be slain without reason.

86.—By the Same

I too rear, not sumptuously, but still I rear children, a wife, a slave, poultry and a dog—for no flatterer sets foot in my house.

87.—By the Same

If we do not laugh at life the runaway, and Fortune the strumpet shifting with the current, we cause ourselves constant pain seeing the unworthy luckier than ourselves.

[1] *i.e.* Pagans.   [2] *cp.* No. 90.

88.—ΤΟΥ ΑΥΤΟΥ

Σῶμα, πάθος ψυχῆς, ἅδης, μοῖρ᾽, ἄχθος, ἀναγκη,
καὶ δεσμὸς κρατερός, καὶ κόλασις βασάνων.
ἀλλ᾽ ὅταν ἐξέλθῃ τοῦ σώματος, ὡς ἀπὸ δεσμῶν
τοῦ θανάτου, φεύγει πρὸς θεὸν ἀθάνατον.

89.—ΤΟΥ ΑΥΤΟΥ

Εἰ θεὸς ἡ Φήμη, κεχολωμένη ἐστὶ καὶ αὐτὴ
῞Ελλησι, σφαλεροῖς ἐξαπατῶσα λόγοις.
Φήμη δ᾽, ἄν τι πάθῃς, ἀναφαίνεται εὐθὺς ἀληθής·
πολλάκι καὶ Φήμην ἔφθασεν ἡ ταχυτής.

90.—ΤΟΥ ΑΥΤΟΥ

῍Ω τῆς μεγίστης τοῦ φθόνου πονηριας·
τὸν εὐτυχῆ μισεῖ τις, ὃν θεὸς φιλεῖ.
οὕτως ἀνόητοι τῷ φθόνῳ πλανώμεθα,
οὕτως ἑτοίμως μωρίᾳ δουλεύομεν.
῞Ελληνές ἐσμεν ἄνδρες ἐσποδωμένοι,   5
νεκρῶν ἔχοντες ἐλπίδας τεθαμμένας·
ἀνεστράφη γὰρ πάντα νῦν τὰ πράγματα.

91.—ΤΟΥ ΑΥΤΟΥ

῞Οταν στυγῇ τις ἄνδρα, τὸν θεὸς φιλεῖ,
οὗτος μεγίστην μωρίαν κατεισάγει·
φανερῶς γὰρ αὐτῷ τῷ θεῷ κορύσσεται,
χόλον μέγιστον ἐκ φθόνου δεδεγμένος,
δεῖ γὰρ φιλεῖν ἐκεῖνον, ὃν θεὸς φιλεῖ.   5

---

[1] No doubt this and No. 89 refer to the contemporary persecution of the Pagans by the Christians under Theodosius. Greek here means non-Christian, as Palladas was himself.

88.—By the Same

The body is an affliction of the soul, it is Hell,
Fate, a burden, a necessity, a strong chain and a
tormenting punishment. But when the soul issues
from the body as from the bonds of death, it flies to
the immortal God.

89.—By the Same

If Rumour be a goddess, she too as well as the
other gods is wroth with the Greeks and cozens
them with deceptive words. Rumour, if any evil
befall thee, at once is proved to be true, and often
the rapidity of events anticipates her.

90.—By the Same

Alas for the extreme malice of envy! A man
hates the fortunate whom God loves. So senselessly
are we led astray by envy; so ready are we to be the
slaves of folly. We Greeks are men reduced to ashes,
having the buried hopes of the dead; for to-day
everything is turned upside down.[1]

91.—By the Same

He who detests a man whom God loves, is guilty
of the greatest folly, for he manifestly takes up arms
against God himself, being gifted by envy with
excessive spite. One should rather love him whom
God loves.

It is hard, however, to find any connexion in thought
between lines 1–4 and what follows, and I quite fail to see
any point in No. 89.

49

92.—ΤΟΥ ΑΥΤΟΥ

Εἰς ἄρχοντα

Ἐπεὶ δικάζεις καὶ σοφιστεύεις λόγοις,
κἀγὼ φέρω σοι τῆς ἐμῆς ἀηδόνος
ἐπίγραμμα σεμνόν, ἄξιον παρρησίας·
ὁ γὰρ σὲ μέλπων τῆς Δίκης ὕμνους χέει.[1]

93.—ΤΟΥ ΑΥΤΟΥ

Βέλτερόν ἐστι τύχης καὶ θλιβομένης ἀνέχεσθαι
ἢ τῶν πλουτούντων τῆς ὑπερηφανίης.

94.—ΤΟΥ ΑΥΤΟΥ

Εἶναι νομίζω φιλόσοφον καὶ τὸν θεόν.
βλασφημίαις τὸν εὐθὺς οὐ θυμούμενον,
χρόνῳ δ᾽ ἐπαυξάνοντα τὰς τιμωρίας
τὰς τῶν πονηρῶν καὶ ταλαιπώρων βροτῶν.

95.—ΤΟΥ ΑΥΤΟΥ

Μισῶ τὸν ἄνδρα τὸν διπλοῦν πεφυκότα,
χρηστὸν λόγοισι, πολέμιον δὲ τοῖς τρόποις.

96.—ΤΟΥ ΑΥΤΟΥ

Ὅταν λογισμοῖς καταμάθω τὰ πράγματα,
καὶ τὰς ἀκαίρους μεταβολὰς τὰς τοῦ βίου,
καὶ ῥεῦμ᾽ ἄπιστον τῆς ἀνωμάλου Τύχης,
πῶς τοὺς πένητας πλουσίους ἐργάζεται,
καὶ τοὺς ἔχοντας χρημάτων ἀποστερεῖ,   5

---

[1] So Jacobs : οὐ γὰρ σὲ μέλπων τῆς Δίκης ὕπνους ἔχει MS.
This would mean, if anything, " For he who sings not of
thee is asleep to Justice."

92.—By the Same
To a Magistrate

Since thou givest judgments and art a subtle speaker, I bring thee too this grave epigram of my nightingale worthy of one who speaks freely ; for he who sings of thee pours forth the praises of Justice.[1]

93.—By the Same

It is better to endure even straitened Fortune rather than the arrogance of the wealthy.

94.—By the Same

I think God is a philosopher too, as he does not wax wroth at once with blasphemy, but with the advance of time increases the punishment of wicked and miserable men.

95.—By the Same

I hate the man who is double-minded, kind in words, but a foe in his conduct.

96.—By the Same

When I think over things, observing the inopportune changes of life and the fickle current of unfair Fortune, how she makes the poor rich and deprives its possessors of wealth, then blinded in my own

---

[1] Referring of course to another epigram or collection of epigrams he is sending.

τότε κατ' ἐμαυτὸν τῇ πλάνῃ σκοτούμενος
μισῶ τὰ πάντα, τῆς ἀδηλίας χάριν.
ποίῳ τρόπῳ γὰρ περιγένωμαι τῆς Τύχης,
τῆς ἐξ ἀδήλου φαινομένης ἐν τῷ βίῳ,
πόρνης γυναικὸς τοὺς τρόπους κεκτημένης;   10

97.—ΤΟΥ ΑΥΤΟΥ

Λίτραν ἐτῶν ζήσας μετὰ γραμματικῆς βραχυμόχθου,
βουλευτὴς νεκύων πέμπομαι εἰς ἀΐδην.

98.—ΤΟΥ ΑΥΤΟΥ

Πᾶς τις ἀπαίδευτος φρονιμώτατός ἐστι σιωπῶν,
τὸν λόγον ἐγκρύπτων, ὡς πάθος αἰσχρότατον.

99.—ΤΟΥ ΑΥΤΟΥ

Πολλάκι, Σέξστ', ἔστησα τεὴν φιλότητα καὶ ὕβριν·
καὶ πολὺ κουφοτέρην τὴν φιλότητα μαθών,
λοιδορίην δὲ ῥέπουσαν, ἐχωρίσθην φιλότητος,
μηκέτι βαστάζων ὕβριν ἀτιμοτάτην.

100.—ΑΝΤΙΦΑΝΟΥΣ

Ἀνθρώποις ὀλίγος μὲν ὁ πᾶς χρόνος, ὅν ποτε δειλοὶ
ζῶμεν, κἢν πολιὸν γῆρας ἅπασι μένῃ·
τῆς δ' ἀκμῆς καὶ μᾶλλον. ὅτ' οὖν χρόνος ὥριος ἡμῖν,
πάντα χύδην ἔστω, ψαλμός, ἔρως, προπόσεις.
χειμὼν τοὐντεῦθεν γήρως βαρύς· οὐδὲ δέκα μνῶν   5
στύσεις· τοιαύτη σ' ἐκδέχετ' ὀρχιπέδη.

---

¹ i.e. 72 years, there were 72 solidi in the pound. He
means that he had sought a seat in the Senate of some town
but in vain.

mind by the error I hate everything owing to the obscurity of all. For how shall I get the better of Fortune, who keeps on appearing in life from no one knows where, behaving like a harlot.

97.—By the Same

Having lived a pound of years[1] with toiling Grammar I am sent to Hell to be senator of the dead.

98.—By the Same

Every uneducated man is wisest if he remains silent, hiding his speech like a disgraceful disease.

99.—By the Same

I often, Sextus, weighed on the balance your kindness and insolence, and finding your kindness much the lightest and your abusive speech ever sinking the scale, I abandoned your friendship, unable to support any longer your most dishonouring insults.

100.—ANTIPHANES

Brief would be the whole span of life that we wretched men live, even if grey old age awaited us all, and briefer yet is the space of our prime. Therefore, while the season is ours, let all be in plenty, song, love, carousal. Henceforth is the winter of heavy eld. Thou wouldst give ten minae[2] to be a man, but no! such fetters shall be set on thy manhood.

---

[2] Roughly fifty pounds [about the year 1918].

101.—ΒΙΑΝΟΡΟΣ

Ηνίδε καὶ χέρσου τὸ γεωτόμον ὅπλον ἐρέσσει
  καὶ τὸν ὑπουθατίαν μόσχον ἄγει δάμαλις,
βούταν μὲν τρομέουσα διώκτορα, τὸν δὲ μένουσα
  νήπιον, ἀμφοτέρων εὔστοχα φειδομένη.
ἴσχες, ἀροτροδίαυλε, πεδώρυχε, μηδὲ διώξης   5
  τὰν διπλοῖς ἔργοις διπλὰ βαρυνομέναν.

102.—ΒΑΣΣΟΥ

Μήτε με χείματι πόντος ἄγοι θρασύς, οὐδὲ γαλήνης
  ἀργῆς ἠσπασάμην τὴν πάλι νηνεμίην.
αἱ μεσότητες ἄρισται· ὅπη δέ τε πρήξιες ἀνδρῶν,
  καὶ πάλι μέτρον ἐγὼ τἄρκιον ἠσπασάμην.
τοῦτ' ἀγάπα, φίλε Λάμπι, κακὰς δ' ἔχθαιρε θυέλ-
  λας·   5
  εἰσὶ τινὲς πρηεῖς καὶ βιοτου Ζέφυροι.

103.—ΦΙΛΟΔΗΜΟΥ

Τὴν †προτερον θυμέλην μήτ' ἔμβλεπε, μήτε παρέλθης[1]·
  νῦν ἄπαγε δραχμῆς εἰς κολοκορδόκολα.
καὶ σῦκον δραχμῆς ἓν γίνεται· ἢν δ' ἀναμείνης,
  χίλια.   τοῖς πτωχοῖς ὁ χρόνος ἐστὶ θεός.

104.—ΚΡΑΤΗΤΟΣ ΦΙΛΟΣΟΦΟΥ

Χαῖρε θεὰ δέσποιν', ἀνδρῶν ἀγαθῶν ἀγάπημα,
  Εὐτελίη, κλεινῆς ἔγγονε Σωφροσύνης·
σὴν ἀρετὴν τιμῶσιν ὅσοι τὰ δίκαι' ἀσκοῦσιν.

---

[1] Lines 1 and 2 are hopeless.

101.—BIANOR

Look, the heifer draws the instrument that cuts the earth, and is followed by the calf she is suckling! She dreads the husbandman at her heels, and waits for her little one, sagaciously careful of both. Thou who followest the plough up and down the field, who turnest up the soil, hold thy hand, nor drive her who bears the double burden of two labours.

102.—BASSUS

I would not have the fierce sea drive me in storm, nor do I welcome the dull windless calm that follows. The mean is best, and so likewise where men do their business, I welcome the sufficient measure. Be content with this, dear Lampis, and hate evil tempests; there are gentle Zephyrs in life too.

103.—PHILODEMUS

Neither look into nor pass by (the place where they sell scarce delicacies?). Now be off to the tripe-stall to spend a drachma.[1] One fig too at times may cost a drachma, but if you wait, it will buy you a thousand. Time is the poor man's god.

104.—CRATES THE PHILOSOPHER

Hail! divine lady Simplicity, child of glorious Temperance, beloved by good men. All who practise righteousness venerate thy virtue.[2]

[2] An extract from Crates' *Hymn to Simplicity*, the whole of which we have.

105.—ΣΙΜΩΝΙΔΟΤ

Χαίρει τις Θεόδωρος, ἐπεὶ θάνον· ἄλλος ἐπ' αὐτῷ
χαιρήσει. θανάτῳ πάντες ὀφειλόμεθα.

106.—ΑΔΗΛΟΝ

Πολλοί τοι ναρθηκοφόροι, παῦροι δε τε βάκχοι.

107.—ΕΤΡΙΠΙΔΟΤ

Θεοῦ μὲν οὐδεὶς ἐκτὸς εὐτυχεῖ βροτός.
φεῦ τῶν βροτείων ὡς ἀνώμαλοι τύχαι·
οἱ μὲν γὰρ εὖ πράσσουσι, τοῖς δὲ συμφοραὶ
σκληραὶ πάρεισιν εὐσεβοῦσι πρὸς θεούς.

108.—ΑΔΗΛΟΝ

Ζεῦ βασιλεῦ, τὰ μὲν ἐσθλὰ καὶ εὐχομένοις καὶ
ἀνεύκτοις
ἄμμι δίδου· τὰ δὲ λυγρὰ καὶ εὐχομένων ἀπερύκοις.

109.—ΑΔΗΛΟΝ

Πᾶς λόγος ἐστὶ μάταιος ὁ μὴ τετελεσμένος ἔργῳ·
καὶ πᾶσα πρᾶξις τὸν λόγον ἀρχὸν ἔχοι.[1]

110.—ΑΙΣΧΤΛΟΤ

Οὐ χρὴ λέοντος σκύμνον ἐν πόλει τρέφειν·
μάλιστα μὲν λέοντα μὴ πόλει τρέφειν·
ἢν δ' ἐκτραφῇ τις, τοῖς τρόποις ὑπηρετεῖν.

[1] ἔργον ἔχει MS.: corr. Jacobs.

---

[1] cp. Horace's " Debemur morti nos nostraque."
[2] A well-known proverb quoted by Plato in the *Phaedo*
(69 c). [3] *Fragments* 684 and 1025.

56

105.—SIMONIDES

A CERTAIN Theodorus rejoices because I am dead
Another shall rejoice at his death. We are all owed
to death.[1]

106.—ANONYMOUS

MANY are the thyrsus-bearers but few the initiated.[2]

107.—EURIPIDES[3]

No man is fortunate unless God will it. Alas! how
unequal is the lot of men. Some are prosperous
and on others who reverence the gods fall cruel
misfortunes

108.—ANONYMOUS [4]

ZEUS the king, give us good things whether we
pray for them or not, and keep evil things away from
us even if we pray for them.

109.—ANONYMOUS

EVERY word is vain that is not completed by deed,
and let every deed spring from reason.[5]

110.—AESCHYLUS

A LION cub should not be reared in the city.
First and foremost bring up no lion in the city, but
if one be reared, submit to his ways.[6]

[4] Quoted as such by Plato, *Alcib.* ii. p. 142 e.
[5] The play on the two senses of Logos, speech and reason,
cannot be rendered.
[6] Spoken by Aeschylus in Aristophanes, *Frogs* 1425, with
reference to Alcibiades.

111.—ΑΔΗΛΟΝ

Ὁ φθόνος αὐτὸς ἑαυτὸν ἑοῖς βελέεσσι δαμάζει.

112.—ΑΔΕΣΠΟΤΟΝ

Οἶνος καὶ τὰ λοετρὰ καὶ ἡ περὶ Κύπριν ἐρωή
ὀξυτέρην πέμπει τὴν ὁδὸν εἰς ἀΐδην.

113.—ΑΔΕΣΠΟΤΟΝ

Οὐκ ἐθέλω πλουτεῖν, οὐκ εὔχομαι· ἀλλά μοι εἴη
ζῆν ἐκ τῶν ὀλίγων μηδὲν ἔχοντα κακον.

114.—ΑΔΗΛΟΝ

Ἡ κρίσις ἐστὶ κάτω καὶ Τάνταλος· οὐδὲν ἀπιστῶ,
τῇ πενίῃ μελετῶν τὴν ὑπὸ γῆν κόλασιν.

115.—ΑΔΗΛΟΝ

Ζῆσον λογισμῷ, καὶ μενεῖς ἀνενδεής.

116.—ΑΔΗΛΟΝ

" Οὐκ ἔστι γήμας, ὅστις οὐ χειμάζεται,"
λέγουσι πάντες, καὶ γαμοῦσιν εἰδότες.

117.—ΦΩΚΥΛΙΔΟΥ

Γνήσιός εἰμι φίλος, καὶ τον φίλον ὡς φίλον οἶδα,
τοὺς δὲ κακοὺς διόλου πάντας ἀποστρέφομαι·
οὐδένα θωπεύω πρὸς ὑπόκρισιν· οὓς δ᾽ ἄρα τιμῶ,
τούτους ἐξ ἀρχῆς μέχρι τέλους ἀγαπῶ.

---

[1] Found also engraved on a stone (*Corp. Inscrr.* No. 1935).

111.—ANONYMOUS [1]

ENVY slays itself by its own arrows.

112.—ANONYMOUS

WINE and baths and venerean indulgence make the road to Hades more precipitous.

113.—ANONYMOUS [2]

I DO not wish or pray to be wealthy, but I would live on a little, suffering no evil.

114.—ANONYMOUS

BELOW in Hell are judgment and Tantalus. I do not disbelieve it, training for the infernal torments by my poverty.

115.—ANONYMOUS

LIVE by reason, and thou shalt not be in want.

116.—ANONYMOUS

" No married man but is tempest-tossed " they all say and marry knowing it. [3]

117.—PHOCYLIDES

I AM a genuine friend, and I know a friend to be a friend, but I turn my back on all evil-doers. I flatter no one hypocritically, but those whom I honour I love from beginning to end.

[2] From Theognis (v. 1155) with differences.
[3] Doubtless from a comic poet.

118.—ΑΔΗΛΟΝ

Πῶς γενόμην; πόθεν εἰμί; τίνος χάριν ἦλθον;
ἀπελθεῖν;
πῶς δύναμαί τι μαθεῖν, μηδὲν ἐπιστάμενος;
οὐδὲν ἐὼν γενόμην· πάλιν ἔσσομαι ὡς πάρος ἦα·
οὐδὲν καὶ μηδὲν τῶν μερόπων τὸ γένος.
ἀλλ' ἄγε μοι Βάκχοιο φιλήδονον ἔντυε νᾶμα·   5
τοῦτο γάρ ἐστι κακῶν φάρμακον ἀντίδοτον.

C. Merivale, in *Collections from the Greek Anthology*, 1833,
p. 240.

119.—ΑΔΗΛΟΝ

Σώματα πολλὰ τρέφειν, καὶ δώματα πόλλ' ἀνεγείρειν
ἀτραπὸς εἰς πενίην ἐστὶν ἑτοιμοτάτη.

H. Wellesley, in *Anthologia Polyglotta*, p. 159.

120.—ΑΔΗΛΟΝ

Πᾶσα γυνὴ φιλέει πλέον ἀνέρος· αἰδομένη δὲ
κεύθει κέντρον ἔρωτος, ἐρωμανέουσα καὶ αὐτή.

121.—ΡΑΡΟΥ

Οὐχ οὕτω βλάπτει μισεῖν ὁ λέγων ἀναφανδόν,
ὥσπερ ὁ τὴν καθαρὰν ψευδόμενος φιλίαν.
τὸν μὲν γὰρ μισοῦντα προειδότες ἐκτρεπόμεσθα,
τὸν δὲ λέγοντα φιλεῖν οὐ προφυλασσόμεθα.
ἐχθρὸν ἐγὼ κρίνω κεῖνον βαρύν, ὅς ποτε λάθρη   5
τὴν ἀπὸ τῆς φιλίας πίστιν ἔχων ἀδικεῖ.

---

[1] Mackail compares the paradox in Plato's *Euthydemus*
that it is impossible to learn what one does not know
already, and hence impossible to learn at all.

118.—Anonymous

How was I born? Whence am I? Why came I here? To depart again? How can I learn aught, knowing nothing?[1] I was nothing and was born; again I shall be as at first. Nothing and of no worth is the race of men. But serve me the merry fountain of Bacchus; for this is the antidote of ills.

119.—Anonymous

To feed many slaves and erect many houses is the readiest road to poverty

120.—Anonymous

Every woman loves more than a man loves; but out of shame she hides the sting of love, although she be mad for it.[2]

121.—RARUS

He who says openly that he hates us does not hurt us so much as the man who simulates pure friendship. For having previous knowledge of him who hates us, we avoid him, but we do not guard ourselves against him who says he loves us. Him I judge a grievous enemy, who, when we trust him as a friend, does us injury by stealth.

[2] From Nonnus, *Dionys.* xlii. 209.

122.—ΛΟΥΚΙΛΛΙΟΥ

Πολλὰ τὸ δαιμόνιον δύναται, κἂν ἦ παράδοξα·
τοὺς μικροὺς ἀνάγει, τοὺς μεγάλους κατάγει·
καὶ σοῦ τὴν ὀφρὺν καὶ τὸν τῦφον καταπαύσει,
κἂν ποταμὸς χρυσοῦ νάματά σοι παρέχῃ.
οὐ θρύον, οὐ μαλάχην ἄνεμός ποτε, τὰς δὲ μεγίστας 5
ἢ δρύας ἢ πλατάνους οἶδε χαμαὶ κατάγειν.

123.—ΑΙΣΩΠΟΥ

Πῶς τις ἄνευ θανάτου σε φύγοι, βίε; μυρία γάρ σευ
λυγρά· καὶ οὔτε φυγεῖν εὐμαρές, οὔτε φέρειν.
ἡδέα μὲν γάρ σου τὰ φύσει καλά, γαῖα, θάλασσα,
ἄστρα, σεληναίης κύκλα καὶ ἠελίου·
τἆλλα δὲ πάντα φόβοι τε καὶ ἄλγεα· κἤν τι πάθῃ
τις
5
ἐσθλόν, ἀμοιβαίην ἐκδέχεται Νέμεσιν.

A. J. Butler, *Amaranth and Asphodel*, p. 79; J. A. Pott,
Greek Love Songs and Epigrams, i. p. 111.

124.—ΓΛΥΚΩΝΟΣ

Πάντα γέλως, καὶ πάντα κόνις, καὶ πάντα τὸ μηδέν·
πάντα γὰρ ἐξ ἀλόγων ἐστὶ τὰ γινόμενα.

124Α.—ΑΔΗΛΟΝ

Φροντίδες οἱ παῖδες· μέγα μὲν κακόν, εἴ τι πάθοιεν·
εἰσὶ δὲ καὶ ζῶντες φροντίδες οὐκ ὀλίγαι.
ἡ γαμετή, χρηστὴ μὲν ἔχει τινὰ τέρψιν ἐν αὐτῇ,
ἡ δὲ κακὴ πικρὸν τὸν βίον ἀνδρὶ φέρει.

122.—LUCILIUS

HEAVEN can do many things even though they be unlikely; it exalteth the little and casteth down the great. Thy lofty looks and pride it shall make to cease, even though a river bring thee streams of gold. The wind hurts not the rush or the mallow, but the greatest oaks and planes it can lay low on the ground.

123.—AESOP

LIFE, how shall one escape thee without death; for thou hast a myriad ills and neither to fly from them nor to bear them is easy. Sweet are thy natural beauties, the earth, the sea, the stars, the orbs of the sun and moon. But all the rest is fear and pain, and if some good befall a man, an answering Nemesis succeeds it.

124.—GLYCON

ALL is laughter, all is dust, all is nothing, for all that is cometh from unreason.

124A.—ANONYMOUS

CHILDREN are a trouble; it is a great evil if anything happens to them, and even if they live they are no small trouble. A wife if she be good hath something in her that delights, but a bad one brings a man a bitter life.

125.—ΑΔΗΛΟΝ

Πρᾶγμα μέν ἐσθ᾽ ὁ φίλος πάνυ δύσκολον· εἰσὶ δὲ
πολλοί,
καὶ σχεδὸν οἱ πάντες, μέχρι προσηγορίας.

126.—ΑΔΗΛΟΝ

Χρησαμένῳ θεράπων ὁ χρήσιμός ἐστ᾽ ἀγαθόν τι·
αὐτάρκης δὲ κακὸν τῶνδ᾽ ὁ πονηρότερος.[1]

[1] κακῶν ἐστιν ἀπειρότερος Brunck, and so I render

125.—Anonymous

A FRIEND is a very difficult thing to find, but many or nearly all are friends only in name.

126.—Anonymous

A USEFUL servant is a good thing for him who makes use of him, but a man who is self-sufficient experiences less evil.

BOOK XI

THE CONVIVIAL AND SATIRICAL EPIGRAMS

This book is divided in the MS. into two sections, the Convivial Epigrams, Nos. 1–64, and the Satirical Epigrams, No. 65 to the end, the former section, not exclusively convivial, being in part at least derived from the *Stephanus* of Philippus (8–9, 23–46, 49–50) and the Cycle of Agathias (57–61, 63–64). The second section, the Satirical poems, while containing much of the work of Palladas, with whom readers became acquainted in the preceding Book, a very limited number of poems from the *Stephanus* of Philippus (158, 168, 318–322, 324–327, 346–348) and a few by Agathias and Macedonius, is largely the work of two writers much allied in style, Lucilius and Nicarchus (we may add Ammianus), whose contributions are not derived from the main sources of the *Anthology*. Lucilius lived in the time of Nero, and Nicarchus probably was contemporary. They both very much remind us of Martial, who probably had read them. There is plenty of evidence that Nicarchus wrote in Alexandria, and I think the same may be true of Lucilius (see No. 212). There are very few epigrams in this book (195, 218, 223, 362–3) from the *Stephanus* of Meleager.

ΙΑ

ΕΠΙΓΡΑΜΜΑΤΑ ΣΥΜΡΟΤΙΚΑ ΚΑΙ ΣΚΩΠΤΙΚΑ

1.—ΝΙΚΑΡΧΟΥ

Ἑρμαίοις ἡμῖν Ἀφροδίσιος ἐξ χόας οἴνου
αἴρων, προσκόψας πένθος ἔθηκε μέγα.
οἶνος καὶ Κένταυρον ἀπώλεσεν· ὡς ὄφελεν δὲ
χἠμᾶς· νῦν δ' ἡμεῖς τοῦτον ἀπωλέσαμεν.

2.—ΚΑΛΛΙΚΤΗΡΟΣ

Αἰσχυλίδα Θεόδωρε, τί μοι μεμάχηνται ἄριστοι;
οὐ διακωλύσεις; πάντες ἔχουσι λίθους.

3.—ΑΔΕΣΠΟΤΟΝ

Ἤθελον ἂν πλουτεῖν, ὡς πλούσιος ἦν ποτε Κροῖσος,
καὶ βασιλεὺς εἶναι τῆς μεγάλης Ἀσίης·
ἀλλ' ὅταν ἐμβλέψω Νικάνορα τὸν σοροπηγόν,
καὶ γνῶ πρὸς τί ποιεῖ ταῦτα τὰ γλωσσόκομα,
ἀκτήν που πάσσας καὶ ταῖς κοτύλαις ὑποβρέξας,   5
τὴν Ἀσίην πωλῶ πρὸς μύρα καὶ στεφάνους.

---

[1] About nine gallons.
[2] It was the cause of their fatal fight with the Lapithae.
[3] Or "killed."

BOOK XI

THE CONVIVIAL AND SATIRICAL
EPIGRAMS

1.—NICARCHUS

At the feast of Hermes, Aphrodisius, as he was
carrying six choes[1] of wine, stumbled and threw us
into deep mourning. " Wine was the death even of
the Centaurs." [2] Would it had been ours ; but now
it is it we have lost.[3]

2.—CALLICTER

Theodorus, son of Aeschylus, why do the leaders
fight with me ? Won't you stop them ? They all
have stones.[4]

3.—Anonymous

I would have liked to be as rich as Croesus once
was, and to be king of great Asia.   But when I look
at Nicanor the coffin-maker and learn what these
flute-cases[5] he is making are meant for, I sprinkle
my flour[6] no matter where, and moistening it with
my pint of wine I sell Asia for scent and garlands.

[4] We cannot tell the occasion of this epigram, but
Theodorus seems to be a doctor and the joke turns on
"stones."

[5] So he facetiously calls the coffins.

[6] Flour kneaded and soaked in wine was a common drink.

4.—ΠΑΡΜΕΝΙΩΝΟΣ

Αὐτῷ τις γήμας πιθανὴν τῷ γείτονι, ῥέγχει
καὶ τρέφεται· τοῦτ᾽ ἦν εὔκολος ἐργασία,
μὴ πλεῖν, μὴ σκάπτειν, ἀλλ᾽ εὐστομάχως ἀπορέγ
χειν,
ἀλλοτρίᾳ δαπάνῃ πλούσια βοσκόμενον.

5.—ΚΑΛΛΙΚΤΗΡΟΣ ΜΑΝΤΙΣΙΟΥ[1]

῞Οστις ἔσω πυροὺς καταλαμβάνει οὐκ ἀγοράζων,
κείνου ᾽Αμαλθείας ἁ γυνά ἐστι κέρας.

6.—ΤΟΥ ΑΥΤΟΥ

Πτωχοῦ ἐστι γάμος κυνέα μάχα, εὐθὺ κυδοιμός,
λοιδορίαι, πλαγαί, ζημία, ἔργα, δίκαι.

7.—ΝΙΚΑΡΧΟΥ[2]

Οὐδεὶς τὴν ἰδίην συνεχῶς, Χαρίδημε, γυναῖκα
βινεῖν[3] ἐκ ψυχῆς τερπόμενος δύναται·
οὕτως ἡ φύσις ἐστὶ φιλόκνισος, ἀλλοτριόχρως,
καὶ ζητεῖ διόλου τὴν ξενοκυσθαπάτην.

8.—ΑΔΕΣΠΟΤΟΝ

Μὴ μύρα, μὴ στεφάνους λιθίναις στήλαισι χαρίζου,
μηδὲ τὸ πῦρ φλέξῃς· ἐς κενὸν ἡ δαπάνη.
ζῶντί μοι, εἴ τι θέλεις, χάρισαι· τέφρην δὲ μεθύσκων
πηλὸν ποιήσεις, κοὐχ ὁ θανὼν πίεται.

---

[1] It is unknown what this means.
[2] I write ΝΙΚΑΡΧΟΥ : Νικάνδρου MS.
[3] κινεῖν MS.: I correct.

---

[1] In late and modern Greek, horns have the sense familiar
from Shakespeare. *cp.* No. 278 below.

4.--PARMENION

A CERTAIN man, having married a woman who is complaisant to his neighbour only, snores and feeds. That was the way to get a living easily—not to go to sea, not to dig, but to snore off one's dinner with a comfortable stomach, fattened richly at the expense of another.

5.—CALLICTER

HE who finds wheat at home without buying it has a wife who is " a horn [1] " of plenty.

6.—BY THE SAME

A POOR man's marriage is a dog-fight, at once the roar of battle, abuse, blows, damage, trouble and law-suits.

7.—NICARCHUS

No one, Charidemus, can constantly poke his own wife and take heart-felt pleasure in it. Our nature is so fond of titillation, such a luster after foreign flesh, that it persists in whoring stealthily after strange quims.

8.—ANONYMOUS

BESTOW not scent and crowns on stone columns, nor set the fire ablaze ; [2] the outlay is in vain. Give me gifts, if thou wilt, when I am alive, but by steeping ashes in wine thou wilt make mud, and the dead shall not drink thereof.[3]

[2] By pouring ointments on it. The fire is the funeral fire.
[3] These striking verses were found also engraved (with a few unimportant variants) on the tomb of Cerellia Fortunata near Rome.

9.—ΛΕΩΝΙΔΑ

Μὴ πάλι μοι μετὰ δόρπον, ὅτ' οὐκέτι γαστέρα πείθω,
οὔθατα καὶ χοίρων ἄντα τίθει τεμάχη·
οὐδὲ γὰρ ἐργοπόνοισι μετὰ στάχυν ὄμβρος ἄκαιρος
χρήσιμος, οὐ ναύταις ἐν λιμένι Ζέφυρος.

10.—ΛΟΥΚΙΛΛΙΟΥ

Τὸν τοῦ δειπναρίου νόμον οἴδατε· σήμερον ὑμᾶς,
Αὖλε, καλῶ καινοῖς δόγμασι συμποσίου.
οὐ μελοποιὸς ἐρεῖ κατακείμενος· οὔτε παρέξεις
οὔθ' ἕξεις αὐτὸς πράγματα γραμματικά.

11.—ΤΟΥ ΑΥΤΟΥ

Οὐκ ᾔδειν σε τραγῳδόν, Ἐπίκρατες, οὐδὲ χοραύλην,
οὐδ' ἄλλ' οὐδὲν ὅλως, ὧν χορόν ἔστιν ἔχειν·
ἀλλ' ἐκάλουν σε μόνον· σὺ δ' ἔχων χορὸν οἴκοθεν
ἥκεις
ὀρχηστῶν, αὐτοῖς πάντα διδοὺς ὀπίσω.
εἰ δ' οὕτω τοῦτ' ἐστί, σὺ τοὺς δούλους κατάκλινον,   5
ἡμεῖς δ' αὖ τούτοις πρὸς πόδας ἐρχόμεθα.

12.—ΑΛΚΑΙΟΥ

Οἶνος καὶ Κένταυρον, Ἐπίκρατες, οὐχὶ σὲ μοῦνον,
ὤλεσεν, ἠδ' ἐρατὴν Καλλίου ἡλικίην.
ὄντως οἰνοχάρων ὁ μονόμματος, ᾧ σὺ τάχιστα
τὴν αὐτὴν πέμψαις ἐξ Ἀΐδεω πρόποσιν.

---

[1] By "dancing" he means only "very active in their
attendance on you."   [2] See No. 1 above.

[3] Epicrates the comic poet and Callias the tragic poet

9.—LEONIDAS OF ALEXANDRIA

SET not before me after supper, when I can no longer persuade my belly, udders and slices of pork. For neither to labourers after harvest is rain out of season useful, nor the Zephyr to mariners in port.

10.—LUCILIUS

You know the rule of my little banquets. To-day, Aulus, I invite you under new convivial laws. No lyric poet shall sit there and recite, and you yourself shall neither trouble us nor be troubled with literary discussions.

11.—BY THE SAME

I NEVER knew, Epicrates, that you were a tragedian or a choral flute-player or any other sort of person whose business it is to have a chorus with them. But I invited you alone ; you, however, came bringing with you from home a chorus of dancing slaves,[1] to whom you hand all the dishes over your shoulder as a gift. If this is to be so, make the slaves sit down at table and we will come and stand at their feet to serve.

12.—ALCAEUS OF MESSENE

"WINE slew the Centaur"[2] too, Epicrates,[3] not yourself alone and Callias in his lovely prime. Truly the one-eyed monster is the Charon of the wine-cup. Send him right quickly from Hades the same draught.

were both said to have been poisoned by King Philip, son of Demetrius. This Philip was not, like Philip II., one-eyed, but Alcaeus means that he was a Cyclops in his cruelty.

GREEK ANTHOLOGY

13.—AMMIANOY

Ἠὼς ἐξ ἠοῦς παραπέμπεται, εἶτ', ἀμελούντων
ἡμῶν, ἐξαίφνης ἥξει ὁ πορφύρεος,
καὶ τοὺς μὲν τήξας, τοὺς δ' ὀπτήσας, ἐνίους δὲ
φυσήσας, ἄξει πάντας ἐς ἓν βάραθρον.

14.—ΤΟΥ ΑΥΤΟΥ

Ἐχθές ἐπὶ ξενίαν κληθείς, ὅτε καιρὸς ὕπνου μοι,
τύλῃ ἐπεκλίνθην Γοργόνος ἢ Νιόβης,
ἣν οὐδεὶς ὕφηνεν, ἀπέπρισε δ', ἢ πελεκήσας
ἐκ τῶν λατομιῶν ἤγαγεν εἰς τὰ Πρόκλου.
ἐξ ἧς εἰ μὴ θᾶττον ἐπηγέρθην, Πρόκλος ἄν μοι   5
τὴν τύλην στήλην ἢ σορὸν εἰργάσατο.

15.—ΤΟΥ ΑΥΤΟΥ

Εἰ μὲν τοὺς ἀπὸ ἄλφα μόνους κέκρικας κατορύσσειν,
Λούκιε, βουλευτὰς καὶ τὸν ἀδελφὸν ἔχεις·
εἰ δ', ὅπερ εὔλογόν ἐστι, κατὰ στοιχεῖον ὁδεύεις,
ἤδη, σοὶ προλέγω, Ὠριγένης λέγομαι.

16. <ΤΟΥ ΑΥΤΟΥ>

Κύλλος καὶ Λεῦρος, δύο Θεσσαλοὶ ἐγχεσίμωροι·
Κύλλος δ' ἐκ τούτων ἐγχεσιμωρότερος.

---

[1] *i.e.* killing us by consumption, fever or dropsy.
[2] The Gorgon turned to stone, Niobe was turned to stone herself.
[3] I take Lucius to be the brother of the author and probably a doctor.   Several senators whose names began with A had by chance died under his treatment, and Ammi-

13.—AMMIANUS

Dawn after dawn goes by, and then, when we take
no heed shall come the Dark One. Melting some of
us, roasting some and puffing out others,[1] he shall
bring us all to the same pit.

14.—By the Same

Invited to dinner yesterday, when it was time for
my siesta, I rested my head on the Gorgon's pillow
or Niobe's,[2] a pillow which none wove, but someone
sawed or hacked out of the quarry and brought to
Proclus' house. If I had not woke up very soon and
left it, Proclus would have made his pillow into a
grave-stone or coffin for me.

15.—By the Same

Lucius, if you have decided to bury only the
senators whose names begin with Alpha, you have
your brother (Ammianus) too. But if, as is reason-
able to suppose, you proceed in alphabetical order,
my name, I beg to state, is now Origenes.[3]

16.—By the Same

Cyllus and Leurus, two Thessalian bounders with
the spear, and Cyllus the bigger bounder of the two.[4]

anus says that if he is going to confine himself to the A's it
is his own turn; otherwise if Lucius adopts alphabetical
order, he changes his name to one beginning with Omega,
the last letter.

[4] He treats the Homeric word ἐγχεσίμωρος, which is lauda-
tory, as if derived from μῶρος—a fool.

17.—ΝΙΚΑΡΧΟΥ

Ἦν Στέφανος πτωχὸς κηπεύς θ' ἅμα· νῦν δὲ προ-
κόψας
πλουτεῖ, καὶ γεγένητ' εὐθὺ Φιλοστέφανος,
τέσσαρα τῷ πρώτῳ Στεφάνῳ καλὰ γράμματα
προσθείς·
ἔσται δ' εἰς ὥρας Ἱπποκρατιππιάδης,
ἢ διὰ τὴν σπατάλην Διονυσιοπηγανόδωρος·   5
ἐν δ' ἀγορανομίῳ παντὶ μένει Στέφανος.

18.—ΤΟΥ ΑΥΤΟΥ

Οὐκ ἐν γαστρὶ λαβοῦσα Φιλαίνιον Ἡλιοδώρῳ
θήλειαν τίκτει παῖδ' ἀπὸ ταὐτομάτου.
τοῦ δ' ἐπὶ θηλείᾳ λυπουμένου, ἐξ διαλείπει
ἤματα, καὶ τίκτειν ἄρσενα παῖδ' ἔφατο.
οὕτως Βούβαστις καταλύεται· εἰ γὰρ ἑκάστη   5
τέξεται ὡς αὐτή, τίς θεοῦ ἐστι λόγος;

19.—ΣΤΡΑΤΩΝΟΣ

Καὶ πίε νῦν καὶ ἔρα, Δαμόκρατες· οὐ γὰρ ἐς αἰεὶ
πιόμεθ', οὐδ' αἰεὶ παισὶ συνεσσόμεθα.
καὶ στεφάνοις κεφαλὰς πυκασώμεθα, καὶ μυρίσωμεν
αὑτούς, πρὶν τύμβοις ταῦτα φέρειν ἑτέρους.
νῦν ἐν ἐμοὶ πιέτω μέθυ τὸ πλέον ὀστέα τἀμά·   5
νεκρὰ δὲ Δευκαλίων αὐτὰ κατακλυσάτω.

---

[1] Hippocratippiades is a comic name invented by the author
as indicative of great wealth and position owing to its very
horsey sound. Dionysiodorus is another name of very aris-
tocratic sound, spoilt however by the malicious introduction

17.—NICARCHUS

STEPHANUS was poor and a gardener, but now having got on well and become rich, he has suddenly turned into Philostephanus, adding four fine letters to the original Stephanus, and in due time he will be Hippocratippiades or, owing to his extravagance, Dionysiopeganodorus.[1] But in all the market he is still Stephanus.

18.—BY THE SAME

PHILAENIS without conceiving bore a girl child to Heliodorus spontaneously, and when he was vexed at its being a girl she let six days pass and said she had borne a boy. So it is all over with Bubastis ;[2] for if every woman is brought to bed like Philaenis, who will pay any attention to the goddess ?

19.—STRATO

DRINK and love now, Damocrates, for we shall not drink for ever or be for ever with the lads. Let us bind our heads with garlands and scent ourselves before others bear flowers and scent to our tombs. Now may my bones inside me drink mostly wine, and when they are dead let Deucalion's flood[3] cover them.

of "pegano" (rue, a common pot-herb) in allusion to Stephanus' former profession.
   [2] The Egyptian representative of Diana presiding over childbirth.   [3] We should say "Noah's flood."

20.—ΑΝΤΙΠΑΤΡΟΥ ΘΕΣΣΑΛΟΝΙΚΕΩΣ

Φεύγεθ' ὅσοι λόκκας ἢ λοφνίδας ἢ καμασῆνας
    ᾄδετε, ποιητῶν φῦλον ἀκανθολόγων,
οἵ τ' ἐπέων κόσμον λελυγισμένον ἀσκήσαντες,
    κρήνης ἐξ ἱερῆς πίνετε λιτὸν ὕδωρ.
σήμερον Ἀρχιλόχοιο καὶ ἄρσενος ἦμαρ Ὁμήρου   5
    σπένδομεν· ὁ κρητὴρ οὐ δέχεθ' ὑδροπότας.

21.—ΣΤΡΑΤΩΝΟΣ

Πρῴην τὴν σαύραν Ἀγάθων ῥοδοδάκτυλον εἶχεν·
    νῦν δ' αὐτὴν ἤδη καὶ ῥοδόπηχυν ἔχει.

22.—ΤΟΥ ΑΥΤΟΥ

Ἔστι Δράκων τις ἔφηβος, ἄγαν καλός· ἀλλά,
    δράκων ὤν,
πῶς εἰς τὴν τρώγλην ἄλλον ὄφιν δέχεται;

23.—ΑΝΤΙΠΑΤΡΟΥ

Ὠκύμορόν με λέγουσι δαήμονες ἀνέρες ἄστρων·
    εἰμὶ μέν, ἀλλ' οὔ μοι τοῦτο, Σέλευκε, μέλει.
εἰς ἀΐδην μία πᾶσι καταίβασις· εἰ δὲ ταχίων
    ἡμετέρη, Μίνω θᾶσσον ἐποψόμεθα.
πίνωμεν· καὶ δὴ γὰρ ἐτήτυμον, εἰς ὁδὸν ἵππος   5
    οἶνος, ἐπεὶ πεζοῖς ἀτραπὸς εἰς ἀΐδην.

---

[1] All obsolete words, such as those used by Lycophron and other affected poets.

[2] The pretty Homeric adjectives are made to minister to a

20.—ANTIPATER OF THESSALONICA

Away with you who sing of loccae[1] (cloaks) or lophnides[1] (torches) or camasenes[1] (fish), race of thorn-gathering poets; and you who practising effeminately decorative verse drink only simple water from the holy fount. To-day we pour the wine in honour of the birthday of Archilochus and virile Homer. Our bowl receives no water-drinkers.

21.—STRATO

Agathon's lizard was rosy-fingered the other day; now it is already even rosy-armed.[2]

22.—By the Same

There's a certain young man, Master Serpent by name, very handsome indeed. But since he is a serpent, how does he take another serpent into his hole?

23.—ANTIPATER OF SIDON

Men learned in the stars say I am short-lived. I am, Seleucus, but I care not. There is one road down to Hades for all, and if mine is quicker, I shall see Minos all the sooner. Let us drink, for this is very truth, that wine is a horse for the road, while foot-travellers take a by-path to Hades.[3]

vile joke, the reference being to the relative length of the finger's breadth and cubit (length of the fore-arm), both well-known measures.

[3] He will go by the royal road and mounted (on wine); the pedestrians are those who do not drink.

24.—ΤΟΥ ΑΥΤΟΥ

'Ω 'Ελικὼν Βοιωτέ, σὺ μέν ποτε πολλάκις ὕδωρ
εὐεπὲς ἐκ πηγέων ἔβλυσας Ἡσιόδῳ·
νῦν δ' ἡμῖν ἔθ' ὁ κοῦρος ὁμώνυμος Αὔσονα Βάκχον
οἰνοχοεῖ κρήνης ἐξ ἀμεριμνοτέρης.
βουλοίμην δ' ἂν ἔγωγε πιεῖν παρὰ τοῦδε κύπελλον   5
ἓν μόνον, ἢ παρὰ σεῦ χίλια Πηγασίδος.

25.—ΑΠΟΛΛΩΝΙΔΟΥ

Ὑπνώεις, ὦ 'ταῖρε· τὸ δὲ σκύφος αὐτὸ βοᾷ σε·
ἔγρεο, μὴ τέρπου μοιριδίῃ μελέτῃ.
μὴ φείσῃ, Διόδωρε· λάβρος δ' εἰς Βάκχον ὀλισθών,
ἄχρις ἐπὶ σφαλεροῦ ζωροπότει γόνατος.
ἔσσεθ' ὅτ' οὐ πιόμεσθα, πολὺς πολύς· ἀλλ' ἄγ'
ἐπείγου·   5
ἡ συνετὴ κροτάφων ἅπτεται ἡμετέρων.

26.—ΑΡΓΕΝΤΑΡΙΟΥ

Σφάλλομαι ἀκρήτῳ μεμεθυσμένος· ἀλλὰ τίς ἆρα
σώσει μ' ἐκ Βρομίου γυῖα σαλευόμενον;
ὡς ἄδικον θεὸν εὗρον, ὁθείνεκεν αὐτὸς ἐγὼ σέ,
Βάκχε, φέρων ὑπὸ σοῦ τἄμπαλι παρφέρομαι.

27.—ΜΑΚΗΔΟΝΙΟΥ

Συρρέντου τρηχεῖα μυρίπνοε, χαῖρε, κονίη,
καὶ Πολλεντίνων γαῖα μελιχροτάτη,
Ἀστῆ θ' ἡ τριπόθητος, ἀφ' ἧς βρομώδεα πηλὸν
φύρησαν Βάκχῳ τριζυγέες Χάριτες,

24.—By the Same

On a cup-bearer named Helicon

O Boeotian Helicon, once didst thou often shed from thy springs the water of sweet speech for Hesiod. But still for us does the boy who bears thy name pour out Italian wine from a fountain that causes less care. Rather would I drink one cup only from his hand than a thousand of Castalia from thine.

25.—APOLLONIDES

Thou art asleep, my friend, but the cup itself is calling to thee : "Awake, and entertain not thyself with this meditation on death." Spare not, Diodorus, but slipping greedily into wine, drink it unmixed until thy knees give way. The time shall come when we shall not drink—a long, long time ; but come, haste thee ; the age of wisdom is beginning to tint our temples.

26.—ARGENTARIUS

I reel drunk with wine ; but who shall save me from Bacchus who makes my limbs totter? How unjust a god have I encountered, since while I carry thee, Bacchus, by thee, in return, I am carried astray.

27.—MACEDONIUS

Rough, sweet-scented dust of Sorrento, hail, and hail, thou earth of Pollenza most honied and Asta's soil thrice desired from which the triple band of Graces knead for Bacchus the clay that is akin to

πλούτου καὶ πενίης κοινὸν κτέαρ· οἷς μὲν ἀνάγκης   5
σκεῦος, τοῖς δὲ τρυφῆς χρῆσι περισσοτέρη.

28.—ΑΡΓΕΝΤΑΡΙΟΤ

Πέντε θανὼν κείσῃ κατέχων πόδας, οὐδὲ τὰ τερπνὰ
ζωῆς, οὐδ' αὐγὰς ὄψεαι ἠελίου·
ὥστε λαβὼν Βάκχου ζωρὸν δέπας ἕλκε γεγηθώς,
Κίγκιε, καλλίστην ἀγκὰς ἔχων ἄλοχον.
εἰ δέ σοι ἀθανάτου σοφίης νόος, ἴσθι Κλεάνθης   5
καὶ Ζήνων ἀΐδην τὸν βαθὺν ὡς ἔμολον.

29.—ΑΤΤΟΜΕΔΟΝΤΟΣ

Πέμπε, κάλει· πάντ' ἐστὶν ἕτοιμά σοι. ἢν δέ τις
ἔλθῃ,
τί πρήξεις; σαυτῷ δὸς λόγον, Αὐτόμεδον.
αὕτη γὰρ λαχάνου σισαρωτέρη, ἡ πρὶν ἀκαμπὴς
ζῶσα, νεκρὰ μηρῶν πᾶσα δέδυκεν ἔσω.
πόλλ' ἐπὶ σοὶ γελάσουσιν, ἀνάρμενος ἂν παρα-
βάλλῃ   5
πλώειν, τὴν κώπην μηκέτ' ἔχων ἐρέτης.

30.—ΦΙΛΟΔΗΜΟΤ

Ὁ πρὶν ἐγὼ καὶ πέντε καὶ ἐννέα, νῦν, Ἀφροδίτη,
ἓν μόλις ἐκ πρώτης νυκτὸς ἐς ἠέλιον·
οἴμοι καὶ . . τοῦτο κατὰ βραχὺ (πολλάκι δ' ἤδη
ἡμιθανὲς) θνήσκει· τοῦτο τὸ τερμέριον.
ὦ γῆρας, γῆρας, τί ποθ' ὕστερον, ἢν ἀφίκηαι,   5
ποιήσεις, ὅτε νῦν ὧδε μαραινόμεθα;

---

[1] He addresses the different soils from which the clay
considered most suitable for wine-jars came.

wine! Hail, common possession of wealth and poverty, to the poor a necessary vessel, to the rich a more superfluous instrument of luxury![1]

28.—ARGENTARIUS

DEAD, five feet of earth shall be thine and thou shalt not look on the delights of life or on the rays of the sun. So take the cup of unmixed wine and drain it rejoicing, Cincius, with thy arm round thy lovely wife. But if thou deemest wisdom to be immortal, know that Cleanthes and Zeno went to deep Hades.

29.—AUTOMEDON

SEND and summon her; you have everything ready. But if she comes, what will you do? Think over that, Automedon. For this thing, which before stayed unbending, but is now flabbier than a boiled carrot, has shrunk wholly into my thighs dead and gone. They will laugh at you much if you venture to put to sea without any tackle, an oarsman who no longer has his oar.

30.—PHILODEMUS

YES, my dear Aphrodite, I who could once do it five and nine times can manage hardly one from early night to sunrise. And, oh dear, this thing (it has often been half-dead) is gradually drying outright. This is the calamity of Termerus[2] that I suffer. Old age, old age, what shalt thou do later, if thou comest, since already I am thus languid?

[2] A proverbial expression for an appropriate punishment. The robber Termerus used to kill his victims by butting them with his head, and Heracles broke his head.

31.—ΑΝΤΙΠΑΤΡΟΥ

Οὔ μοι Πληϊάδων φοβερὴ δύσις, οὐδὲ θαλάσσης
ὠρύον στυφελῷ κῦμα περὶ σκοπέλῳ,
οὐδ᾽ ὅταν ἀστράπτῃ μέγας οὐρανός, ὡς κακὸν ἄνδρα
ταρβέω, καὶ μύθων μνήμονας ὑδροπότας.

32.—ΟΝΕΣΤΟΥ

Μούσης νουθεσίην φιλοπαίγμονος εὕρετο Βάκχος,
ᾧ Σικυών, ἐν σοὶ κῶμον ἄγων Χαρίτων·
δὴ γὰρ ἔλεγχον ἔχει γλυκερώτατον, ἔν τε γέλωτι
κέντρον· χὠ μεθύων ἀστὸν ἐσωφρόνισεν.

33.—ΦΙΛΙΠΠΟΥ

Λάθριον ἑρπηστὴν σκολιὸν πόδα, κισσέ, χορεύσας,
ἄγχεις τὴν Βρομίου βοτρυόπαιδα χάριν·
δεσμεῖς δ᾽ οὐχ ἡμᾶς, ὀλέκεις δὲ σέ· τίς γὰρ ἕλοιτ᾽ ἂν
κισσὸν ἐπὶ κροτάφοις, μὴ κεράσας Βρόμιον;

34.—ΦΙΛΟΔΗΜΟΥ

Λευκοΐνους πάλι δὴ καὶ ψάλματα, καὶ πάλι Χίους
οἴνους, καὶ πάλι δὴ σμύρναν ἔχειν Συρίην,
καὶ πάλι κωμάζειν, καὶ ἔχειν πάλι διψάδα πόρνην
οὐκ ἐθέλω· μισῶ ταῦτα τὰ πρὸς μανίην.
ἀλλά με ναρκίσσοις ἀναδήσατε, καὶ πλαγιαύλων 5
γεύσατε, καὶ κροκίνοις χρίσατε γυῖα μύροις,
καὶ Μυτιληναίῳ τὸν πνεύμονα τέγξατε Βάκχῳ,
καὶ συζεύξατέ μοι φωλάδα παρθενικήν.

---

[1] A season unfavourable for navigation.

31.—ANTIPATER OF THESSALONICA

I DREAD not the setting of the Pleiads,[1] nor the waves of the sea that roar round the stubborn rock, nor the lightning of great heaven so much as I dread a wicked man and water-drinkers who remember all our words.[2]

32.—HONESTUS

BACCHUS, leading the rout of the Graces, instituted in thee, Sicyon, the sermons of the jolly Muse.[3] Indeed, very sweet are his rebukes and in laughter is his sting. A man in his cups teaches wisdom to a clever man of the town.

33.—PHILIPPUS

SECRETLY advancing, O ivy, thy twisted creeping foot, thou throttlest me, the vine, sweet gift of Bacchus, mother of clusters. But thou dost not so much fetter me as thou dost destroy thine own honour; for who would set ivy on his brows without pouring out wine?

34.—PHILODEMUS

I WISH no garlands of white violets again, no lyre-playing again, no Chian wine again, no Syrian myrrh again, no revelling again, no thirsty whore with me again. I hate these things that lead to madness. But bind my head with narcissus and let me taste the slanting flute, and anoint my limbs with saffron ointment, wet my gullet with wine of Mytilene and mate me with a virgin who will love her nest.

---

[2] cp. the proverb μισῶ μνάμονα συμπόταν, "I hate a boon-companion with a good memory."

[3] i.e. the Satyric drama. See Book VII. 707.

35.—ΤΟΥ ΑΥΤΟΥ

Κράμβην Ἀρτεμίδωρος, Ἀρίσταρχος δὲ τάριχον,
  βολβίσκους δ' ἡμῖν δῶκεν Ἀθηναγόρας,
ἡπάτιον Φιλόδημος, Ἀπολλοφάνης δὲ δύο μνᾶς
  χοιρείου, καὶ τρεῖς ἦσαν ἀπ' ἐχθὲς ἔτι.
ᾠόν, καὶ στεφάνους, καὶ σάμβαλα, καὶ μύρον ἡμῖν   5
  λάμβανε, καὶ δεκάτης εὐθὺ θέλω παράγειν.

36.—ΦΙΛΙΠΠΟΥ

Ἡνίκα μὲν καλὸς ἦς, Ἀρχέστρατε, κἀμφὶ παρειαῖς
  οἰνωπαῖς ψυχὰς ἔφλεγες ἠιθέων,
ἡμετέρης φιλίης οὐδεὶς λόγος· ἀλλὰ μετ' ἄλλων
  παίζων, τὴν ἀκμὴν ὡς ῥόδον ἠφάνισας.
ὡς δ' ἐπιπερκάζεις μιαρῇ τριχί, νῦν φίλον ἕλκων,   5
  τὴν καλάμην δωρῇ, δοὺς ἑτέροις τὸ θέρος.

37.—ΑΝΤΙΠΑΤΡΟΥ

Ἤδη τοι φθινόπωρον, Ἐπίκλεες, ἐκ δὲ Βοώτου
  ζώνης Ἀρκτούρου λαμπρὸν ὄρωρε σέλας·
ἤδη καὶ σταφυλαὶ δρεπάνης ἐπιμιμνήσκονται,
  καί τις χειμερινὴν ἀμφερέφει καλύβην.
σοὶ δ' οὔτε χλαίνης θερμὴ κροκύς, οὔτε χιτῶνος   5
  ἔνδον· ἀποσκλήσῃ δ' ἀστέρα μεμφόμενος.

38.—ΠΟΛΕΜΩΝΟΣ ΒΑΣΙΛΕΩΣ

Ἡ πτωχῶν χαρίεσσα πανοπλίη ἀρτολάγυνος
  αὕτη, καὶ δροσερῶν ἐκ πετάλων στέφανος,

35.—By the Same

ARTEMIDORUS gave us a cabbage, Aristarchus caviare, Athenagoras little onions, Philodemus a small liver, and Apollophanes two pounds of pork, and there were three pounds still over from yesterday Go and buy us an egg and garlands and sandals[1] and scent, and I wish them to be here at four o'clock sharp.

36.—PHILIPPUS

WHEN you were pretty, Archestratus, and the hearts of the young men were burnt for your wine-red cheeks, there was no talk of friendship with me, but sporting with others you spoilt your prime like a rose. Now, however, when you begin to blacken with horrid hair, you would force me to be your friend, offering me the straw after giving the harvest to others.

37.—ANTIPATER OF SIDON

IT is already autumn, Epicles, and from the girdle of Bootes springs the bright flame of Arcturus. Already the vines bethink them of the pruning-hook and men build winter huts to shelter them. But you have no warm woollen cloak nor tunic indoors, and you will grow stiff, blaming the star.

38.—KING POLEMO

On a relief representing a jar, a loaf, a crown, and a skull

THIS is the poor man's welcome armour against hunger—a jar and a loaf, here is a crown of dewy

---

[1] Worn especially at table by the Romans. *cp.* Hor. *Ep.* i. 13. 15.

καὶ τοῦτο φθιμενοιο προάστιον ἱερὸν ὀστεῦν
ἐγκεφάλου, ψυχῆς φρούριον ἀκρότατον.
"Πῖνε," λέγει τὸ γλύμμα, "καὶ ἔσθιε καὶ περίκεισο   5
ἄνθεα· τοιοῦτοι γινόμεθ' ἐξαπίνης."

39.—ΜΑΚΗΔΟΝΙΟΤ ΘΕΣΣΑΛΟΝΙΚΕΩΣ

Ἐχθές μοι συνέπινε γυνή, περὶ ἧς λόγος ἔρρει
οὐχ ὑγιής.   παῖδες, θραύσατε τὰς κύλικας.

40.—ΑΝΤΙΣΤΙΟΤ

Εὐμένεος Κλεόδημος ἔτι βραχύς· ἀλλὰ χορεύει
σὺν παισὶν βαιῷ μικρὸς ἔτ' ἐν θιάσῳ·
ἠνίδε καὶ στικτοῖο δορὴν ἐζώσατο νεβροῦ,
καὶ σείει ξανθῆς κισσὸν ὑπὲρ κεφαλῆς·
ὦνα σύ μιν Καδμεῖε τίθει μέγαν, ὡς ἂν ὁ μύστης   5
ὁ βραχὺς ἡβήτας αὖθις ἄγοι θιάσους.

41.—ΦΙΛΟΔΗΜΟΤ

Ἑπτὰ τριηκόντεσσιν ἐπέρχονται λυκάβαντες,
ἤδη μοι βιότου σχιζόμεναι σελίδες·
ἤδη καὶ λευκαί με κατασπείρουσιν ἔθειραι,
Ξανθίππη, συνετῆς ἄγγελοι ἡλικίης.
ἀλλ' ἔτι μοι ψαλμός τε λάλος κῶμοί τε μέλονται,   5
καὶ πῦρ ἀπλήστῳ τύφετ' ἐνὶ κραδίῃ.
αὐτὴν ἀλλὰ τάχιστα κορωνίδα γράψατε, Μοῦσαι,
ταύτην ἡμετέρης, δεσπότιδες, μανίης.

42.—ΚΡΙΝΑΓΟΡΟΤ

Εἰ καί σοι ἑδραῖος ἀεὶ βίος, οὐδὲ θάλασσαν
ἔπλως, χερσαίας τ' οὐκ ἐπάτησας ὁδούς,

---

[1] Not of course that technically called *os sacrum*, but a skull.

leaves, and this is the holy bone,[1] outwork of a dead brain, the highest citadel of the soul. "Drink," says the sculpture, "and eat, and surround thee with flowers, for like to this we suddenly become." [2]

39.—MACEDONIUS OF THESSALONICA

YESTERDAY a woman was drinking with me about whom an unpleasant story is current. Break the cups, slaves.

40.—ANTISTIUS

CLEODEMUS, Eumenes' boy, is still small, but tiny as he is, he dances with the boys in a little company of worshippers. Look! he has even girt on the skin of a dappled fawn and he shakes the ivy on his yellow hair. Make him big, Theban King,[3] so that thy little servant may soon lead holy dances of young men.

41.—PHILODEMUS

SEVEN years added to thirty are gone already like so many pages torn out of my life; already, Xanthippe, my head is sprinkled with grey hairs, messengers of the age of wisdom. But still I care for the speaking music of the lyre and for revelling, and in my insatiate heart the fire is alive. But ye Muses, my mistresses, bring it to a close at once with the words "Xanthippe is the end of my madness."

42.—CRINAGORAS

THOUGH thy life be always sedentary, and thou hast never sailed on the sea or traversed the high

[2] The distich has been found engraved on a gem beneath a skull and table spread with food. (Boeckh. *C.I.G.* 7298.)

[3] *i.e.* Bacchus.

ἔμπης Κεκροπίης ἐπιβήμεναι, ὄφρ᾽ ἂν ἐκείνας
 Δήμητρος μεγάλας νύκτας ἴδης ἱερῶν,
τῶν ἄπο κὴν ζωοῖσιν ἀκηδέα, κεῦτ᾽ ἂν ἵκηαι   5
 ἐς πλεόνων, ἕξεις θυμὸν ἐλαφρότερον.

43.—ΖΩΝΑ

Δός μοι τοὺκ γαίης πεπονημένον ἀδὺ κύπελλον,
 ἇς γενόμην, καὶ ὑφ᾽ ᾇ κείσομ᾽ ἀποφθίμενος.

44.—ΦΙΛΟΔΗΜΟΥ

Αὔριον εἰς λιτήν σε καλιάδα, φίλτατε Πείσων,
 ἐξ ἐνάτης ἕλκει μουσοφιλὴς ἔταρος,
εἰκάδα δειπνίζων ἐνιαύσιον· εἰ δ᾽ ἀπολείψεις
 οὔθατα καὶ Βρομίου χιογενῆ πρόποσιν,
ἀλλ᾽ ἑτάρους ὄψει παναληθέας, ἀλλ᾽ ἐπακούσῃ   5
 Φαιήκων γαίης πουλὺ μελιχρότερα·
ἢν δέ ποτε στρέψῃς καὶ ἐς ἡμέας ὄμματα, Πείσων,
 ἄξομεν ἐκ λιτῆς εἰκάδα πιοτέρην.

45.—ΟΝΕΣΤΟΥ

Αὐτοθελὴς ἥδιστος ἀεὶ πότος· ὃς δέ κ᾽ ἀνάγκῃ,
 ὑβριστὴς οἴνῳ τ᾽ ἐστὶ καὶ οἰνοπότῃ.
τὸν μὲν γὰρ γαίῃ προχέει κρύφα· τὸν δ᾽ ὑπὸ γαίῃ
 πολλάκι πρὸς Λήθης ἤγαγε πικρὸν ὕδωρ.
πουλυμεθεῖς χαίροιτε· τὸ δ᾽ ὁππόσον ἡδὺ ποθῆναι,   5
 μέτρον ἐμοὶ πάσης ἄρκιον εὐφροσύνης.

---

[1] L. Cornelius Piso, Cicero's adversary. It is in the villa
of the Pisos at Herculaneum that all Philodemus' works
were found.

[2] The birthday of Epicurus, to whose sect Philodemus and
Piso belonged.

roads of the land, yet set thy foot on the Attic soil, that thou mayest see those long nights of Demeter's holy rites, whereby while thou art among the living thy mind shall be free from care, and when thou goest to join the greater number it shall be lighter.

43.—ZONAS

Give me the sweet beaker wrought of earth, earth from which I was born, and under which I shall lie when dead.

44.—PHILODEMUS

To-morrow, dearest Piso,[1] your friend, beloved by the Muses, who keeps our annual feast of the twentieth[2] invites you to come after the ninth hour to his simple cottage. If you miss udders and draughts of Chian wine, you will see at least sincere friends and you will hear things far sweeter than the land of the Phaeacians.[3] But if you ever cast your eyes on me,[4] Piso, we shall celebrate the twentieth richly instead of simply.

45.—HONESTUS

Drink which we wish ourselves is ever the sweetest; what is forced on us does outrage to the wine as well as to the drinker. The drinker will spill the wine on the earth secretly, and, if he drink it, it will often take him under the earth to the bitter water of Lethe. Farewell, ye topers; as much as I like to drink is to me the sufficient measure of all enjoyment.

[3] *i.e.* sweeter discourse than the story of Ulysses which he told in Phaeacia.

[4] He seeks his patronage and support.

46.—ΑΥΤΟΜΕΔΟΝΤΟΣ ΚΥΖΙΚΗΝΟΥ

Ἄνθρωποι δείλης, ὅτε πίνομεν· ἢν δὲ γένηται
ὄρθρος, ἐπ᾽ ἀλλήλους θῆρες ἐγειρόμεθα.

47.—ΑΝΑΚΡΕΟΝΤΟΣ

Οὔ μοι μέλει τὰ Γύγεω,
τοῦ Σαρδίων ἄνακτος,
οὔθ᾽ αἱρέει με χρυσός,
οὐκ αἰνέω τυράννους·
ἐμοὶ μέλει μύροισι   5
καταβρέχειν ὑπήνην·
ἐμοὶ μέλει ῥόδοισι
καταστέφειν κάρηνα.
τὸ σήμερον μέλει μοι·
τὸ δ᾽ αὔριον τίς οἶδεν;   10

48.—ΤΟΥ ΑΥΤΟΥ

Τὸν ἄργυρον τορεύσας
Ἥφαιστέ μοι ποίησον
πανοπλίαν μὲν οὐχί,
ποτήριον δὲ κοῖλον
ὅσον δύνῃ βάθυνον.   5
ποίει δέ μοι κατ᾽ αὐτοῦ
μηδ᾽ ἄστρα, μηδ᾽ ἀμάξας,
μὴ στυγνὸν Ὠρίωνα,
ἀλλ᾽ ἀμπέλους χλοώσας,
καὶ βότρυας γελῶντας,   10
σὺν τῷ καλῷ Λυαίῳ.

46.—AUTOMEDON OF CYZICUS

WE are men in the evening when we drink together, but when day-break comes, we get up wild beasts preying on each other.

47.—ANACREON

I CARE not for the wealth of Gyges the King of Sardis, nor does gold take me captive, and I praise not tyrants. I care to drench my beard with scent and crown my head with roses. I care for to-day; who knows to-morrow?

48.—BY THE SAME

MOULDING the silver make me, Hephaestus, no suit of armour, but fashion as deep as thou canst a hollow cup, and work on it neither stars nor chariots nor hateful Orion,[1] but blooming vines and laughing clusters with lovely Bacchus.

[1] Alluding to the shield of Achilles described by Homer.

49.—ΕΥΗΝΟΥ

Βάκχου μέτρον ἄριστον, ὃ μὴ πολυ, μηδ' ἐλάχιστον·
ἔστι γὰρ ἢ λύπης αἴτιος ἢ μανίης.
χαίρει κιρνάμενος δὲ τρισὶν Νύμφαισι τέταρτος·
τῆμος καὶ θαλάμοις ἐστὶν ἑτοιμότατος·
εἰ δὲ πολὺς πνεύσειεν, ἀπέστραπται μὲν Ἔρωτας,   5
βαπτίζει δ' ὕπνῳ γείτονι τοῦ θανάτου.

50.—ΑΥΤΟΜΕΔΟΝΤΟΣ

Εὐδαίμων, πρῶτον μὲν ὁ μηδενὶ μηδὲν ὀφείλων·
εἶτα δ' ὁ μὴ γήμας· τὸ τρίτον, ὅστις ἄπαις.
ἢν δὲ μανεὶς γήμῃ τις, ἔχει χάριν, ἢν κατορύξῃ
εὐθὺς τὴν γαμετήν, προῖκα λαβὼν μεγάλην.
ταῦτ' εἰδὼς σοφὸς ἴσθι· μάτην δ' Ἐπίκουρον ἔασον   5
ποῦ τὸ κενὸν ζητεῖν, καὶ τίνες αἱ μονάδες.

51.—ΑΔΗΛΟΝ

Τῆς ὥρας ἀπόλαυε· παρακμάζει ταχὺ πάντα·
ἓν θέρος ἐξ ἐρίφου τρηχὺν ἔθηκε τράγον.

52.—ΑΔΗΛΟΝ

Παιδείῳ, Θρασύβουλε, σαγηνευθεὶς ὑπ' ἔρωτι
ἀσθμαίνεις, δελφὶς ὥς τις ἐπ' αἰγιαλοῦ
κύματος ἱμείρων· δρέπανον δέ σοι οὐδὲ τὸ Περσέως
ἀρκεῖ ἀποτμῆξαι δίκτυον ᾧ δέδεσαι.

---

[1] i.e. to be mixed in the proportion of one quarter to three
of water.

49.—EVENUS

THE best measure of wine is neither much nor very little; for it is the cause of either grief or madness. It pleases the wine to be the fourth, mixed with three Nymphs.[1] Then it is most suited for the bridal chamber too, but if it breathe too fiercely, it puts the Loves to flight and plunges us in a sleep which is neighbour to death.

50.—AUTOMEDON

BLEST is he first who owes naught to anyone, next he who never married, and thirdly he who is childless. But if a man be mad enough to marry, it is a blessing for him if he buries his wife at once after getting a handsome dowry. Knowing this, be wise, and leave Epicurus to enquire in vain where is the void and what are the atoms.

51.—ANONYMOUS

ENJOY the season of thy prime; all things soon decline: one summer turns a kid into a shaggy he-goat.

52.—ANONYMOUS

CAUGHT, Thrasybulus, in the net of a boy's love, thou gaspest like a dolphin on the beach, longing for the waves, and not even Perseus' sickle[2] is sharp enough to cut through the net that binds thee.

[2] The sickle-shaped knife with which he was armed and with which he liberated Andromeda.

53.—ΑΔΗΛΟΝ

Τό ῥόδον ἀκμάζει βαιὸν χρόνον· ἢν δὲ παρέλθῃ,
ζητῶν εὑρήσεις οὐ ῥόδον, ἀλλὰ βάτον.

J. A. Pott, *Greek Love Songs and Epigrams*, i. p. 141.

54.—ΠΑΛΛΑΔΑ

Γηραλέον με γυναῖκες ἀποσκώπτουσι, λέγουσαι
εἰς τὸ κάτοπτρον ὁρᾶν λείψανον ἡλικίης.
ἀλλ' ἐγὼ εἰ λευκὰς φορέω τρίχας, εἴτε μελαίνας,
οὐκ ἀλέγω, βιότου πρὸς τέλος ἐρχόμενος.
εὐόδμοις δὲ μύροισι καὶ εὐπετάλοις στεφάνοισι   5
καὶ Βρομίῳ παύω φροντίδας ἀργαλέας.

55.—ΤΟΥ ΑΥΤΟΥ

Δὸς πιέειν, ἵνα Βάκχος ἀποσκεδάσειε μερίμνας,
ἂψ ἀναθερμαίνων ψυχομένην κραδίην.

56.—ΑΔΗΛΟΝ

Πῖνε καὶ εὐφραίνου· τί γὰρ αὔριον, ἢ τί τὸ μέλλον,
οὐδεὶς γινώσκει. μὴ τρέχε, μὴ κοπία,
ὡς δύνασαι, χάρισαι, μετάδος, φάγε, θνητὰ λογίζου·
τὸ ζῆν τοῦ μὴ ζῆν οὐδὲν ὅλως ἀπέχει.
πᾶς ὁ βίος τοιόσδε, ῥοπὴ μόνον· ἂν προλάβῃς, σοῦ,   5
ἂν δὲ θάνῃς, ἑτέρου πάντα, σὺ δ' οὐδὲν ἔχεις.

J. A. Pott, *Greek Love Songs and Epigrams*, ii. p. 128.

57.—ΑΓΑΘΙΟΥ ΣΧΟΛΑΣΤΙΚΟΥ

Γαστέρα μὲν σεσάλακτο γέρων εὐώδεϊ Βάκχῳ
Οἰνοπίων, ἔμπης δ' οὐκ ἀπέθηκε δέπας·

53.—Anonymous

THE rose blooms for a little season, and when
that goes by thou shalt find, if thou seekest, no
rose, but a briar.[1]

54.—PALLADAS

THE women mock me for being old, bidding me
look at the wreck of my years in the mirror.   But I,
as I approach the end of my life, care not whether I
have white hair or black, and with sweet-scented
ointments and crowns of lovely flowers and wine I
make heavy care to cease.

55.—By the Same

GIVE me to drink, that wine may scatter my
troubles, warming again my chilled heart.

56.—Anonymous

DRINK and take thy delight ; for none knows what
is to-morrow or what is the future.   Hasten not and
toil not ; be generous and give according to thy power,
eat and let thy thoughts befit a mortal : there is
no difference between living and not living.   All life
is such, a mere turn of the scale ; all things are thine
if thou art beforehand, but if thou diest, another's,
and thou hast nothing.

57.—AGATHIAS SCHOLASTICUS

OLD Oenopion had loaded his belly with sweet-
scented wine, but yet he did not lay aside the cup,

[1] This distich also occurs annexed to another in Book XII.
No. 29, *q.v.*

ἀλλ' ἔτι διψώων ἰδίῃ κατεμέμφετο χειρί,
  ὡς ἀπὸ κρητῆρος μηδὲν ἀφυσσαμένῃ.
οἱ δὲ νέοι ῥέγχουσι, καὶ οὐ σθένος οὐδ' ἀπ' ἀριθμοῦ 5
  τὰς κύλικας γνῶναι τὰς ἔτι πινομένας.
πῖνε, γέρον, καὶ ζῆθι· μάτην δ' ἄρα θεῖος Ὅμηρος
  τείρεσθαι πολιὴν ἐκ νεότητος ἔφη.

58.—ΜΑΚΗΔΟΝΙΟΤ ὙΠΑΤΟΤ

Ἤθελον οὐ χρυσόν τε καὶ ἄστεα μυρία γαίης,
  οὐδ' ὅσα τὰς Θήβας εἶπεν Ὅμηρος ἔχειν·
ἀλλ' ἵνα μοι τροχόεσσα κύλιξ βλύσσειε λυαίῳ,
  χείλεος ἀενάῳ νάματι λουομένου,
καὶ γεραρῶν συνέπινε λάλος χορός, οἱ δὲ περισσοὶ 5
  ἀνέρες ἐργατίναι κάμνον ἐφ' ἡμερίσιν.
οὗτος ἐμοὶ πολὺς ὄλβος, ἀεὶ φίλος· οὐδ' ἀλεγίζω
  τῶν χρυσέων ὑπάτων, τὴν φιάλην κατέχων.

59.—ΤΟΥ ΑΥΤΟΥ

Χανδοπόται, βασιλῆος ἀεθλητῆρες Ἰάκχου,
  ἔργα κυπελλομάχου στήσομεν εἰλαπίνης,
Ἰκαρίου σπένδοντες ἀφειδέα δῶρα Λυαίου·
  ἄλλοισιν μελέτω Τριπτολέμοιο γέρα,
ᾗχι βόες, καὶ ἄροτρα, καὶ ἱστοβοεύς, καὶ ἐχέτλη, 5
  καὶ στάχυς, ἁρπαμένης ἴχνια Φερσεφόνης.
εἴ ποτε δὲ στομάτεσσι βαλεῖν τινα βρῶσιν ἀνάγκη,
  ἀσταφὶς οἰνοπόταις ἄρκιος ἢ Βρομίου.

60.—ΠΑΤΛΟΤ ΣΙΛΕΝΤΙΑΡΙΟΤ

Σπείσομεν οἰνοποτῆρες ἐγερσιγέλωτι Λυαίῳ
  ᾄσομεν ἀνδροφί νον φροντίδα ταῖς φιάλαις,

still thirsty and blaming his own hand for not having ladled anything out of the crater. But the young men are snoring, and none has strength to reckon the number of the cups he goes on drinking. Drink, old man, and live. It was a vain saying of divine Homer's that grey hairs are hard pressed by youth.

58.—MACEDONIUS THE CONSUL

I WISH not for gold, nor for the myriad cities of the world, nor for all that Homer said Thebes contained, but I would have the rounded bowl overflow with wine and my lips be bathed by a perpetual stream. I would have the gossiping company of those I revere drink with me while over-industrious folk labour at the vines. That for me is the great wealth ever dear to me, and when I hold the bowl I care naught for consuls resplendent with gold.

59.—BY THE SAME

WE deep drinkers, champions of Bacchus the king, will initiate the exploits of our banquet, the war of cups, pouring out copiously the gift of the Icarian god. Let the rites of Triptolemus be the concern of others, there where the oxen are and the ploughs and the pole and the share and the corn-ears, relics of the rape of Persephone. But if we are ever forced to put any food in our mouths, the raisins of Bacchus suffice for wine-bibbers.

60.—PAULUS SILENTIARIUS

WE wine-drinkers will pour a libation to Bacchus the awakener of laughter, with the cups we will expel

σιτοδόκῳ δ' ἄγραυλος ἀνὴρ βαρύμοχθος ἰάλλοι
    γαστρὶ μελαμπέπλου μητέρα Φερσεφόνης·
ταυροφόνων δ' ἀμέγαρτα καὶ αἱμαλέα κρέα δόρπων 5
    θηρσὶ καὶ οἰωνοῖς λείψομεν ὠμοβόροις·
ὀστέα δ' αὖ νεπόδων ταμεσίχροα χείλεσι φωτῶν
    εἰξάτω οἷς Ἀΐδης φίλτερος ἠελίου·
ἡμῖν δ' ὀλβιόδωρον ἀεὶ μέθυ καὶ βόσις ἔστω
    καὶ ποτόν· ἀμβροσίην δ' ἄλλος ἔχειν ἐθέλοι. 10

61.—ΜΑΚΗΔΟΝΙΟΤ ΤΠΑΤΟΤ

Χθιζὸν ἐμοὶ νοσέοντι παρίστατο δήϊος ἀνὴρ
    ἰητρός, δεπάων νέκταρ ἀπειπάμενος·
εἶπε δ' ὕδωρ πίνειν· ἀνεμώλιος, οὐδ' ἐδιδάχθη,
    ὅττι μένος μερόπων οἶνον Ὅμηρος ἔφη.

62.—ΠΑΛΛΑΔΑ

Πᾶσι θανεῖν μερόπεσσιν ὀφείλεται, οὐδέ τις ἐστὶν
    αὔριον εἰ ζήσει θνητὸς ἐπιστάμενος.
τοῦτο σαφῶς, ἄνθρωπε, μαθὼν εὔφραινε σεαυτόν,
    λήθην τοῦ θανάτου τὸν Βρόμιον κατέχων.
τέρπεο καὶ Παφίῃ, τὸν ἐφημέριον βίον ἕλκων· 5
    τᾆλλα δὲ πάντα Τύχῃ πράγματα δὸς διέπειν.

63.—ΜΑΚΗΔΟΝΙΟΤ ΤΠΑΤΟΤ

Ανέρες, οἷσι μέμηλεν ἀπήμονος ὄργια Βάκχου,
    ἐλπίσιν ἡμερίδων ῥίψατε τὴν πενίην.
αὐτὰρ ἐμοὶ κρητὴρ μὲν ἔοι δέπας, ἄγχι δὲ ληνὸς
    ἀντὶ πίθου, λιπαρῆς ἔνδιον εὐφροσύνης.

man-killing care. Let toiling rustics supply their bread-tolerating bellies with the mother of black-robed Persephone,[1] and we will leave to wild beasts and birds that feed on raw flesh the copious and bloody banquets of meat of slain bulls. Let us surrender the bones of fish that cut the skin to the lips of men to whom Hades is dearer than the sun. But for us let wine the bountiful be ever food and drink, and let others long for ambrosia.

61.—MACEDONIUS THE CONSUL

A PHYSICIAN, a foeman, stood by me yesterday when I was ill, forbidding me the nectar of the cups, and told me to drink water, an empty-headed fellow who had never learnt that Homer calls wine the strength of men.[2]

62.—PALLADAS

DEATH is a debt due by all men and no mortal knows if he shall be alive to-morrow. Take this well to heart, O man, and make thee merry, since thou possessest wine that is oblivion of death. Take joy too in Aphrodite whilst thou leadest this fleeting life, and give up all else to the control of Fortune.

63.—MACEDONIUS THE CONSUL

YE men who care for the rites of harmless Bacchus, cast away poverty by the hope the vine inspires. Let me have a punch-bowl for a cup, and instead of a cask a wine-vat at hand, the home of bright jollity. Then

i.e. Demeter, and hence bread.　　[2] *Il.* xi. 706.

αὐτίκα δ᾽ ἡμετέροιο πιὼν κρητῆρα Λυαίου   5
παισὶ Καναστραίοις μάρναμαι, ἢν ἐθέλῃς.
οὐ τρομέω δὲ θάλασσαν ἀμείλιχον, οὐδὲ κεραυνούς,
πιστὸν ἀταρβήτου θάρσος ἔχων Βρομίου.

64.—ΑΓΑΘΙΟΥ ΣΧΟΛΑΣΤΙΚΟΥ

Ἡμεῖς μὲν πατέοντες ἀπείρονα καρπὸν Ἰάκχου
ἄμμιγα βακχευτὴν ῥυθμὸν ἀνεπλέκομεν.
ἤδη δ᾽ ἄσπετον οἶδμα κατέρρεεν· οἷα δὲ λέμβοι
κισσύβια γλυκερῶν νήχεθ᾽ ὑπὲρ ῥοθίων,
οἷσιν ἀρυσσάμενοι σχέδιον ποτὸν ἤνομεν ἤδη,   5
θερμῶν Νηϊάδων οὐ μάλα δευόμενοι.
ἡ δὲ καλὴ ποτὶ ληνὸν ὑπερκύπτουσα Ῥοδάνθη
μαρμαρυγῇς κάλλους νᾶμα κατηγλάϊσεν.
πάντων δ᾽ ἐκδεδόνηντο θοαὶ φρένες, οὐδέ τις ἡμέων
ἦεν, ὃς οὐ Βάκχῳ δάμνατο καὶ Παφίῃ.   10
τλήμονες, ἀλλ᾽ ὁ μὲν εἷρπε παραὶ ποσὶν ἄφθονος ἡμῖν·
τῆς δ᾽ ἄρ᾽ ὑπ᾽ ἐλπωρῇ μοῦνον ἐπαιζόμεθα.

Love in Idleness, p. 175.

<Εἰς γραίας>

65.—ΠΑΡΜΕΝΙΩΝΟΣ

Λιμοῦ καὶ γραίης χαλεπὴ κρίσις. ἀργαλέον μὲν
πεινῆν, ἡ κοίτη δ᾽ ἔστ᾽ ὀδυνηροτέρα.
πεινῶν εὔχετο γραῦν· κοιμώμενος εὔχετο λιμὸν
Φίλλις· ἴδ᾽ ἀκλήρου παιδὸς ἀνωμαλίην.

A promontory on the borders of Macedonia and Thrace,
said to have been the home of the giants

straight when I have drunk a bowl of my wine I will fight with the giants, the sons of Canastra,[1] if thou wilt. I dread not the ruthless sea nor the thunderbolt, having the sure courage of fearless Bacchus.

64.—AGATHIAS SCHOLASTICUS

WE treading the plenteous fruit of Bacchus were weaving in a band the rythmic revellers' dance. Already a vast flood was running down, and the cups like boats were swimming on the sweet surges. Dipping therewith we soon had improvised a carouse in no great need of the hot Naiads.[2] But pretty Rhodanthe stooping over the vat made the stream glorious with the radiance of her beauty. The alert spirits of all were shaken from their seat, nor was there one who was not conquered by Bacchus and the Paphian. Poor wretches, his stream flowed at our feet in abundance, but we were mocked by hope alone of her.

There is here a space with a line of asterisks in the MS. indicating the conclusion of the strictly convivial epigrams.

On Old Women (65-74)

65.—PARMENION

IT is difficult to choose between famine and an old woman. To hunger is terrible, but her bed is still more painful. Phillis when starving prayed to have an elderly wife, but when he slept with her he prayed for famine. Lo the inconstancy of a portionless son !

[2] *i.e.* hot water to mix with the wine.

GREEK ANTHOLOGY

66.—ΑΝΤΙΦΙΛΟΥ ΒΥΖΑΝΤΙΟΥ

Κἢν τείνῃς ῥακόεντα πολυτμήτοιο παρειῆς
χρῶτα, καὶ ἀβλεφάρους ὦπας ἐπανθρακίσῃς,
καὶ λευκὴν βάψῃς μέλανι τρίχα, καὶ πυρίφλεκτα
βόστρυχια κροτάφοις οὖλα περικρεμάσῃς,
οὐδὲν ταῦτα, γελοῖα, καὶ ἢν ἔτι πλείονα ῥέξῃς,   5

*　　*　　*　　*

67.—ΜΥΡΙΝΟΥ

Ὗ τετρηκόσι' ἐστίν· ἔχεις δὲ σὺ τοὺς ἐνιαυτοὺς
δὶς τόσσους, τρυφερὴ Λαΐ κορωνεκάβη,
Σισύφου ὦ μάμμη, καὶ Δευκαλίωνος ἀδελφή.
βάπτε δὲ τὰς λευκάς, καὶ λέγε πᾶσι τατᾶ.

68.—ΛΟΥΚΙΛΛΙΟΥ

Τὰς τρίχας, ὦ Νίκυλλα, τινὲς βάπτειν σε λέγουσιν,
ἃς σὺ μελαινοτάτας ἐξ ἀγορᾶς ἐπρίω.

69.—ΤΟΥ ΑΥΤΟΥ

Τὰς πολιὰς βάψασα Θεμιστονόη τρικόρωνος
γίνεται ἐξαπίνης οὐ νέα, ἀλλὰ Ῥέα.

70.—ΛΕΩΝΙΔΑ ΑΛΕΞΑΝΔΡΕΩΣ

Γρῆῦν ἔγημε Φιλῖνος, ὅτ' ἦν νέος· ἡνίκα πρέσβυς,
δωδεκέτιν· Παφίῃ δ' ὥριος οὐδέποτε.
τοιγὰρ ἄπαις διέμεινε ποτὲ σπείρων ἐς ἄκαρπα·
νῦν δ' ἑτέροις γήμας, ἀμφοτέρων στέρεται.

---

[1] The point of this is not obvious.
[2] The crow was supposed to live nine times as long as a man, and Hecuba is often cited as an example of a very old woman.

66.—ANTIPHILUS OF BYZANTIUM

EVEN if you smoothen the wrinkled skin of your many-trenched cheeks, and blacken with coal your lidless eyes, and dye your white hair black, and hang round your temples curly ringlets crisped by fire, this is useless and even ridiculous, and even if you go further

67.—MYRINUS

THE letter υ signifies four hundred,[1] but your years are twice as much, my tender Lais, as old as a crow and Hecuba put together,[2] grandmother of Sisyphus and sister of Deucalion. But dye your white hair and say "tata"[3] to everyone.

68.—LUCILIUS

SOME say, Nicylla, that you dye your hair, but you bought it as black as coal in the market.

69.—BY THE SAME

THEMISTONOE, three times a crow's age, when she dyes her grey hair becomes suddenly not young (*nea*) but Rhea.[4]

70.—LEONIDAS OF ALEXANDRIA

PHILINUS when he was young married an old woman, in his old age he married a girl of twelve, but he never knew Venus at the right season. Therefore sowing formerly in barren land he remained childless, and now has married a wife for others to enjoy and is deprived of both blessings.

[3] A child's word, "papa." *cp.* Mart. i. 101.
[4] The mother of the gods.

71.—ΝΙΚΑΡΧΟΥ

Ἤκμασε Νικονόη· κἀγὼ λέγω· ἤκμασε δ' αὐτὴ
ἡνίκα Δευκαλίων ἄπλετον εἶδεν ὕδωρ.
ταῦτα μὲν οὖν ἡμεῖς οὐκ οἴδαμεν, ἀλλ' ὅτι ταύτην
οὐκ ἄνδρα ζητεῖν νῦν ἔδει, ἀλλὰ τάφον.

72.—ΒΑΣΣΟΥ ΣΜΥΡΝΑΙΟΥ

Ἡ πολιὴ κροτάφοισι Κυτώταρις, ἡ πολύμυθος
γραῖα, δι' ἣν Νέστωρ οὐκέτι πρεσβύτατος,
ἡ φάος ἀθρήσασ' ἐλάφου πλέον, ἡ χερὶ λαιῇ
γῆρας ἀριθμεῖσθαι δεύτερον ἀρξαμένη,
ζώει καὶ λεύσσουσα καὶ ἀρτίπος, οἷά τε νύμφη,   5
ὥστε με διστάζειν, μή τι πέπονθ' Ἀΐδης.

73.—ΝΙΚΑΡΧΟΥ

Γραῖα καλὴ (τί γάρ;) οἶσθας ὅτ' ἦν νέα· ἀλλὰ τότ'
ᾔτει,
νῦν δ' ἐθέλει δοῦναι μισθὸν ἐλαυνομένη.
εὑρήσεις τεχνῖτιν· ὅταν δὲ πίῃ, τότε μᾶλλον
εἰς ὃ θέλεις αὐτὴν εὐεπίτακτον ἔχεις.
πίνει γὰρ καὶ τρεῖς καὶ τέσσαρας, ἢν ἐθελήσῃς,   5
ξέστας, κἀκ τούτου γίνετ' ἄνω τὰ κάτω·
κολλᾶται, κνίζει, παθικεύεται· ἤν τι διδῷ τις,
λαμβάνει· ἢν μὴ δῷ, μισθὸν ἔχει τὸ πάθος.

---

[1] Stags were supposed to live four times as long as crows.
[2] The fingers of the right hand were used for counting
hundreds and thousands, those of the left for decades and

71.—NICARCHUS

Niconoe was once in her prime, I admit that, but her prime was when Deucalion looked on the vast waters. Of those times we have no knowledge, but of her now we know that she should seek not a husband, but a tomb.

72.—BASSUS OF SMYRNA

Cytotaris with her grey temples, the garrulous old woman, who makes Nestor no longer the oldest of men, she who has looked on the light longer than a stag [1] and has begun to reckon her second old age on her left hand,[2] is alive and sharp-sighted and firm on her legs like a bride, so that I wonder if something has not befallen Death.

73.—NICARCHUS

A handsome old woman (why deny it?) you know she was, when she was young; but then she asked for money while now she is ready to pay her mount. You will find her an artist, and when she has had something to drink then all the more you will have her submissive to whatever you want. For she drinks, if you consent, three or four pints, and then things are all topsy-turvy with her; she clings, she scratches, she plays the pathic; and if one gives her anything, she accepts, if not, the pleasure is her payment.

units. The meaning then, I suppose, is that she has reached a thousand and is now counting the years of the first century of her next thousand which he calls her second old age.

74.—ΤΟΥ ΑΥΤΟΥ

Τὴν δύσκωφον γραῖαν, Ὀνήσιμε, πρὸς Διός, ἔξω
ἔκβαλε· πολλὰ λίην πράγματά μοι παρέχει.
ἢν αὐτῇ τυροὺς ἁπαλοὺς εἴπωμεν ἐνέγκαι,
οὐ τυροὺς, πυροὺς δ᾽ ἔρχετ᾽ ἔχουσα νέους.
πρώην τὴν κεφαλὴν ἐπόνουν, καὶ πήγανον αὐτὴν   5
ᾔτουν· ἡ δ᾽ ἔφερεν τήγανον ὀστράκινον.
ἂν †ὁπὸν αἰτήσω, δοκὸν εἰσφέρει· ἂν, "Λάχανόν μοι."
εἴπω "δός" πεινῶν, εὐθὺ φέρει λάσανον.
ὄξος ἐὰν αἰτῶ, τόξον φέρει· ἂν δέ γε τόξον,
ὄξος· ὅλως δ᾽ ὃ λέγω οὔποτ᾽ ἐπαισθάνεται.   10
αἰσχρὸν τῆς γραός με χάριν κήρυκα γενέσθαι,
καὶ μελετᾶν ἔξω, νυκτὸς ἐγειρόμενον.

Εἰς πύκτας

75.—ΛΟΥΚΙΛΛΙΟΥ

Οὗτος ὁ νῦν τοιοῦτος Ὀλυμπικὸς εἶχε, Σεβαστε,
ῥῖνα, γένειον, ὀφρῦν, ὠτάρια, βλέφαρα·
εἶτ᾽ ἀπογραψάμενος πύκτης ἀπολώλεκε πάντα,
ὥστ᾽ ἐκ τῶν πατρικῶν μηδὲ λαβεῖν τὸ μέρος·
εἰκόνιον γὰρ ἀδελφὸς ἔχων προενήνοχεν αὐτοῦ,   5
καὶ κέκριτ᾽ ἀλλότριος, μηδὲν ὅμοιον ἔχων.

76.—ΤΟΥ ΑΥΤΟΥ

Ῥύγχος ἔχων τοιοῦτον, Ὀλυμπικέ, μήτ᾽ ἐπὶ κρήνην
ἔλθῃς, μήτ᾽ ἐνόρα πρός τι διαυγὲς ὕδωρ.
καὶ σὺ γάρ, ὡς Νάρκισσος, ἰδὼν τὸ πρόσωπον ἐναργές,
τεθνήξῃ, μισῶν σαυτὸν ἕως θανάτου.

74.—By the Same

Turn out that stone-deaf old woman, Onesimus, for God's sake, she is such a nuisance to me. If we tell her to bring soft cheeses (*turoi*), she comes not with cheeses, but with fresh grains of wheat (*puroi*). The other day I had a headache and asked her for rue (*peganon*) and she brought me an earthenware frying-pan (*teganon*); if I ask her for —— she brings me a rafter; if I say when I am hungry, " Give me some greens " (*lachanon*), she at once brings a night-stool (*lasanon*). If I ask for vinegar (*oxos*), she brings me a bow (*toxon*), and if I ask for a bow, she brings vinegar ; in fact she does not comprehend a word I say. It would disgrace me to become a crier all for the sake of the old woman, and to get up at night and practise outside the town.

On Prizefighters (75-81)

75.—LUCILIUS

This Olympicus who is now such as you see him, Augustus, once had a nose, a chin, a forehead, ears and eyelids. Then becoming a professional boxer he lost all, not even getting his share of his father's inheritance ; for his brother presented a likeness of him he had and he was pronounced to be a stranger, as he bore no resemblance to it.

76.—By the Same

Having such a mug, Olympicus, go not to a fountain nor look into any transparent water, for you, like Narcissus, seeing your face clearly, will die, hating yourself to the death.

77.—ΤΟΥ ΑΥΤΟΥ

Εἰκοσέτους σωθέντος Ὀδυσσέος εἰς τὰ πατρῷα
ἔγνω τὴν μορφὴν Ἄργος ἰδὼν ὁ κύων·
ἀλλὰ σὺ πυκτεύσας, Στρατοφῶν, ἐπὶ τέσσαρας ὥρας,
οὐ κυσὶν ἄγνωστος, τῇ δὲ πόλει γέγονας.
ἢν ἐθέλῃς τὸ πρόσωπον ἰδεῖν ἐς ἔσοπτρον ἑαυτοῦ,   5
"Οὐκ εἰμὶ Στρατοφῶν," αὐτὸς ἐρεῖς ὀμόσας.

78.—ΤΟΥ ΑΥΤΟΥ

Κόσκινον ἡ κεφαλή σου, Ἀπολλόφανες, γεγένηται,
ἢ τῶν σητοκόπων βιβλαρίων τὰ κάτω·
ὄντως μυρμήκων τρυπήματα λοξὰ καὶ ὀρθά,
γράμματα τῶν λυρικῶν Λύδια καὶ Φρύγια.
πλὴν ἀφόβως πύκτευε· καὶ ἢν τρωθῇς γὰρ ἄνωθεν,   5
ταῦθ' ὅσ' ἔχεις, ἕξεις· πλείονα δ' οὐ δύνασαι.

79.—ΤΟΥ ΑΥΤΟΥ

Πύκτης ὢν κατέλυσε Κλεόμβροτος· εἶτα γαμήσας
ἔνδον ἔχει πληγῶν Ἴσθμια καὶ Νέμεα,
γραῦν μαχίμην, τύπτουσαν Ὀλύμπια, καὶ τὰ παρ'
    αὐτῷ
μᾶλλον ἰδεῖν φρίσσων ἢ ποτὲ τὸ στάδιον.
ἂν γὰρ ἀναπνεύσῃ, δέρεται τὰς παντὸς ἀγῶνος   5
πληγάς, ὡς ἀποδῷ· κἂν ἀποδῷ, δέρεται.

80.—ΤΟΥ ΑΥΤΟΥ

Οἱ συναγωνισταὶ τὸν πυγμάχον ἐνθάδ' ἔθηκαν
Ἄπιν· οὐδένα γὰρ πώποτ' ἐτραυμάτισεν.

77.—By the Same

When Ulysses after twenty years came safe to his home, Argos the dog recognised his appearance when he saw him, but you, Stratophon, after boxing for four hours, have become not only unrecognisable to dogs but to the city. If you will trouble to look at your face in a glass, you will say on your oath, "I am not Stratophon."

78.—By the Same

Your head, Apollophanes, has become a sieve, or the lower edge of a worm-eaten book, all exactly like ant-holes, crooked and straight, or musical notes Lydian and Phrygian. But go on boxing without fear; for even if you are struck on the head you will have the marks you have—you can't have more.

79.—By the Same

Cleombrotus ceased to be a pugilist, but afterwards married and now has at home all the blows of the Isthmian and Nemean games, a pugnacious old woman hitting as hard as in the Olympian fights, and he dreads his own house more than he ever dreaded the ring. Whenever he gets his wind, he is beaten with all the strokes known in every match to make him pay her his debt [1]; and if he pays it, he is beaten again.

80.—By the Same

His competitors set up here the statue of Apis the boxer, for he never hurt anyone.

[1] *i.e.* his marital devoir.

81.—ΤΟΥ ΑΥΤΟΥ

Πᾶσαν ὅσαν Ἕλληνες ἀγωνοθετοῦσιν ἄμιλλαν
  πυγμῆς, Ἀνδρόλεως πᾶσαν ἀγωνισάμαν·
ἔσχον δ᾽ ἐν Πίσῃ μὲν ἐν ὠτίον, ἐν δὲ Πλαταιαῖς
  ἐν βλέφαρον· Πυθοῖ δ᾽ ἄπνοος ἐκφέρομαι·
Δαμοτέλης δ᾽ ὁ πατὴρ καρύσσετο σὺν πολιήταις   5
  ἆραί με σταδίων ἢ νεκρὸν ἢ κολοβόν.

Εἰς δρομέας

82.—ΝΙΚΑΡΧΟΥ

Πέντε μετ᾽ ἄλλων Χάρμος ἐν Ἀρκαδίᾳ δολιχεύων,
  θαῦμα μέν, ἀλλ᾽ ὄντως ἕβδομος ἐξέπεσεν.
"Ἐξ ὄντων," τάχ᾽ ἐρεῖς, "πῶς ἕβδομος"; εἷς
    φίλος αὐτοῦ,
  "Θάρσει, Χάρμε," λέγων, ἦλθεν ἐν ἱματίῳ.
ἕβδομος οὖν οὕτω παραγίνεται· εἰ δ᾽ ἔτι πέντε   5
  εἶχε φίλους, ἦλθ᾽ ἄν, Ζωῖλε, δωδέκατος.

83.—ΛΟΥΚΙΛΛΙΟΥ

Τὸν σταδιῇ πρῴην Ἐρασίστρατον ἡ μεγάλη γῆ,
  πάντων σειομένων, οὐκ ἐσάλευσε μόνον.

84.—ΤΟΥ ΑΥΤΟΥ

Οὔτε τάχιον ἐμοῦ τις ἐν ἀντιπάλοισιν ἔπιπτεν,
  οὔτε βράδιον ὅλως ἔδραμε τὸ στάδιον·
δίσκῳ μὲν γὰρ ὅλως οὐδ᾽ ἤγγισα, τοὺς δὲ πόδας μου
  ἐξᾶραι πηδῶν ἴσχυον οὐδέποτε·
κυλλὸς δ᾽ ἠκόντιζεν ἀμείνονα· πέντε δ᾽ ἀπ᾽ ἄθλων   5
  πρῶτος ἐκηρύχθην πεντετριαζόμενος.

---

[1] As was done after a battle.
[2] He is ridiculing of course the runner's extreme slowness.

81.—By the Same

I, Androleos, took part in every boxing contest that the Greeks preside over, every single one. At Pisa I saved one ear, and in Plataea one eyelid, but at Delphi I was carried out insensible. Damoteles, my father, and my fellow-townsmen had been summoned by herald[1] to bear me out of the stadion either dead or mutilated.

On Runners (82-86)
82.—NICARCHUS

Charmus in Arcadia in the long race with five others came in (wonderful to say, but it is a fact) seventh. "As there were six," you will probably say, "how seventh?" A friend of his came in his overcoat calling out "Go it, Charmus," so that thus he ran in seventh and if he had had five more friends, Zoilus, he would have come in twelfth.

83.—LUCILIUS

Of late the great earth made everything quake, but only the runner Erasistratus it did not move from his place.[2]

84.—By the Same

None among the competitors was thrown quicker than myself and none ran the race slower. With the quoit I never came near the rest, I never was able to lift my legs for a jump and a cripple could throw the javelin better than I. I am the first who out of the five events was proclaimed beaten in all five.[3]

[3] He pretends that this athlete had entered for the pentathlon, which consisted of wrestling, running, quoit throwing, jumping, and throwing the javelin.

85.—ΤΟΥ ΑΥΤΟΥ

Νύκτα μέσην ἐποίησε τρέχων ποτὲ Μάρκος ὁπλίτης,
 ὥστ᾽ ἀποκλεισθῆναι πάντοθε τὸ στάδιον.
οἱ γὰρ δημόσιοι κεῖσθαί τινα πάντες ἔδοξαν
 ὁπλίτην τιμῆς εἵνεκα τῶν λιθίνων.
καὶ τί γάρ; εἰς ὥρας ἠνοίγετο· καὶ τότε Μάρκος   5
 ἦλθε, προσελλείπων τῷ σταδίῳ στάδιον.

86—ΑΔΗΛΟΝ

Τὸ στάδιον Περικλῆς εἴτ᾽ ἔδραμεν, εἴτ᾽ ἐκάθητο,
 οὐδεὶς οἶδεν ὅλως· δαιμόνιος βραδυτής.
ὁ ψόφος ἦν ὕσπληγος ἐν οὔασι, καὶ στεφανοῦτο
 ἄλλος, καὶ Περικλῆς δάκτυλον οὐ προέβη.

87.—ΛΟΥΚΙΛΛΙΟΥ

Τιμόμαχον τὸν μακρὸν ὁ πεντόργυιος ἐχώρει
 οἶκος, ὑπὲρ γαίης πάντοτε κεκλιμένον·
στῆναι δ᾽ εἴ ποτ᾽ ἔχρῃζεν, ἔδει τοὺς παῖδας ἀπ᾽ ὄρθρου
 τὴν ὀροφὴν τρῆσαι πέντ᾽ ἐπὶ πέντε πόδας.

88.—ΤΟΥ ΑΥΤΟΥ

Τὴν μικρὴν παίζουσαν Ἐρώτιον ἥρπασε κώνωψ·
 ἡ δέ· "Τί," φησί, "πάθω; Ζεῦ πάτερ, ἦ μ᾽ ἐθέλεις";

89.—ΤΟΥ ΑΥΤΟΥ

Ὁ βραχὺς Ἑρμογένης, ὅταν ἐκβάλῃ εἰς τὸ χαμαί τι,
 ἕλκει πρὸς τὰ κάτω τοῦτο δορυδρεπάνῳ.

---

[1] *i.e.* the whole length of the course. He had not moved at all.

[2] This phrase, meaning that the signal for the start had long been given, is quoted from an older epigram (Book XVI. 53).

85.—By the Same

Marcus once running in armour, went on until it was midnight, so that the course was closed on all sides; for the public servants all thought that he was one of the honorary stone statues of men in armour set up there. What happened? Why next year they opened, and Marcus came in, but a whole stadion [1] behind.

86.—Anonymous

No one knows if Pericles ran or sat in the stadion race. Marvellous slowness! "The noise of the barrier's fall was in our ears [2]" and another was receiving the crown and Pericles had not advanced an inch.

Chiefly on Defects of Stature (87–111)

87.—LUCILIUS

The house five fathoms long had room for tall Timomachus if he always lay on the floor; but if he ever wanted to stand, his slaves had to bore a hole in the roof in the morning five feet by five.

88.—By the Same

A gnat carried off little Erotion as she was playing. "What is going to happen to me?" she said, "Dost thou want me, father Zeus?" [3]

89.—By the Same

Short Hermogenes when he lets anything fall on the ground pulls it down with a halbert. [4]

---

[3] Alluding to the story of Ganymede, who was carried off by an eagle to serve Zeus.

[4] An absurd hyperbole. Even things on the ground are too high for him to get at.

90.—ΤΟΥ ΑΥΤΟΥ

Τῷ πατρὶ θυμωθείς, Διονύσιε, Μάρκος ὁ μικρός,
πυρῆνα στήσας, αὐτὸν ἀπηγχόνισεν.

91.—ΤΟΥ ΑΥΤΟΥ

Ἐν καλάμῳ πήξας ἀθέρα Στρατονικος ὁ λεπτός,
καὶ τριχὸς ἐκδήσας, αὐτὸν ἀπηγχόνισεν·
καὶ τί γάρ; οὐχὶ κάτω βρῖσεν βαρύς· ἀλλ' ὑπὲρ αὐτῶν,
νηνεμίας οὔσης, νεκρὸς ἄνω πέταται.

92.—ΤΟΥ ΑΥΤΟΥ

Γάϊος ἐκπνεύσας τὸ πανύστατον ἐχθὲς ὁ λεπτὸς
εἰς τὴν ἐκκομιδὴν οὐδὲν ἀφῆκεν ὅλως·
καὶ πέρας εἰς ἀΐδην καταβὰς οἷόσπερ ὅτ' ἔζη,
τῶν ὑπὸ γῆν σκελετῶν λεπτότατος πέταται.
τὴν δὲ κενὴν κλίνην οἱ φράτορες ἦραν ἐπ' ὤμων,   5
ἐγγράψαντες ἄνω· "Γάϊος ἐκφέρεται."

93.—ΤΟΥ ΑΥΤΟΥ

Τῶν Ἐπικουρείων ἀτόμων ποτὲ Μάρκος ὁ λεπτός,
τῇ κεφαλῇ τρήσας, εἰς τὸ μέσον διέβη.

94.—ΤΟΥ ΑΥΤΟΥ

Σαλπίζων ἔπνευσεν ὅσον βραχὺ Μάρκος ὁ λεπτός,
καὶ κατὰ τῆς κεφαλῆς ὀρθὸς ἀπῆλθε κάτω.

95.—ΤΟΥ ΑΥΤΟΥ

Τὸν μικρὸν Μάκρωνα θέρους κοιμώμενον εὑρὼν
εἰς τρώγλην μικρὸς τοῦ ποδὸς εἵλκυσε μῦς.
ὃς δ' ἐν τῇ τρώγλῃ ψιλὸς τὸν μῦν ἀποπνίξας,
"Ζεῦ πάτερ," εἶπεν, "ἔχεις δεύτερον Ἡρακλέα."

90.—BY THE SAME

Do you know, Dionysius, that little Marcus, being angry with his father, set on end a probe and hanged himself on it.

91.—BY THE SAME

THIN Stratonicus fixed on a reed a spike of corn and attaching himself to it by a hair hanged himself. And what happened ? He was not heavy enough to hang down, but his dead body flies in the air above his gallows, although there is no wind.

92.—BY THE SAME

LEAN Gaius, when he breathed his last yesterday, left absolutely nothing to be carried to the grave, and finally going down to Hades just as he was when alive flutters there the thinnest of the skeletons under earth. His kinsmen bore on their shoulders his empty bier, writing above it "This is the funeral of Gaius."

93.—BY THE SAME

LEAN Marcus once made a hole with his head in one of Epicurus' atoms and went through the middle of it.

94.—BY THE SAME

LEAN Marcus sounding a trumpet just blew into it and went straight headforemost down it.

95.—BY THE SAME

A SMALL mouse finding little Macron asleep one summer's day dragged him into its hole by his foot. But he in the hole, though unarmed, strangled the mouse and said, "Father Zeus, thou hast a second Heracles."

96.—ΝΙΚΑΡΧΟΥ

Ἀρκάδας οὐχ οὕτω Στυμφαλίδες, ὡς ἐμὲ κίχλαι
   αἱ νέκυες ξηροῖς ἤκαχον ὀσταρίοις,
Ἅρπυιαι, δραχμῆς ξηρὴ δεκάς. ὢ ἐλεειναὶ
   λειμώνων ἐτύμως, ἔρρετε, νυκτερίδες.

97.—ΑΜΜΙΑΝΟΥ

Τῷ Στρατονικείῳ πόλιν ἄλλην οἰκοδομεῖτε,
   ἢ τούτοις ἄλλην οἰκοδομεῖτε πόλιν.

98.—ΤΟΥ ΑΥΤΟΥ

Ἔστω μητρόπολις πρῶτον πόλις, εἶτα λεγέσθω
   μητρόπολις· μὴ νῦν, ἡνίκα μηδὲ πόλις.

99.—ΛΟΥΚΙΛΛΙΟΥ

Τὸν λεπτὸν φυσῶντα τὸ πῦρ Πρόκλον ἦρεν ὁ καπνός,
   καὶ διὰ τῶν θυρίδων ἔνθεν ἀπῆλθεν ἔχων.
ἀλλὰ μόλις νεφέλῃ προσενήξατο, καὶ δι᾽ ἐκείνης
   προσκατέβη τρωθεὶς μυρία ταῖς ἀτόμοις.

100.—ΤΟΥ ΑΥΤΟΥ

Οὕτω κουφότατος πέλε Γάϊος, ὥστ᾽ ἐκολύμβα
   τοῦ ποδὸς ἐκκρεμάσας ἢ λίθον ἢ μόλιβον.

101.—ΤΟΥ ΑΥΤΟΥ

Ῥιπίζων ἐν ὕπνοις Δημήτριος Ἀρτεμιδώραν
   τὴν λεπτήν, ἐκ τοῦ δώματος ἐξέβαλεν.

---

[1] Presumably this ridicules the man's arrogance and the airs he gave himself.

96.—NICARCHUS

THE birds of Stymphalus vexed not so the Arcadians, as those dead thrushes vexed me with their dry bones, very harpies, ten of them, a dry drachma's worth. Out on you, wretched creatures, true bats of the fields.

97.—AMMIANUS

BUILD another city for the man from Stratonicea, or build another for the inhabitants of this one.[1]

98.—BY THE SAME

LET a city first be a metropolis and then be called so, but not now when it is not even a city.

99.—LUCILIUS

As thin little Proclus was blowing the fire the smoke took him up and went off with him from here through the window. With difficulty he swum to a cloud and came down through it wounded in a thousand places by the atomies.

100.—BY THE SAME

GAIUS was so very light that he used to dive with a stone or lead hung from his foot.

101.—BY THE SAME

DEMETRIUS, fanning slight little Artemidora in her sleep, fanned her off the roof.[2]

---

[2] i.e. the flat roof on which people sleep in the East.

102.—ΑΜΜΙΑΝΟΥ, οἱ δὲ ΝΙΚΑΡΧΟΥ

Ἐξαίρων ποτ' ἄκανθαν ὁ λεπτακινὸς Διόδωρος
αὐτὸς ἐτρύπησεν τῷ ποδὶ τὴν βελόνην.

103.—ΛΟΥΚΙΛΛΙΟΥ

Ἐξ ἀτόμων Ἐπίκουρος ὅλον τὸν κόσμον ἔγραψεν
εἶναι, τοῦτο δοκῶν, Ἄλκιμε, λεπτότατον.
εἰ δὲ τότ' ἦν Διόφαντος, ἔγραψεν ἂν ἐκ Διοφάντου,
τοῦ καὶ τῶν ἀτόμων πουλύ τι λεπτοτέρου,
ἢ τὰ μὲν ἄλλ' ἔγραψε συνεστάναι ἐξ ἀτόμων ἄν,   5
ἐκ τούτου δ' αὐτάς, Ἄλκιμε, τὰς ἀτόμους.

104.—ΤΟΥ ΑΥΤΟΥ

Ἱππεύων μύρμηκι Μενέστρατος, ὡς ἐλέφαντι,
δύσμορος ἐξαπίνης ὕπτιος ἐξετάθη,
λακτισθεὶς δ' ὡς εἶχε τὸ καίριον, "Ὦ φθόνε," φησίν
" οὕτως ἱππεύων ὤλετο καὶ Φαέθων."

Rendered by Ausonius, *Ep.* 122.

105.—ΤΟΥ ΑΥΤΟΥ

Τὸν μέγαν ἐζήτουν Εὐμήκιον· ὃς δ' ἐκάθευδεν
μικρῷ ὑπ' ὀξυβάφῳ τὰς χέρας ἐκτανύσας.

106.--ΤΟΥ ΑΥΤΟΥ

Ἀρθεὶς ἐξ αὔρης λεπτῆς ἐποτᾶτο δι' αἴθρης
Χαιρήμων, ἀχύρου πολλὸν ἐλαφρότερος·

102.—AMMIANUS or NICARCHUS

THIN little Diodorus once in taking a thorn out made a hole in the needle with his foot.[1]

103.—LUCILIUS

EPICURUS wrote that all the world consisted of atoms, thinking, Alcimus, that an atom was the most minute thing. But if Diophantus had existed then he would have written that it consisted of Diophantus, who is much more minute than the atoms. Or he would have written that other things were composed of atoms, but the atoms themselves, Alcimus, of Diophantus.

104.—BY THE SAME

POOR Menestratus once, riding on an ant as if it were an elephant, was suddenly stretched on his back. When it trod on him and he was breathing his last, "O Envy!" he exclaimed, "thus riding perished Phaethon too."

105.—BY THE SAME

I WAS looking for great Eumecius, and he was asleep with his arms stretched out under a small saucer.

106.—BY THE SAME

CHAEREMON caught by a slight breeze was floating in the air, much lighter than a straw. He would

[1] *i.e.* instead of piercing his foot with the needle.

καὶ τάχ᾽ ἂν ἐρροίζητο δι᾽ αἰθέρος, εἰ μὴ ἀράχνη
τοὺς πόδας ἐμπλεχθεὶς ὕπτιος ἐκρέματο.
αὐτοῦ δὴ νύκτας τε καὶ ἤματα πέντε κρεμασθεὶς   5
ἐκταῖος κατέβη νήματι τῆς ἀράχνης.

107.—ΤΟΥ ΑΥΤΟΥ

Αἰγείρου φύλλῳ πεφορημένῳ ἐξ ἀνέμοιο
πληγεὶς Χαιρήμων ὕπτιος ἐξετάθη.
κεῖται δ᾽ ἡ Τιτυῷ ἐναλίγκιος, ἢ πάλι κάμπῃ,
ἁπλώσας κατὰ γῆς σῶμα τὸ καννάβινον.

108.—ΑΔΗΛΟΝ

Κόνων δίπηχυς, ἡ γυνὴ δὲ τεσσάρων·
ἐν τῇ κλίνῃ δὲ τῶν ποδῶν ἰσουμένων,
σκόπει Κόνωνος ποῦ τὸ χεῖλος ἔρχεται.

109.—ΑΛΛΟ

Οὐδ᾽ ἐπικύψαι ἔχει Δημήτριος οὐδὲν ὁ μικρός·
ἀλλ᾽ †ἔρριπται χαμαὶ πάντοτ᾽ ἐπαιρόμενος.

110.—ΝΙΚΑΡΧΟΥ

Τρεῖς λεπτοὶ πρῴην περὶ λεπτοσύνης ἐμάχοντο,
τίς προκριθεὶς εἴη λεπτεπιλεπτότερος.
ὧν ὁ μὲν εἷς, Ἕρμων, μεγάλην ἐνεδείξατο τέχνην,
καὶ διέδυ ῥαφίδος τρῆμα, λίνον κατέχων·
Δημᾶς δ᾽ ἐκ τρώγλης βαίνων ἐς ἀράχνιον ἔστη,   5
ἡ δ᾽ ἀράχνη νήθουσ᾽ αὐτὸν ἀπεκρέμασεν.
Σωσίπατρος δ᾽ ἐβόησεν· "Ἐμὲ στεφανώσατ᾽· ἐγὼ
        γὰρ
εἰ βλέπομ᾽, ἥττημαι· πνεῦμα γάρ εἰμι μόνον."

soon have been swept away through the air, if he had not caught his feet in a spider's web and hung there on his back. Here he hung for five days and nights, and on the sixth day came down by a thread of the web.

107.—By the Same

Chaeremon fell flat on his back, struck by a poplar leaf carried by the wind, and he lies on the ground like Tityus or rather like a caterpillar, stretching on the ground his skeleton [1] body.

108.—Anonymous

(By some attributed to Julian the Apostate)

Conon is two cubits tall, his wife four. In bed, then, with their feet on a level, reckon where Conon's face is.

109.—Anonymous

Little Demetrius has not wherewith to stoop, but always lies flat on the ground trying to get up.

110.—NICARCHUS

Three thin men were competing the other day about thinness, to see which of them would be adjudged the very thinnest. The one, Hermon, ex-hibited great skill and went through the eye of a needle holding the thread. But Demas coming out of a hole stopped at a spider's web, and the spider spinning hung him from it. But Sosipater exclaimed, "Give me the prize, for I lose it if I am seen, since I am nothing but air."

[1] The word *canabos* means the block round which a sculptor moulds his clay.

111. <ΤΟΥ ΑΥΤΟΥ>

Βουλόμενός ποθ' ὁ λεπτὸς ἀπάγξασθαι Διόφαντος,
νῆμα λαβὼν ἀράχνης αὑτὸν ἀπηγχόνισεν.

Εἰς ἰατρούς
112.—ΤΟΥ ΑΥΤΟΥ

Πρίν σ' ἐναλείψασθαι, Δημόστρατε, " Χαῖρ', ἱερὸν
φῶς,"
εἰπὲ τάλας· οὕτως εὔσκοπός ἐστι Δίων.
οὐ μόνον ἐξετύφλωσεν Ὀλυμπικόν, ἀλλὰ δι' αὐτοῦ
εἰκόνος ἧς εἶχεν τὰ βλέφαρ' ἐξέβαλεν.

113.—ΤΟΥ ΑΥΤΟΥ

Τοῦ λιθίνου Διὸς ἐχθὲς ὁ κλινικὸς ἥψατο Μάρκος·
καὶ λίθος ὢν καὶ Ζεύς, σήμερον ἐκφέρεται.

114.—ΤΟΥ ΑΥΤΟΥ

Ἑρμογένην τὸν ἰατρὸν ὁ ἀστρολόγος Διόφαντος
εἶπε μόνους ζωῆς ἐννέα μῆνας ἔχειν.
κἀκεῖνος γελάσας, " Τί μὲν ὁ Κρόνος ἐννέα μηνῶν,"
φησί, " λέγει, σὺ νόει· τἀμὰ δὲ σύντομά σοι."
εἶπε, καὶ ἐκτείνας μόνον ἥψατο· καὶ Διόφαντος   5
ἄλλον ἀπελπίζων, αὐτὸς ἀπεσκάρισεν.

cp. Ausonius, Ep. 73.

115.—ΤΟΥ ΑΥΤΟΥ

Ἤν τιν' ἔχῃς ἐχθρόν, Διονύσιε, μὴ καταράσῃ
τὴν Ἶσιν τούτῳ, μηδὲ τὸν Ἁρποκράτην,
μηδ' εἴ τις τυφλοὺς ποιεῖ θεός, ἀλλὰ Σίμωνα·
καὶ γνώσῃ, τί θεός, καὶ τί Σίμων δύναται.

111.—By the Same

Lean Diophantus once wishing to hang himself
took a thread from a spider's web and did so.

On Physicians (112–126)
112.—By the Same

Before he anoints your eyes, Demostratus, say
" Adieu dear light," so successful is Dion.   Not only
did he blind Olympicus, but through his treatment
of him put out the eyes of the portrait of himself
he had.

113.—By the Same

The physician Marcus laid his hand yesterday on
the stone Zeus, and though he is of stone and Zeus
he is to be buried to-day.

114.—By the Same

The astrologer Diophantus told Hermogenes the
doctor that he had only nine months to live, and he,
smiling, said, " You understand what Saturn says will
happen in nine months, but my treatment is more
expeditious for you."   Having said so he reached out
his hand and only touched him, and Diophantus,
trying to drive another to despair, himself gave his
last gasp.

115.—By the Same

If you have an enemy, Dionysius, call not down on
him the curse of Isis or Harpocrates or of any god
who blinds men, but call on Simon and you will see
what a god's power is and what Simon's is.

116.—ΤΟΥ ΑΥΤΟΥ

Εἰς Ἄϊδος κατέπεμψε πάλαι ποτέ, δέσποτα Καῖσαρ,
  ὡς λόγος, Εὐρυσθεὺς τὸν μέγαν Ἡρακλέα·
νῦν δ᾽ ἐμὲ Μηνοφάνης ὁ κλινικός· ὥστε λεγέσθω
  κλινικὸς Εὐρυσθεύς, μηκέτι Μηνοφάνης.

117.—ΣΤΡΑΤΩΝΟΣ

Ἰητρὸς Καπίτων Χρύσην ἐνέχρισεν, ὁρῶντα
  ὀκτὼ μὲν μακρὸν πύργον ἀπὸ σταδίων,
ἄνδρα δ᾽ ἀπὸ σταδίου, διὰ δώδεκα δ᾽ ὄρτυγα πηχῶν,
  φθεῖρα δ᾽ ἀπὸ σπιθαμῶν καὶ δύο δερκόμενον.
νῦν δ᾽ ἀπὸ μὲν σταδίου πόλιν οὐ βλέπει, ἐκ δὲ δι-
      πλέθρου   5
  καιόμενον κατιδεῖν τὸν φάρον οὐ δύναται·
ἵππον ἀπὸ σπιθαμῆς δὲ μόλις βλέπει, ἀντὶ δὲ τοῦ πρὶν
  ὄρτυγος οὐδὲ μέγαν στρουθὸν ἰδεῖν δύναται.
ἂν δὲ προσεγχρίσας αὐτὸν φθάσῃ, οὐδ᾽ ἐλέφαντα
  οὐκέτι μήποτ᾽ ἴδῃ πλησίον ἑσταότα.   10

118.—ΚΑΛΛΙΚΤΗΡΟΣ

Οὔτ᾽ ἔκλυσεν Φείδων μ᾽, οὔθ᾽ ἥψατο· ἀλλὰ πυρέξας
  ἐμνήσθην αὐτοῦ τοὔνομα, κἀπέθανον.

119.—ΤΟΥ ΑΥΤΟΥ

Ἰητρὸς τὴν γραῦν εἴτ᾽ ἔκλυσεν, εἴτ᾽ ἀπέπνιξεν,
  οὐδεὶς γινώσκει· δαιμόνιον τὸ τάχος.
ὁ ψόφος ἦν κλυστῆρος ἐν οὔασι, καὶ στεφανοῦτο
  ἡ σορός, οἱ δ᾽ ἄλλοι τὸν φακὸν ηὐτρέπισαν.

116.—By the Same

Lord Caesar, as they tell, Eurystheus once sent down great Heracles to the house of Hades; but now Menophanes the physician has sent me. So let him be called Doctor Eurystheus and no longer Doctor Menophanes.

117.—STRATO

The physician Capito anointed Chryses' eyes then when he could see a high tower from a mile off and a man from a furlong and a quail from ten yards and a louse even from a foot. Now from a furlong he cannot see the town and from two hundred feet cannot see that the lighthouse is alight; he scarcely sees a horse from half a foot off and as for the quail he once saw, he can't even see a large ostrich. If he manages to give him another dose, he won't ever after be able to see even an elephant standing close to him.

118.—CALLICTER

Phidon did not purge me with a clyster or even feel me, but feeling feverish I remembered his name and died.

119.—By the Same

Whether the doctor purged or strangled the old woman no one knows, but it was terribly sudden. The noise of the clyster was in our ears[1] and her bier was being crowned and the rest prepared the pease-pudding.[2]

[1] cp. No. 86 which this parodies.   [2] A funeral dish.

120.—ΤΟΥ ΑΥΤΟΥ

Ὀρθῶσαι τὸν κυρτὸν ὑποσχόμενος Διόδωρον
Σωκλῆς τετραπέδους τρεῖς ἐπέθηκε λίθους
τοῦ κυρτοῦ στιβαροὺς ἐπὶ τὴν ῥάχιν· ἀλλὰ πιεσθεὶς
τέθνηκεν, γέγονεν δ᾽ ὀρθότερος κανόνος.

121.—ΤΟΥ ΑΥΤΟΥ

Χειρουργῶν ἔσφαξεν Ἀκεστορίδην Ἀγέλαος·
  " Ζῶν γὰρ χωλεύειν," φησίν, " ἔμελλε τάλας."

122.—ΤΟΥ ΑΥΤΟΥ

Πέντ᾽ ἰητρὸς Ἄλεξις ἅμ᾽ ἔκλυσε, πέντ᾽ ἐκάθηρε,
  πέντ᾽ ἴδεν ἀρρώστους, πέντ᾽ ἐνέχρισε πάλιν·
καὶ πᾶσιν μία νύξ, ἓν φάρμακον, εἷς σοροπηγός,
  εἷς τάφος, εἷς Ἀΐδης, εἷς κοπετὸς γέγονεν.

123.—ΗΔΥΛΟΥ

Ἆγις Ἀρισταγόρην οὔτ᾽ ἔκλυσεν, οὔτ᾽ ἔθιγ᾽ αὐτοῦ·
  ἀλλ᾽ ὅσον εἰσῆλθεν, κᾤχετ᾽ Ἀρισταγόρης.
ποῦ τοίην ἀκόνιτος ἔχει φύσιν; ὦ σοροπηγοί,
  Ἆγιν καὶ μίτραις βάλλετε καὶ στεφάνοις.

124.—ΝΙΚΑΡΧΟΥ

α. Ξεῖνε, τί μὰν πεύθη; β. Τίνες ἐν χθονὶ τοῖσδ᾽
  ὑπὸ τύμβοις;
  α. Οὓς γλυκεροῦ φέγγους Ζώπυρος ἐστέρισεν,

128

120.—By the Same

Socles, promising to set Diodorus' crooked back straight, piled three solid stones, each four feet square, on the hunchback's spine. He was crushed and died, but he has become straighter than a ruler.

121.—By the Same

Agelaus by operating killed Acestorides, for he said, " If he had lived the poor fellow would have been lame."

122.—By the Same

Alexis the physician purged by a clyster five patients at one time and five others by drugs; he visited five, and again he rubbed five with ointment. And for all there was one night, one medicine, one coffin-maker, one tomb, one Hades, one lamentation.

123.—HEDYLUS

Agis neither purged Aristagoras, nor touched him, but no sooner had he come in than Aristagoras was gone. What aconite has such natural virtue ? Ye coffin-makers, throw chaplets and garlands on Agis.

124.—NICARCHUS

A. Stranger, what dost thou seek to know ?
B. Who are here in earth under these tombs ?
A. All those whom Zopyrus robbed of the sweet day-

Δᾶμις, Ἀριστοτέλης, Δημήτριος, Ἀρκεσίλαος,
Σώστρατος, οἵ τ᾽ ὀπίσω μέχρι Παραιτονίου.
κηρύκιον γὰρ ἔχων ξύλινον, καὶ πλαστὰ πέδιλα,   5
ὡς Ἑρμῆς, κατάγει τοὺς θεραπευομένους.

125.—ΑΔΕΣΠΟΤΟΝ

Ἰητρὸς Κρατέας καὶ Δάμων ἐνταφιαστὴς
κοινὴν ἀλλήλοις θέντο συνωμοσίην.
καί ῥ᾽ ὁ μὲν οὓς κλέπτεσκεν ἀπ᾽ ἐνταφίων τελαμῶνας
εἰς ἐπιδεσμεύειν πέμπε φίλῳ Κρατέᾳ·
τὸν δ᾽ ἀπαμειβόμενος Κρατέας εἰς ἐνταφιάζειν   5
πέμπεν ὅλους αὐτῷ τοὺς θεραπευομένους.

W. Shepherd, in Wellesley's *Anthologia Polyglotta*, p. 21.

126.—ΑΔΗΛΟΝ

Οὐ μήλη, τριόδοντι δ᾽ ἐνήλειψέν με Χαρῖνος,
σπόγγον ἔχων καινὸν τῶν γραφικῶν πινάκων·
τὴν μήλην δ᾽ ἕλκων, ἐξέσπασε τὸ βλέφαρόν μου
ῥιζόθεν· ἡ μήλη δ᾽ ἔνδον ἔμεινεν ὅλη.
ἂν δὲ δὶς ἐγχρίσῃ με, πονῶν πάλιν οὐκ ἐνοχλήσω   5
ὀφθαλμοὺς αὐτῷ· πῶς γὰρ ὁ μηκέτ᾽ ἔχων;

Εἰς ποιητάς

127.—ΠΩΛΛΙΑΝΟΥ

Εἰσὶ καὶ ἐν Μούσῃσιν Ἐρινύες, αἵ σε ποιοῦσιν
ποιητήν, ἀνθ᾽ ὧν πολλὰ γράφεις ἀκρίτως.
τοίνυν, σοῦ δέομαι, γράφε πλείονα· μείζονα γάρ σοι
εὔξασθαι ταύτης οὐ δύναμαι μανίαν.

---

[1] On the Egyptian coast a considerable distance west of
Alexandria. The cemetery of Alexandria did not of course
extend so far.

light, Damis, Aristoteles, Demetrius, Arcesilaus, Sostratus, and the next ones so far as Paraetonium.[1] For with a wooden herald's staff and counterfeit sandals,[2] like Hermes, he leads down his patients to Hell.

125.—Anonymous

The physician Crateas and the sexton Damon made a joint conspiracy. Damon sent the wrappings he stole from the grave-clothes to his dear Crateas to use as bandages and Crateas in return sent him all his patients to bury.

126.—Anonymous

Charinus anointed my eye not with a spatula, but with a three-pronged fork, and he had a new sponge like those used for paintings. In pulling out the spatula he tore out my eye from the roots and the whole spatula remained inside. But if he anoints me twice, I shall not trouble him any more by suffering from sore eyes ; for how can a man who no longer has eyes do so ?

On Poets (127-137)
127.—POLLIANUS

There are among the Muses too Avengers, who make you a poet, and therefore you write much and without judgment. Now, I entreat you, write still more, for no greater madness can I beseech the gods to give you than that.

---

[2] Attributes of Hermes Psychopompus ; but there is some point here which eludes us.

128.—ΤΟΥ ΑΥΤΟΥ

Εἰ μὴ χαίρω, Φλῶρε, γενοίμην δάκτυλος ἢ πούς
εἰς τῶν σῶν τούτων τῶν κατατεινομένων.
χαίρω, νὴ τὸν κλῆρον, ὃν εὐκλήρησας ἐν ἄθλοις,
ὡς περὶ χοιρείας τοῦ στεφάνου μερίδος.
τοιγὰρ θάρσει, Φλῶρε, καὶ εὔθυμος πάλι γίνου·   5
οὕτω νικῆσαι καὶ δόλιχον δύνασαι.

129.—ΚΕΡΕΑΛΙΟΥ

Ποιητὴς ἐλθὼν εἰς Ἴσθμια πρὸς τὸν ἀγῶνα,
εὑρὼν ποιητάς, εἶπε παρίσθμι' ἔχειν.
μέλλει δ' ἐξορμᾶν εἰς Πύθια· κἂν πάλιν εὕρῃ,
εἰπεῖν οὐ δύναται, "Καὶ παραπύθι' ἔχω."

130.—ΠΩΛΛΙΑΝΟΥ

Τοὺς κυκλίους τούτους, τοὺς αὐτὰρ ἔπειτα λεγοντας,
μισῶ, λωποδύτας ἀλλοτρίων ἐπέων.
καὶ διὰ τοῦτ' ἐλέγοις προσέχω πλέον· οὐδὲν ἔχω γὰρ
Παρθενίου κλέπτειν ἢ πάλι Καλλιμάχου.
θηρὶ μὲν οὐατόεντι γενοίμην, εἴ ποτε γράψω,   5
εἴκελος, ἐκ ποταμῶν χλωρὰ χελιδόνια.
οἱ δ' οὕτως τὸν Ὅμηρον ἀναιδῶς λωποδυτοῦσιν,
ὥστε γράφειν ἤδη μῆνιν ἄειδε, θεά.

---

[1] On a bad poet who won a prize owing to the incapacity of the other competitors, and who expected congratulations.
[2] "Parapythia" of course has no meaning.

128.—By the Same[1]

If I am not pleased, Florus, may I become a dactyl or a foot, one of those that you torture. Yes, I swear by the happy lot you drew in the contest, I am as pleased at your crown as if it were a joint of pork. Therefore be of good heart, Florus, and become cheerful again ; in this fashion you can win the long race as well.

129.—CEREALIUS

A poet coming to the Isthmian games to the contest, when he found other poets there said he had paristhmia (mumps). He is going to start off for the Pythian games, and if he finds poets there again he can't say he has parapythia[2] as well.

130.—POLLIANUS

I hate these cyclic[3] poets who say "natheless eftsoon," filchers of the verses of others, and so I pay more attention to elegies, for there is nothing I want to steal from Callimachus or Parthenius. Let me become like an "eared beast"[4] if ever I write "from the rivers yellow king-cup."[5] But these epic poets strip Homer so shamelessly that they already write "Sing, O Goddess, the wrath."[6]

[3] Contemporary writers of epic poems.
[4] So Callimachus calls a donkey.
[5] Probably from Parthenius. He like Callimachus, wrote elegies. The flower is usually the so-called "greater celandine."
[6] *i.e.* the very first words of his poem.

131.—ΛΟΥΚΙΛΛΙΟΥ

Οὔτ' ἐπὶ Δευκαλίωνος ὕδωρ, ὅτε πάντ' ἐγενήθη,
οὔθ' ὁ καταπρήσας τοὺς ἐπὶ γῆς Φαέθων,
ἀνθρώπους ἔκτεινεν ὅσους Ποτάμων ὁ ποιητής,
καὶ χειρουργήσας ὤλεσεν Ἑρμογένης.
ὥστ' ἐξ αἰῶνος κακὰ τέσσαρα ταῦτ' ἐγενήθη,   5
Δευκαλίων, Φαέθων, Ἑρμογένης, Ποτάμων.

132.—ΤΟΥ ΑΥΤΟΥ

Μισῶ, δέσποτα Καῖσαρ, ὅσοις νέος οὐδέποτ' οὐδεὶς
ἤρεσε, κἂν εἴπῃ, μῆνιν ἄειδε θεά,
ἀλλ' ἢν μὴ Πριάμου τις ἔχῃ χρόνον ἡμιφάλακρος,
ἢ καὶ κυρτὸς ἄγαν, οὐ δύνατ' ἄλφα γράφειν.
εἰ δ' ὄντως οὕτως τοῦτ' ἔστ' ἔχον, ὦ ὕπατε Ζεῦ,   5
εἰς τοὺς κηλήτας ἔρχεται ἡ σοφία.

133.—ΤΟΥ ΑΥΤΟΥ

Τέθνηκ' Εὐτυχίδης ὁ μελογράφος. οἱ κατὰ γαῖαν
φεύγετ'· ἔχων ᾠδὰς ἔρχεται Εὐτυχίδης·
καὶ κιθάρας αὑτῷ διετάξατο συγκατακαῦσαι
δώδεκα, καὶ κίστας εἰκοσιπέντε νόμων.
νῦν ὑμῖν ὁ Χάρων ἐπελήλυθε· ποῦ τις ἀπέλθῃ   5
λοιπόν, ἐπεὶ χᾴδην Εὐτυχίδης κατέχει;

134.—ΤΟΥ ΑΥΤΟΥ

Ἀρχόμεθ', Ἡλιόδωρε; ποιήματα παίζομεν οὕτω
ταῦτα πρὸς ἀλλήλους; Ἡλιόδωρε, θέλεις;
ἆσσον ἴθ', ὥς κεν θᾶσσον ὀλέθρου . . . καὶ γὰρ ἔμ'
                                                ὄψει
μακροφλυαρητὴν Ἡλιοδωρότερον.

131.—LUCILIUS

Nor water in Deucalion's day when all became water, nor Phaethon who burned up the inhabitants of the earth, slew so many men as Potamon the poet and Hermogenes by his surgery killed. So from the beginning of the ages there have been these four curses, Deucalion, Phaethon, Hermogenes and Potamon.

132.—By the Same

I hate, Lord Caesar, those who are never pleased with any young writer, even if he says "Sing, O Goddess, the wrath," but if a man is not as old as Priam, if he is not half bald and not so very much bent, they say he can't write a b c. But, Zeus most high, if this really be so, wisdom visits but the ruptured.

133.—By the Same

Eutychides the lyric poet is dead. Fly, ye people who dwell under earth; Eutychides is coming with odes, and he ordered them to burn with him twelve lyres and twenty-five cases of music. Now indeed Charon has got hold of you. Where can one depart to in future, since Eutychides is established in Hades too?

134.—By the Same

Shall we begin, Heliodorus? Shall we play thus at these poems together? Do you wish it, Heliodorus? "Come near, that swifter thou mayst reach Death's goal";[1] for you will see in me a master of tedious twaddle more Heliodorian than yourself.

---

[1] From *Iliad* vi. 143.

135.—ΤΟΥ ΑΥΤΟΥ

Μηκέτι, μηκέτι, Μάρκε, τὸ παιδίον, ἀλλ' ἐμὲ κόπτου
τὸν πολὺ τοῦ παρὰ σοὶ νεκρότερον τεκνίου.
εἰς ἐμὲ νῦν ἐλέγους ποίει πάλιν, εἰς ἐμὲ θρήνους,
δῆμιε, τὸν στιχίνῳ σφαζόμενον θανάτῳ.
τοῦ σοῦ γὰρ πάσχω νεκροῦ χάριν, οἷα πάθοιεν   5
οἱ καταδείξαντες βιβλία καὶ καλάμους.

136.—ΤΟΥ ΑΥΤΟΥ

Οὐχ οὕτω κακοεργὸν ἐχαλκεύσαντο μάχαιραν
ἄνθρωποι, διὰ τὰς ἐξαπίνης ἐνέδρας,
οἷον ἀκήρυκτον, Καλλίστρατε, καὶ σὺ προσελθὼν
ποιεῖς μοι φονικῶν ἐξαμέτρων πόλεμον.
σάλπιγξον ταχέως ἀνακλητικόν· εἰς ἀνοχὰς γὰρ   5
καὶ Πρίαμος κλαύσας †ἡμερίων ἔτυχεν.

137.—ΤΟΥ ΑΥΤΟΥ

Ὠμοβοείου μοι παραθεὶς τόμον, Ἡλιόδωρε,
καὶ τρία μοι κεράσας ὠμοβιειότερα,
εὐθὺ κατακλύζεις ἐπιγράμμασιν. εἰ δ' ἀσεβήσας
βεβρώκειν τινὰ βοῦν τῶν ἀπὸ Τρινακρίας,
βούλομ' ἅπαξ πρὸς κῦμα χανεῖν . . . εἰ δ' ἐστὶ τὸ κῦμα   5
ἔνθε μακράν, ἄρας εἰς τὸ φρέαρ με βάλε.

---

[1] This and the following two are skits on versifiers who insisted on reciting to their friends.

[2] A parody of Aratus, *Phaen.* 131.

135.--By the Same

No longer, Marcus, no longer lament the boy, but
me, who am much more dead than that child of yours.
Make elegies, hangman, now for me, make dirges
for me who am slain by this versy death. For all
for the sake of that dead child of yours I suffer what
I would the inventors of books and pens might
suffer.[1]

136.—By the Same

No sword so maleficent was ever forged by man for
sudden treacherous attack as is the undeclared war
of murderous hexameters, Callistratus, that you come
to wage with me. Sound the retreat on the bugle
at once, for even Priam by his tears gained his foes'
consent (?) to an armistice.[2]

137.—By the Same

You serve me a slice of raw beef, Heliodorus,
and pour me out three cups of wine rawer than the
beef, and then you wash me out at once with
epigrams. If sinning against heaven I have eaten
one of the oxen from Trinacria, I would like to gulp
down the sea at once [3]—but if the sea is too far
from here, take me up and throw me into a well.

---

[3] To drown like the companions of Ulysses in punishment
for eating the oxen of the Sun in the island Trinacria.

GREEK ANTHOLOGY

138.—ΤΟΥ ΑΥΤΟΥ

Ἂν τοῦ γραμματικοῦ μνησθῶ μόνον Ἡλιοδώρου,
εὐθὺ σολοικίζον τὸ στόμα μου δέδεται.

139.—ΤΟΥ ΑΥΤΟΥ

Γραμματικὸν Ζηνωνὶς ἔχει πώγωνα Μένανδρον,
τὸν δ' υἱὸν τούτῳ φησὶ συνεστακέναι.
τὰς νύκτας δ' αὐτῇ μελετῶν οὐ παύεται οὗτος
πτώσεις, συνδέσμους, σχήματα, συζυγίας.

140.—ΤΟΥ ΑΥΤΟΥ

Τούτοις τοῖς παρὰ δεῖπνον ἀοιδομάχοις λογολέ-
σχαις,
τοῖς ἀπ' Ἀριστάρχου γραμματολικριφίσιν,
οἷς οὐ σκῶμμα λέγειν, οὐ πεῖν φίλον, ἀλλ' ἀνά-
κεινται
νηπυτιευόμενοι Νέστορι καὶ Πριάμῳ,
μή με βάλῃς κατὰ λέξιν ἕλωρ καὶ κύρμα γενέσθαι·   5
σήμερον οὐ δειπνῶ μῆνιν ἄειδε θεά.

141.—ΤΟΥ ΑΥΤΟΥ

Χοιρίδιον καὶ βοῦν ἀπολώλεκα, καὶ μίαν αἶγα,
ὧν χάριν εἴληφας μισθάριον, Μενέκλεις·

---

[1] cp. No. 148 below.   [2] Literally "falls."
[3] Quoted from *Odyssey* iii. 271.

On Grammarians (138–140)

138.—By the Same

If I only think of the grammarian Heliodorus, my tongue at once commits solecisms and I suffer from impediment of speech.[1]

139.—By the Same

Zenonis keeps Menander the bearded grammar-teacher, and says she has entrusted her son to him; but he never stops at night making her practise cases,[2] conjunctions, figures, and conjugations.

140.—By the Same

To these praters, these verse-fighters of the supper table, these slippery dominies of Aristarchus' school who care not for making a joke or drinking, but lie there playing infantile games with Nestor and Priam, cast me not literally "to be their prey and spoil."[3] To-day I don't sup on "Sing, O Goddess, the wrath."

On Rhetors (141–152)

141.—By the Same[4]

I lost a little pig and a cow and one nanny-goat, and on account of them you received your little fee,

---

[4] He is ridiculing lawyers who were fond of dragging classical allusions into their speeches. Martial vi. 19 should be compared.

οὔτε δέ μοι κοινόν τι πρὸς Ὀθρυάδαν γεγένηται,
οὔτ᾽ ἀπάγω κλέπτας τοὺς ἀπὸ Θερμοπυλῶν·
ἀλλὰ πρὸς Εὐτυχίδην ἔχομεν κρίσιν· ὥστε τί ποιεῖ 5
ἐνθάδε μοι Ξέρξης καὶ Λακεδαιμόνιοι;
πλὴν κἀμοῦ μνήσθητι νόμου χάριν, ἢ μέγα κράξω·
"᾽Άλλα λέγει Μενεκλῆς, ἄλλα τὸ χοιρίδιον."

142.—ΤΟΥ ΑΥΤΟΥ

"Πολλοῦ δεῖ" καὶ "σφίν" καὶ τρὶς παρ᾽ ἕκαστα
  "δικασταὶ
ἄνδρες," καὶ "λέγε δὴ τὸν νόμον ἐνθάδε μοι,"
καὶ "ταυτί" καὶ "μῶν" καὶ "τετταράκοντα" καὶ
  "ἄττα"
σκεψάμενος, καί τοι "νὴ Δία," καὶ "μὰ Δία,"
ῥήτωρ ἐστὶ Κρίτων, καὶ παιδία πολλὰ διδάσκει· 5
προσθήσει δ᾽ αὐτοῖς "γρῦ," "φαθί" καὶ "μίν" ἔτι.

143.—ΤΟΥ ΑΥΤΟΥ

Οὐ δέχεται Μάρκον τὸν ῥήτορα νεκρὸν ὁ Πλούτων,
εἰπών, "᾽Αρκείτω Κέρβερος ὧδε κύων.
εἰ δ᾽ ἐθέλεις πάντως, Ἰξίονι καὶ Μελίτωνι
τῷ μελοποιητῇ, καὶ Τιτυῷ μελέτα.
οὐδὲν γὰρ σοῦ χεῖρον ἔχω κακόν, ἄχρις ἂν ἐλθὼν 5
ὧδε σολοικίζῃ Ῥοῦφος ὁ γραμματικός."

144.—ΚΕΡΕΑΛΙΟΥ

Οὐ τὸ λέγειν παράσημα καὶ Ἀττικὰ ῥήματα πέντε,
εὐζήλως ἐστὶν καὶ φρονίμως μελετᾶν·

---

[1] He is here ridiculing rhetors who ornamented their
speeches with phrases from Demosthenes and the old orators.

Menecles. I never had anything in common with
Othryades nor do I prosecute the three hundred
from Thermopylae for theft; my suit is against
Eutychides, so that here how do Xerxes and the
Spartans help me? I beg you just to mention me
for form's sake, or I will call out loud "One thing
says Menecles, and another thing says the piggie."

142.—By the Same[1]

AFTER having studied "Far be it," and sphin[2] and
thrice in each period, "Gentlemen of the jury," and
"Here, usher, repeat the law for me," and "These
presents," and "I put it to you," and "two score,"
and "certain alleged," and indeed "By heaven," and
"'Sdeath," Crito is an orator and teaches numbers of
children, and to these phrases he will add gru,[3]
phathi,[2] and min.[2]

143.—By the Same

PLUTO will not receive the rhetor Marcus when
dead, saying, "Let our one dog Cerberus be enough
here; but if thou wilt come in at any cost, declaim
to Ixion, Melito[4] the lyric poet, and Tityus. For I
have no evil worse than thee, until the day when
Rufus the grammarian shall come here with his
solecisms."

144.—CEREALIUS

To use out-of-the-way words and four or five Attic
ones is not to study with proper fervour and wisdom.

[2] Obsolete forms.
[3] οὐδὲ γρῦ, "not a word," used by Demosthenes.
[4] See No. 246.

οὐδὲ γὰρ εἰ "κάρκαιρε,"¹ καὶ εἰ "κοναβεῖ" τό τε
  "σίζει"
καὶ "κελάρυζε" λέγεις, εὐθὺς Ὅμηρος ἔσῃ.
νοῦν ὑποκεῖσθαι δεῖ τοῖς γράμμασι, καὶ φράσιν
  αὐτῶν   5
εἶναι κοινοτέραν, ὥστε νοεῖν ἃ λέγεις.

145.—ΑΔΗΛΟΝ

Εἰκὼν ἡ Σέξστου μελετᾷ, Σέξστος δὲ σιωπᾷ.
εἰκὼν ἦν ῥήτωρ, ὁ δὲ ῥήτωρ εἰκόνος εἰκών.

146.—ΑΜΜΙΑΝΟΥ

Ἑπτὰ σολοικισμοὺς Φλάκκῳ τῷ ῥήτορι δῶρον
  πέμψας, ἀντέλαβον πεντάκι διακοσίους·
καὶ "Νῦν μέν," φησίν, "τούτους ἀριθμῷ σοι
  ἔπεμψα,
τοῦ λοιποῦ δὲ μέτρῳ, πρὸς Κύπρον ἐρχόμενος."

147.—ΤΟΥ ΑΥΤΟΥ

Ῥήτωρ ἐξαπίνης Ἀσιατικός· οὐδὲν ἄπιστον·
καὶ τοῦτ᾽ ἐν Θήβαις νῦν γέγονεν τὸ τέρας.

148.—ΛΟΥΚΙΛΛΙΟΥ

Μηδὲ λαλῶν πρῴην ἐσολοίκισε Φλάκκος ὁ ῥήτωρ,
  καὶ μέλλων χαίνειν, εὐθὺς ἐβαρβάρισεν,
καὶ τῇ χειρὶ τὰ λοιπὰ σολοικίζει διανεύων,
  κἀγὼ δ᾽ αὐτὸν ἰδών—τὸ στόμα μου δέδεται.

¹ *Il.* xx. 157, only used here. The other words cited are
more common in Homer.

---

¹ *cp.* No. 151. The point is that though Sextus can assume
a rhetorical attitude as in the picture, he finds nothing to say.
² His home, where much worse Greek was talked.

For not even if you say " quaked," and " clangs,"
and " hisses," and " gurgled," will you be a Homer
at once. Sense should underlie literature, and its
phraseology be more vulgar so that people may
understand what you say.

145.—ANONYMOUS

SEXTUS' picture declaims, but Sextus is silent.
The picture is a rhetor and the rhetor the image of
his picture.[1]

146.—AMMIANUS

I SENT Flaccus the rhetor a present of seven
solecisms and received back five times two hundred.
And "Now," he says, "I send you these by the
hundred, but in future when I get to Cyprus [2] I will
send them by the bushel."

147.—BY THE SAME

ASIATICUS has suddenly become an orator. Nothing
incredible in that ! It is only another miracle in
Thebes.[3]

148.—LUCILIUS

FLACCUS the rhetor made solecisms the other day
without even speaking, and when he was about to
yawn at once was guilty of a barbarism, and now
goes on making solecisms by signs with his hand,
and I, seeing him, am tongue-tied.[4]

[3] Where so many marvels had occurred. He was pre-
sumably a Theban.

[4] *cp.* No. 138, where the same phrase is used. In both
cases it means "I dare not open my mouth for fear of making
a solecism."

149.—ΑΔΗΛΟΝ

Αὐτὸν ὁρῶ σέ, Μέδον, τὸν ῥήτορα. φεῦ, τί τὸ
θαῦμα;
στειλάμενος σιγᾷς· οὐδὲν ὁμοιότερον.

150.—ΑΜΜΙΑΝΟΥ

"Ἀρκαδικὸν πῖλον κατ᾽ ἐνύπνιον Ἀρκάδι δῶρον
Ἑρμείη ῥήτωρ θῆκεν Ἀθηναγόρας."
εἰ μὲν καὶ ῥήτωρ κατ᾽ ἐνύπνιον, οἴσομεν Ἑρμῇ·
εἰ δ᾽ ὕπαρ, ἀρκείτω· "Θῆκεν Ἀθηναγόρας."

151.—ΑΔΕΣΠΟΤΟΝ

Ῥήτορος ἅδ᾽ εἰκών· ὁ δὲ ῥήτωρ, εἰκόνος εἰκών.
καὶ πῶς; οὐ λαλέει· οὐδὲν ὁμοιότερον.

152.—ΑΜΜΙΑΝΟΥ

Εἰ βούλει τὸν παῖδα διδάξαι ῥήτορα, Παῦλε,
ὡς οὗτοι πάντες, γράμματα μὴ μαθέτω.

Εἰς φιλοσόφους
153.—ΛΟΥΚΙΛΛΙΟΥ

Εἶναι μὲν Κυνικόν σε, Μενέστρατε, κἀνυπόδητον,
καὶ ῥιγοῦν οὐδεὶς ἀντιλέγει καθόλου·
ἂν δὲ παραρπάξῃς ἄρτους καὶ κλάσματ᾽ ἀναιδῶς,
κἀγὼ ῥάβδον ἔχω, καὶ σὲ λέγουσι κύνα.

---

[1] The meaning, I think, is simply that if Athenagoras is a real orator, he need not announce that he is one.

149.—ANONYMOUS

I SEE the very image of you, Medon the rhetor. Well, what is there surprising in that? You have arranged your dress effectively and you are silent. Nothing could be more like.

150.—AMMIANUS

"THE rhetor Athenagoras in consequence of a dream dedicated an Arcadian hat to Arcadian Hermes." If he is a rhetor, too, in a dream only, we will take it so inscribed to Hermes, but if he is a real one, let "Athenagoras dedicated this" suffice.[1]

151.—ANONYMOUS

THIS is the image of a rhetor, but the rhetor is the image of his image. How is that? He does not speak. Nothing could be more life-like.[2]

152.—AMMIANUS

IF you want, Paulus, to teach your son to be a rhetor like all these, don't let him learn his letters.

On Philosophers (153-158)
153.—LUCILIUS

No one at all denies, Menestratus, that you are a cynic and bare-footed and that you are shivering. But if you shamelessly steal loaves and broken pieces on the sly, I have a stick, and they call you a dog.[3]

[2] *cp.* No. 145.
[3] *i.e.* as you are a dog (*i.e.* a cynic) I will beat you.

154.—ΤΟΥ ΑΥΤΟΥ

Πᾶς ὃς ἂν ᾖ πτωχὸς καὶ ἀγράμματος, οὐκέτ᾽ ἀλήθει,
  ὡς τὸ πρίν, οὐδ᾽ αἴρει φορτία μισθαρίου·
ἀλλὰ τρέφει πώγωνα, καί, ἐκ τριόδου ξύλον ἄρας,
  τῆς ἀρετῆς εἶναι φησὶν ὁ πρωτοκύων.
Ἑρμοδότου τόδε δόγμα τὸ πάνσοφον· εἴ τις
  ἀχαλκεῖ,   5
  μηκέτι πεινάτω, θεὶς τὸ χιτωνάριον.

155.—ΤΟΥ ΑΥΤΟΥ

Οὗτος ὁ τῆς ἀρετῆς ἀδάμας βαρύς, οὗτος ὁ πάντη
  πᾶσιν ἐπιπλήσσων, οὗτος ὁ ῥιγομάχος,
καὶ πώγωνα τρέφων, ἑάλω. Τί γάρ; Ἀπρεπὲς
  εἰπεῖν·
ἀλλ᾽ ἑάλω ποιῶν ἔργα κακοστομάτων.

156.—ΑΜΜΙΑΝΟΥ

Οἴει τὸν πώγωνα φρενῶν ποιητικὸν εἶναι,
  καὶ διὰ τοῦτο τρέφεις, φίλτατε, μυιοσόβην.
κεῖρον ἐμοὶ πεισθεὶς ταχέως· οὗτος γὰρ ὁ πώγων
  φθειρῶν ποιητής, οὐχὶ φρενῶν γέγονεν.

157.—ΤΟΥ ΑΥΤΟΥ

"Ὦ 'γαθέ" καὶ "μῶν οὖν" καὶ "ποῖ δὴ καὶ πόθεν
  ὦ 'τάν"
καὶ "θαμά" καὶ "φέρε δή" καὶ "κομιδῇ" καὶ
  "ἴθι,"
καὶ στόλιον, μάλιον, πωγώνιον, ὦμιον ἔξω,
  ἐκ τούτων ἡ νῦν εὐδοκιμεῖ σοφία.

---

[1] The cynics went without tunics.

154.—By the Same

EVERYONE who is poor and illiterate does not grind corn as formerly or carry burdens for small pay, but grows a beard and picking up a stick from the cross-roads, calls himself the chief dog of virtue. This is the sage pronouncement of Hermodotus, " If anyone is penniless, let him throw off his shirt[1] and no longer starve."

155.—By the Same

"THIS solid adamant of virtue, this rebuker of everyone, this fighter with the cold, with his long beard, has been caught."   " At what ? "   " It is not proper to say at what, but he was caught doing things that foul-mouthed people do."

156.—AMMIANUS

Do you suppose that your beard creates brains and therefore you grow that fly-flapper ? Take my advice and shave it off at once ; for that beard is a creator of lice and not of brains.

157.—By the Same

" GOOD Sir " and " Can it be ? " and " Whence, sirrah, and whither ? " and " Right off " and " Go to " and " Quite so " and " Hie ye " and cloakie and little lock and beardie, and " Keep your little shoulder bare " — that is what present-day philosophy flourishes on.[2]

---

[1] He is ridiculing two affectations of the philosophers of his day, the use of archaic forms of speech and that of diminutives.   The cynics went bare-shouldered.

158.—ΑΝΤΙΠΑΤΡΟΥ

Αἰάζει πήρη τε, καὶ Ἡράκλειον ἄριστον
βριθὺ Σινωπίτου Διογένευς ῥόπαλον,
καὶ τὸ χύδην ῥυπόεντι πίνῳ πεπαλαγμένον ἔσθος
διπλάδιον, κρυερῶν ἀντίπαλον νιφάδων,
ὅττι τεοῖς ὤμοισι μιαίνεται· ἢ γὰρ ὁ μέν που   5
οὐράνιος, σὺ δ᾽ ἔφυς οὐν σποδιῇσι κύων.
ἀλλὰ μέθες, μέθες ὅπλα τὰ μὴ σέθεν· ἄλλο λεόντων,
ἄλλο γενειητῶν ἔργον ὄρωρε τράγων.

Εἰς μάντεις

159.—ΛΟΥΚΙΛΛΙΟΥ

Τῷ πατρί μου τὸν ἀδελφὸν οἱ ἀστρολόγοι μακρό-
γηρων
πάντες ἐμαντεύσανθ᾽ ὡς ἀφ᾽ ἑνὸς στόματος·
ἀλλ᾽ Ἑρμοκλείδης αὐτὸν μόνος εἶπε πρόμοιρον·
εἶπε δ᾽, ὅτ᾽ αὐτὸν ἔσω νεκρὸν ἐκοπτόμεθα.

H. Wellesley, in *Anthologia Polyglotta*, p. 365.

160.—ΤΟΥ ΑΥΤΟΥ

Πάντες ὅσοι τὸν Ἄρην καὶ τὸν Κρόνον ὡροθετοῦσιν,
ἄξιοί εἰσι τυχεῖν πάντες ἑνὸς τυπάνου.
ὄψομαι οὐ μακρὰν αὐτοὺς τυχὸν εἰδότας ὄντως
καὶ τί ποεῖ ταῦρος, καὶ τί λέων δύναται.

161.—ΤΟΥ ΑΥΤΟΥ

Πρὸς τὸν μάντιν Ὄλυμπον Ὀνήσιμος ἦλθεν ὁ
πύκτης,
εἰ μέλλει γηρᾶν βουλόμενος προμαθεῖν.
κἀκεῖνος, "Ναί," φησίν, "ἐὰν ἤδη καταλύσῃς·
ἂν δέ γε πυκτεύῃς, ὡροθετεῖ σε Κρόνος."

158.—ANTIPATER

THE wallet laments, and the fine sturdy Heracles club of Sinopian Diogenes and the double coat, foe of the cold clouds, befouled all over with encrusted dirt, lament likewise because they are polluted by thy shoulders.   Verily I take Diogenes himself to be the dog of heaven, but thou art the dog that lies in the ashes.   Put off, put off the arms that are not thine. The work of lions is one thing, and that of bearded goats another

On Prophets (159–164)

159.—LUCILIUS

ALL the astrologers as it were with one voice prophesied to my father a ripe old age for his brother.   Hermoclides alone foretold his premature death, but he foretold it when we were lamenting over his corpse in the house.

160.—BY THE SAME

ALL those who take horoscopes from observing Mars and Saturn are deserving of one cudgelling. I shall see them perhaps at no distant date really learning what a bull can do and how strong a lion is.[1]

161.—BY THE SAME

ONESIMUS the boxer came to the prophet Olympus wishing to learn if he were going to live to old age. And he said, " Yes, if you give up the ring now, but if you go on boxing, Saturn[2] is your horoscope."

[1] *i.e.* exposed to beasts in the theatre.
[2] The most unlucky of the planets.

162.—ΝΙΚΑΡΧΟΥ

Εἰς 'Ρόδον εἰ πλεύσει τις 'Ολυμπικὸν ἦλθεν ἐρωτῶν
τὸν μάντιν, καὶ πῶς πλεύσεται ἀσφαλέως.
χὼ μάντις, " Πρῶτον μέν," ἔφη, " καινὴν ἔχε τὴν
ναῦν,
καὶ μὴ χειμῶνος, τοῦ δὲ θέρους ἀνάγου.
τοῦτο γὰρ ἂν ποιῇς, ἥξεις κάκεῖσε καὶ ὧδε,   5
ἂν μὴ πειρατὴς ἐν πελάγει σε λάβῃ."

163.—ΛΟΥΚΙΛΛΙΟΥ

Πρὸς τὸν μάντιν Ὄλυμπον 'Ονήσιμος ἦλθ' ὁ πα-
λαιστής,
καὶ πένταθλος Ὕλας, καὶ σταδιεὺς Μενεκλῆς,
τίς μέλλει νικᾶν αὐτῶν τὸν ἀγῶνα θέλοντες
γνῶναι.   κἀκεῖνος τοῖς ἱεροῖς ἐνιδών,
" Πάντες," ἔφη, " νικᾶτε, μόνον μή τις σὲ παρέλθῃ,   5
καὶ σὲ καταστρέψῃ, καὶ σὲ παρατροχάσῃ."

cp. Ausonius, *Ep.* 91.

164.—ΤΟΥ ΑΥΤΟΥ

Εἶπεν ἐληλυθέναι τὸ πεπρωμένον, αὐτὸς ἑαυτοῦ
τὴν γένεσιν διαθεὶς Αὖλος ὁ ἀστρολόγος,
καὶ ζήσειν ὥρας ἔτι τέσσαρας· ὡς δὲ παρῆλθεν
εἰς πέμπτην, καὶ ζῆν εἰδότα μηδὲν ἔδει,
αἰσχυνθεὶς Πετόσιριν ἀπήγξατο· καὶ μετέωρος   5
θνήσκει μέν, θνήσκει δ' οὐδὲν ἐπιστάμενος.

Εἰς μικρολόγους
165.—ΤΟΥ ΑΥΤΟΥ

Οὐ γλήχωνι Κρίτων ὁ φιλάργυρος, ἀλλὰ διχάλκῳ
αὐτὸν ἀποσφραίνει, θλιβομένου στομάχου.

162.—NICARCHUS

ONE came to ask the prophet Olympicus if he should take ship for Rhodes and how to sail there safely. And the prophet said, "First have a new ship and don't start in winter, but in summer. If you do this you will go there and back, unless a pirate catches you at sea."

163.—LUCILIUS

ONESIMUS the wrestler and the pentathlist Hylas and the runner Menecles came to the prophet Olympus wishing to know which of them was going to win at the games, and he, after inspecting the sacrifice, said, "You will all win—unless anyone passes you, Sir, or unless anyone throws you, Sir, or unless anyone runs past you, Sir."

164.—BY THE SAME

AULUS the astrologer, after making out his own nativity, said that the fatal hour had come and that he had still four hours to live. When it reached the fifth hour and he had to go on living convicted of ignorance, he grew ashamed of Petosiris[1] and hanged himself, and there up in the air he is dying, but he is dying ignorant.

On Misers (165-173)

165.—BY THE SAME

CRITO the miser, when he has a pain in his stomach refreshes himself by smelling not mint, but a penny piece.

[1] An astrological writer.

166.—ΑΔΗΛΟΝ

Πλουτεῖν φασί σε πάντες, ἐγὼ δέ σέ φημι πένεσθαι·
χρῆσις γὰρ πλούτου μάρτυς, Ἀπολλόφανες.
ἂν μετέχῃς αὐτῶν σύ, σὰ γίνεται· ἂν δὲ φυλάττῃς
κληρονόμοις, ἀπὸ νῦν γίνεται ἀλλότρια.

167.—ΠΩΛΛΙΑΝΟΤ

Χαλκὸν ἔχων, πῶς οὐδὲν ἔχεις μάθε. πάντα δανείζεις·
οὕτως οὐδὲν ἔχεις αὐτός, ἵν' ἄλλος ἔχῃ.

168.—ΑΝΤΙΦΑΝΟΤΣ

Ψηφίζεις, κακόδαιμον· ὁ δὲ χρόνος, ὡς τόκον, οὕτω
καὶ πολιὸν τίκτει γῆρας ἐπερχόμενος·
κοὔτε πιών, οὔτ' ἄνθος ἐπὶ κροτάφοις ἀναδήσας,
οὐ μύρον, οὐ γλαφυρὸν γνούς ποτ' ἐρωμένιον,
τεθνήξῃ, πλουτοῦσαν ἀφεὶς μεγάλην διαθήκην,   5
ἐκ πολλῶν ὀβολὸν μοῦνον ἐνεγκάμενος.

169.—ΝΙΚΑΡΧΟΤ

Ἐχθὲς ἀπάγχεσθαι μέλλων Δείναρχος ὁ φείδων,
Γλαῦκε, δι' ἐξ χαλκοῦς δύσμορος οὐκ ἔθανεν·
ἐξ χαλκῶν ἦν γὰρ τὸ σχοινίον· ἀλλ' ἐδυσώνει,
εὔωνον ζητῶν ἄλλον ἴσως θάνατον.
τοῦτο φιλαργυρίας δεινῆς ὅρος, ὅς γ' ἀποθνήσκων,   5
Γλαῦκε, δι' ἐξ χαλκοῦς δύσμορος οὐκ ἔθανεν.

166.—ANONYMOUS

ALL say you are rich, but I say you are poor, for, Apollophanes, their use is the proof of riches. If you take your share of them, they are yours, but if you keep them for your heirs, they are already someone else's.

167.—POLLIANUS

You have money, but I will tell you how it is you have nothing. You lend all; so that in order that another may have some, you have none yourself.

168.—ANTIPHANES.

THOU reckonest up thy money, poor wretch ; but Time, just as it breeds interest, so, as it overtakes thee, gives birth to grey old age. And so having neither drunk wine, nor bound thy temples with flowers, having never known sweet ointment or a delicate little love, thou shalt die, leaving a great and wealthy testament, and of all thy riches carrying away with thee but one obol.[1]

169.—NICARCHUS

YESTERDAY, Glaucus, Dinarchus the miser being about to hang himself, did not die, poor fellow, all for the sake of sixpence ; for the rope cost sixpence, but he tried to drive a hard bargain, seeking perhaps some other cheap death. This is the very height of wretched avarice, for a man to be dying, Glaucus, and not able to die, poor fellow, all for the sake of sixpence.

[1] That which it was customary to put in the corpse's mouth.

170.—ΤΟΥ ΑΥΤΟΥ

Δακρύει Φείδων ὁ φιλάργυρος, οὐχ ὅτι θνήσκει,
  ἀλλ' ὅτι πέντε μνῶν τὴν σορὸν ἐπρίατο.
τοῦτ' αὐτῷ χαρίσασθε, καί, ὡς τόπος ἐστὶν ἐν αὐτῇ,
  τῶν πολλῶν τεκνίων ἔν τι προσεμβάλετε.

171.—ΛΟΥΚΙΛΛΙΟΥ

Θνήσκων Ἑρμοκράτης ὁ φιλάργυρος ἐν διαθήκαις
  αὐτὸν τῶν ἰδίων ἔγραφε κληρονόμον.
ψηφίζων δ' ἀνέκειτο πόσον δώσει διεγερθεὶς
  ἰητροῖς μισθοῦ, καὶ τί νοσῶν δαπανᾷ·
ὡς δ' εὗρε πλείω δραχμὴν μίαν, ἢν διασωθῇ,   5
  " Λυσιτελεῖ θνήσκειν," εἶπε, καὶ ἐξετάθη.
κεῖται δ' οὐδὲν ἔχων ὀβολοῦ πλέον· οἱ δὲ τὰ κείνου
  <χρήματα κληρονόμοι ἥρπασαν ἀσπασίως>.

172.—ΤΟΥ ΑΥΤΟΥ

Γεννηθὲν τέκνον κατεπόντισεν Αὖλος ὁ κνιπός,
  ψηφίζων αὐτοῦ σωζομένου δαπάνας.

173.—ΦΙΛΙΠΠΟΥ

Εἰ τὸ μὲν ἐκδεδάνεικας, ὃ δ' ἄρτι δίδως, ὃ δὲ μέλλεις,
  οὐδέποτ' εἶ τοῦ σοῦ κύριος ἀργυρίου.

Εἰς κλέπτας

174.—ΛΟΥΚΙΛΛΙΟΥ

Τὰν ἀναδυομέναν ἀπὸ ματέρος ἄρτι θαλάσσας
  Κύπριν ὅλην χρυσῆν ἐχθὲς ἔκλεψε Δίων·

170.—By the Same

Phido the miser weeps not because he is dying, but because he paid thirty pounds for his coffin. Let him off this, and as there is room in it, put one of his many little children into it besides.

171.—LUCILIUS

Hermocrates the miser when he was dying wrote himself his own heir in his will, and he lay there reckoning what fee he must pay the doctors if he leaves his bed and how much his illness costs him. But when he found it cost one drachma more if he were saved, " It pays," he said, " to die," and stiffened himself out. Thus he lies, having nothing but an obol, and his heirs were glad to seize on his wealth.

172.—By the Same

Aulus the miser drowned in the sea a child that was born to him, reckoning how much it would cost him if he kept it.

173.—PHILIPPUS

If you have lent out some of it, and give some now, and are going to give some more, you are never master of your money.

On Thieves (174–184)
174.—LUCILIUS

Dio yesterday stole Cypris all of gold, just risen from her mother sea, and he also pulled down with

καὶ χερὶ προσκατέσυρεν ὁλοσφύρητον Ἄδωνιν,
καὶ τὸ παρεστηκὸς μικρὸν Ἐρωτάριον.
αὐτοὶ νῦν ἐρέουσιν ὅσοι ποτὲ φῶρες ἄριστοι·   5
"Οὐκέτι σοὶ χειρῶν εἰς ἔριν ἐρχόμεθα."

175.—ΤΟΥ ΑΥΤΟΥ

Τὸν θεὸν αὐτὸν ἔκλεψεν, ὃν ὁρκίζεσθαι ἔμελλεν
Εὐτυχίδης, εἰπών· "Οὐ δύναμαί σ' ὁμόσαι."

176.—ΤΟΥ ΑΥΤΟΥ

Τὸν πτανὸν Ἑρμᾶν, τὸν θεῶν ὑπηρέταν,
τὸν Ἀρκάδων ἄνακτα, τὸν βοηλάταν,
ἐστῶτα τῶνδε γυμνασίων ἐπίσκοπον,
ὁ νυκτικλέπτας Αὖλος εἶπε βαστάσας·
"Πολλοὶ μαθηταὶ κρείσσονες διδασκάλων."   5

177.—ΤΟΥ ΑΥΤΟΥ

Τὸν τῶν κλεπτόντων μανύτορα Φοῖβον ἔκλεψεν
Εὐτυχίδης, εἰπών, "Μὴ πάνυ πολλὰ λάλει,
σύγκρινον δὲ τέχνην τέχνῃ, καὶ χείρεσι χρησμούς,
καὶ μάντιν κλέπτῃ, καὶ θεὸν Εὐτυχίδῃ·
τῶν δ' ἀχαλινώτων στομάτων χάριν αὐτίκα πραθείς,   5
τοῖς ὠνησαμένοις πᾶν ὃ θέλεις με λέγε."

178.—ΤΟΥ ΑΥΤΟΥ

Βουκόλε, τὰν ἀγέλαν πόρρω νέμε, μή σε Περικλῆς
ὁ κλέπτης αὐταῖς βουσὶ συνεξελάσῃ.

---

[1] This epigram is a parody of a subsequent one, *App.
Plan.* 178, which should be read with it.

his hand Adonis of beaten gold and the little Love that stood by.   Even the best thieves that ever were will now say, " No longer do we enter into a contest of dexterity with you." [1]

175.—By the Same

Eutychides stole the god himself by whom he was about to swear, saying, " I can't swear by you." [2]

176.—By the Same

As he carried off the winged Hermes, the servant of the gods, the Lord of the Arcadians, the cattle-raider, who stood here as curator of this gymnasium, Aulus the night-thief said, " Many pupils are cleverer than their teachers."

177.—By the Same

Eutychides stole Phoebus the detector of thieves, saying, " Speak not too much, but compare thy art with mine and thy oracles with my hands and a prophet with a thief and a god with Eutychides. And because of thy unbridled tongue thou shalt be sold at once, and then say of me what thou wilt to thy purchasers."

178.—By the Same

Herdsman, feed thy flock far away, lest Pericles the thief drive thee and thy cattle off together.

[2] I suppose the point is, " I can't well swear by you that I did not steal you and thus get into trouble with you for perjury."

179.—ΤΟΥ ΑΥΤΟΥ

Εἰ πόδας εἶχε Δίων οἵας χέρας, οὐκέτ᾽ ἂν Ἑρμῆς
πτηνὸς ἐν ἀνθρώποις, ἀλλὰ Δίων ἐκρίθη.

180.—ΑΜΜΙΑΝΟΥ

Εἰδοὺς οὐ κρίνει Πολέμων, νώναις κατακρίνει·
κἂν δῷς, κἂν μὴ δῷς, ἔστιν ἀεὶ Πολέμων.

181.—ΤΟΥ ΑΥΤΟΥ

Ἤδειμεν, Πολέμων, Ἀντώνιον ὄντα σε πάντες·
ἐξαπίνης τρία σοι γράμματα πῶς ἔλιπεν;

182.—ΔΙΟΝΥΣΙΟΥ

ΧΟΙΡΙ μέν, οὐκ ΙΔΙΟΝ δέ με θύετε· καί με καλεῖτε
ΧΟΙΡΙΔΙΟΝ, φανερῶς εἰδότες οὐκ ἴδιον.

183.—ΛΟΥΚΙΛΛΙΟΥ

Τὴν γένεσιν λυποῦντα μαθὼν Κρόνον Ἡλιόδωρος,
   νύκτωρ ἐκ ναοῦ χρύσεον ἦρε Κρόνον,
"Τίς πρῶτος κακοποιὸς ἐλήλυθε πείρασον," εἰπών,
" δέσποτα, καὶ γνώσῃ τίς τίνος ἐστὶ Κρόνος·
ὃς δ᾽ ἄλλῳ κακὰ τεύχει, ἐῷ κακὸν ἥπατι τεύχει·   5
   εὑρών μοι τιμήν, πᾶν ἀνάτελλ᾽ ὃ θέλεις."

---

[1] cp. Book XII. 75.   [2] The play is on the Latin non.
[3] i.e. his character never changes. This Antonius Polemon
the sophist, whose life by Philostratus we have, held office in
Smyrna, where, as we see, he had enemies.

179.—By the Same

If Dio had feet like his hands, Dio, and Hermes no longer, would be distinguished among men as winged.[1]

180.—AMMIANUS

On the Ides (or "if you give") Polemon does not decide the suit, on the Nones (or "if you say 'No'[2]") he condemns you. Whether you give or don't give, he is always Polemon.[3]

181.—By the Same

We all knew, Polemon, that your name was Antonius. How is it that three letters are suddenly missing?[4]

182.—DIONYSIUS

You are killing me, a pig but not your own, and you call me "piggie" (or "our own pig"), knowing well that I am not your own.[5]

183.—LUCILIUS

Heliodorus, hearing that Saturn troubles nativities, carried off the golden Saturn at night from the temple, saying: "Experience by fact, my Lord, which of us anticipated the other in working evil, and thou shalt know which of us is the Saturn of which. 'Who works evil for another, works it for his own heart.'[6] Fetch me a good price and portend what thou wilt by thy rising."

[4] How is it that instead of Antonius you have become "onios," which in Greek means "venal"?
[5] The pig was a stolen one. [6] A line of Callimachus.

184.—ΤΟΥ ΑΥΤΟΥ

Ἐκ τῶν Ἑσπερίδων τῶν τοῦ Διὸς ἦρε Μενίσκος,
    ὡς τὸ πρὶν Ἡρακλέης, χρύσεα μῆλα τρία.
καὶ τί γάρ; ὡς ἑάλω, γέγονεν μέγα πᾶσι θέαμα,
    ὡς τὸ πρὶν Ἡρακλέης ζῶν κατακαιόμενος.

Εἰς κιθαρῳδοὺς ἀλλὰ μὴν καὶ τραγῳδοὺς καὶ κωμῳδούς

185.—ΤΟΥ ΑΥΤΟΥ

Ἑλλήνων ἀπέλυε πόλιν ποτέ, δέσποτα Καῖσαρ,
    εἰσελθὼν ἆσαι Ναύπλιον Ἡγέλοχος.
Ναύπλιος Ἕλλήνεσσιν ἀεὶ κακόν· ἢ μέγα κῦμα
    <νηυσὶν ἐπεμβάλλων,> ἢ κιθαρῳδὸν ἔχων.

186.—ΝΙΚΑΡΧΟΥ

Νυκτικόραξ ᾄδει θανατηφόρον· ἀλλ' ὅταν ᾄσῃ
    Δημόφιλος, θνήσκει καὐτὸς ὁ νυκτικόραξ.

187.—ΛΕΩΝΙΔΑ

Σιμύλος ὁ ψάλτης τοὺς γείτονας ἔκτανε πάντας
    νυκτὸς ὅλης ψάλλων, πλὴν ἑνὸς Ὠριγένους·
κωφὸν γὰρ φύσις αὐτὸν ἐθήκατο· τοὔνεκεν αὐτῷ
    ζωὴν ἀντ' ἀκοῆς δῶκε περισσοτέρην.

188.—ΑΜΜΙΑΝΟΥ

Νικήτης ᾄδων τῶν ᾠδῶν ἐστιν Ἀπόλλων·
    ἂν δ' ἰατρεύῃ, τῶν θεραπευομένων.

---

[1] He probably means " from the Emperor's garden."

184.—By the Same

From the Hesperides' Garden of Zeus,[1] Meniscus, as Heracles did formerly, carried off three golden apples. Well, what happened? When he was caught he became a famous spectacle for all, burning alive, like Heracles of old.

On Singers and Actors (185–189)

185.—By the Same

Hegelochus, my Lord Caesar, once emptied a Greek city by appearing to sing the part of Nauplius.[2] Nauplius is ever an evil to the Greeks, either sending a great wave on their ships or having a lyre-singer to play his part.

186.—NICARCHUS

The night-raven's song bodes death, but when Demophilus sings the night-raven itself dies.

187.—LEONIDAS OF ALEXANDRIA

Simylus the lyre-player killed all his neighbours by playing the whole night, except only Origenes, whom Nature had made deaf, and therefore gave him longer life in the place of hearing.

188.—AMMIANUS

Nicetas when he sings is the Apollo[3] of the songs, and when he doctors, of the patients.

[2] Nauplius caused the destruction of the Greek fleet on its return from Troy by exhibiting deceptive beacons.
[3] *i.e.* perdition. The god's name is often interpreted as Destroyer.

189.—ΛΟΥΚΙΛΛΙΟΥ

Πεντ' ὀβολῶν πέπρακεν Ἀπολλοφάνης ὁ τραγῳδὸς
πέντε θεῶν σκευήν, Ἡρακλέους ῥόπαλον,
Τισιφόνης τὰ φόβητρα, Ποσειδῶνος τριόδοντα,
ὅπλον Ἀθηναίης, Ἀρτέμιδος φαρέτρην.
οἱ δὲ θεοὶ πὰρ Ζηνὶ καθήμενοι ἐξεδύθησαν   5
εἰς βραχὺ σιταρίου κέρμα καὶ οἰναρίου.

Εἰς κουρέας

190.—ΤΟΥ ΑΥΤΟΥ

Τὸν δασὺν Ἑρμογένην ζητεῖ πόθεν ἄρξεθ' ὁ κουρεὺς
κείρειν τὴν κεφαλήν, ὄνθ' ὅλον ὡς κεφαλήν.

191.—ΤΟΥ ΑΥΤΟΥ

Ἄρες Ἄρες βροτολοιγέ, μιαιφόνε, παύεο, κουρεῦ,
τέμνων· οὐ γὰρ ἔχεις οὐκέτι πού με τεμεῖς·
ἀλλ' ἤδη μεταβὰς ἐπὶ τοὺς μύας ἢ τὰ κάτωθεν
τῶν γονάτων, οὕτω τέμνε με, καὶ παρέχω.
νῦν μὲν γὰρ μυιῶν ὁ τόπος γέμει· ἢν δ' ἐπιμείνῃς,   5
ὄψει καὶ γυπῶν ἔθνεα καὶ κοράκων.

Εἰς φθονερούς

192.—ΤΟΥ ΑΥΤΟΥ

Μακροτέρῳ σταυρῷ σταυρούμενον ἄλλον ἑαυτοῦ
ὁ φθονερὸς Διοφῶν ἐγγὺς ἰδὼν ἐτάκη.

193.—ΑΔΕΣΠΟΤΟΝ

Ὁ φθόνος ὡς κακόν ἐστιν· ἔχει δέ τι καλὸν ἐν αὑτῷ·
τήκει γὰρ φθονερῶν ὄμματα καὶ κραδίην.

189.—LUCILIUS

APOLLOPHANES the tragedian sold for five obols the stage property of five gods, the club of Heracles, Tisiphone's instruments of terror, the trident of Poseidon, the shield of Athena, and the quiver of Artemis. "And the gods that sit beside Zeus"[1] were stripped to get a few coppers to buy a little bread and wine.

On Barbers (190-191)

190.—BY THE SAME

THE barber is puzzled to know where to begin to shave the head of hairy Hermogenes, as he seems to be all head.

191.—BY THE SAME

"ARES, Ares, destroyer of men, blood-fiend,"[2] cease, barber, from cutting me, for you have no place left in which to cut me. But change now to my muscles and my legs below the knees, and cut me there, and I will let you. For even now the shop is full of flies, and if you persist, you will see the tribes of vultures and ravens here.

On Envy (192-193)

192.—BY THE SAME

ENVIOUS Diophon, seeing another man near him crucified on a higher cross than himself, fell into a decline.

193.—ANONYMOUS

WHAT an evil is Envy! but it has something good in it; for it wastes away the eyes and heart of the envious.

---

[1] From Hom. *Il.* iv. 1.   [2] Hom. *Il.* v. 455.

194.—ΛΟΥΚΙΛΛΙΟΥ

Πανὶ φιλοσπήλυγγι καὶ οὐρεοφοιτάσι Νύμφαις,
καὶ Σατύροις, ἱεραῖς τ' ἔνδον Ἀμαδρυάσιν,
σὺν κυσὶ καὶ λόγχαις συοφόντισι Μάρκος . . .
μηδὲν ἑλών, αὐτοὺς τοὺς κύνας ἐκρέμασεν.

195.—ΔΙΟΣΚΟΡΙΔΟΥ

Γάλλον Ἀρισταγόρης ὠρχήσατο· τοὺς δὲ φιλόπλους
Τημενίδας ὁ καμὼν πολλὰ διῆλθον ἐγώ.
χὠ μὲν τιμηθεὶς ἀπεπέμπετο· τὴν δὲ τάλαιναν
Ὑρνηθὼ κροτάλων εἰς ψόφος ἐξέβαλεν.
εἰς πῦρ ἡρώων ἴτε πρήξιες· ἐν γὰρ ἀμούσοις   5
καὶ κόρυδος κύκνου φθέγξετ' ἀοιδότερον.

Εἰς αἰσχρούς

196.—ΛΟΥΚΙΛΛΙΟΥ

Ῥύγχος ἔχουσα Βιτὼ τριπιθήκινον, οἷον ἰδοῦσαν
τὴν Ἑκάτην αὐτὴν οἴομ' ἀπαγχονίσαι,
"Εἰμί," λέγει, "σώφρων, Λουκίλλιε, καὶ μονοκοιτῶ."
αἰδεῖται γὰρ ἴσως, "Παρθένος εἰμί," λέγειν.
εἰ δέ γέ τις μισεῖ με, κακὸν τοιοῦτο γαμήσας,   5
τῆς αὐτῆς σχοίη τέκνα σαοφροσύνης.

197.—ΤΟΥ ΑΥΤΟΥ

Ἤθελε ΔΡΙΜΥΣ ἄγαν τὸ πρόσθ' Ἱερώνυμος εἶναι·
νῦν δὲ τὸ ΔΡΙ μὲν ἔχει, ΛΟΣ δὲ τὸ ΜΥΣ γέγονεν.

---

[1] A eunuch priest of Rhea.
[2] The Temenidae of Euripides dealt with the jealousy of
their sister Hyrnetho on the part of King Temenos' sons.

194.—LUCILIUS

To Pan who loves the cave, and the Nymphs that haunt the hills, and to the Satyrs and to the holy Hamadryads within the cave, Marcus ..., having killed nothing with his dogs and boar-spears, hung up the dogs themselves.

195.—DIOSCORIDES

ARISTAGORAS danced the part of a Gallus,[1] while I, with great labour, went through the story of the warlike Temenidae. He was dismissed with honour, but one unceasing storm of rattles sent poor Hyrnetho off the boards.[2] Into the fire with you, ye exploits of the heroes! for among the illiterate even a lark sings more musically than a swan.

On Ugly People (196–204)

196.—LUCILIUS

BITO, with a face three times worse than a monkey's, enough to make even Hecate hang herself for envy if she saw it, says, " I am chaste, Lucilius, and sleep alone ; " for perhaps she is ashamed of saying " I am a virgin." But may whoever hates me marry such a horror and have children of similar chastity.

197.—BY THE SAME

HIERONYMUS formerly wanted to be too *drimys* (strict); now he has the *dri,* but the *mys* has turned into *los.*[3]

The complainant here had been dancing in the pantomime the part of Hyrnetho.
   [3] He has become *drilos* (i.e. stript, peeled for copulation), the opposite of what he wished.

198.—ΘΕΟΔΩΡΟΥ

Ἑρμοκράτης τᾶς ῥινός· ἐπεί, τὰν ῥῖνα λέγοντες
Ἑρμοκράτους, μικροῖς μακρὰ χαριζόμεθα.

199.—ΛΕΩΝΙΔΑ

Ἰχθῦν ὁ γρυπὸς Σωσίπτολις οὐκ ἀγοράζει,
   προῖκα δ' ἔχει πολλὴν ἐξ ἁλὸς εὐβοσίην,
οὐ λίνον, οὐ κάλαμον προσάγων, τῇ ῥινὶ δὲ προσθεὶς
   ἄγκιστρον, σύρει πάντα τὰ νηχόμενα.

200.—ΤΟΥ ΑΥΤΟΥ

Ζηνογένους οἶκος κατεκαίετο, πολλὰ δ' ἐμόχθει
   ἐκ θυρίδος ζητῶν αὐτὸν ὑπεκχαλάσαι·
ἰκρία συμπήξας οὐκ ἔφθανεν· ὀψὲ δ' ἐπιγνούς,
   τὴν ῥῖν' Ἀντιμάχου κλίμακα θεὶς ἔφυγεν.

201.—ΑΜΜΩΝΙΔΟΥ

Ἀντιπάτραν γυμνὴν εἴ τις Πάρθοισιν ἔδειξεν,
   ἔκτοθεν ἂν στηλῶν Ἡρακλέους ἔφυγον.

202.—ΑΔΗΛΟΝ

Τὴν γραῦν ἐκκομίσας, φρονίμως πάνυ Μόσχος ἔγημε
   παρθένον· ἡ φερνὴ δ' ἔνδον ἔμεινεν ὅλη.
ἄξιον αἰνῆσαι Μόσχου φρένας, ὃς μόνος οἶδε
   καὶ τίνα δεῖ κινεῖν καὶ τίνα κληρονομεῖν.

198.—THEODORUS

"The nose's Hermocrates"—for if we say "Hermocrates' nose," we give long things to little ones.[1]

199.—LEONIDAS OF ALEXANDRIA

Hook-nosed Sosipolis does not buy fish, but gets plenty of good fare from the sea for nothing ; bringing no line and rod, but attaching a hook to his nose, he pulls out everything that swims.

200.—By the Same

Zenogenes' house was on fire, and he was toiling sore in his efforts to let himself down from a window By fixing planks together he could not reach far enough, but at length, when it struck him, he set Antimachus' nose as a ladder and escaped.

201.—AMMONIDES

If anyone had shown Antipatra naked to the Parthians, they would have fled outside the Pillars of Heracles.

202.—Anonymous

After burying his old woman, Moschus very sensibly married a young girl, his first wife's whole dowry remaining intact in his house.   Moschus deserves to be praised for his good sense, in that he alone knows whom to poke and from whom to inherit.

[1] Probably a proverbial phrase.

203.—ΑΛΛΟ

Ἡ ῥὶς Κάστορός ἐστιν, ὅταν σκάπτῃ τι, δίκελλα·
σάλπιγξ δ᾽, ἂν ῥέγχῃ· τῇ δὲ τρύγῃ, δρέπανον·
ἐν πλοίοις ἄγκυρα· κατασπείροντι δ᾽ ἄροτρον·
ἄγκιστρον ναύταις· ὀψοφάγοις κρεάγρα·
ναυπηγοῖς σχένδυλα· γεωργοῖς δὲ πρασόκουρον· 5
τέκτοσιν ἀξίνη· τοῖς δὲ πυλῶσι κόραξ.
οὕτως εὐχρήστου σκεύους Κάστωρ τετύχηκε,
ῥῖνα φέρων πάσης ἄρμενον ἐργασίης.

204.—ΠΑΛΛΑΔΑ

Ῥήτορα Μαῦρον ἰδὼν ἐτεθήπεα, ῥυγχελέφαντα,
χείλεσι λιτραίοις φθόγγον ἱέντα φόνον.

Εἰς ἀπλήστους

205.—ΛΟΥΚΙΛΛΙΟΥ

Οὐδὲν ἀφῆκεν ὅλως, Διονύσιε, λείψανον Αὔλῳ
Εὐτυχίδης δειπνῶν, ἦρε δὲ πάντ᾽ ὀπίσω·
καὶ νῦν Εὐτυχίδης μὲν ἔχει μέγα δεῖπνον ἐν οἴκῳ,
μὴ κληθεὶς δ᾽ Αὖλος ξηροφαγεῖ καθίσας.

206.—ΤΟΥ ΑΥΤΟΥ

Οὕτω σοι πέψαι, Διονύσιε, ταῦτα γένοιτο
πάντα· νόμου δὲ χάριν, δός τι καὶ ὧδε φαγεῖν·
κἀγὼ κέκλημαι, κἀμοὶ παρέθηκέ τι τούτων
γεύσασθαι Πόπλιος, κἀμὸν ἔπεστι μέρος·

203.—Anonymous

Castor's nose is a hoe for him when he digs any-
thing, a trumpet when he snores and a grape-sickle
at vintage time, an anchor on board ship, a plough
when he is sowing, a fishing-hook for sailors, a flesh-
hook for feasters, a pair of tongs for ship-builders,
and for farmers a leek-slicer, an axe for carpenters
and a handle for his door. Such a serviceable im-
plement has Castor the luck to possess, wearing a
nose adaptable for any work.

204.—PALLADAS

I was thunderstruck when I saw the rhetor
Maurus, with a snout like an elephant, emitting a
voice that murders one from lips weighing a pound
each.

On Gluttons (205–209)

205.—LUCILIUS

Eutychides when he came to supper, Dionysius,
did not leave Aulus[1] a single scrap, but handed
everything to his servant behind him, and now
Eutychides has a great supper in his house, and
Aulus, not invited, sits eating dry bread.[2]

206.—By the Same

So may you be able, Dionysius, to digest all these
things you are eating, but for custom's sake give
us something to eat here too. I was invited also, and
Publius served some of these things for me too to
taste, and my portion too is on the board. Unless,

---

[1] His host.   [2] *cp.* Martial ii. 37.

εἰ μὴ λεπτὸν ἰδών με δοκεῖς κατακεῖσθαι ἄρωστον, 5
εἶθ᾽ οὕτως τηρεῖς, μή σε λαθών τι φάγω.

207.—ΤΟΥ ΑΥΤΟΥ

Καὶ τρώγεις ὅσα πέντε λύκοι, Γάμε, καὶ τὰ περισσά,
οὐ τὰ σά, τῶν δὲ πέριξ, πάντα δίδως ὀπίσω.
πλὴν μετὰ τοῦ κοφίνου τοῦ πρὸς πόδας αὔριον ἔρχου,
τρίσματα καὶ σπόγγον καὶ σαρὸν εὐθὺς ἔχων.

208.—ΤΟΥ ΑΥΤΟΥ

Ἢν βραδὺς Εὐτυχίδας σταδιοδρόμος· ἀλλ᾽ ἐπὶ
      δεῖπνον
ἔτρεχεν, ὥστε λέγειν· "Εὐτυχίδας πέταται."

209.—ΑΜΜΙΑΝΟΥ

Κἂν μέχρις Ἡρακλέους στηλῶν ἔλθῃς παρορίζων,
γῆς μέρος ἀνθρώποις πᾶσιν ἴσον σε μένει,
κείσῃ δ᾽ Ἴρῳ ὅμοιος, ἔχων ὀβολοῦ πλέον οὐδέν,
εἰς τὴν οὐκέτι σὴν γῆν ἀναλυόμενος.

Εἰς δειλούς

210.—ΛΟΥΚΙΛΛΙΟΥ

Ἄνθρακα καὶ δάφνην παραβύεται ὁ στρατιώτης
Αὖλος, ἀποσφίγξας μήλινα λωμάτια.

---

[1] It looks a little as if Dionysius, the greedy guest he addresses, were a doctor.

[2] So it appears we should understand "the man who stands at your feet."

thin, you think I was ill when I sat
and so watch me thus in case I eat
noticed by you.[1]

5

207.—BY THE SAME

as much as five wolves, Gamus, and you
ur slave behind you all that is over, not
own portion, but that of those round you.
to-morrow with your slave's[2] basket, and
wdust and a sponge and a broom.[3]

208.—BY THE SAME

5

a racer Eutychides was slow, but he ran to
er so quickly that they said, "Eutychides is
ng."

209.—AMMIANUS

Even if thou removest thy neighbour's boundaries
till thou reachest the Pillars of Heracles, a portion
of earth equal to that of all men awaits thee, and
thou shalt lie like Irus,[4] with no more than an obol
on thee,[5] dissolving into the earth that is no more
thine.

On Cowards (210–211)

210.—LUCILIUS

Aulus the soldier stops his ears when he sees
charcoal or laurel, wrapping his yellow duds tight

[3] *i.e.* to sweep up all the fragments; he is even told to
bring the sawdust which it was customary to sprinkle
before sweeping.　　　[4] The beggar in the *Odyssey.*
[5] The obol it was customary to place in the mouth of the
corpse.

φρίσσει καὶ τὸ μάτην ἴδιον ξίφος.   ἦν δέ ποτ
 " Ἔρχοντ'," ἐξαπίνης ὕπτιος ἐκτέταται.
οὐδενὶ δ' οὐ Πολέμωνι προσέρχεται, οὐ Σ
    κλείδη·
ἀλλὰ φίλῳ χρῆται πάντοτε Λυσιμάχῳ.

211.—ΤΟΥ ΑΥΤΟΥ

Γραπτὴν ἐν τοίχῳ Καλπούρνιος ὁ στρατιώτης,
    ὡς ἔθος ἐστίν, ἰδὼν τὴν ἐπὶ ναυσὶ μάχην,
ἄσφυκτος καὶ χλωρὸς ὁ θούριος ἐξετανύσθη,
    " Ζωγρεῖτε," κράξας, " Τρῶες ἀρηΐφιλοι."
καὶ μὴ τέτρωται κατεμάνθανε, καὶ μόλις ἔγνω
    ζῆν, ὅτε τοῖς τοίχοις ὡμολόγησε λύτρα.

Εἰς ζωγράφου
212.—ΤΟΥ ΑΥΤΟΥ

<Τεκνίον εὔμορφον, Διόδωρε, γράφειν σ' ἐκέλευσα·>
    ἀλλὰ σύ μοι προφερεῖς τεκνίον ἀλλότριον,
τὴν προτομὴν αὐτῷ περιθεὶς κυνός· ὥστε με κλάειν
    πῶς μοι Ζωπυρίων ἐξ Ἑκάβης γέγονεν.
καὶ πέρας ἐξ δραχμῶν Ἐρασίστρατος ὁ κρεοπώλης   5
    ἐκ τῶν Ἰσείων υἱὸν Ἄνουβιν ἔχω.

213.—ΛΕΩΝΙΔΑ

Εἰκόνα Μηνοδότου γράψας Διόδωρος ἔθηκεν
    πλὴν τοῦ Μηνοδότου πᾶσιν ὁμοιοτάτην.

---

[1] This is the only meaning I can elicit from this possibly
corrupt couplet.   The soldier is supposed to be afraid of the
crackling of charcoal or laurel when lighted.   Yellow was a
military colour.
[2] He wants no friend whose name suggests war (*polemos*) or

172

round his head,[1] and he shudders at his own useless sword; and if you ever say, "They are coming," he falls flat on his back. No Polemo or Stratoclides will he approach, but always has Lysimachus for a friend.[2]

211.—By the Same

When Calpurnius the soldier saw the battle by the ships[3] painted on a wall, as is the custom, the warrior lay stretched out pulseless and pale, calling out, "Quarter, ye Trojans dear to Ares." Then he enquired if he had been wounded, and with difficulty believed he was alive when he had agreed to pay ransom to the wall.

On Painters (212-215)

212.—By the Same

I ordered you, Diodorus, to paint a pretty child, but you produce a child strange to me, putting a dog's head on his shoulders, so that I weep to think how my Zopyrion was born to me by Hecuba.[4] And finally I, Erasistratus the butcher, have got for six drachmae a son Anubis[5] from the shrines of Isis.

213.—LEONIDAS OF ALEXANDRIA

Diodorus, painting Menodotus' portrait, made it very like everyone except Menodotus.

armies (*stratos*), but associates with Lysimachus (deliverer from battle). [3] At Troy.
[4] Said to have been changed into a dog.
[5] The dog-headed god worshipped together with Isis. In Ἰσείων there is probably a pun on the Latin *insicia*, "sausage-meat."

214.—ΛΟΥΚΙΛΛΙΟΥ

Γράψας Δευκαλίωνα, Μενέστρατε, καὶ Φαέθοντα,
  ζητεῖς τίς τούτων ἄξιός ἐστι τίνος.
τοῖς ἰδίοις αὐτοὺς τιμήσομεν· ἄξιος ὄντως
  ἐστὶ πυρὸς Φαέθων, Δευκαλίων δ᾽ ὕδατος.

215.—ΤΟΥ ΑΥΤΟΥ

Εἴκοσι γεννήσας ὁ ζωγράφος Εὔτυχος υἱούς,
  οὐδ᾽ ἀπὸ τῶν τέκνων οὐδὲν ὅμοιον ἔχει.

Εἰς ἀσελγεῖς

216.—ΤΟΥ ΑΥΤΟΥ

Τὸν φιλόπαιδα Κράτιππον ἀκούσατε· θαῦμα γὰρ
      ὑμῖν
  καινὸν ἀπαγγέλλω· πλὴν μεγάλαι Νεμέσεις.
τὸν φιλόπαιδα Κράτιππον ἀνεύρομεν ἄλλο γένος τι
  τῶν ἑτεροζήλων. ἤλπισα τοῦτ᾽ ἂν ἐγώ;
ἤλπισα τοῦτο, Κράτιππε· μανήσομαι εἰ, λύκος εἶναι 5
  πᾶσι λέγων, ἐφάνης ἐξαπίνης ἔριφος;

217.—ΤΟΥ ΑΥΤΟΥ

Φεύγων τὴν ὑπόνοιαν Ἀπολλοφάνης ἐγάμησεν,
  καὶ διὰ τῆς ἀγορᾶς νυμφίος ἦλθε μέσης,
" Αὔριον εὐθύ," λέγων, " ἔξω τέκνον." εἶτα προῆλθεν
  αὔριον, ἀντὶ τέκνου τὴν ὑπόνοιαν ἔχων.

174

214.—LUCILIUS

HAVING painted Deucalion and Phaethon, Menestratus, you enquire which of them is worth anything. We will appraise them according to their own fate. Phaethon is truly worthy of the fire and Deucalion of the water.

215.—BY THE SAME

EUTYCHUS the painter was the father of twenty sons, but never got a likeness even among his children.

On Lewd Livers (216–223)

216.—BY THE SAME

You have heard of Cratippus as a lover of boys. It is a great marvel I have to tell you, but great goddesses are the Avengers. We discovered that Cratippus, the lover of boys, belongs now to another variety of those persons whose tastes lie in an inverse direction. Would I ever have expected this? I expected it, Cratippus. Shall I go mad because, while you told everyone you were a wolf, you suddenly turned out to be a kid?

217.—BY THE SAME

To avoid suspicion, Apollophanes married and walked as a bridegroom through the middle of the market, saying, "To-morrow at once I will have a child." Then when to-morrow came he appeared carrying the suspicion instead of a child.

GREEK ANTHOLOGY

218.—ΚΡΑΤΗΤΟΣ

Χοίριλος 'Αντιμάχου πολὺ λείπεται· ἀλλ' ἐπὶ πᾶσιν
Χοίριλον Εὐφορίων εἶχε διὰ στόματος,
καὶ κατάγλωσσ' ἐπόει τὰ ποιήματα, καὶ τὰ Φιλητᾶ
ἀτρεκέως ᾔδει· καὶ γὰρ Ὁμηρικὸς ἦν.

219.—ΑΝΤΙΠΑΤΡΟΥ

Οὐ προσέχω, καίτοι πιστοί τινες· ἀλλὰ μεταξύ,
πρὸς Διός, εἴ με φιλεῖς, Πάμφιλε, μή με φίλει.

220.—ΑΔΗΛΟΝ

'Αλφειοῦ στόμα φεῦγε· φιλεῖ κόλπους 'Αρεθούσης,
πρηνὴς ἐμπίπτων ἁλμυρὸν ἐς πέλαγος.

221.—ΑΜΜΙΑΝΟΥ

Οὐχ ὅτι τὸν κάλαμον λείχεις, διὰ τοῦτό σε μισῶ,
ἀλλ' ὅτι τοῦτο ποιεῖς καὶ δίχα τοῦ καλάμου.

222.—ΑΔΕΣΠΟΤΟΝ

ΧΕΙΛΩΝ καὶ ΛΕΙΧΩΝ ἴσα γράμματα. ἐς τί δὲ τοῦτο;
ΛΕΙΧΕΙ γὰρ ΧΕΙΛΩΝ, κἂν ἴσα, κἂν ἄνισα.

---

[1] Choerilus of Samos, epic poet of the fifth century B.C.
[2] Obscure words.
[3] Such is the meaning the epigram bears on its face, but
several somewhat improper puns give it the following one,
reflecting not on the style but on the morals of Euphorion :
But Euphorion always and everywhere had a woman's sow

176

218.—CRATES

CHOERILUS[1] is far inferior to Antimachus, but on all occasions Euphorion would ever talk of Choerilus and made his poems full of glosses,[2] and knew those of Philetas well, for he was indeed a follower of Homer.[3]

219.—ANTIPATER

I DON'T pay any attention, although some people are to be trusted; but in the meantime, for God's sake, if you love me, Pamphilus, don't kiss me.

220.—ANONYMOUS

AVOID the mouth of Alpheus; he loves the bosom of Arethusa, falling headlong into the salt sea.[4]

221.—AMMIANUS

I DON'T dislike you because you lick the sugar cane, but because you do this, too, without the cane.

222.—ANONYMOUS

XEIΛΩN (Chilon) and ΛEIXΩN (licking) have the same letters. But what does that matter? For Chilon licks whether they are the same or not.

in his mouth, and he used to make his poems all tongue-kissings, and knew with expert accuracy the tricks of osculation; for he was indeed the real thigh-man.

[4] Alluding to the story of the love of the river for the fountain Arethusa; but this epigram has also another meaning.

223.—ΜΕΛΕΑΓΡΟΥ

Εἰ βινεῖ Φαβωρῖνος ἀπιστεῖς· μηκέτ᾽ ἀπίστει·
αὐτός μοι βινεῖν εἶπ᾽ ἰδίῳ στόματι.

224.—ΑΝΤΙΠΑΤΡΟΥ

Ἑστηκὸς τὸ Κίμωνος ἰδὼν πέος, εἶφ᾽ ὁ Πρίηπος·
" Οἴμοι, ὑπὸ θνητοῦ λείπομαι ἀθάνατος."

225.—ΣΤΡΑΤΩΝΟΣ

Ἡ κλίνη πάσχοντας ἔχει δύο, καὶ δύο δρῶντας,
οὓς σὺ δοκεῖς πάντας τέσσαρας· εἰσὶ δὲ τρεῖς.
ἢν δὲ πύθῃ, πῶς τοῦτο; τὸν ἐν μέσσῳ δὶς ἀρίθμει,
κοινὰ πρὸς ἀμφοτέρους ἔργα σαλευόμενον.

226.—ΑΜΜΙΑΝΟΥ

Εἴη σοι κατὰ γῆς κούφη κόνις, οἰκτρὲ Νέαρχε,
ὄφρα σε ῥηϊδίως ἐξερύσωσι κύνες.

227.—ΤΟΥ ΑΥΤΟΥ

Θᾶττον ποιήσει μέλι κάνθαρος ἢ γάλα κώνωψ,
ἢ σύ τι ποιήσεις, σκορπίος ὤν, ἀγαθόν.
οὔτε γὰρ αὐτὸς ἑκοντὶ ποιεῖς, οὔτ᾽ ἄλλον ἀφίης,
ὡς ἀστὴρ Κρονικὸς πᾶσιν ἀπεχθόμενος.

228.—ΤΟΥ ΑΥΤΟΥ

Μητέρα τις, πατέρ᾽ ἄλλος ἀπέκτανεν, ἄλλος ἀδελφόν·
Πωλιανὸς τοὺς τρεῖς, πρῶτος ἀπ᾽ Οἰδίποδος.

223.—MELEAGER

You wonder whether Favorinus pokes or not; don't wonder any longer; he told me himself that he pokes with his own mouth.

224.—ANTIPATER

When Priapus saw Cimon's prick standing upright, said he: " Oh dear! I an immortal am left behind by a mortal."

225.—STRATO

The bed holds two submissive, and two in action— and you think they are four in all. But they're three! If you ask " How so? " count the one in the middle twice—he's jerked in a see-saw action shared by both the others.

226.—AMMIANUS

May the dust lie light on thee when under earth, wretched Nearchus, so that the dogs may easily drag thee out.

227.—By the Same

Sooner shall a beetle make honey or a mosquito milk than thou, being a scorpion, shalt do any good. For neither dost thou do good willingly thyself, nor dost thou allow another to do it, hated as thou art by all like Saturn's star.

228.—By the Same

One man killed his mother, another his father, a third his brother, but Polianus all three, the first since Oedipus.

229.—ΤΟΥ ΑΥΤΟΥ

Ὀψέ ποθ' ἡ ποδάγρα τὸν ἑαυτῆς ἄξιον εὗρεν,
ὃν ποδαγρᾶν πρὸ ἐτῶν ἄξιον ἦν ἑκατόν.

230.—ΤΟΥ ΑΥΤΟΥ

Μασταύρων ἀφελὼν δύο γράμματα, Μάρκε, τὰ πρῶτα,
ἄξιος εἶ πολλῶν τῶν ὑπολειπομένων.

231.—ΤΟΥ ΑΥΤΟΥ

Θηρίον εἶ παρὰ γράμμα, καὶ ἄνθρωπος διὰ γράμμα·
ἄξιος εἶ πολλῶν, ὧν παρὰ γράμμα γράφῃ.

232.—ΚΑΛΛΙΟΥ ΑΡΓΕΙΟΥ

Αἰεὶ χρυσίον ἦσθα, Πολύκριτε· νῦν δὲ πεπωκώς,
ἐξαπίνης ἐγένου λυσσομανές τι κακόν·
αἰεί μοι δοκέεις κακὸς ἔμμεναι. οἶνος ἐλέγχει
τὸν τρόπον· οὐκ ἐγένου νῦν κακός, ἀλλ' ἐφάνης.

233.—ΛΟΥΚΙΛΛΙΟΥ

Φαῖδρος πραγματικὸς καὶ ζωγράφος ἤρισε Ῥοῦφος
τίς θᾶσσον γράψει καὶ τίς ὁμοιότερον.
ἀλλ' ἐν ὅσῳ Ῥοῦφος τρίβειν τὰ χρώματ' ἔμελλεν,
Φαῖδρος ἔγραψε λαβὼν εἰκονικὴν ἀποχήν.

---

[1] i.e. many crosses (stauroi).
[2] Addressed to Marcos. Take M away and it becomes

229.—By the Same

Late in the day has the gout found him who deserved it, him who deserved to be gouty a hundred years ago.

230.—By the Same

Take away, Marcus, the two first letters from Mastauron, and you deserve many of what is left.[1]

231.—By the Same

You are a wild beast all but a letter and a man by a letter, and you deserve many of the beasts that you are all but a letter.[2]

232.—CALLIAS OF ARGOS

You were always, Polycritus, as good as gold, but now after drinking you have suddenly become a sort of rabid curse. I believe you are always wicked; wine is the test of character; it is not now that you become wicked, but now you have been shown to be so.

233.—LUCILIUS

Phaedrus the man of business and the painter Rufus contended as to which of them would copy quickest and most truly. But while Rufus was about to mix his paints Phaedrus took and wrote out a renouncement of Rufus' claim faithful as a picture.[3]

---

arcos, a late form of the word arctos, "bear." He deserves many bears to tear him in pieces.

[3] *i.e.* admirably forged. Phaedrus owed Rufus money.

234.—ΤΟΥ ΑΥΤΟΥ

Τοὺς πόδας εἰ Κρατερὸς καὶ τὰς χέρας εἶχ᾽ ὁλο-
κλήρους,
οὐκ αὖ τὴν κεφαλὴν εἶχε, τοιαῦτα γράφων.

235.—ΔΗΜΟΔΟΚΟΤ

Καὶ τόδε Δημοδόκου· Χῖοι κακοί· οὐχ ὁ μέν, ὃς δ᾽ οὔ·
πάντες, πλὴν Προκλέους· καὶ Προκλέης δὲ Χίος.

236.—ΤΟΥ ΑΥΤΟΥ

Πάντες μὲν Κίλικες κακοὶ ἀνέρες· ἐν δὲ Κίλιξιν
εἷς ἀγαθὸς Κινύρης, καὶ Κινύρης δὲ Κίλιξ.

237.—ΤΟΥ ΑΥΤΟΥ

Καππαδόκην ποτ᾽ ἔχιδνα κακὴ δάκεν· ἀλλὰ καὶ αὐτὴ
κάτθανε, γευσαμένη αἵματος ἰοβόλου.

238.—ΤΟΥ ΑΥΤΟΥ

Καππαδόκαι φαῦλοι μὲν ἀεί, ζώνης δὲ τυχόντες
φαυλότεροι, κέρδους δ᾽ εἵνεκα φαυλότατοι.
ἢν δ᾽ ἄρα δὶς καὶ τρὶς μεγάλης δράξωνται ἀπήνης,
δή ῥα τότ᾽ εἰς ὥρας φαυλεπιφαυλότατοι.
μή, λίτομαι, βασιλεῦ, μὴ τετράκις, ὄφρα μὴ αὐτὸς 5
κόσμος ὀλισθήσῃ καππαδοκιζόμενος.

---

[1] Demodocus of Leros lived previously to Aristotle who
mentions him.   There is another couplet identical with this
except that the Lerians are substituted for the Chians and
that the saying is attributed to Phocylides.   Bentley's para-

234.—By the Same

If Craterus' feet and hands were sound, his head was not, when he wrote such stuff.

235.—DEMODOCUS

This, too, is by Demodocus: "The Chians are bad, not one bad and another not, but all bad except Procles, and Procles is a Chian."[1]

236.—By the Same

All Cilicians are bad men, but among the Cilicians the only good man is Cinyras, and Cinyras is a Cilician.

237.—By the Same

An evil viper once bit a Cappadocian, but it died itself, having tasted the venomous blood.

238.—By the Same

The Cappadocians are always bad, but when they get a belt[2] they are worse, and for the sake of gain they are the worst of all, and if once or twice they get hold of a large carriage[3] they are as bad as bad can be for a year. I implore thee, O King, let it not be four times, lest the whole world slide to ruin, becoming cappadocianified.[4]

phrase, "The Germans in Greek are sadly to seek, Except only Hermann, and Hermann's a German," is well known.

[2] When they became soldiers.

[3] When they hold high office.

[4] The epigram must refer to some Cappadocian who looked forward to a fourth term of office.

239.—ΛΟΥΚΙΛΛΙΟΥ

Οὔτε Χίμαιρα τοιοῦτον ἔπνει κακὸν ἡ καθ' Ὅμηρον,
οὐκ ἀγέλη ταύρων, ὡς ὁ λόγος, πυρίπνους,
οὐ Λῆμνος σύμπασα, καὶ Ἁρπυιῶν τὰ περισσά,
οὐδ' ὁ Φιλοκτήτου πούς ἀποσηπόμενος·
ὥστε σε παμψηφεὶ νικᾶν, Τελέσιλλα, Χιμαίρας,   5
σηπεδόνας, ταύρους, ὄρνεα, Λημνιάδας.

240.—ΤΟΥ ΑΥΤΟΥ

Οὐ μόνον αὐτὴ πνεῖ Δημοστρατίς, ἀλλὰ δὴ αὐτῆς
τοὺς ὀσμησαμένους πνεῖν πεποίηκε τράγου.

241.—ΝΙΚΑΡΧΟΥ

Τὸ στόμα χὠ πρωκτὸς ταὐτόν, Θεόδωρε, σοῦ ὄζει,
ὥστε διαγνῶναι τοῖς φυσικοῖς καλὸν ἦν.
ἢ γράψαι σε ἔδει ποῖον στόμα, ποῖον ὁ πρωκτός.
νῦν δὲ λαλοῦντός σου <βδεῖν σ' ἐνόμιζον ἐγώ>.

242.—ΤΟΥ ΑΥΤΟΥ

Οὐ δύναμαι γνῶναι, πότερον χαίνει Διόδωρος,
ἢ βδῆσ'· ἓν γὰρ ἔχει πνεῦμα κάτω καὶ ἄνω.

243.—ΤΟΥ ΑΥΤΟΥ

Λούσασθαι πεπόρευται Ὀνήσιμος εἰς βαλανεῖον
δωδεκάτῃ δύστρου μηνός, ἐπ' Ἀντιφίλου,
παῖδα λιπὼν οἴκοις ἐπιτίτθιον, ὃν δύο τέκνων
ἄλλων εὑρήσει λουσάμενος πατέρα.

*   *   *   *   *

ἥξειν δ' εἰς ὥρας ἡμῖν γράφει· οἱ βαλανεῖς γὰρ   5
εἰς τότε τάσσονται τὴν πυρίαν καθελεῖν.

---

[1] The women of Lemnos, who had killed their husbands,
were afflicted by Venus with an evil odour.
[2] See Vergil, Aen. iii. 244.

239.—LUCILIUS

Not Homer's Chimaera breathed such foul breath, not the fire-breathing herd of bulls of which they tell, not all Lemnos[1] nor the excrements of the Harpies,[2] nor Philoctetes' putrefying foot. So that in universal estimation, Telesilla, you surpass Chimerae, rotting sores, bulls, birds, and the women of Lemnos.

240.—By the Same

Demostratis not only breathes herself the stink of a he-goat, but makes those who smell her breathe the same.

241.—NICARCHUS

Your mouth and your breech, Theodorus, smell the same, so that it would be a famous task for men of science to distinguish them. You ought really to write on a label which is your mouth and which your breech, but now when you speak I think you break wind.

242.—By the Same

I can't tell whether Diodorus is yawning or has broken wind, for he has one breath above and below.

243.—By the Same

Onesimus went to the bath to bathe on the twelfth of the month Dystrus in the year of Antiphilus, leaving at home a child at the breast, whom when he has finished bathing he will find to be the father of two other children. . . . He writes us to say he will go again next year, for the bath-men promise to take off the heat then.[3]

[3] The joke is evidently about a bath which it took an enormous time to heat. There appears to be something missing after the second couplet.

244.—ΑΔΗΛΟΝ

Ἠγόρασας χαλκοῦν μιλιάριον, Ἡλιόδωρε,
τοῦ περὶ τὴν Θράκην ψυχρότερον Βορέου.
μὴ φύσα, μὴ κάμνε· μάτην τὸν καπνὸν ἐγείρεις·
εἰς τὸ θέρος χαλκῆν βαύκαλιν ἠγόρασας.

245.—ΛΟΥΚΙΛΛΙΟΥ

Οἱ τοῖχοι, Διόφαντε, τὰ κύματα πάντα δέχονται,
καὶ διὰ τῶν θυρίδων Ὠκεανὸς φέρεται·
δελφίνων δ' ἀγέλαι καὶ Νηρέος ἀγλαὰ τέκνα
ἐν τῷ πλοίῳ σου νηχόμενα βλέπεται.
ἂν δ' ἀναμείνωμεν, πλεύσει τάχα καί τις ἐν ἡμῖν·   5
οὐ γὰρ ἔνεστιν ὕδωρ οὐκέτι τῷ πελάγει.

246.—ΤΟΥ ΑΥΤΟΥ

Ἐκ ποίων ἔταμες, Διονύσιε, τὰ ξύλα ταῦτα
λατομιῶν; ποίων τὸ σκάφος ἐστὶ μύλων;
εἰ γὰρ ἐγώ τι νοῶ, μολίβου γένος, οὐ δρυός ἐστιν,
οὐδ' ἐλάτης, μικροῦ ῥιζοβολεῖ τὰ κάτω·
καὶ τυχὸν ἐξαπίνης ἔσομαι λίθος· εἶτα, τὸ χεῖρον,   5
γράψει μ' ὡς Νιόβην δρᾶμα σαπρὸν Μελίτων.

247.—ΤΟΥ ΑΥΤΟΥ

Ἢ[1] πέλαγος πλέομεν, Διονύσιε, καὶ γεγέμισται
τὸ πλοῖον παντὸς πανταχόθεν πελάγους.

¹ εἰ MS.: corr. Boissonade.

---

[1] The ship is supposed to be speaking.

244.—Anonymous

You bought a brass boiler, Heliodorus, colder than Thracian Boreas. Don't blow the fire, don't put yourself out; it is in vain you stir up the smoke. What you bought was a brass wine-cooler for summer.

245.—LUCILIUS

The sides of the ship, Diophantes, let in all the waves, and through the ports ocean enters; and we see swimming in your ship herds of dolphins and the bright children of Nereus. But if we wait longer someone will soon be sailing inside this our ship, for there is no more water left in the sea.

246.—By the Same [1]

From what quarry, Dionysius, did you hew these timbers? Of what mill-stones is the ship built? For if I know anything about it, it is a kind of lead, not oak or pine, and the lower part of me is nearly taking root. [2] Perhaps I shall suddenly become a stone, and then the worst of it is Melito will write a rotten drama about me as if I were Niobe.

247.—By the Same

Of a truth, Dionysius, we the seas [3] sail, and the ship is full of every sea from all parts. The Adriatic,

[1] Like the Phaeacian ship in the *Odyssey* (xiii. 162) which Poseidon changed into a rock.
[3] πέλαγος may be taken either as accusative or nominative. In the former case the meaning is " we sail the seas," in the latter " we, the seas, are sailing."

ἀντλεῖται δ' Ἀδρίας, Τυρρηνικός, Ἰσσικός, Αἴγων·
οὐ πλοῖον, πηγὴ δ' Ὠκεανοῦ ξυλίνη.
ὁπλίζου, Καῖσαρ· Διονύσιος ἄρχεται ἤδη   5
οὐκέτι ναυκληρεῖν, ἀλλὰ θαλασσοκρατεῖν.

248.—ΒΙΑΝΟΡΟΣ

Τὸ σκάφος οὐ βυθὸς εἷλε (πόθεν βυθός; οὐ γὰρ
ἔπλωσεν),
οὐδὲ Νότος, πρὸ Νότου δ' ὤλετο καὶ πελάγευς.
ἤδη γάρ μιν ἅπασαν ἐπὶ ζυγὰ γομφωθεῖσαν
ἤλειφον πεύκης τῇ λιπαρῇ νοτίδι·
πίσσα δ' ὑπερβρασθεῖσα πυρὸς φλογὶ τὴν ἁλὶ
πιστὴν   5
τευχομένην γαίῃ δεῖξεν ἀπιστοτέρην.

249.—ΛΟΥΚΙΛΛΙΟΥ

Ἀγρὸν Μηνοφάνης ὠνήσατο, καὶ διὰ λιμὸν
ἐκ δρυὸς ἀλλοτρίας αὑτὸν ἀπηγχόνισεν.
γῆν δ' αὐτῷ τεθνεῶτι βαλεῖν οὐκ ἔσχον ἄνωθεν,
ἀλλ' ἐτάφη μισθοῦ πρός τινα τῶν ὁμόρων.
εἰ δ' ἔγνω τὸν ἀγρὸν τὸν Μηνοφάνους Ἐπίκουρος,   5
πάντα γέμειν ἀγρῶν εἶπεν ἄν, οὐκ ἀτόμων.

250.—ΑΔΕΣΠΟΤΟΝ

Τὸν παχὺν εὖ ἔγραψ' ὁ ζωγράφος· ἀλλ' ἀπόλοιτο,
εἰ δύο μισητοὺς ἀνθ' ἑνὸς ὀψόμεθα.

251.—ΝΙΚΑΡΧΟΥ

Δυσκώφῳ δύσκωφος ἐκρίνετο· καὶ πολὺ μᾶλλον
ἦν ὁ κριτὴς τούτων τῶν δύο κωφότερος.

the Tyrrhene Sea, the Gulf of Issa, the Aegean, are
running dry. This is no ship, but a wooden fountain
of ocean. To arms, Caesar! Dionysius begins already
not to command a ship, but to command the seas.

248.—BIANOR

It was not the depths that took the ship (how the
depths, when she had never sailed?) nor the south
wind, but she perished before encountering south
wind and sea. Already completely built, even as far
as the benches, they were anointing her with the fat
juice of the pine; and the pitch, overboiling with
the flame of the fire, showed that she, who was being
built to serve the sea faithfully, was less faithful to
the land.[1]

249.—LUCILIUS

Menophanes bought a field, and from hunger hanged
himself on another man's oak. When he was dead
they had no earth to throw over him from above, but
he was buried for payment in the ground of one of
his neighbours. If Epicurus had known of Meno-
phanes' field he would have said that everything is
full of fields, not of atoms.

250.—Anonymous

The artist painted the fat man well, but to Hell
with him if we shall look on two guzzlers instead
of one.

251.—NICARCHUS

A stone-deaf man went to law with another stone-
deaf man, and the judge was much deafer than the

[1] *i.e.* deceived the expectations of those on the land who
were building her.

ὧν ὁ μὲν ἀντέλεγεν τὸ ἐνοίκιον αὐτὸν ὀφείλειν
μηνῶν πένθ'· ὁ δ' ἔφη νυκτὸς ἀληλεκέναι.
ἐμβλέψας δ' αὐτοῖς ὁ κριτὴς λέγει, "'Ες τί μάχεσθε; 5
μήτηρ ἔσθ' ὑμῶν· ἀμφότεροι τρέφετε."

G. C. Swayne, in *The Greek Anthology* (Bohn), p. 383;
J. A. Pott, *Greek Love Songs and Epigrams*, ii. p. 81.

252.—ΤΟΥ ΑΥΤΟΥ

Εἴ με φιλεῖς, μισεῖς με· καὶ εἰ μισεῖς, σὺ φιλεῖς με·
εἰ δέ με μὴ μισεῖς, φίλτατε, μή με φίλει.

253.—ΛΟΥΚΙΛΛΙΟΥ

'Εκ ποίων ὁ πατήρ σε δρυῶν τέτμηκεν, 'Αρίστων,
ἢ ποίων σε μύλου κόψατο λατομιῶν;
ἢ γὰρ ἀπὸ δρυὸς ἐσσὶ παλαιφάτου ἢ ἀπὸ πέτρης
ὀρχηστής, Νιόβης ἔμπνοον ἀρχέτυπον·
ὥστε με θαυμάζοντα λέγειν, ὅτι "Καὶ σύ τι Λητοῖ 5
ἤρισας· οὐ γὰρ ἂν ἦς αὐτομάτως λίθινος."

254.—ΤΟΥ ΑΥΤΟΥ

Πάντα καθ' ἱστορίην ὀρχούμενος, ἐν τὸ μέγιστον
τῶν ἔργων παριδὼν ἡνίασας μεγάλως.
τὴν μὲν γὰρ Νιόβην ὀρχούμενος, ὡς λίθος ἔστης,
καὶ πάλιν ὢν Καπανεύς, ἐξαπίνης ἔπεσες·
ἀλλ' ἐπὶ τῆς Κανάκης ἀφυῶς, ὅτι καὶ ξίφος ἦν σοι 5
καὶ ζῶν ἐξῆλθες· τοῦτο παρ' ἱστορίην.

---

[1] Probably to avoid certain dues.
[2] There is a play which cannot be rendered on the two
meanings of *philein*, to love and to kiss.
[3] Hom. *Od.* xix. 163.

pair of them. One of them contended that the other owed him five months' rent, and the other said that his opponent had ground corn at night.[1] Says the judge, looking at them : " Why are you quarrelling ? She is your mother; you must both maintain her."

252.—By the Same

If you kiss me you hate me, and if you hate me you kiss me. But if you don't hate me, dear friend, don't kiss me ![2]

253.—LUCILIUS

From what oak-trees did your father cut you, Aristo, or from what mill-stone quarry did he hew you ? For indeed you are a dancer "made of a venerable tree or of stone,"[3] the living original of Niobe ; so that I wonder and say : "You, too, must have had some quarrel with Leto, or else you would not have been naturally made of stone."

254.—By the Same

You played in the ballet everything according to the story, but by overlooking one very important action you highly displeased us. Dancing the part of Niobe you stood like a stone, and again when you were Capaneus[4] you suddenly fell down. But in the case of Canace[5] you were not clever, for you had a sword, but yet left the stage alive; that was not according to the story.

[4] Who fell from the scaling-ladder struck by lightning in the legendary story of the Seven against Thebes.

[5] She killed herself when her incestuous attachment to her brother, Macareus, was discovered.

255.—ΠΑΛΛΑΔΑ

Δάφνην καὶ Νιόβην ὠρχήσατο Μέμφις ὁ σιμός,
  ὡς ξύλινος Δάφνην, ὡς λίθινος Νιόβην.

R. Garnett, *A Chaplet from the Greek Anthology*, cxxxi.

256.—ΛΟΥΚΙΛΛΙΟΥ

Λούεσθαί σε λέγουσι πολὺν χρόνον, Ἡλιοδώρα,
  γραῖαν ἐτῶν ἑκατὸν μὴ καταλυομένην.
πλὴν ἔγνωκα τίνος ποιεῖς χάριν· ὡς ὁ παλαιὸς
  ἐλπίζεις Πελίας ἑψομένη νεάσαι.

257.—ΤΟΥ ΑΥΤΟΥ

Ἑρμογένη τὸν ἰατρὸν ἰδὼν Διόφαντος ἐν ὕπνοις
  οὐκέτ' ἀνηγέρθη, καὶ περίαμμα φέρων.

cp. Martial vi. 53.

258.—ΤΟΥ ΑΥΤΟΥ

Τῷ Πίσης μεδέοντι τὸ κρανίον Αὖλος ὁ πύκτης,
  ἓν καθ' ἓν ἀθροίσας ὀστέον, ἀντίθεται.
σωθεὶς δ' ἐκ Νεμέας, Ζεῦ δέσποτα, σοὶ τάχα θήσει
  καὶ τοὺς ἀστραγάλους τοὺς ἔτι λειπομένους.

259.—ΤΟΥ ΑΥΤΟΥ

Θεσσαλὸν ἵππον ἔχεις, Ἐρασίστρατε, ἀλλὰ σαλεῦσαι
  οὐ δύνατ' αὐτὸν ὅλης φάρμακα Θεσσαλίης,
ὄντως δούριον ἵππον, ὃν εἰ Φρύγες εἷλκον ἅπαντες
  σὺν Δαναοῖς, Σκαιὰς οὐκ ἂν ἐσῆλθε πύλας·
ὃν στήσας ἀνάθημα θεοῦ τινος, εἰ προσέχεις μοι,   5
  τὰς κριθὰς ποίει τοῖς τεκνίοις πτισάνην.

255.—PALLADAS

SNUB-NOSED Memphis danced the parts of Daphne [1] and Niobe, Daphne as if he were wooden, and Niobe as if he were of stone.

256.—LUCILIUS

THEY say you spend a long time in the bath, Heliodora, an old woman of a hundred not yet retired from the profession. But I know why you do it. You hope to grow young, like old Pelias, by being boiled.

257.—BY THE SAME

DIOPHANTUS saw Hermogenes the doctor in his sleep and never woke up again, although he was wearing an amulet.

258.—BY THE SAME

AULUS the boxer dedicates to the Lord of Pisa [2] his skull, having collected the bones one by one And if he escapes from Nemea, Lord Zeus, he will perchance dedicate to thee also the vertebrae he still has left.

259.—BY THE SAME

YOU have a Thessalian horse, Erasistratus, but all the magic of Thessaly cannot make him stir; truly a wooden horse which would never have got through the Scaean gates, if all the Trojans and Greeks together had dragged it. If you take my advice, put him up as a votive statue to some god and make his barley into gruel for your children.

[1] Changed into a laurel tree.   [2] The Olympian Zeus.

260.—ΑΔΗΛΟΝ

Τοῦτο τὸ "οὐλεύειν" εἶχες πάλαι, ἀλλὰ τὸ Βῆτα
οὐκ ἐπιγινώσκω· Δέλτα γὰρ ἐγράφετο.

261.—ΑΔΗΛΟΝ

Ὑἱὸς Πατρικίου μάλα κόσμιος, ὃς διὰ Κύπριν
οὐχ ὁσίην ἑτάρους πάντας ἀποστρέφεται.

262.—ΑΔΗΛΟΝ

Αἰθερίην διὰ νύκτα νέοι κατάγουσι Σελήνην
ἤθεοι Φαρίης ἄνδιχα τεμνομένην.

263.—ΠΑΛΛΑΔΑ

Παύλῳ κωμῳδῷ κατ' ὄναρ στὰς εἶπε Μένανδρος·
"Οὐδὲν ἐγὼ κατὰ σοῦ, καὶ σὺ κακῶς με λέγεις."

264.—ΛΟΥΚΙΛΛΙΟΥ

Ποιήσας δαπάνην ἐν ὕπνοις ὁ φιλάργυρος Ἕρμων
ἐκ περιωδυνίας αὑτὸν ἀπηγχόνισεν.

265.—ΤΟΥ ΑΥΤΟΥ

Εἰ μὲν ἐπ' ἀττελάβους ἄγεται στρατός, ἢ κυνομυίας,
ἢ μύας, ἢ ψυλλῶν ἱππικὸν ἢ βατράχων,
Γάϊε, καὶ σὺ φοβοῦ μὴ καί σέ τις ἐγκαταλέξῃ,
ὡς ἂν τῆς τούτων ἄξιον ὄντα μάχης.
εἰ δ' ἀρετῆς ἀνδρῶν ἄγεται στρατός, ἄλλο τι παῖζε· 5
Ῥωμαίοις δ' οὐδεὶς πρὸς γεράνους πόλεμος.

---

[1] *cp.* No. 337.
[2] Selene (Moon) was the name of a courtesan. The
words may mean "bring down the half-moon by magic," but
as applied to Selene they have an improper meaning.

260.—ANONYMOUS[1]

THIS Ouleuein you had long ago, but I don't recognise the "b" (*bouleuein,* to be a senator), for it used to be written "d" (*douleuein,* to be a slave).

261.—ANONYMOUS

PATRICIUS' son is very well behaved, as he avoids all his fellows because of impure indulgence.

262.—ANONYMOUS

THE young men of Alexandria bring down Selene[2] divided in two in the ethereal night.

263.—PALLADAS

MENANDER, standing over the comedian Paulus in his sleep, said : "I never did you any harm, and you speak me ill."

264.—LUCILIUS

HERMON the miser, having spent money in his sleep, hanged himself from vexation.

265.—BY THE SAME

IF an army is being led against locusts, or dog-flies, or mice, or the cavalry of fleas or frogs, you too should be afraid, Gaius, of someone enrolling you as being worthy of fighting with such foes. But if an army of brave men is being despatched, amuse yourself with something else ; but the Romans do not fight against cranes.[3]

[3] *i.e.* the Romans are not like the Pygmies, who made war on cranes, so there is no chance of their requiring your services.

266.—ΤΟΥ ΑΥΤΟΥ

Ψευδὲς ἔσοπτρον ἔχει Δημοσθενίς· εἰ γὰρ ἀληθὲς
ἔβλεπεν, οὐκ ἂν ὅλως ἤθελεν αὐτὸ βλέπειν.

267.—ΑΔΗΛΟΝ

Κερκίδος οὐ χρῄζεις ὁ λογιστικός, οὐδὲ μέλει σοι·
καὶ γὰρ ἀβασκάντως ῥῖνα τρίπηχυν ἔχεις.

268.—ΑΛΛΟ

Οὐ δύναται τῇ χειρὶ Πρόκλος τὴν ῥῖν' ἀπομύσσειν·
τῆς ῥινὸς γὰρ ἔχει τὴν χέρα μικροτέρην·
οὐδὲ λέγει Ζεῦ σῶσον ἐὰν πταρῇ· οὐ γὰρ ἀκούει
τῆς ῥινός· πολὺ γὰρ τῆς ἀκοῆς ἀπέχει.

269.—ΑΔΗΛΟΝ

Ὁ τοῦ Διὸς παῖς καλλίνικος Ἡρακλῆς
οὐκ εἰμὶ Λούκιος, ἀλλ' ἀναγκάζουσί με.

270.—ΑΔΗΛΟΝ

Εἰς εἰκόνα Ἀναστασίου βασιλέως ἐν τῷ Εὐρίπῳ

Εἰκόνα σοι, βασιλεῦ κοσμοφθόρε, τήνδε σιδήρου
ἄνθεσαν, ὡς χαλκοῦ πολλὸν ἀτιμοτέρην,
ἀντὶ φόνου, πενίης τ' ὀλοῆς, λιμοῦ τε, καὶ ὀργῆς,
οἷς πάντα φθείρεις ἐκ φιλοχρημοσύνης.

---

[1] A lampoon on a statue of Hercules from which Commodus had removed the head and substituted his own, inscribing it "Lucius Commodus Hercules."

266.—By the Same

DEMOSTHENIS has a lying mirror, for if she saw the truth she would not want to look into it at all.

267.—Anonymous

You, Mathematician, don't require a measuring rod, and it is no concern of yours, for you have a nose three cubits long which no one grudges you.

268.—Anonymous

PROCLUS cannot wipe his nose with his hand, for his arm is shorter than his nose; nor does he say "God preserve us" when he sneezes, for he can't hear his nose, it is so far away from his ears.

269.—Anonymous

I "VICTORIOUS Heracles the son of Zeus" am not Lucius but they compel me to be so.[1]

270.—Anonymous

On a Statue of the Emperor Anastasius on the Euripus.[2]

KING, destroyer of the world, they set up this iron statue of thee as being much less precious than bronze, in return for the bloodshed, the fatal poverty and famine and wrath, by which thou destroyest all things owing to thy avarice.

A place in the Circus at Constantinople so called.

271.—ΑΛΛΟ

Ἐγγύθι τῆς Σκύλλης χαλεπὴν στήσαντο Χάρυβδιν,
ἄγριον ὠμηστὴν τοῦτον Ἀναστάσιον.
δείδιθι καὶ σύ, Σκύλλα, τεαῖς φρεσί, μὴ σὲ καὶ αὐτὴν
βρώξῃ, χαλκείην δαίμονα κερματίσας.

272.—ΑΔΗΛΟΝ

Εἰς κιναίδους

Ἀνέρας ἠρνήσαντο, καὶ οὐκ ἐγένοντο γυναῖκες·
οὔτ' ἄνδρες γεγάασιν, ἐπεὶ πάθον ἔργα γυναικῶν·
οὔτε γυναῖκες ἔασιν, ἐπεὶ φύσιν ἔλλαχον ἀνδρῶν.
ἀνέρες εἰσὶ γυναιξί, καὶ ἀνδράσιν εἰσὶ γυναῖκες.

273.—ΑΔΗΛΟΝ

Χωλὸν ἔχεις τὸν νοῦν, ὡς τὸν πόδα· καὶ γὰρ ἀληθῶς
εἰκόνα τῶν ἐντὸς σὴ φύσις ἐκτὸς ἔχει.

274.—ΛΟΥΚΙΑΝΟΥ

Εἰπέ μοι εἰρομένῳ, Κυλλήνιε, πῶς κατέβαινεν
Λολλιανοῦ ψυχὴ δῶμα τὸ Φερσεφόνης ;
θαῦμα μέν, εἰ σιγῶσα· τυχὸν δέ τι καὶ σὲ διδάσκειν
ἤθελε. φεῦ, κείνου καὶ νέκυν ἀντιάσαι.

275.—ΑΠΟΛΛΩΝΙΟΥ ΓΡΑΜΜΑΤΙΚΟΥ

Καλλίμαχος τὸ κάθαρμα· τὸ παίγνιον· ὁ ξύλινος
νοῦς. αἴτιος ὁ γράψας Αἴτια Καλλίμαχος.

---

[1] There must have been a statue of Scylla at the place.

[2] Callimachus, author of *Causes* or *Origins* (fragments are edited and translated by C. A. Trypanis, in Callimachus, *Aitia* etc. L.C.L. No. 421) was a librarian at Alexandria c. 250 B.C.

271.—Anonymous

Nigh to Scylla[1] they set up cruel Charybdis, this savage ogre Anastasius. Fear in thy heart, Scylla, lest he devour thee too, turning a brazen goddess into small change.

272.—Anonymous

On Cinaedi

They denied their manhood and did not become women, nor were they born men, as they have suffered what women do; nor are they women, since a man's nature was theirs. They are men to women and women to men.

273.—Anonymous

Your mind is as lame as your foot, for truly your nature bears outside the image of what is inside.

274.—LUCIAN

Tell me, I ask you, Hermes, how did the soul of Lollianus go down to the house of Persephone? If in silence, it was a marvel, and very likely he wanted to teach you also something. Heavens, to think of meeting that man even when one is dead!

275.—APOLLONIUS (RHODIUS)

Callimachus. garbage; petty toy; wooden head.

Cause, the. he who wrote the *Causes*:—Callimachus.[2]

and quarrelled with his pupil the epic poet Apollonius, who, I take it, hitting at Callimachus, pretends to give two items from a word-dictionary; and I translate accordingly. The last word of the epigram is perhaps Καλλιμάχου—E. H. W.]

276.—ΛΟΥΚΙΛΛΙΟΥ

Εἰς φυλακὴν βληθείς ποτε Μάρκος ὁ ἀργός, ἑκοντί,
ὀκνῶν ἐξελθεῖν, ὡμολόγησε φόνον.

277.—ΤΟΥ ΑΥΤΟΥ

Τῆς νυκτὸς τροχάσας ἐν ὕπνοις ποτὲ Μάρκος ὁ ἀργός,
οὐκέτ' ἐκοιμήθη μὴ πάλι που τροχάσῃ.

278.—ΤΟΥ ΑΥΤΟΥ

Εἰς γραμματικὸν κερασφόρον

Ἔξω παιδεύεις Πάριδος κακὰ καὶ Μενελάου.
ἔνδον ἔχων πολλοὺς σῆς Ἑλένης Πάριδας.

279.—ΤΟΥ ΑΥΤΟΥ

Οὐδεὶς γραμματικῶν δύναταί ποτε <ἄρτιος> εἶναι,
ὀργήν, καὶ μῆνιν, καὶ χόλον εὐθὺς ἔχων.

280.—ΠΑΛΛΑΔΑ

Βέλτερον Ἡγέμονος ληστοκτόνου ἐς κρίσιν ἐλθεῖν,
ἢ τοῦ χειρουργοῦ Γενναδίου παλάμας.
ὃς μὲν γὰρ φονέας ὁσίως στυγέων κατατέμνει·
ὃς δὲ λαβὼν μισθοὺς εἰς ἀίδην κατάγει.

281.—ΤΟΥ ΑΥΤΟΥ

Εἰς Μάγνον ἰατροσοφιστήν

Μάγνος ὅτ' εἰς Ἀίδην κατέβη, τρομέων Ἀϊδωνεὺς
εἶπεν· "Ἀναστήσων ἤλυθε καὶ νέκυας."

276.—LUCILIUS

INDOLENT Marcus once, when cast into prison, confessed to a murder of his own accord, being too lazy to come out.

277.—BY THE SAME

LAZY Marcus, having once run in his sleep, never went to sleep again lest he should chance to run once more.

278.—BY THE SAME

On a Cuckold Grammarian

OUTSIDE you teach the woes of Paris and Menelaus, having at home plenty of Parises for your Helen.

279.—BY THE SAME

NONE of the grammarians can ever be moderate, as from the very beginning he has wrath, and spite, and bile.[1]

280.—PALLADAS

BETTER to be judged by Hegemon, the slayer of robbers, than to fall into the hands of the surgeon Gennadius. For he executes murderers in just hatred, but Gennadius takes a fee for sending you down to Hades.

281.—BY THE SAME

On Magnus the Expert Physician

WHEN Magnus went down to Hades, Pluto trembled and said: "He has come to set the dead, too, on their legs."

[1] Alluding to the opening of the *Iliad.*

282.—ΑΛΛΟ

Τοὺς καταλείψαντας γλυκερὸν φάος οὐκέτι θρηνῶ,
τοὺς δ' ἐπὶ προσδοκίῃ ζῶντας ἀεὶ θανάτου.

W. Cowper, *Works* (Globe ed.), p. 501.

283.—ΠΑΛΛΑΔΑ

Εἰς Δαμόνικον ὕπαρχον

Πολλοὶ πολλὰ λέγουσιν, ὅμως δ' οὐ πάντα δύνανται
ῥήμασιν ἐξειπεῖν ῥεύματα σῶν παθέων·
ἐν δ' ἐπὶ σοῦ παράδοξον ἐθαυμάσαμεν καὶ ἄπιστον,
δάκρυα πῶς κλέπτων εἶχες ἑτοιμότατα.
Χαλκίδος ἐκ γαίης ἀπεχάλκισε τὴν πόλιν ἡμῶν,   5
κλέπτων, καὶ κλέπτων δάκρυσι κερδαλέοις.

284.—ΤΟΥ ΑΥΤΟΥ

Ἐκ γῆς Λωτοφάγων μέγας ὄρχαμος ἦλθε Λυκάων
Χαλκίδος ἐκ γαίης ἀντιοχευόμενος.

285.—ΤΟΥ ΑΥΤΟΥ

Θηλυφανὲς παράδοξον ἐθαυμάσαμεν πάθος ἄλλο·
ἔκλαιεν κλέπτων, κλεπτομένους ἐλεῶν,
ὃς κλέπτων ἤγνευε, καὶ ἁγνεύων ἀπεσύλα,
μηδὲν ἔχων καθαρόν, μηδὲ τὸ σῶμα ῥύπου.

---

[1] Chalcis in Euboea. Here it probably only means the
Brazen land or the land of Avarice, for which the Chalcidians
were famous. We need not suppose that this magistrate
was a native of Chalcis. In the next epigram he is said to

282.—Anonymous

I lament no longer those who have left the sweet daylight, but those who ever live in expectation of death.

283.—PALLADAS

On Demonicus the Prefect

Many people say many things, but yet they cannot express in words all the currents of your vices. But there is one strange and incredible thing I marvelled at in you : how, while you were stealing, you had tears ready to hand. Coming from the land of Chalcis [1] he deprived our city of brass, stealing and stealing with profitable tears.

284.—By the Same

On the Same

From the land of the Lotophagi came the great leader Lycaon, from the land of Chalcis a fellow who gets mounted behind.[2]

285.—By the Same

On the Same

We marvelled at another strange, effeminate characteristic. He wept while stealing, pitying those he was robbing ; he who, while robbing, observed ceremonial purity, and while thus affecting purity went on despoiling, a man with nothing clean about him, not even his person free of dirt.

come also from the Lotos-eaters' land, which was placed in North Africa.

[2] In the last word there is a play on Antioch. The prefect is here, I suppose, called Lycaon as being wolfish.

286.—ΤΟΥ ΑΥΤΟΥ

Οὐδὲν γυναικὸς χεῖρον, οὐδὲ τῆς καλῆς·
δούλου δὲ χεῖρον οὐδέν, οὐδὲ τοῦ καλοῦ·
χρήζεις ὅμως οὖν τῶν ἀναγκαίων κακῶν.
εὔνουν νομίζεις δοῦλον εἶναι δεσπότῃ;
καλὸς δ᾽ ἂν εἴη δοῦλος ὁ τὰ σκέλη κλάσας.

287.—ΤΟΥ ΑΥΤΟΥ

Ὁ τὴν γυναῖκα τὴν ἄμορφον δυστυχῶν,
λύχνους ἀνάψας ἑσπέρας σκότος βλέπει.

288.—ΤΟΥ ΑΥΤΟΥ

Κουρεὺς καὶ ῥαφιδεὺς κατεναντίον ἦλθον ἀγῶνος,
καὶ τάχα νικῶσιν τὸ ξυρὸν αἱ ῥαφίδες.

289.—ΤΟΥ ΑΥΤΟΥ

Ὦ τῆς ταχίστης ἁρπαγῆς τῆς τοῦ βίου·
ἀνὴρ δανειστής, τῶν χρόνων γλύφων τόκους,
τέθνηκεν εὐθὺς ἐν ῥοπῆς καιρῷ βραχεῖ,
ἐν δακτύλοισι τοὺς τόκους σφίγγων ἔτι.

290.—ΤΟΥ ΑΥΤΟΥ

Δακτυλικὴν ψῆφόν τις ἔχων πέρι δάκτυλα χειρῶν
ψήφῳ τοῦ θανάτου προὔλαβεν εἰς ἀΐδην.
ζῇ δ᾽ ἡ ψῆφος νῦν τοῦ ψηφίζοντος ἐρήμη,
ψυχῆς ἁρπαγίμης ἔνθεν ἐλαυνομένης.

---

[1] A verse of Menander's.

[2] And consequently was incapable of doing any mischief.

[3] He seems to be ridiculing a barber whose razors were blunt.

[4] He must have been counting out the money with his left hand and marking down the amount with his right.

286.—By the Same

"Nothing is worse than a woman, even a good one";[1] and nothing is worse than a slave, even a good one. But still one requires necessary evils. Do you suppose a slave bears his master affection? A good slave would be he who broke both his legs.[2]

287.—By the Same

He who is cursed with an ugly wife sees darkness when he lights the lamps in the evening.

288.—By the Same

A barber and a tailor came to blows with each other, and soon the needles got the better of the razor.[3]

289.—By the Same

O swiftest ravishment of life! A money-lender, while marking down on his tablets the interest of years, died instantly in the space of a moment, still grasping his interest in his fingers.[4]

290.—By the Same

One holding in his fingers a reckoning counter for the fingers went by the counter-vote[5] of death in double-quick time to Hades. The counter now lives bereaved of the reckoner, whose soul is rapidly driven from hence.[6]

[5] There is a play on the two senses of *psephos*, "vote" and "counter."

[6] This epigram seems to refer to the same incident as the preceding, but is very obscure. Palladas evidently uses δακτυλικὴ ψῆφος in some sense that eludes us. What, again, is the point of his saying that the counter (or vote) is alive?

291.—ΤΟΥ ΑΥΤΟΥ

Τί ὠφέλησας τὴν πόλιν στίχους γράφων,
χρυσὸν τοσοῦτον λαμβάνων βλασφημίας,
πωλῶν ἰάμβους, ὡς ἔλαιον ἔμπορος;

292.—ΤΟΥ ΑΥΤΟΥ

Εἴς τινα φιλόσοφον γενόμενον ὕπαρχον πόλεως ἐπὶ
Βαλεντινιανοῦ καὶ Βάλεντος

Ἄντυγος οὐρανίης ὑπερήμενος, ἐς πόθον ἦλθες
ἄντυγος ἀργυρέης· αἶσχος ἀπειρέσιον·
ἦσθά ποτε κρείσσων· αὖθις δ' ἐγένου πολὺ χείρων.
δεῦρ' ἀνάβηθι κάτω· νῦν γὰρ ἄνω κατέβης.

293.—ΤΟΥ ΑΥΤΟΥ

Ἵππον ὑποσχόμενός μοι Ὀλύμπιος ἤγαγεν οὐράν,
ἧς ὀλιγοδρανέων ἵππος ἀπεκρέματο.

294.—ΛΟΥΚΙΛΛΙΟΥ

Πλοῦτον μὲν πλουτοῦντος ἔχεις, ψυχὴν δὲ πένητος,
ὦ τοῖς κληρονόμοις πλούσιε, σοὶ δὲ πένης.

295.—ΤΟΥ ΑΥΤΟΥ

Εἴ τιν' ἔχεις Διόνυσον ἐνὶ μεγάροισι τεοῖσι,
τὸν κισσὸν ἀφελών, θριδάκων φύλλοις στεφάνωσον.

---

[1] *i.e.* the official carriage.
[2] The last line is merely a very frigid repetition of the opinion that the philosopher (by some said to be Themistius) demeaned himself by accepting office.

291.—By the Same

WHAT good do you do to the city by writing verses, getting so much gold for your slanders, selling iambic verses as a shopman sells oil?

292.—By the Same

On a certain Philosopher who became Prefect of Constantinople in the reign of Valentinian and Valens

THOU, seated above the heavenly wheel, hast desired a silver wheel.[1] Oh, infinite shame! Erst thou wast of higher station and hast straight become much lower. Ascend hither to the depths; for now thou hast descended to the heights.[2]

293.—By the Same

OLYMPIUS promised me a horse, but brought me a tail from which hung a horse at its last gasp.

294.—LUCILIUS

THOU hast the wealth of a rich man, but the soul of a pauper, thou who art rich for thy heirs and poor for thyself.

295.—By the Same

IF thou hast any Dionysus in thy house, take off the ivy from his head and crown him with lettuce leaves.[3]

---

[3] Addressed to a man who had given him bad wine. Lettuce, I suppose, because the wine was like vinegar. *cp.* No. 396.

GREEK ANTHOLOGY

296.—ΤΙΜΩΝΟΣ

Εἰς Κλεάνθην

Τίς δ' οὗτος κτίλος ὡς ἐπιπωλεῖται στίχας ἀνδρῶν;
μωλύτης, ἐπέων λίθος Ἄσσιος, ὅλμος ἄτολμος.

297.—ΑΔΗΛΟΝ

Εἰς γυναῖκα μεθυστρίδα

a. Πῶς φιλέεις, ὦ μῆτερ, ἐμοῦ πλέον υἱέος οἶνον;
  δὸς πιέειν οἴνοιο, ἐπεὶ γάλα τὸ πρὶν ἔδωκας.
β. Ὦ παῖ, σὴν μὲν δίψαν ἐμὸν γάλα τὸ πρὶν ἔπαυσε·
  νῦν ἴθι πῖνε ὕδωρ, καὶ παύεο δίψαν ἑοῖο.

298.—ΑΛΛΟ

Δέρκεο πῶς διψῶν υἱὸς χέρα μητέρι τείνει·
ἡ δὲ γυνή, ἄτε πᾶσα γυνή, κεκρατημένη οἴνῳ,
ἐν λαγύνῳ πίνουσα, τόδ' ἔννεπε λοξὸν ἰδοῦσα·
" Ἐκ βρόχθου ὀλίγοιο τί σοι δῶ, τέκνον ἐμεῖο ;
ξέστας γὰρ τριάκοντα μόνους λάγυνός γ' ὅδε χωρεῖ." 5

" Μῆτερ, μητρυιῆς χαλεπὸν τρόπον ἀντικρατοῦσα,
ἀμπέλου ἡδυτάτης τάδε δάκρυα δός μοι ἀφύσσειν."

" Μῆτερ ἐμή, δύσμητερ, ἀπηνέα θυμὸν ἔχουσα,
εἰ φιλέεις με τὸν υἷα, δίδου μέ τι τυτθὸν ἀφύσσειν."

299.—ΠΑΛΛΑΔΑ

Ὑβρίζεις· τί τὸ θαῦμα; τί δυσχερές; ἀλλὰ φέρω σε·
τῶν γὰρ ὑβριζόντων ἡ θρασύτης κόλασις.

296.—TIMON

On Cleanthes the Philosopher

Who is this who like a ram stalks through the ranks of men, a slow-coach, an Assian mill-stone of words, a spiritless block?

297.—ANONYMOUS

On a Tippling Old Woman[1]

A. How is it, mother, that thou lovest wine more than me, thy son? Give me wine to drink since once thou didst give me milk. *B.* My son, my milk once stilled thy thirst, but now drink water and still thy own thirst.

298.—ANONYMOUS

See how the son athirst reaches out his hand to his mother, and the woman, being a thorough woman, overcome by wine, drinking from a jar, spoke thus, looking askance: "How shall I give thee to drink, my son, from a little droppie, for this jar holds but thirty pints."

———

"Mother, who hast rather the harsh nature of a step-mother, give me to quaff these tears of the sweetest vine."

———

"Mother, evil mother, pitiless at heart, if thou lovest me, thy son, give me but a little to quaff."

299.—PALLADAS

Thou waxest wanton! What wonder? Does it distress me? No, I bear with thee. For the boldness of the wanton is their punishment.

———

[1] These and the following verses (No. 298) seem to have been inspired by a picture.

300.—ΤΟΥ ΑΥΤΟΥ

Πολλὰ λαλεῖς, ἄνθρωπε, χαμαὶ δὲ τίθῃ μετὰ μικρόν.
σίγα, καὶ μελέτα ζῶν ἔτι τὸν θάνατον.

301.—ΤΟΥ ΑΥΤΟΥ

Ἥλιος ἀνθρώποις αὐγῆς θεός· εἰ δὲ καὶ αὐτὸς
ὕβριζεν φαίνων, οὐδὲ τὸ φῶς ἐπόθουν.

302.—ΤΟΥ ΑΥΤΟΥ

Οὐκ ἐμέ, τὴν πενίην δὲ καθύβρισας· εἰ δὲ καὶ ὁ Ζεὺς
ἦν ἐπὶ γῆς πτωχός, καὐτὸς ἔπασχεν ὕβριν.

303.—ΤΟΥ ΑΥΤΟΥ

Εἰ πένομαι, τί πάθω; τί με μισεῖς οὐκ ἀδικοῦντα;
πταῖσμα τόδ᾽ ἐστὶ Τύχης, οὐκ ἀδίκημα τρόπων.

304.—ΤΟΥ ΑΥΤΟΥ

Πάντες μὲν δειλοὶ καὶ ἀλαζόνες εἰσί, καὶ εἴ τι
ἐν τοῖς ἀνθρώποις ἄλλο πέφυκε πάθος·
ἀλλ᾽ ὁ λογισμὸν ἔχων τῷ πλησίον οὐκ ἀναφαίνει,
ἔνδον ἀποκρύπτων τῇ συνέσει τὸ πάθος.
σῆς δὲ θύρα ψυχῆς ἀναπέπταται· οὐδένα λήθεις   5
οὔτε καταπτήσσων, οὔτε θρασυνόμενος.

305.—ΤΟΥ ΑΥΤΟΥ

Τέκνον ἀναιδείης, ἀμαθέστατε, θρέμμα μορίης,
εἰπέ, τί βρενθύῃ μηδὲν ἐπιστάμενος;

300.—By the Same

Thou speakest much, O man, but in a little thou shalt be laid on the ground. Silence! and while thou yet livest get into practice for death.

301.—By the Same

The Sun to men is the god of light, but if he too were insolent to them in his shining, they would not desire even light.

302.—By the Same

Thou hast not insulted me, but my poverty; but if Zeus dwelt on earth in poverty, he himself also would have suffered insult.

303.—By the Same

If I am poor, what shall it harm me? Why dost thou hate me who do no wrong? This is the fault of Fortune, not a vice of character.

304.—By the Same

All are cowards and braggarts and whatever other fault there may be among men, yet he who has reason does not expose his fault to his neighbour, but in his wisdom hides it within. But thy soul's door is flung wide open, and it is evident to all when thou crouchest in terror or art too brazen.

305.—By the Same

Child of shamelessness, most ignorant of men, nursling of folly, tell why dost thou hold thy head high, knowing nothing? Among the grammarians

ἐν μὲν γραμματικοῖς ὁ πλατωνικός· ἂν δὲ Πλά-
τωνος
δόγματά τις ζητῇ, γραμματικὸς σὺ πάλιν.
ἐξ ἑτέρου φεύγεις ἐπὶ θάτερον· οὔτε δὲ τέχνην   5
οἶσθα γραμματικήν, οὔτε πλατωνικὸς εἶ.

306.—ΤΟΥ ΑΥΤΟΥ

Ἂν μετ' Ἀλεξάνδρειαν ἐς Ἀντιόχειαν ἀπέλθῃς,
καὶ μετὰ τὴν Συρίην Ἰταλίας ἐπιβῇς,
τῶν δυνατῶν οὐδείς σε γαμήσει· τοῦτο γὰρ αἰεὶ
οἰομένη πηδᾷς εἰς πόλιν ἐκ πόλεως.

307.—ΤΟΥ ΑΥΤΟΥ

Υἱὸν ἔχεις τὸν Ἔρωτα, γυναῖκα δὲ τὴν Ἀφροδίτην·
οὐκ ἀδίκως, χαλκεῦ, τὸν πόδα χωλὸν ἔχεις.

308.—ΛΟΥΚΙΛΛΙΟΥ

Τὸν πόδα τῇ βελόνῃ τρυπῶν Κλεόνικος ὁ λεπτός,
αὐτὸς ἐτρύπησεν τῷ ποδὶ τὴν βελόνην.

309.—ΤΟΥ ΑΥΤΟΥ

Θαρσύμαχε, πλοῦτον πολὺν ὤλεσας ἐξ ἐπιβουλῆς,
εἰς οὐδὲν δ' ἥκεις ἄθλιος ἐξαπίνης,
φεισάμενος, δανίσας, τοκίσας τόκον, ὑδροποτήσας,
πολλάκι μηδὲ φαγών, ὥστε τι πλεῖον ἔχειν.
ἀλλ' εἴ μοι λογίσαιο τὸ πεινῆν καὶ τότε καὶ νῦν,   5
οὐδὲν ἔλαττον ἔχεις ὧν τότ' ἔδοξας ἔχειν.

310.—ΤΟΥ ΑΥΤΟΥ

Ἠγόρασας πλοκάμους, φῦκος, μέλι, κηρόν, ὀδόντας·
τῆς αὐτῆς δαπάνης ὄψιν ἂν ἠγόρασας.

thou art the Platonist, and if anyone enquire as to Plato's doctrines thou art again a grammarian. From one thing thou takest refuge in another, and thou neither knowest the Art of Grammar nor art thou a Platonist.

306.—By the Same

THOUGH you leave Alexandria for Antioch, and after Syria land in Italy, no man in power will ever wed you. The fact is you always are fancying that some one will, and therefore skip from city to city.

307.—By the Same

YOUR son is called Eros and your wife Aphrodite, and so, blacksmith, it is quite fair you should have a lame leg.[1]

308.—LUCILIUS

LEAN Cleonicus, making a hole in his foot with the needle, himself made a hole in the needle with his foot.[2]

309.—By the Same

THRASYMACHUS, you lost great wealth by a plot, and, poor fellow, you have suddenly come to naught after all your economising, lending, exacting interest, drinking water, often not even eating, so as to have a little more money. But if you calculate what starvation was then and what it is now, you have no less now than you then seemed to have.

310.—By the Same

YOU bought hair, rouge, honey, wax, and teeth. For the same outlay you might have bought a face.

[1] *i.e.* like Hephaestus.   [2] *cp.* No. 102.

311.—ΤΟΥ ΑΥΤΟΥ

Οὕτως ἔστ' ἀργὸς Πανταίνετος, ὥστε πυρέξας
μηκέτ' ἀναστῆναι παντὸς ἐδεῖτο θεοῦ.
καὶ νῦν οὐκ ἐθέλων μὲν ἐγείρεται, ἐν δέ οἱ αὐτῷ
κωφὰ θεῶν ἀδίκων οὔατα μεμφόμενος.

312.—ΤΟΥ ΑΥΤΟΥ

Οὐδενὸς ἐνθάδε νῦν τεθνηκότος, ὦ παροδῖτα,
Μάρκος ὁ ποιητὴς ᾠκοδόμηκε τάφον,
καὶ γράψας ἐπίγραμμα μονόστιχον, ὧδ' ἐχάραξε·
" Κλαύσατε δωδεκέτη Μάξιμον ἐξ Ἐφέσου."
οὐδὲ γὰρ εἶδον ἐγώ τινα Μάξιμον· εἰς δ' ἐπίδειξιν   5
ποιητοῦ κλαίειν τοῖς παριοῦσι λέγω.

313.—ΤΟΥ ΑΥΤΟΥ

Ἀργυρέη λιμῷ τις, ἐς εἰλαπίνην με καλέσσας,
ἔκτανε, πειναλέους τοὺς πίνακας προφέρων.
ὀχθήσας δ' ἄρ' ἔειπον ἐν ἀργυροφεγγέϊ λιμῷ·
" Ποῦ μοι χορτασίη ὀστρακίνων πινάκων; "

314.—ΤΟΥ ΑΥΤΟΥ

Ἐζήτουν πινάκων πόθεν οὔνομα τοῦτο καλέσσω,
καὶ παρὰ σοὶ κληθείς, εὗρον ὅθεν λέγεται.
πείνης γὰρ μεγάλης μεγάλους πίνακας παρέθηκας,
ὄργανα τοῦ λιμοῦ πειναλέους πίνακας.

315.—ΤΟΥ ΑΥΤΟΥ

Εἴσιδεν Ἀντίοχος τὴν Λυσιμάχου ποτὲ τύλην,
κοὐκέτι τὴν τύλην εἴσιδε Λυσίμαχος.

311.—By the Same

Pantaenetus is so lazy that when he fell sick of a fever he prayed to every god never to get up again. And now he leaves his bed unwillingly, and in his heart blames the deaf ears of the unjust gods.

312.—By the Same

Though there is no one dead here now, O passer-by, Marcus the poet built a tomb here, and writing an inscription of one line as follows, engraved it: "Weep for twelve year old Maximus from Ephesus." I (says the tomb) never even saw any Maximus, but to show off the poet's talent I bid the passer-by weep.[1]

313.—By the Same

One, bidding me to a banquet, killed me with silver hunger, serving famished dishes. And in wrath I spoke amid the silver sheen of hunger: "Where is the plenty of my earthenware dishes?"

314.—By the Same

I sought whence I should say the word *pinakes* (dishes) was derived, and on being invited by you I found out why they are so called. For you placed before me great *pinakes* of great *peina* (hunger), famished dishes, instruments of famine.

315.—By the Same

Antiochus once set eyes on Lysimachus' cushion, and Lysimachus never set eyes on it again.

[1] This phrase in Greek has also the sense of "to send to the deuce."

316.—ΑΛΛΟ

Εἰς ἱερόν ποτ' ἀγῶνα Μίλων μόνος ἦλθ' ὁ παλαιστής·
τὸν δ' εὐθὺς στεφανοῦν ἀθλοθέτης ἐκάλει.
προσβαίνων δ' ὤλισθεν ἐπ' ἰσχίον· οἱ δ' ἐβόησαν
τοῦτον μὴ στεφανοῦν, εἰ μόνος ὢν ἔπεσεν.
ἀνστὰς δ' ἐν μέσσοις ἀντέκραγεν· "Οὐχὶ τρί' ἐστίν· 5
ἐν κεῖμαι· λοιπὸν τἄλλα μέ τις βαλέτω."

317.—ΠΑΛΛΑΔΑ

Ἀντίσπαστον ἐμοί τις ὄνον μακρόθυμον ἔδωκεν,
τῶν βασταζομένων ὅρμον ὁδοιπορίης,
υἱὸν τῆς βραδυτῆτος ὄνον, πόνον, ὄκνον, ὄνειρον,
τῶν ἀνακαμπτόντων ὑστάτιον πρότερον.

318.—ΦΙΛΟΔΗΜΟΥ

Ἀντικράτης ᾔδει τὰ σφαιρικὰ μᾶλλον Ἀράτου
πολλῷ, τὴν ἰδίην δ' οὐκ ἐνόει γένεσιν·
διστάζειν γὰρ ἔφη, πότερ' ἐν κριῷ γεγένηται
ἢ διδύμοις, ἢ τοῖς ἰχθύσιν ἀμφοτέροις.
εὕρηται δὲ σαφῶς ἐν τοῖς τρισί· καὶ γὰρ ὀχευτὴς 5
καὶ μωρὸς μαλακός τ' ἐστὶ καὶ ὀψοφάγος.

319.—ΑΥΤΟΜΕΔΟΝΤΟΣ

Ἀνθρακίων δέκα μέτρα φέρων, ἔσο καὶ σὺ πολίτης·
ἢν δὲ καὶ ὗν ἀγάγῃς, αὐτὸς ὁ Τριπτόλεμος.

---

[1] To win the match one had to throw one's adversary
three times.

[2] The metrical foot *antispastus* was so called because it
was composed of an iambus and a trochee, which have
opposite movements.

216

316.—Anonymous

Milo the wrestler was once the only one who came
to the sacred games, and the steward of the games
called him to crown him at once. But as he was ap-
proaching he slipped and fell on his back, and the
people called out: "Do not crown this man, as he
got a fall when he was alone!" But he, standing up
in their midst, shouted back: "Are there not three
falls?[1] I fell once; now let someone give me the
other two."

317.—PALLADAS

Someone gave me a long-suffering donkey that
moves backwards as much as forward[2] their journey's
haven to those who ride on it; a donkey, the son of
slowness, a labour, a delay, a dream,[3] but first instead
of last[4] for those who are retiring.

318.—PHILODEMUS

Anticrates knew the constellations much better
than Aratus, but could not tell his own nativity; for
he said he was in doubt whether he was born in the
Ram or the Twins, or in both the Fishes. But it was
clearly found to be in all three, for he is a tupper
and a fool, and effeminate, and fond of fish.[5]

319.—AUTOMEDON

If you bring ten sacks of charcoal you, too, will
be a citizen, and if you bring a pig, also, you will be

---

[3] These are puns that cannot be reproduced.
[4] Here there is a play on the figure of speech *hysteron-proteron*, or inversion of words.
[5] As μαλακός certainly refers to δίδυμοι (= *Gemini*, or twin testicles) I think both ὀχευτής and μωρός must refer to the Ram.

δεῖ δὲ καὶ Ἡρακλείδῃ ὑφηγητῆρι δοθῆναι
ἢ καυλοὺς κράμβης, ἢ φακόν, ἢ κοχλίας.
ταῦτ' ἔχε, καὶ λέγε σαυτὸν Ἐρεχθέα, Κέκροπα,
Κόδρον,   5
ὃν κ' ἐθέλῃς· οὐδεὶς οὐδὲν ἐπιστρέφεται.

320.—ΑΡΓΕΝΤΑΡΙΟΥ

Ἀντιγόνην ἔστεργε Φιλόστρατος· ἦν δὲ παλαισταῖς
ὁ τλήμων Ἴρου πέντε πενιχρότερος.
εὗρε δ' ὑπὸ κρυμοῦ γλυκὺ φάρμακον· ἀντία γὰρ σχὼν
γούνατ' ἐκοιμήθη, ξεῖνε, μετ' Ἀντιγόνης.

321.—ΦΙΛΙΠΠΟΥ

Γραμματικοὶ Μώμου στυγίου τέκνα, σῆτες ἀκανθῶν,[1]
τελχῖνες βίβλων, Ζηνοδότου σκύλακες,
Καλλιμάχου στρατιῶται, ὃν ὡς ὅπλον ἐκτανύσαντες,
οὐδ' αὐτοῦ κείνου γλῶσσαν ἀποστρέφετε,
συνδέσμων λυγρῶν θηρήτορες, οἷς τὸ "μὶν" ἢ "σφὶν"   5
εὔαδε, καὶ ζητεῖν εἰ κύνας εἶχε Κύκλωψ,
τρίβοισθ' εἰς αἰῶνα κατατρύζοντες ἀλιτροὶ
ἄλλων· ἐς δ' ἡμᾶς ἰὸν ἀποσβέσατε.

322.—ΑΝΤΙΦΑΝΟΥΣ

Γραμματικῶν περίεργα γένη, ῥιζώρυχα μούσης
ἀλλοτρίης, ἀτυχεῖς σῆτες ἀκανθοβάται,

---

[1] So Scaliger : ἀπάντων MS. cp. Nos. 322 and 347.

[1] Ancient Athenian heroes.
[2] He is satirizing the facility with which the Athenians granted citizenship.

Triptolemus himself, and to Heraclides your intro-
ducer must be given either some cabbage castocks,
or lentils, or snails. Have these with you and call
yourself Erechtheus, Cecrops, Codrus,[1] whoever you
like; no one minds a rap about it.[2]

320.—ARGENTARIUS

PHILOSTRATUS loved Antigone. He was poorer by
five cubits, poor fellow, than Irus. The cold, how-
ever, taught him a sweet remedy; for tucking up his
knees (with *antia gonata*) he slept so, stranger, with
Antigone.

321.—PHILIPPUS

GRAMMARIANS, ye children of Stygian Momus, ye
book-worms feeding on thorns,[3] demon foes of books,
cubs of Zenodotus,[4] soldiers of Callimachus[5] from
whom, though you hold him out as a shield, you do
not refrain your tongue, hunters of melancholy con-
junctions who take delight in *min*[6] and *sphin*[6] and in
enquiring if the Cyclops had dogs, may ye wear
yourselves away for all eternity, ye wretches,
muttering abuse of others; then come and quench
your venom in me.

322.—ANTIPHANES

IDLY curious race of grammarians, ye who dig up
by the roots the poetry of others; unhappy book-
worms that walk on thorns, defilers of the great,

[3] On thorny passages of authors, as we should say.
[4] The celebrated grammarian.
[5] Callimachus is a difficult poet, owing to his recondite
learning.   [6] Obsolete pronouns.

τῶν μεγάλων κηλῖδες, ἐπ' Ἠρίννῃ δὲ κομῶντες,
πικροὶ καὶ ξηροὶ Καλλιμάχου πρόκυνες,
ποιητῶν λῶβαι, παισὶ σκότος ἀρχομένοισιν,   5
ἔρροιτ', εὐφώνων λαθροδάκναι κόριες.

323.—ΠΑΛΛΑΔΑ

Ῥῶ καὶ Λάμβδα μόνον κόρακας κολάκων διορίζει·
λοιπὸν ταὐτὸ κόραξ βωμολόχος τε κόλαξ.
τοὔνεκά μοι, βέλτιστε, τόδε ζῶον πεφύλαξο,
εἰδὼς καὶ ζώντων τοὺς κόλακας κόρακας.

324.—ΑΥΤΟΜΕΔΟΝΤΟΣ

α. Δέξαι, Φοῖβε, τὸ δεῖπνον, ὅ σοι φέρω. β. Ἢν τις
      ἐάσῃ,
δέξομαι. α. Εἶτα φοβῇ καὶ σύ τι, Λητοΐδη;
β. Οὐδένα τῶν ἄλλων, πλὴν Ἄρριον· οὗτος ἔχει
      γὰρ
ἅρπαγος ἰκτίνου χεῖρα κραταιοτέρην,
ἀκνίσου βωμοῖο νεωκόρος· ἢν τελέσῃ δὲ   5
τὴν πομπήν, ἄρας ᾤχεθ' ἅπαντα πάλιν.
ἐν Διὸς ἀμβροσίῃ πολλὴ χάρις· εἰς γὰρ ἂν ὑμέων
ἤμην, εἰ λιμοῦ καὶ θεὸς ᾐσθάνετο.

325.—ΤΟΥ ΑΥΤΟΥ

Ἐχθὲς δειπνήσας τράγεον πόδα, καὶ δεκαταῖον
κανναβίνης κράμβης μήλινον ἀσπάραγον,
εἰπεῖν τὸν καλέσαντα φυλάσσομαι· ἔστι γὰρ ὀξύς,
καὶ φόβος οὐχ ὁ τυχὼν μή με πάλιν καλέσῃ.

---

[1] She was reckoned among the Alexandrian poets, and
hence is mentioned here together with Callimachus.
[2] i.e. not, like other crows, the dead.

proud of your Erinna,[1] bitter and dry dogs set on by Callimachus, bane of poets, darkness to little beginners, away with you, bugs that secretly bite the eloquent.

323.—PALLADAS

Corakes (crows) and *colakes* (flatterers) are only distinguished by *Rho* and *Lambda*. Therefore a crow and a lick-spittle flatterer are the same thing. So, my good sir, beware of this beast, knowing that flatterers are crows that pick the living too.[2]

324.—AUTOMEDON

A. Accept, Phoebus, the supper I bring thee. *B.* I will accept it if someone lets me. *A.* Then, Son of Leto, is there something that thou too dost fear? *B.* No one else but only Arrius, for he, that ministrant of an altar that smells not of fat,[3] has a more powerful claw than a robber-hawk, and once he has celebrated the procession[4] he walks back carrying off everything. There is great virtue in Jove's ambrosia, for I should be one of you[5] if a god, too, could feel hunger.

325.—By the Same

Having supped yesterday on a leg of an old goat and the yellow stalk, ten days old, of a cabbage like hemp, I am shy of mentioning the man who invited me; for he is short-tempered, and I am not a little afraid of his asking me again.

[3] Because he carries all the meat away and never lets the altar smell of fat.
[4] A procession accompanying a victim for sacrifice.
[5] A mortal and liable to die of starvation.

326.—ΤΟΥ ΑΥΤΟΥ

Πώγων, καὶ λάσιαι μηρῶν τρίχες, ὡς ταχὺ πάντα
ὁ χρόνος ἀλλάσσει· Κόννιχε, τοῦτ' ἐγένου.
οὐκ ἔλεγον; "Μὴ πάντα βαρὺς θέλε μηδὲ βάναυσος
εἶναι· καὶ κάλλους εἰσί τινες Νεμέσεις."
ἦλθες ἔσω μάνδρης, ὑπερήφανε· νῦν ὅτι βούλει   5
οἴδαμεν· ἀλλ' ἐξῆν καὶ τότ' ἔχειν σε φρένας.

327.—ΑΝΤΙΠΑΤΡΟΥ ΘΕΣΣΑΛΟΝΙΚΕΩΣ

Τὴν ξηρὴν ἐπὶ νῶτα Λυκαινίδα, τὴν Ἀφροδίτης
λώβην, τὴν ἐλάφου παντὸς ἀπυγοτέρην,
αἰπόλος ᾗ μεθύων οὐκ ἄν ποτε, φασί, συνῴκει,
γοῖ, γοῖ. τοιαῦται Σιδονίων ἄλοχοι.

328.—ΝΙΚΑΡΧΟΥ

Τὴν μίαν Ἑρμογένης κἀγώ ποτε καὶ Κλεόβουλος
ἤγομεν εἰς κοινὴν κύπριν Ἀριστοδίκην·
ἧς ἔλαχον μὲν ἐγὼ πολιὴν ἅλα ναιέμεν αὐτός·
εἷς γὰρ ἕν, οὐ πάντες πάντα, διειλόμεθα.
Ἑρμογένης δ' ἔλαχε στυγερὸν δόμον εὐρώεντα,   5
ὕστατον, εἰς ἀφανῆ χῶρον ὑπερχόμενος,
ἔνθ' ἀκταὶ νεκύων, καὶ ἐρινεοὶ ἠνεμόεντες
δινεῦνται πνοιῇ δυσκελάδων ἀνέμων.
Ζῆνα δὲ θὲς Κλεόβουλον, ὃς οὐρανὸν εἰσαναβαίνειν,
τὸ ψολόεν κατέχων ἐν χερὶ πῦρ, ἔλαχεν.   10
γῆ δ' ἔμενε ξυνὴ πάντων· ψίαθον γὰρ ἐν αὐτῇ
στρώσαντες, τὴν γραῦν ὧδε διειλόμεθα.

326.—By the Same

BEARD and rough hair on the thighs, how quickly time changes all! Connichus, is this what you have become? Did I not say, " Be not in all things harsh and discourteous; Beauty has its own Avenging Deities "? So you have come into the pen,[1] proud youth; we know that you wish for it now; but then, too, you might have had sense.

327.—ANTIPATER OF THESSALONICA (?)[2]

LYCAENIS with the dry back, the disgrace of Aphrodite, with less haunches than any deer, with whom, as the saying is, a drunken goatherd would not live. G-r-r, g-r-r! such are the wives of the Sidonians.

328.—NICARCHUS

ONE day, Hermogenes and I and Cleobulus took one and the same dame, Aristodice, to a love-bed which we all shared. I myself was allotted a hoary sea to stay in—for we divided the business into one part each, not all of us getting the whole thing. But Hermogenes got a dismal mouldy lodging—the last place on earth; he dipped into an obscure spot where lie the shores which the dead haunt and breeze-tossed figs rock and roll around in the blast of horrid raucous winds. But Cheobulus—imagine him to be Zeus who was fated to climb to heaven's roof holding glowing fire in his hand. However, earth remained common ground to us all. For we spread a rush-mat on it; and that's how we parcelled out the old girl.

---

[1] *i.e.* as I think, " You have become tame." Commentators interpret, " You have become like a goat."
[2] Surely by the Sidonian.

329.—ΤΟΥ ΑΥΤΟΥ

Δημῶναξ, μὴ πάντα κάτω βλέπε, μηδὲ χαρίζου
  τῇ γλώσσῃ· δεινὴν χοῖρος ἄκανθαν ἔχει.
καὶ σὺ ζῇς †ἡμῖν, ἐν Φοινίκῃ δὲ καθεύδεις,
  κοὐκ ὢν ἐκ Σεμέλης μηροτραφὴς γέγονας.

330.—ΤΟΥ ΑΥΤΟΥ

Ἐκλήθην ἐχθές, Δημήτριε· σήμερον ἦλθον
  δειπνεῖν. μὴ μέμψῃ, κλίμακ᾽ ἔχεις μεγάλην·
ἐν ταύτῃ πεποίηκα πολὺν χρόνον· οὐδ᾽ ἂν ἐσώθην
  σήμερον, ἀλλ᾽ ἀνέβην κέρκον ὄνου κατέχων.
ἦψαι τῶν ἄστρων· Ζεὺς ἡνίκα τὸν Γανυμήδην   5
  ἥρπασε, τῇδ᾽ αὐτόν, φαίνετ᾽, ἔχων ἀνέβη.
ἔνθεν δ᾽ εἰς Ἀΐδην πότ᾽ ἀφίξεαι; οὐκ ἀφυὴς εἶ
  εὕρηκας τέχνην πῶς ἔσῃ ἀθάνατος.

331.—ΤΟΥ ΑΥΤΟΥ

Εἶχε Φίλων λέμβον Σωτήριχον· ἀλλ᾽ ἐν ἐκείνῳ
  σωθὴν οὐδὲ Ζεὺς αὐτὸς ἴσως δύναται.
οὔνομα γὰρ μόνον ἦν Σωτήριχος, οἱ δ᾽ ἐπιβάντες
  ἔπλεον ἢ παρὰ γῆν, ἢ παρὰ Φερσεφόνην.

332.—ΤΟΥ ΑΥΤΟΥ

Οὐ πλεῖν, ἀλλ᾽ ἀντλεῖν ἡμᾶς Εὔκανδρος ὁ πρωρεὺς
  εἰς τὴν εἰκόσορον φαίνεται ἐμβιβάσας·
οὐκ ὀλίγον γὰρ ἔνεστιν ὕδωρ ἔσω, ἀλλ᾽ ὁ Ποσειδῶν
  ἐν ταύτῃ διαπλεῖν φαίνεται εἰς τὸ πέραν·

---

[1] = the female part. For the reference to Phoenicia see
Φοινικίζω in L. and S.

329.—By the Same

Demonax, do not always turn down your eyes, nor indulge your tongue; the pig¹ has a formidable thorn. And you live . . . and sleep in Phoenicia, and though not Semele's son,² art nourished by a thigh.

330.—By the Same

I was invited yesterday, Demetrius, and came to supper to-day. Don't find fault with me; you have a long staircase. I spent an age on it, and I should not have got safe up it to-day only I came up holding on to a donkey's tail. You touch the stars: Zeus, it seems, when he ran away with Ganymede, went up with him by this route. But from here how long will it take you to reach Hades? You are not wanting in cleverness; you have hit on a trick for being immortal.

331.—By the Same

Philo had a boat called the "Saviour," but in it perhaps not even Zeus himself can be saved. Its name only was Saviour, but the passengers sailed either close to land or to Persephone.

332.—By the Same

Icander the captain embarked us, it seems, on his twenty-oarer, not for a sail, but to bale her out. For the water in her is not little, but Poseidon seems to sail over in her to the opposite shore. It is

---

² Dionysus, who was said to have come to maturity as a baby in the thigh of Zeus.

νῦν πρῶτον ναῦς ὦπται ὑδρωπική, ἀλλά γε [δείδω] 5
μὴ σορὸν οὖσαν ἴδης τὴν πάλαι εἰκόσορον.

333.—ΚΑΛΛΙΚΤΗΡΟΣ

Φαρμακίοισι 'Ρόδων λέπραν καὶ χοιράδας αἴρει·
τἆλλα δὲ πάντ' αἴρει καὶ δίχα φαρμακίων.

334.—ΑΔΕΣΠΟΤΟΝ

Δαμαγόραν καὶ λοιμὸν ἰσόψηφον τις ἀκούσας
ἔστησ' ἀμφοτέρων τὸν τρόπον ἐκ κανόνος·
εἰς τὸ μέρος δὲ καθείλκετ' ἀνελκυσθὲν τὸ τάλαντον
Δαμαγόρου, λοιμὸν δ' εὗρεν ἐλαφρότερον.

335.—ΑΔΕΣΠΟΤΟΝ

'Ω τλῆμον Κυνέγειρε, καὶ ἐν ζωοῖς καὶ ἀπελθών,
ὡς αἰεὶ κόπτῃ ῥήμασι καὶ κοπίσιν.
πρόσθε μὲν ἐν πολέμοισι τεῇ πέσε μαρναμένη χείρ·
νῦν δέ σ' ὁ γραμματικὸς καὶ ποδὸς ἐστέρισεν.

336.—ΑΔΕΣΠΟΤΟΝ

Τῆς 'Ασίης τὰ λάφυρα λαβὼν ἔπλευσε Καρῖνος
ἤματι χειμερίῳ, δυομένων ἐρίφων·
εἶδε καὶ 'Αδράστεια τὸ φορτίον· ὃς δ' ἐφορώσης
ᾤχετο, καὶ πελάγους δαίμοσιν ἐγγελάσας.

---

¹ There is a play on *eikosoros* and *soros* (coffin).
² *i.e.* he is a thief.
³ Reckoning the letters as numbers, each comes to 420

the first time a ship with the dropsy has been seen. But I, at least, fear lest you may see what was once a long boat turn into our long home.[1]

333.—CALLICTER

RHODO removes leprosy and scrofula by drugs, but he removes everything else even without drugs.[2]

334.—ANONYMOUS

SOMEONE, hearing that "Damagoras" and "pestilence" were numerical equivalents,[3] weighed the character of both from the beam of the balance. But the scale, when raised, was pulled down on Damagoras' side, and he found pestilence lighter.

335.—ANONYMOUS

O UNHAPPY Cynegirus,[4] how among the living and in death art thou hacked by words and axes! Formerly thy hand fell fighting in the war, and now the grammarian has deprived thee of a foot.

336.—ANONYMOUS

CARINUS,[5] after receiving the spoils of Asia, set sail on a winter's day at the setting of the Kids. Nemesis, too, saw the cargo, but he departed in her sight and laughing at the gods of the sea.

[4] A famous fighter at the battle of Marathon. The correct form of the name is Cynaegirus, the second syllable being long. The grammarian had misspelt it and made it short.
[5] If he be the emperor of this name, nothing is known of the circumstance to which this epigram alludes.

337.—ΑΔΕΣΠΟΤΟΝ

Βουλεύεις, Ἀγαθῖνε· τὸ βῆτα δὲ τοῦτ᾽ ἐπρίω νῦν,
εἰπέ, πόσης τιμῆς; δέλτα γὰρ ἦν πρότερον.

338.—ΑΔΕΣΠΟΤΟΝ

Τὴν φωνὴν ἐνοπήν σε λέγειν ἐδίδαξεν Ὅμηρος·
τὴν γλῶσσαν δ᾽ ἐνοπὴν τίς σ᾽ ἐδίδαξεν ἔχειν;

339.—ΑΔΕΣΠΟΤΟΝ

Τὴν κεφαλὴν σείεις, καὶ τὴν πυγὴν ἀνασείεις·
ἐν μὲν μαινομένου, ἐν δὲ περαινομένου.

340.—ΠΑΛΛΑΔΑ

Ὤμοσα μυριάκις ἐπιγράμματα μηκέτι ποιεῖν·
πολλῶν γὰρ μωρῶν ἔχθραν ἐπεσπασάμην.
ἀλλ᾽ ὁπόταν κατίδω τοῦ Παφλαγόνος τὸ πρόσωπον
Πανταγάθου, στέξαι τὴν νόσον οὐ δύναμαι.

341.—ΤΟΥ ΑΥΤΟΥ

Αἰνίζειν μὲν ἄριστον, ὁ δὲ ψόγος ἔχθεος ἀρχή·
ἀλλὰ κακῶς εἰπεῖν, Ἀττικόν ἐστι μέλι.

342.—ΑΔΕΣΠΟΤΟΝ

Κήλην κηλήτου μὴ φαινομένου προτέθεικας.
μή μοι τὴν κήλην· αὐτὸν ἰδεῖν δέομαι.

337.—Anonymous

You are a senator, Agathinus, but tell me how much you paid now for the Beta, for formerly it was Delta.[1]

338.—Anonymous

Homer taught you to call the voice *enope*, but who taught you to have your tongue *enope* (i.e. in a hole)?

339.—Anonymous

You wobble your head and upwaggle your backside. One's a sign of raving at the top, the other of ravishing at the bottom.

340.—PALLADAS

I swore ten thousand times to make no more epigrams, for I had brought on my head the enmity of many fools, but when I set eyes on the face of the Paphlagonian Pantagathus I can't repress the malady.

341.—By the Same

It is best to praise, and blaming is the cause of enmity, but yet to speak ill of others is Attic honey.

342.—Anonymous

You put the ruptured man's rupture in front of him, he himself not being visible. Don't present me to the rupture; I want to see the man himself.

---

[1] See note to the similar epigram, No. 260.

343.—ΑΛΛΟ

Σιλβανὸς δύο παῖδας ἔχων, Οἶνόν τε καὶ Ὕπνον,
οὐκέτι τὰς Μούσας, οὐδὲ φίλους φιλέει·
ἀλλ' ὁ μὲν ἐκ λεχέων νιν ἐύρροος ἐς φρένα θέλγει,
ἄλλος δ' ἐς θαλάμους ῥεγχόμενον κατέχει.

344.—ΑΛΛΟ

Εἰς Μητρόδοτον Βένετον ἔχοντα πρασίνην τράπεζαν

Μητρόδοτος στυγέων πρασίνων αἰώνιον ἄχθος,
μνημοσύνην μίσους τήνδε τράπεζαν ἔχει.

345.—ΑΛΛΟ

Μητρόφανες, κύκνοψι, δασύθριξ, δῖε πελαργέ,
τῇ καὶ τῇ κραδάων κεφαλὴν γεράνοισιν ὁμοίην,
μηκεδανὸν καράκαλλον ὑπὲκ δαπέδοιο κομίζεις.

346. —ΑΥΤΟΜΕΔΟΝΤΟΣ

Μέχρι τίνος, Πολύκαρπε, κενῆς παράσιτε τραπέζης,
λήσῃ κερματίοις χρώμενος ἀλλοτρίοις;
οὐ γὰρ ἔτ' εἰν ἀγορῇ σε βλέπω πολύν· ἀλλ' ὑπο-
κάμπτεις
ἤδη, καὶ ζητεῖς ποῖ σε φέρωσι πόδες.
πᾶσιν ἐπαγγέλλῃ· "Κόμισαι τὸ σὸν αὔριον· ἔρχου 5
καὶ λάβε·" κοὐδ' ὀμόσας, οὐκέτι πίστιν ἔχεις.
Κυζικόθεν σε φέρων ἄνεμος Σαμόθραξι πέλασσεν·
τοῦτό σε τοῦ λοιποῦ τέρμα μένει βιότου.

---

[1] The Veneti, or Blues, were one of the factions of the Circus, the others being the Greens and Whites.

343.—ANONYMOUS

SILVANUS has two servants, Wine and Sleep; he no longer loves either the Muses or his friends, but the one flowing copiously into his head charms him from bed, and the other keeps him in his bedroom snoring.

344.—ANONYMOUS

On Metrodotus, one of the Veneti [1] who had a Green Table

METRODOTUS, detesting the eternal burden of the Greens, has this table to keep him mindful of his hatred.

345.—ANONYMOUS

METROPHANES, swan-faced, shock-headed, lovely stork, shaking your head this way and that like a crane's, you drag your long hood over the ground.[2]

346.—AUTOMEDON

How long, Polycarpus, sitting to feast at an empty table,[3] shall you live undetected on the savings of others? I no longer see you much in the market-place, but you now turn up side streets and try to think where your feet shall carry you. You promise all, "Come, take yours to-morrow. Come and get it": but not even if you take your oath do you continue to keep faith. "The wind bearing thee from Cyzicus brought thee to Samothrace": this is the goal that awaits you for the rest of your life.

[1] There is no point appreciable by us in these derisive lines addressed to an unknown person.
[3] *i.e.* his bank. The allusion in l. 7, which is partly a parody of Homer, is quite obscure.

347.—ΦΙΛΙΠΠΟΥ

Χαίροιθ' οἱ περὶ κόσμον ἀεὶ πεπλανηκότες ὄμμα,
οἵ τ' ἀπ' Ἀριστάρχου σῆτες ἀκανθολόγοι.
ποῖ γὰρ ἐμοὶ ζητεῖν, τίνας ἔδραμεν ἥλιος οἴμους,
καὶ τίνος ἦν Πρωτεύς, καὶ τίς ὁ Πυγμαλίων;
γινώσκοιμ' ὅσα λευκὸν ἔχει στίχον· ἡ δὲ μέλαινα   5
ἱστορίη τήκοι τοὺς Περικαλλιμάχους.

348.—ΑΝΤΙΦΑΝΟΥΣ

Ὦ θηρῶν βροτὲ μᾶλλον ἀνήμερε, πάντα σε μισεῖ,
πατρολέτωρ· πάντη δ' ἐκδέχεταί σε μόρος.
ἢν ἐπὶ γῆς φεύγῃς, ἀγχοῦ λύκος· ἢν δὲ πρὸς ὕψος
δενδροβατῆς, ἀσπὶς δεῖμ' ὑπὲρ ἀκρεμόνων.
πειράζεις καὶ Νεῖλον· ὁ δ' ἐν δίναις κροκόδειλον   5
ἔτρεφεν, εἰς ἀσεβεῖς θῆρα δικαιότατον.

349.—ΠΑΛΛΑΔΑ

Εἰπὲ πόθεν σὺ μετρεῖς κόσμον καὶ πείρατα γαίης
ἐξ ὀλίγης γαίης σῶμα φέρων ὀλίγον.
σαυτὸν ἀρίθμησον πρότερον καὶ γνῶθι σεαυτόν,
καὶ τότ' ἀριθμήσεις γαῖαν ἀπειρεσίην.
εἰ δ' ὀλίγον πηλὸν τοῦ σώματος οὐ καταριθμεῖς,   5
πῶς δύνασαι γνῶναι τῶν ἀμέτρων τὰ μέτρα;

350.—ΑΓΑΘΙΟΥ ΣΧΟΛΑΣΤΙΚΟΥ

Εἰς δικολόγον ἀδικοῦντα

Νήπιε, πῶς σε λέληθε Δίκης ζυγόν, οὐ νοέεις δὲ
ἀνδράσιν οὐχ ὁσίοις ψῆφον ὀφειλομένην;

347.—PHILIPPUS

FAREWELL ye whose eyes ever range over the
universe, and ye thorn-gathering book-worms of
Aristarchus' school. What serves it me to enquire
what path the Sun has run, and whose son was
Proteus and who Pygmalion ? Let me know works
whose lines are clear,[1] but let dark lore waste away
the devotees of Supercallimachuses.

348.—ANTIPHANES

O PARRICIDE, man more savage than the beasts, all
things hate thee, everywhere thy fate awaits thee.
If thou fliest on the land, the wolf is near ; and if
thou climbest high on trees, the asp on the branches
is a terror. Thou makest trial of the Nile, too, but
he nourishes in his eddies the crocodile, a brute most
just to the impious.

349.—PALLADAS

TELL me whence comes it that thou measurest the
Universe and the limits of the Earth, thou who
bearest a little body made of a little earth ? Count[2]
thyself first and know thyself, and then shalt thou
count this infinite Earth. And if thou canst not
reckon thy body's little store of clay, how canst
thou know the measures of the immeasurable ?

350.—AGATHIAS SCHOLASTICUS

On a Lawyer guilty of Malpractice

FOOL, how hast thou failed to notice the balance
of Justice and dost not know the sentence due to

---

[1] Lit. " white." [2] We should say " measure."

ῥήτρῃ πιστεύεις πυκινόφρονι, σῇ τε μενοινῇ
ποικίλον αὐδῆσαι μῦθον ἐπισταμένῃ.
ἐλπίζειν ἔξεστι· Θέμιν δ᾽ οὐκ οἶδεν ἀμεῖψαι   5
τῆς σῆς ἠλεμάτου παίγνια φαντασίης.

351.—ΠΑΛΛΑΔΑ

Τῷ πτισάνην πωλοῦντι τὸ κελλίον ἐχθὲς ἔδωκα,
  καὶ φοβερὸν πύκτην σήμερον εὗρον ἔσω.
ὡς δ᾽ ἔλεγον, "Σὺ τίς εἶ; πόθεν ἤλυθες ἡμέτερον δῶ;"
  πυγμαχίης κατ᾽ ἐμοῦ χεῖρας ἀνέσχεν ἄνω.
ψύττα δ᾽ ἐγὼ κατέτεινα, φοβεύμενος ἄγριον ἄνδρα, 5
  τὸν πτιστὴν πύκτην ἐξαπίνης ὁρόων.
ἀλλά σε, πρὸς πύκτου Πολυδεύκεος ἠδὲ καὶ αὐτοῦ
  Κάστορος, ἱκνοῦμαι, καὶ Διὸς ἱκεσίου,
τὸν πύκτην ἀπόκρουσον, ἐμὸν χόλον· οὐ δύναμαι γὰρ
  πυκτεύειν καθάπαξ μηνὸς ἐπερχομένου.   10

352.—ΑΓΑΘΙΟΥ ΣΧΟΛΑΣΤΙΚΟΥ

Τὸν σοφὸν ἐν κιθάρῃ, τὸν μουσικὸν Ἀνδροτίωνα
  εἴρετό τις τοίην κρουματικὴν σοφίην·
"Δεξιτερὴν ὑπάτην ὁπότε πλήκτροισι δόνησας,
  ἡ λαιὴ νήτη πάλλεται αὐτομάτως
λεπτὸν ὑποτρίζουσα, καὶ ἀντίτυπον τερέτισμα   5
  πάσχει, τῆς ἰδίης πλησσομένης ὑπάτης·
ὥστε με θαυμάζειν πῶς ἄπνοα νεῦρα ταθέντα
  ἡ φύσις ἀλλήλοις θήκατο συμπαθέα."
ὃς δὲ τὸν ἐν πλήκτροισιν Ἀριστόξεινον ἀγητὸν
  ὤμοσε μὴ γνῶναι τήνδε θεημοσύνην·   10
"Ἔστι δ᾽," ἔφη, "λύσις ἥδε· τὰ νευρία πάντα τέ-
      τυκται
  ἐξ ὄϊος χολάδων ἄμμιγα τερσομένων·

impious men! Thou trustest in thy subtle rhetoric
and thy trained mind, which knows how to utter
a fallacious argument. Thou mayest hope if thou
wilt, but the play of thy vain fancy cannot change
Themis.

351.—PALLADAS

I LET the cell yesterday to a barley-water maker,
and to-day I found a formidable pugilist in it. And
when I said, "Who art thou? Whence didst thou
invade my house?" he up with his hands to box
with me. I went off at the double, afraid of the
savage man, on seeing the brewer suddenly turned
into a bruiser. But by the boxer Pollux and Castor
himself, and Zeus who hearkens to suppliants, keep
the boxer, my aversion, off me; for I can't have a
stand-up fight at the beginning of every month.[1]

352.—AGATHIAS SCHOLASTICUS

SOME one questioned the musician Androtion,
skilled in what concerns the lyre, on a curious piece
of instrumental lore. "When you set the highest
ng on the right in motion with the plectron, the
on the left quivers of its own accord with a
wang, and is made to whisper reciprocally
own highest string is struck; so that
nature made sympathetic to each other
in a state of tension." But he swore
with his admirable knowledge of
w the theoretical explanation of
he said, "is as follows. The
eep's gut dried all together.

call for the rent.
on music.

τοὔνεκεν εἰσὶν ἀδελφά, καὶ ὡς ξύμφυλα συνηχεῖ,
ξυγγενὲς ἀλλήλων φθέγμα μεριζόμενα.
γνήσια γὰρ τάδε πάντα, μιῆς ἅτε γαστρὸς ἐόντα,   15
καὶ τῶν ἀντιτύπων κληρονομεῖ πατάγων.
καὶ γὰρ δεξιὸν ὄμμα κακούμενον ὄμματι λαιῷ
πολλάκι τοὺς ἰδίους ἀντιδίδωσι πόνους."

353.—ΠΑΛΛΑΔΑ

Ἑρμολύκου θυγάτηρ μεγάλῳ παρέλεκτο πιθήκῳ·
ἡ δ' ἔτεκεν πολλοὺς Ἑρμοπιθηκιάδας.
εἰ δ' Ἑλένην ὁ Ζεὺς καὶ Κάστορα καὶ Πολυδεύκην
ἐκ Λήδης ἔτεκεν, κύκνον ἀμειψάμενος,
Ἑρμιόνη γε κόραξ παρελέξατο· ἡ δὲ τάλαινα   5
φρικτῶν δαιμονίων ἑρμαγέλην ἔτεκεν.

354.—ΑΓΑΘΙΟΤ ΣΧΟΛΑΣΤΙΚΟΤ

Ἄλλον Ἀριστοτέλην, Νικόστρατον, ἰσοπλάτωνα,
σκινδαλαμοφράστην αἰπυτάτης σοφίης,
τοῖα περὶ ψυχῆς τις ἀνείρετο· " Πῶς θέμις εἰπεῖν
τὴν ψυχήν; θνητήν, ἢ πάλιν ἀθάνατον;
σῶμα δὲ δεῖ καλέειν, ἢ ἀσώματον; ἐν δὲ νοητοῖς
τακτέον, ἢ ληπτοῖς, ἢ τὸ συναμφότερον;"
αὐτὰρ ὁ τὰς βίβλους ἀνελέξατο τῶν μετεώρων,
καὶ τὸ περὶ ψυχῆς ἔργον Ἀριστοτέλους,
καὶ παρὰ τῷ Φαίδωνι Πλατωνικὸν ὕψος ἐπιγι
πᾶσαν ἐνησκήθη πάντοθεν ἀτρεκίην.
εἶτα περιστέλλων τὸ τριβώνιον, εἶτα γενείου
ἄκρα καταψήχων, τὴν λύσιν ἐξέφερεν·

---

[1] i.e. an ape-like man.

So they are sisters and sound together as if related, sharing each other's family voice. For they are all legitimate children, being the issue of one belly, and they inherit those reciprocal noises. Just so does the right eye, when injured, often convey its own pain to the left eye."

353.—PALLADAS

Hermolycus' daughter slept with a great ape [1] and she gave birth to many little ape-Hermeses. If Zeus, transformed into a swan, got him from Leda Helen, Castor, and Pollux, with Hermione at least a crow lay, and, poor woman, she gave birth to a Hermes-crowd of horrible demons. [2]

354.—AGATHIAS SCHOLASTICUS

One enquired as follows about the soul from Nicostratus, that second Aristotle, that equal of Plato, the straw-splitter of the loftiest philosophy. "How should we describe the soul, as mortal or rather immortal? Must we call it a body or incorporeal? Is it to be classed among intelligible or apprehensible things, or is it both?" But he perused again his books of metaphysic and Aristotle's work on the Soul, and having renewed his acquaintance with Plato's sublimity in the *Phaedo*, armed himself from every source with the complete truth. Then, wrapping his cloak about him and stroking down the end of his beard, he gave utter-

[2] The epigram seems very confused. Is Hermione the same as Hermolycus' daughter, and how did she manage to have such a variety of husbands?

" Εἴπερ ὅλως ἔστι ψυχῆς φύσις (οὐδὲ γὰρ οἶδα),
   ἢ θνητὴ πάντως ἐστὶν ἢ ἀθάνατος,
στεγνοφυὴς ἢ ἄυλος· ὅταν δ᾽ Ἀχέροντα περήσῃς, 15
   κεῖθι τὸ νημερτὲς γνώσεαι ὡς ὁ Πλάτων.
εἰ δ᾽ ἐθέλεις, τὸν παῖδα Κλεόμβροτον Ἀμβρακιώτην
   μιμοῦ, καὶ τεγέων σὸν δέμας ἐκχάλασον·
καὶ κεν ἐπιγνοίης δίχα σώματος αὐτίκα σαυτόν,
   μοῦνον ὅπερ ζητεῖς τοῦθ᾽ ὑπολειπόμενος." 20

355.—ΠΑΛΛΑΔΑ

Πάντα μὲν οἶδα, λέγεις· ἀτελὴς δ᾽ ἐν πᾶσιν ὑπάρχεις,
   γευόμενος πάντων, οὐδὲν ἔχεις ἴδιον.

356.—ΑΔΕΣΠΟΤΟΝ

Εἰς σὲ καὶ ἀψευδὴς ἐψεύσατο βίβλος Ὁμήρου,
   ὁπλοτέρων ἐνέπουσα μετήορα δήνεα φωτῶν.

357.—ΠΑΛΛΑΔΑ

Υἱὸς καὶ γενετὴρ δῆριν φιλόνεικον ἔθεντο,
   τίς πλέον ἐκδαπανῶν κλῆρον ἅπαντα φάγῃ.
καὶ μετὰ τὴν βρῶσιν τὴν χρηματικὴν μάλα πᾶσαν,
   ὕστατον ἀλλήλους λοιπὸν ἔχουσι φαγεῖν.

358.—ΑΛΛΟ

Ῥουφινιανός, Ῥοῦφος ὢν δισύλλαβος,
   συνεξέτεινε τοῖς κακοῖς τὰς συλλαβάς·
οὐ λανθάνει δὲ τὴν δισύλλαβον Δίκην.
   κληθήσεται γὰρ καὶ δισύλλαβος πάλιν,
Ῥοῦφος κακοῦργος καὶ γόης, ὡς ἦν ποτε.

ance to the solution: "If the soul has in truth any nature (for even that I don't know) it is in any case either mortal or immortal, either of a solid nature or immaterial; but when you have passed over Acheron, there you shall learn the precise truth like Plato. Or, if you will, imitate the boy Cleombrotus of Ambracia,[1] and let your body drop from the roof.   Then you would at once recognise what you are, being without a body, and with nothing left you but the thing you are enquiring into."

355.—PALLADAS

You say "I know all things," but you are imperfect in all things.   Tasting of everything, you have nothing that is your own.

356.—ANONYMOUS

THE book of Homer, which never lies, lied about thee, saying the minds of young men are volatile.

357.—PALLADAS

A SON and father started a competitive contest as to which could eat up all the property by spending most, and after devouring absolutely all the money they have at last each other to eat up.

358.—ANONYMOUS

RUFINIANUS was once Rufus in two syllables, but extended his syllables simultaneously with his crimes; but he does not escape the eye of two-syllabled Justice, for he shall again be called in two syllables Rufus the scoundrel and rascal, as he was before.

[1] See Callimachus epigram, Bk. VII. 471.

359.—ΑΛΛΟ

Ὦ τῆς ἀπάσης δυνάμεως ὑπέρτατε,
σῶσόν με τὸν δύστηνον ἐκ παντὸς φθόνου.
θέλεις ἀκοῦσαι, βούλομαι κἀγὼ λέγειν·
τὸ γὰρ θέλημα τὴν χάριν τίκτει διπλῆν,
διπλοῦν τε κάλλος τῷ λόγῳ χαρίζεται   5
λέγοντι κόσμος, καὶ κλύοντι σεμνότης.
φωστὴρ γὰρ εἶ σὺ καὶ λόγων καὶ τῶν νόμων,
νόμοις δικάζων καὶ λόγοισιν ἐκπρέπων.
αἴλουρον εἶδον χρυσίου τὸν πρίγκιπα,
ἢ βδέλλαν ὠμήν, χρυσοκόλλητον χόλον.   10

360.—ΑΛΛΟ

Νῦν ὁ στρατηγὸς Ἑρμανούβης ἐγένετο
κύων, ἀδελφοὺς συλλαβὼν Ἑρμᾶς δύο
ἀσημοκλέπτας, συνδεθέντας σχοινίῳ,
ψυχροὺς ἀώρους Ταρταρίους τε δαίμονας.
οὐκ οἶδα χῶρον τοῦ τρόπου κατήγορον·   5
τρόπον δὲ χώρου τὸν κατήγορον λέγω.

361.—ΑΥΤΟΜΕΔΟΝΤΟΣ

Ἡμίονοι σύγγηροι ἐμὴν κομέουσιν ἀπήνην,
    ταῖσιν Ὁμηρείοις πάντα Λιταῖς ἴκελαι,
χωλαί τε, ῥυσαί τε, παραβλῶπές τ' ὀφθαλμώ,
    Ἡφαίστου πομπή, σκύτινα δαιμόνια,
οὔ ποτε γευσάμεναι, μὰ τὸν Ἥλιον, οὐδ' ἐν ὀνείρῳ,   5
    οὐ θέρεος κριθήν, οὐκ ἔαρος βοτάνην.
τοὔνεκ' ἐμεῦ μὲν ἔκητι βίον ζώοιτε κορώνης
    <ἢ ἐλάφου,> κενεὴν ἠέρα βοσκόμεναι.

---

[1] If the whole really forms one epigram, the first eight
lines are, of course, ironical.

359.—Anonymous

O THOU who art higher than all power, save my
wretched self from all envy. Thou wouldest hear
and I, too, would speak; for the wish gives birth to
double pleasure, while elegance on the speaker's part
and gravity on the hearer's bestow double beauty on
the speech. Thou art the luminary of speech and
of laws, judging by law and excelling in speech.

I saw in this prince a cat-like gold-grabber or a
cruel leech, a mass of bile set in gold.[1]

360.—Anonymous

Now the general has become Hermanubis the dog,
taking with him two brother Hermeses, stealers of
silver, tied together with a rope, cold, prematurely
dead demons of Tartarus.[2] I know no place that
accuses morals, but I say that morals accuse the
place.

361.—AUTOMEDON

Two mules, equally advanced in years, adorn my
carriage, in all things resembling Homer's Prayers[3]:
lame, wrinkled, with squinting eyes, the escort of
Hephaestus,[4] leathery demons who never tasted, I
swear it by the Sun, even in a dream, either barley
in summer or grass in spring. Therefore, as far as I
am concerned, may you live as long as a crow or stag,
feeding on empty air.

[1] This obscure vituperation conveys very little to us.
Were the two brothers members of the general's staff? That
they are all called Hermeses implies that they were thieves.
[3] *Il.* i. 502.   [4] Who was lame.

362.—ΚΑΛΛΙΜΑΧΟΥ

Εὐδαίμων ὅτι τἆλλα μανεὶς ὠρχαῖος Ὀρέστας,
Λεύκαρε, τὰν ἁμὰν οὐκ ἐμάνη μανίην,
οὐδ' ἔλαβ' ἐξέτασιν τῶ Φωκέος, ἅτις ἐλέγχει
τὸν φίλον, ἀλλ' †αἰχ' ἐν δρᾶμ' ἐδίδαξε μόνον.
ἦ τάχα κα τὸν ἑταῖρον ἀπώλεσε τοῦτο ποήσας·   5
κἀγὼ τοὺς πολλοὺς οὐκέτ' ἔχω Πυλάδας.

363.—ΔΙΟΣΚΟΡΙΔΟΥ

Οὐκέτ' Ἀλεξανδρεῦσι τὰ τίμια, χὠ Πτολεμαίου
Μόσχος ἐν ἠϊθέοις λαμπάδι κῦδος ἔχει·
ὁ Πτολεμαίου Μόσχος, ἰὼ πόλι· ποῦ δὲ τὰ μητρὸς
αἴσχεα, πάνδημοί τ' ἐργασίαι τέγεος;
ποῦ δὲ . . . συφόρβια; τίκτετε, πόρναι,   5
τίκτετε, τῷ Μόσχου πειθόμεναι στεφάνῳ.

364.—ΒΙΑΝΟΡΟΣ

Οὗτος ὁ μηδέν, ὁ λιτός, ὁ καὶ λάτρις, οὗτος, ὁρᾶτε,
ἐστί τινος ψυχῆς κύριος ἀλλοτρίης.

Lilla C. Perry, *From the Garden of Hellas*, p. 106.

365.—ΑΓΑΘΙΟΥ ΣΧΟΛΑΣΤΙΚΟΥ

Καλλιγένης ἀγροῖκος, ὅτε σπόρον ἔμβαλε γαίῃ,
οἶκον Ἀριστοφάνους ἦλθεν ἐς ἀστρολόγου,

---

[1] Pylades, the friend of Orestes.
[2] The point of the whole has not been explained, and it is
unfortunate that line 4 is corrupt. The "one drama" must,
I think, mean the *Choephori*. Orestes then would have
offended Pylades had he introduced him into the *Eumenides*

362.—CALLIMACHUS

ORESTES of old, Leucarus, was happy in this, that, mad in other matters, he was not mad with my madness, nor did he have to apply the test to the Phocian,[1] which is the trial of a friend, but taught him a part in one drama only.   Perchance had he done this he would have lost his companion, and, as a fact, I no longer have most of my Pyladeses.[2]

363.—DIOSCORIDES

GONE is the honour of the Alexandrians and Moschus, Ptolemaeus'[3] son, has won glory among the young men in the torch-race, Moschus, Ptolemaeus' son! Woe for my city! And where are his mother's deeds of shame and her public prostitution?[4] Where are the . . .? Where are the pigsties? Bring forth, ye whores, bring forth, persuaded by Moschus' crown.

364.—BIANOR

THIS man, a cypher, mean, yes a slave, this man look ye, is lord of some other's soul.

365.—AGATHIAS SCHOLASTICUS

CALLIGENES the husbandman, when he had cast the seed into the land, came to the house of Aristophanes

also, and Callimachus had offended his friends in some like manner.

  [3] It is scarcely probable that he means the King. The name, of course, is fairly common.

  [4] Literally, "work on the roof." The calling of a prostitute is still called "work" in Greece.

ἤτεε δ' ἐξερέειν, εἴπερ θέρος αἴσιον αὐτῷ
  ἔσται, καὶ σταχύων ἄφθονος εὐπορίη.
ὃς δὲ λαβὼν ψηφῖδας, ὑπὲρ πίνακός τε πυκάζων,   5
  δάκτυλά τε γνάμπτων, φθέγξατο Καλλιγένει·
" Εἴπερ ἐπομβρηθῇ τὸ ἀρούριον ὅσσον ἀπόχρη,
  μηδέ τιν' ὑλαίην τέξεται ἀνθοσύνην,
μηδὲ πάγος ῥήξῃ τὴν αὔλακα, μηδὲ χαλάζῃ
  ἄκρον ἀποδρυφθῇ δράγματος ὀρνυμένου,   10
μηδὲ κεμὰς κείρῃσι τὰ λήϊα, μηδέ τιν' ἄλλην
  ἠέρος ἢ γαίης ὄψεται ἀμπλακίην,
ἐσθλόν σοι τὸ θέρος μαντεύομαι, εὖ δ' ἀποκόψεις
  τοὺς στάχυας· μούνας δείδιθι τὰς ἀκρίδας."

366.—ΜΑΚΗΔΟΝΙΟΤ ΤΠΑΤΟΤ

Φειδωλός τις ἀνὴρ ἀφόων θησαυρὸν ὀνείρῳ,
  ἤθελ' ἀποθνήσκειν, πλούσιον ὕπνον ἔχων·
ὡς δ' ἴδε τὴν προτέρην, σκιόεν μετὰ κέρδος ὀνείρου,
  ἐξ ὕπνου πενίην, ἀντικάθευδε πάλιν.

367.—ΙΟΤΛΙΑΝΟΤ ΑΝΤΙΚΕΝΣΟΡΟΣ

Ὄψιν ἔχεις στρουθῷ πανομοίϊον. ἦ ῥά σε Κίρκη
  ἐς πτηνὴν μετέθηκε φύσιν, κυκεῶνα πιόντα;

368.—ΤΟΥ ΑΥΤΟΥ

Ἀμητὸς πολύς ἐστι τεὴν κατὰ δάσκιον ὄψιν·
  τῷ σε χρὴ δρεπάνοισι, καὶ οὐ ψαλίδεσσι καρῆναι.

369.—ΤΟΥ ΑΥΤΟΥ

Ἀσφαλέως οἴκησον ἐν ἄστεϊ, μή σε κολάψῃ
  αἵματι Πυγμαίων ἡδομένη γέρανος.

H. Wellesley, in *Anthologia Polyglotta*, p. 264.

the astrologer and begged him to tell him if he would have a favourable harvest and great abundance of corn. Taking his counters and spreading them on a tray, and bending his fingers, he said to Calligenes: "If your bit of land receives sufficient rain and produces no crop of wild flowers, if the frost does not break the furrows, if the hail does not nip off the tops of the sprouting ears, if no goat browses on the corn, and if it meet with no other injury by air or earth, I prophesy that your harvest will be excellent and you will cut the ears with success; only look out for the locusts."

366.—MACEDONIUS THE CONSUL

A PARSIMONIOUS man, laying hands on a treasure in a dream, wished to die enjoying a rich sleep. But when after the shadowy gain of the dream he awoke and saw his poverty as it was, he went to sleep again.

367.—JULIAN ANTECESSOR

You have a face just like an ostrich. Did Circe give you a potion to drink and change your nature into that of a bird?

368.—By THE SAME

You have such a heavy crop on your hairy face that you ought to have it cut with scythes and not with scissors.

369.—By THE SAME

To a Dwarf

LIVE in safety in the town, lest the stork who delights in the blood of Pygmies peck you.

370.—ΜΑΚΗΔΟΝΙΟΥ ΥΠΑΤΟΥ

Οὐ λαλέει τὸ κάτοπτρον· ἐγὼ δέ σε †πάλιν ἐλέγξω
  τὴν νοθοκαλλοσύνην φύκεϊ χριομένην.
τοῦτο καὶ ἡδυλύρης ποτὲ Πίνδαρος . . . ἐλέγχων,
  εἶπεν ἄριστον ὕδωρ, φύκεος ἐχθρότατον.

371.—ΠΑΛΛΑΔΑ

Μή με κάλει δίσκων ἐπιΐστορα λιμοφορήων,
  βρωτύν μοι φορέων τὴν κολοκυνθιάδα.
ἀργυρέην ὕλην οὐ τρώγομεν, ἢν παραβάλλεις,
  λιμῷ κρητίζων τοὺς μελέους πίνακας.
ζήτει νηστεύοντας ἐς ἀργυρέην¹ ἐπίδειξιν,   5
  καὶ τότε θαυμάζῃ, κοῦφον ἄσημον ἔχων.

372.—ΑΓΑΘΙΟΥ ΣΧΟΛΑΣΤΙΚΟΥ

Σῶμα φέρων σκιοειδές, ἀδερκέϊ σύμπνοον αὔρῃ,
  μή ποτε θαρσήσῃς ἄγχι τινὸς πελάσαι,
μή τις ἔσω μυκτῆρος ἀναπνείων σε κομίσσῃ
  ἄσματος ἠερίου πολλὸν ἀφαυρότερον.
οὐ σὺ μόρον τρομέεις· τότε γὰρ πάλιν οὐδὲν
    ἀμείψας   5
  ἔσσεαι ὡσαύτως φάσμα, τόπερ τελέθεις.

373.—ΠΑΛΛΑΔΑ

Εἰς ποιητὴν κυβεύοντα

Πάντων μουσοπόλων ἡ Καλλιόπη θεός ἐστιν·
  ἡ σὴ Καλλιόπη Ταβλιόπη λέγεται.

¹ So Scaliger : ἀργαλέην MS.

370.—MACEDONIUS THE CONSUL

THE mirror does not speak, but I will expose you who daub your counterfeit beauty with rouge. Sweet-lyred Pindar, too, once censuring this, said that "Water is best,"[1] water the greatest enemy of rouge.

371.—PALLADAS

Do not invite me to witness your hunger-laden dishes, bringing me pumpkin pie to feast on. We don't eat the solid silver you set before us, defrauding with famine fare the poor trenchers. Seek those who are keeping their fast for your display of silver, and then you will be admired for your lightly loaded plate.

372.—AGATHIAS SCHOLASTICUS

AS you have a body like a shadow, made of breath like the invisible wind, you should never venture to come near anyone, lest in drawing his breath he carry you into his nostrils, more feeble as you are than a breath of air. You have no fear of death, for then, without changing at all, you will again be just as you are, a ghost.

373.—PALLADAS

On a Poet playing at Dice

CALLIOPE is the goddess of all poets : your Calliope is called Tabliope.[2]

[1] *Ol.* i. 1.   [2] *Tabla* is a draught-board.

374.—ΜΑΚΗΔΟΝΙΟΥ ΥΠΑΤΟΥ

Τῷ ψιμύθῳ μὲν ἀεὶ λιποσαρκέα τεῖνε παρειήν,
   Λαοδίκη, λαοῖς ἔνδικα τινυμένη·
μή ποτε δ' εὐρύνῃς σέο χείλεα· τίς γὰρ ὀδόντων
   ὄρχατον ἐμπήξει φαρμακόεντι δόλῳ;
τὴν χάριν ἐξέρρευσας ὅσην ἔχες· οὐκ ἀπὸ πηγῆς [1] 5
   ἀγλαΐη μελέων ἕλκεται ἀενάου.
ὡς δὲ ῥόδον θαλέθεσκες ἐν εἴαρι· νῦν δ' ἐμαράνθης,
   γήραος αὐχμηρῷ καρφομένη θέρεϊ.

375.—ΤΟΥ ΑΥΤΟΥ

Ἔπταρον ἄγχι τάφοιο, καὶ ἤθελον αὐτόθ' ἀκοῦσαι
   οἷά περ ὠϊσάμην, μοῖραν ἐμῆς ἀλόχου.
ἔπταρον εἰς ἀνέμους· ἄλοχον δέ μοι οὔ τι κιχάνει
   λυγρὸν ἐν ἀνθρώποις, οὐ νόσος, οὐ θάνατος.

376.—ΑΓΑΘΙΟΥ ΣΧΟΛΑΣΤΙΚΟΥ

Ῥήτορα πρὸς Διόδωρον ἀνὴρ δείλαιος ἀπελθὼν
   εἵρετό μιν τοίης ἀμφὶ δικασπολίης·
"Ἡμετέρη θεράπαινα φύγεν ποτέ· τὴν δέ τις εὑρών,
   ἀλλοτρίην τ' εἶναι λάτριν ἐπιστάμενος,
ζεῦξεν ἑῷ θεράποντι· τέκεν δ' ὑπὸ παῖδας ἐκείνῳ· 5
   καὶ τίνι δουλεύειν εἰσὶ δικαιότεροι;"
ὃς δ' ὅτε μερμήριξε, καὶ ἔδρακε βίβλον ἑκάστην,
   εἶπεν ἐπιστρέψας γυρὸν ἐπισκύνιον·
"Ἢ σοί, ἢ τῷ ἑλόντι τεὴν θεράπαιναν ἀνάγκη
   δουλεύειν κείνους, ὧν χάριν ἐξερέεις· 10
δίζεο δ' εὐμενέοντα δικασπόλον, αἶψα δ' ἀποίσῃ
   ψῆφον ἀρειοτέρην, εἴ γε δίκαια λέγεις."

       [1] ἀπὸ γαλης MS.: corr. Scaliger.

374.—MACEDONIUS THE CONSUL

Make your fleshless cheeks always smooth with white lead, Laodice (just, indeed, is the penalty you pay the people),[1] but never open your lips wide, for who by cosmetic fraud shall fix a row of teeth there? You have shed all the beauty you had; loveliness of limb cannot be drawn from a perennial fountain. Like a rose you flourished in the spring; now you are withered, dried by the parching summer of old age.

375.—By the Same

I sneezed near a tomb and wished to hear of what I hoped, the death of my wife. I sneezed to the winds, but my wife meets with none of the misfortunes of mankind, neither illness nor death.

376.—AGATHIAS SCHOLASTICUS

An unhappy man, going to the rhetor Diodorus, consulted him about the following case. "My slave-girl ran away once and a certain man found her, and knowing her to be another man's servant married her to his own slave. She bore him children, and I wish to know whose slaves they legally are." When he had considered and looked up every book, he said, twisting his eyebrows into a semi-circle: "Those about whom you enquire must either be your slaves or those of the man who took your slave-girl. Seek a well-disposed judge and you will at once get a more favourable decision, at least if what you say is just."

[1] He puns on her name, *Laos*, people, and *dike*, justice.

377.—ΠΑΛΛΑΔΑ

Ὄρνεον ἠσθίομεν κεκλημένοι ἄθλιον ἄνδρες
ἄλλων ὀρνίθων βρώματα γινόμενοι·
καὶ τὸν μὲν Τιτυὸν κατὰ γῆς δύο γῦπες ἔδουσιν,
ἡμᾶς δὲ ζῶντας τέσσαρες αἰγυπιοί.

378.—ΤΟΥ ΑΥΤΟΥ

Οὐ δύναμαι γαμετῆς καὶ γραμματικῆς ἀνέχεσθαι,
γραμματικῆς ἀπόρου, καὶ γαμετῆς ἀδίκου.
ἀμφοτέρων τὰ πάθη θάνατος καὶ μοῖρα τέτυκται.
τὴν οὖν γραμματικὴν νῦν μόλις ἐξέφυγον·
οὐ δύναμαι δ᾽ ἀλόχου τῆς ἀνδρομάχης ἀναχωρεῖν· 5
εἴργει γὰρ χάρτης καὶ νόμος Αὐσόνιος.

379.—ΑΓΑΘΙΟΥ ΣΧΟΛΑΣΤΙΚΟΥ

Οὔ τις ἀλοιητῆρας ἰδεῖν τέτληκεν ὀδόντας
ὑμετέρους, ἵνα σοῖς ἐν μεγάροις πελάσῃ·
εἰ γὰρ ἀεὶ βούβρωστιν ἔχεις Ἐρυσίχθονος αὐτοῦ,
ναὶ τάχα δαρδάψεις καὶ φίλον ὃν καλέεις.
ἀλλ᾽ οὐ σεῖο μέλαθρά με δέξεται· οὐ γὰρ ἔγωγε 5
βήσομαι ὑμετέρῃ γαστρὶ φυλαξόμενος.
εἰ δέ ποτ᾽ ἐς τεὸν οἶκον ἐλεύσομαι, οὐ μέγ᾽ ἄνυσσεν
Λαρτιάδης Σκύλλης χάσμασιν ἀντιάσας·
ἀλλ᾽ ἔσομαι πολύτλας τις ἐγὼ πλέον, εἰ σὲ περήσω,
Κύκλωπος κρυεροῦ μηδὲν ἐλαφρότερον. 10

380.—ΜΑΚΗΔΟΝΙΟΥ ΥΠΑΤΟΥ

Παρθένος εὐπατέρεια Δίκη, πρέσβειρα πολήων,
οὐ τὸν ἐν εὐσεβίῃ χρυσὸν ἀποστρέφεται·

377.—PALLADAS

WE guests had a miserable fowl to eat and were ourselves devoured by other birds. Two vultures eat Tityus under earth and four vultures eat us alive.[1]

378.—By the Same

I CANNOT put up with a wife and with Grammar too, Grammar that is penniless and a wife who is injurious. What I suffer from both is Death and Fate. Now I have just with difficulty escaped from Grammar, but I cannot escape from this shrewish wife, for our contract and Roman law prevent it.

379.—AGATHIAS SCHOLASTICUS

No one has the courage to look on your grinders so that none approach your house, for if you always have the famine of Erysichthon [2] himself you will even perhaps devour the friend you invite. Your halls will never see me enter them, for I am not going there to be kept for your belly. But if I ever do go to your house it was no great prowess of Ulysses to face the jaws of Scylla. Rather shall I be much more "all-daring" than he, if I manage to get past you who are no less fearful than the heart-chilling Cyclops.

380.—MACEDONIUS THE CONSUL

(*A Reply to* App. Plan. *No.* 314, *which should be read first*)

THE high-born virgin Justice, patroness of cities, does not turn her face away from gold that is asso-

---

[1] It is not clear whom he means by the other birds.
[2] See Ovid, *Met.* viii. 738.

ἀλλὰ καὶ αὐτὰ τάλαντα Διὸς πάγχρυσα τελέσθη,
   οἷσι ταλαντεύει πάντα νόμον βιότου·
" καὶ τότε δὴ χρύσεια πατὴρ ἐτίταινε τάλαντα,"   5
   εἰ μὴ Ὁμηρείων ἐξελάθου χαρίτων.

381.—ΠΑΛΛΑΔΑ

Πᾶσα γυνὴ χόλος ἐστίν· ἔχει δ' ἀγαθὰς δύω ὥρας,
   τὴν μίαν ἐν θαλάμῳ, τὴν μίαν ἐν θανάτῳ.

382.—ΑΓΑΘΙΟΥ ΣΧΟΛΑΣΤΙΚΟΥ

Κεῖτο μὲν Ἀλκιμένης κεκακωμένος ἐκ πυρετοῖο,
   καὶ περὶ λαυκανίην βραγχὰ λαρυγγιόων,
νυσσόμενός τε τὸ πλευρὸν ἅτε ξιφέεσσιν ἀμυχθέν,
   καὶ θαμὰ δυσκελάδοις ἄσθμασι πνευστιόων·
ἦλθε δὲ Καλλίγνωτος ὁ Κῷος, ὁ πλατυλέσχης,   5
   τῆς παιωνιάδος πληθόμενος σοφίης,
πᾶσαν ἔχων πρόγνωσιν ἐν ἄλγεσιν, οὔ τι περιττὸν
   ἄλλο προαγγέλλων ἢ τὸ γενησόμενον.
Ἀλκιμένους δ' ἐδόκευεν ἀνάκλισιν, ἔκ τε προσώπου
   φράζετο, καὶ παλάμης ψαῦεν ἐπισταμένως,   10
καὶ τὸ περὶ κρισίμων φαέων ἐλογίζετο γράμμα,
   πάντ' ἀναπεμπάζων οὐχ ἑκὰς Ἱπποκράτους.
καὶ τότε τὴν πρόγνωσιν ἐς Ἀλκιμένην ἀνεφώνει
   σεμνοπροσωπήσας καὶ σοβαρευόμενος·
" Εἴ γε φάρυγξ βομβεῦσα, καὶ ἄγρια τύμματα
   πλευροῦ,   15
καὶ πυρετῷ λήξει πνεῦμ· δασυνόμενον,
οὐκέτι τεθνήξει πλευρίτιδι· τοῦτο γὰρ ἡμῖν
   σύμβολον ἐσσομένης ἐστὶ· ἀπημοσύνης.

ciated with piety, but the very scales of Zeus with which he weighs every law of life are of solid gold. "Then did the Father hold out the scales of gold," [1] if thou hast not forgotten the beauties of Homer.

381.—PALLADAS

EVERY woman is a source of annoyance, but she has two good seasons, the one in her bridal chamber and the other when she is dead.

382.—AGATHIAS SCHOLASTICUS

ALCIMENES lay in bed sore sick of a fever and giving vent to hoarse wheezings from his wind-pipe, his side pricking him as if he had been pierced by a sword, and his breath coming short in ill-sounding gasps. Then came Callignotus of Cos, with his never-ending jaw, full of the wisdom of the healing art, whose prognosis of pains was complete, and he never foretold anything but what came to pass. He inspected Alcimenes' position in bed and drew conclusions from his face, and felt his pulse scientifically. Then he reckoned up from the treatise on critical days, calculating everything not without his Hippocrates, and finally he gave utterance to Alcimenes of his prognosis, making his face very solemn and looking most serious : " If your throat stops roaring and the fierce attacks of pain in your side cease, and your breathing is no longer made thick by the fever, you will not die in that case of pleurisy, for this is to us a sign of coming freedom

---

[1] *Il.* ix. 69.

θάρσει· τὸν νομικὸν δὲ κάλει, καὶ χρήματα σαυτοῦ
εὖ διαθείς, βιότου λῆγε μεριμνοτόκου,   20
καί με τὸν ἰητρόν, προρρήσιις εἵνεκεν ἐσθλῆς,
ἐν τριτάτῃ μοίρῃ κάλλιπε κληρονόμον."

383.—ΠΑΛΛΑΔΑ

Ἦν ἄρα καὶ κάνθωσι Τύχη χαλεπή τε καὶ ἐσθλή,
καὶ Κρόνος ὡρονομεῖ τετραπόδων γένεσιν.
ἐξότε γὰρ καὶ τοῦτον ὄνον χαλεπὸς χρόνος ἔσχεν,
ἐξ ἀλαβαρχείης γραμματικοῦ γέγονεν.
τλῆθι φέρειν λοιπόν, κανθήλιε· γραμματικοῖς γὰρ 5
οὐδὲ τέλος κριθῇ, κρῖ δὲ μόνον λέγεται.

384.—ΤΟΥ ΑΥΤΟΥ

Εἰ μοναχοί, τί τοσοίδε; τοσοίδε δέ, πῶς πάλι μοῦνοι;
ὦ πληθὺς μοναχῶν ψευσαμένη μονάδα.

385.—ΤΟΥ ΑΥΤΟΥ

Πλαστὸν ἔχεις τὸν ἔρωτα, φόβῳ δὲ φιλεῖς καὶ ἀνάγκῃ·
τοῦ δὲ φιλεῖν οὕτως οὐδὲν ἀπιστότερον.

386.—ΤΟΥ ΑΥΤΟΥ

Στυγνὴν τὴν Νίκην τις ἰδὼν κατὰ τὴν πόλιν ἐχθὲς
εἶπε· "Θεὰ Νίκη, τίπτε πέπονθας ἄρα;"
ἡ δ' ἀποδυρομένη καὶ μεμφομένη κρίσιν, εἶπεν·
"Οὐκ ἔγνως σὺ μόνος; Πατρικίῳ δέδομαι."

---

[1] There is a play on *Cronos* (Saturn) and *Chronos* (Time).

from pain. Cheer up, and summoning your lawyer, dispose well of your property and depart from this life, the mother of care, leaving to me, your doctor, in return for my good prognostic, the third part of your inheritance."

383.—PALLADAS

So for mokes, too, there is sinister and good Fortune, and Saturn rules the nativities of beasts also; for ever since evil time[1] befel this donkey, it has become a grammarian's instead of being in the alabarch's[2] palace. But bear it patiently henceforth, donkey; for grammarians crithe (barley) has no end, but is called only cri.[3]

384.—By the Same

If solitaries (monks), why so many? And if so many, how again are they solitary? O crowd of solitaries who give the lie to solitude!

385.—By the Same

Thy love is counterfeit and thou lovest from fear and by force. But nothing is more treacherous than such love.

386.—By the Same

Yesterday a certain man seeing Victory in town sour-faced, said: "Goddess Victory, what has befallen thee, then?" But she, lamenting and finding fault with the decision, said: "Dost thou alone not know it? I have been given to Patricius." So

[2] The chief magistrate of the Alexandrian Jews.
[3] *Cri* is an epic form of *crithe*.

ἦν ἄρα καὶ Νίκη πολυώδυνος, ἦν παρὰ θεσμὸν   5
Πατρίκιος ναύτης ἥρπασεν ὡς ἄνεμον.

387.—ΤΟΥ ΑΥΤΟΥ

Πάντες ἅπαξ τρώγουσιν· ὅταν δὲ τρέφῃ Σαλαμῖνος,
οἴκαδ' ἀριστῶμεν δεύτερον ἐρχόμενοι.

388.—ΛΟΥΚΙΛΛΙΟΥ

Ἄχρις ἂν ᾖς ἄγαμος, Νουμήνιε, πάντα δοκεῖ σοι
ἐν τῷ ζῆν εἶναι τῶν ἀγαθῶν ἀγαθά·
εἶθ' ὅταν εἰσέλθῃ γαμετή, πάλιν εὐθὺ δοκεῖ σοι
ἐν τῷ ζῆν εἶναι πάντα κακῶν τὰ κακά.
ἀλλὰ χάριν τεκνίων — ἕξεις, Νουμήνιε, τέκνα,   5
χαλκὸν ἔχων· πτωχὸς δ' οὐδὲ τὰ τέκνα φιλεῖ.

389.—ΤΟΥ ΑΥΤΟΥ

Εἰ μὲν ζῆς ἐλάφου ταναὸν χρόνον, ἠὲ κορώνης,
συγγνώμη πλεῖστον πλοῦτον ἀγειρομένῳ·
εἰ δέ τις ἐσσὶ βροτῶν, οὓς αὐτίκα γῆρας ἰάπτει,
μή σέ γ' ἀπειρεσίων οἶστρος ἕλῃ κτεάνων·
μὴ σὺ μὲν ἀτλήτοισιν ἐν ἄλγεσι θυμὸν ὀλέσσῃς,   5
χρήσωνται δ' ἄλλοι σοῖς ἀγαθοῖς ἀπόνως.

390.—ΤΟΥ ΑΥΤΟΥ

Εἴ με φιλεῖς, ἔργῳ με φίλει, καὶ μή μ' ἀδικήσῃς,
ἀρχὴν τοῦ βλάπτειν τὴν φιλίαν θέμενος.

---

[1] The meaning seems to be: If rich and unmarried you

Victory, too, was in deep grief at being illegally caught by the sailor Patricius as if she were a breeze

387.—BY THE SAME

EVERYONE takes but one meal, but when Salaminus feasts us we go home and breakfast a second time.

388.—LUCILIUS

As long as you are unmarried, Numenius, everything in life seems to you the best of the best, but when a wife enters the house everything again in life seems to you at once the worst of the worst. "But I marry for the sake of having children," says he. You will have children, Numenius, if you have money, but a poor man does not even love his children.[2]

389.—BY THE SAME

IF thou livest the long years of a stag or crow thou mayest be pardoned for amassing vast wealth, but if thou art one of mortal men, whom old age right soon assails, let not the furious desire of immeasurable possessions beset thee, lest thou destroy thy soul in insufferable torture and others use thy goods without toiling for them.

390.—BY THE SAME

IF thou lovest me, love me indeed, and do me no evil, making friendship the beginning of injury. For

will have children—people running after your money and wishing you to adopt them; but if poor and married, your children will be a source of trouble.

πᾶσι γὰρ ἀνθρώποισιν ἐγὼ πολὺ κρέσσονα φημὶ
  τὴν φανερὰν ἔχθραν τῆς δολερῆς φιλίας.
φασὶ δὲ καὶ νήεσσιν ἀλιπλανέεσσι χερείους   5
  τὰς ὑφάλους πέτρας τῶν φανερῶν σπιλάδων.

391.—ΤΟΥ ΑΥΤΟΥ

Μῦν Ἀσκληπιάδης ὁ φιλάργυρος εἶδεν ἐν οἴκῳ,
  καὶ "Τί ποιεῖς, φησίν, φίλτατε μῦ, παρ᾽ ἐμοί; "
ἡδὺ δ᾽ ὁ μῦς γελάσας, "Μηδέν, φίλε, φησί, φοβηθῇς,
  οὐχὶ τροφῆς παρὰ σοὶ χρήζομεν, ἀλλὰ μονῆς."

392.—ΤΟΥ ΑΥΤΟΥ

Μύρμηκος πτερόεντος ὑπὲρ νώτοιο καθεσθεὶς
  Ἄδραστος ῥήτωρ τοῖον ἔλεξεν ἔπος·
"Ἵπτασο· τὸν σὸν ἔχεις, ὦ Πήγασε, Βελλεροφόντην,"
  φέρτατον ἡρώων, ἡμιθανῆ σκελετόν.

393.—ΤΟΥ ΑΥΤΟΥ

Οὐκ ἔστιν θυγατρὸς μεῖζον βάρος· εἰ δὲ δοκεῖ σοι,
  Εὐκτήμων, εἶναι κοῦφον, ἄκουσον ἐμοῦ.
ἔστιν σοὶ κήλη, κἀμοὶ θυγάτηρ· λάβε ταύτην,
  καὶ δός μοι κήλας ἀντὶ μιᾶς ἑκατόν.

394.—ΑΛΛΟ

Ποιητὴς πανάριστος ἀληθῶς ἐστιν ἐκεῖνος,
  ὅστις δειπνίζει τοὺς ἀκροασαμένους.
ἢν δ᾽ ἀναγινώσκῃ, καὶ νήστιας οἴκαδε πέμπῃ,
  εἰς αὐτὸν τρεπέτω τὴν ἰδίαν μανίην.

I say that for all men open enmity is much better than deceptive friendship. They say, too, that for seafaring ships sunken reefs are worse than visible rocks.

391.—By the Same

Asclepiades the miser saw a mouse in his house and said: "My dearest mouse, what business have you here with me?" And the mouse said, smiling sweetly: "Fear nothing, my friend, I do not seek board with you, but residence."

392.—By the Same

Adrastus the rhetor, seating himself on the back of a winged ant, spoke as follows: "Fly, O Pegasus, thou hast thy Bellerophon." Yes indeed the most doughty of heroes, a half-dead skeleton.[1]

393.—By the Same

There is no greater burden than a daughter, and if, Euctemon, you think it is a light one, listen to me. You have a hydrocele and I have a daughter; take her and give me a hundred hydroceles instead of one.

394.—By the Same

He is really the most excellent of poets who gives supper to those who have listened to his recitation. But if he reads to them and sends them home fasting, let him turn his own madness[2] on his own head.

[1] *cp.* No. 104.
[2] *i.e.* his passion for making and reciting verse.

395.—ΝΙΚΑΡΧΟΤ

Πορδὴ ἀποκτέννει πολλοὺς ἀδιέξοδος οὖσα·
  πορδὴ καὶ σώζει τραυλὸν ἱεῖσα μέλος.
οὐκοῦν εἰ σώζει, καὶ ἀποκτέννει πάλι πορδή,
  τοῖς βασιλεῦσιν ἴσην πορδὴ ἔχει δύναμιν.

396.—ΛΟΤΚΙΑΝΟΤ

Πολλάκις οἶνον ἔπεμψας ἐμοί, καὶ πολλάκις ἔγνως
  σοὶ χάριν, ἡδυπότῳ νέκταρι τερπόμενος.
νῦν δ' εἴπερ με φιλεῖς, μὴ πέμψῃς· οὐ δέομαι γὰρ
  οἴνου τοιούτου, μηκέτ' ἔχων θρίδακας.

397.—ΤΟΥ ΑΥΤΟΥ

Πολλὰς μυριάδας ψηφίζων Ἀρτεμίδωρος,
  καὶ μηδὲν δαπανῶν, ζῇ βίον ἡμιόνων,
πολλάκις αἱ χρυσοῦ τιμαλφέα φόρτον ἔχουσαι
  πολλὸν ὑπὲρ νώτου, χόρτον ἔδουσι μόνον.

398.—ΝΙΚΑΡΧΟΤ

Τὴν κεφαλὴν βάπτων τις ἀπώλεσε τὰς τρίχας αὐτάς,
  καὶ δασὺς ὢν λίαν, ᾠὸν ἅπας γέγονεν.
τοῦτο βαφεὺς ἐπόησε, τὸ μηκέτι κουρέα τέμνειν
  μήτε κόμην λευκὴν μήτε μελαινομένην.

399.—ΑΠΟΛΛΙΝΑΡΙΟΤ

Γραμματικός ποτ' ὄνῳ ἐποχούμενος ἐξεκυλίσθη,
  καὶ τῆς γραμματικῆς, ὡς λόγος, ἐξέπεσεν·
εἶθ' ἑξῆς ἐβίου κοινὸν βίον, ὡς ἰδιώτης,
  ὧν ἐδίδασκεν ἀεὶ μηδὲν ἐπιστάμενος.

395.—NICARCHUS

A FART which cannot find an outlet kills many a man; a fart also saves, sending forth its lisping music. Therefore if a fart saves, and on the other hand kills, a fart has the same power as kings.

396.—LUCIAN

You often sent me wine and I was often grateful to you, enjoying the draught of sweet nectar. But now if you love me, don't send any, for I don't wish for such wine, not having now any lettuces.[1]

397.—By the Same

ARTEMIDORUS, reckoning his fortune at many times ten thousand, and spending nothing, leads the life of mules, who often, carrying on their backs a heavy and precious load of gold, only eat hay.

398.—NICARCHUS

A MAN, by dyeing his head, destroyed the hair itself, and his head from being very hairy became all like an egg. The dyer attained this result, that no barber now ever cuts his hair be it white or dark.

399.—APOLLINARIUS

A GRAMMARIAN riding on a donkey fell off it, and, they say, lost his memory of grammar; then afterwards he led an ordinary life without any profession, not knowing a word of what he had always been

[1] *i.e.* to make into salad with the vinegar.

ἀλλὰ Γλύκων ἔπαθεν τοὐναντίον· ὧν γὰρ ἄπειρος   5
καὶ κοινῆς γλώττης, οὐχ ὅτι γραμματικῆς,
νῦν Λιβυκοὺς κάνθωνας ὀχούμενος, εἶτ᾽ ἀποπίπτων
πολλάκις, ἐξαίφνης γραμματικὸς γέγονεν.

400—ΛΟΥΚΙΑΝΟΥ

Ἴλαθι, Γραμματικὴ φυσίζοε, ἴλαθι λιμοῦ
φάρμακον εὑρομένη " Μῆνιν ἄειδε θεά."
νηὸν ἐχρῆν καὶ σοὶ περικαλλέα δωμήσασθαι,
καὶ βωμὸν θυέων μή ποτε δευόμενον.
καὶ γὰρ σοῦ μεσταὶ μὲν ὁδοί, μεστὴ δὲ θάλασσα   5
καὶ λιμένες, πάντων δέκτρια Γραμματική.

401.—ΤΟΥ ΑΥΤΟΥ

Ἰητήρ τις ἐμοὶ τὸν ἑὸν φίλον υἱὸν ἔπεμψεν,
ὥστε μαθεῖν παρ᾽ ἐμοὶ ταῦτα τὰ γραμματικά.
ὡς δὲ τὸ "Μῆνιν ἄειδε" καὶ "ἄλγεα μυρί᾽ ἔθηκεν"
ἔγνω, καὶ τὸ τρίτον τοῖσδ᾽ ἀκόλουθον ἔπος
"πολλὰς δ᾽ ἰφθίμους ψυχὰς Ἄϊδι προΐαψεν,"   5
οὐκέτι μιν πέμπει πρός με μαθησόμενον.
ἀλλά μ᾽ ἰδὼν ὁ πατήρ, "Σοὶ μὲν χάρις," εἶπεν,
   "ἑταῖρε·
αὐτὰρ ὁ παῖς παρ᾽ ἐμοὶ ταῦτα μαθεῖν δύναται·
καὶ γὰρ ἐγὼ πολλὰς ψυχὰς Ἄϊδι προϊάπτω,
καὶ πρὸς τοῦτ᾽ οὐδὲν γραμματικοῦ δέομαι."   10

R. Bland, in *Collections from the Greek Anthology*, 1813,
p. 447 ; *Translations, chiefly from the Greek Anthology*, p. 58.

402.—ΤΟΥ ΑΥΤΟΥ

Μηδείς μοι ταύτην, Ἐρασίστρατε, τὴν σπατάλην σου
ποιήσειε θεῶν, ἢ σὺ κατασπαταλᾷς,

teaching. But just the opposite happened to
Glycon; for, having been ignorant of the vulgar
tongue, not to speak of grammar, now, by riding on
Libyan donkeys and often falling off them, he has
suddenly become a grammarian.[1]

400.—LUCIAN

HAIL, Grammar, giver of life! Hail, thou whose
cure for famine is "Sing, O goddess, the wrath"!
Men should build a splendid temple to thee, too,
and an altar never lacking sacrifice. "For the ways
are full of thee, and the sea and its harbours are full
of thee,"[2] Grammar, the hostess of all.

401.—BY THE SAME

A PHYSICIAN sent me his dear son to be taught by
me those elementary lessons. And when he had read
"Sing the Wrath" and "imposed a thousand woes,"
and the third verse that follows these, "Many
strong souls he sped to Hades," his father no longer
sends him to learn from me, but on seeing me
said: "All thanks to you, my friend, but the boy
can learn that at home, for I speed down many souls
to Hades, and for that I have no need of a gram-
marian."

402.—BY THE SAME

MAY none of the gods, Erasistratus, create for me
that luxury in which you riot, monstrously eating

---

[1] A development of the well-known pun, ἀπ' ὄνου (ἀπὸ νοῦ)
πεσών.

[2] Parodied from the outset of Aratus' *Phaenomena*.

ἔσθων ἐκτραπέλως στομάχων κακά, χείρονα λιμοῦ,
οἷα φάγοιεν ἐμῶν ἀντιδίκων τεκνία.
πεινάσαιμι γὰρ αὖθις ἔτι πλέον, ἢ πρὶν ἐπείνων,   5
ἢ χορτασθείην τῆς παρὰ σοὶ σπατάλης.

403.—ΤΟΥ ΑΥΤΟΥ

Εἰς Ποδάγραν

Μισόπτωχε θεά, μούνη πλούτου δαμάτειρα,
ἡ τὸ καλῶς ζῆσαι πάντοτ' ἐπισταμένη,
εἰ δὲ καὶ ἀλλοτρίοις ἐπιΐζομένη ποσὶ χαίρεις,
πιλοφορεῖν [1] τ' οἶδας, καὶ μύρα σοι μέλεται,
τέρπει καὶ στέφανός σε, καὶ Αὐσονίου πόμα Βάκχου. 5
ταῦτα παρὰ πτωχοῖς γίνεται οὐδέποτε.
τοὔνεκα νῦν φεύγεις πενίης τὸν ἀχάλκεον οὐδόν,
τέρπῃ δ' αὖ πλούτου πρὸς πόδας ἐρχομένη.

404.—ΤΟΥ ΑΥΤΟΥ

Οὐδέποτ' εἰς πορθμεῖον ὁ κηλήτης Διόφαντος
ἐμβαίνει μέλλων εἰς τὸ πέραν ἀπίναι·
τῆς κήλης δ' ἐπάνωθε τὰ φορτία πάντα τεθεικὼς
καὶ τὸν ὄνον, διαπλεῖ σινδόν' ἐπαράμενος.
ὥστε μάτην Τρίτωνες ἐν ὕδασι δόξαν ἔχουσιν, 5
εἰ καὶ κηλήτης ταὐτὸ ποιεῖν δύναται.

405.—ΤΟΥ ΑΥΤΟΥ

Ὁ γρυπὸς Νίκων ὀσφραίνεται οἴνου ἄριστα,
οὐ δύναται δ' εἰπεῖν οἷος ἂν ᾖ ταχέως.

[1] So Jacobs : ὁπλοφορεῖν MS.

---

[1] i.e. felt bandages, but with an allusion to the felt cap of
office of the Roman *flamines.*
[2] The point lies in these things being remedies for the gout

plagues of the stomach worse than famine, such as I wish the children of my enemies might eat. I would starve again even more than I used to starve rather than gorge myself with the luxuries of your table.

403.—By the Same

To the Gout

GODDESS who hatest the poor, sole vanquisher of wealth, who ever knowest to live well, even though it is thy joy to sit on the feet of others, thou knowest how to wear felt,[1] and thou art fond of ointments. A garland delights thee and draughts of Italian wine.[2] These things are never found among the poor. Therefore thou fliest the brassless threshold [3] of poverty, and delightest to come to the feet [4] of wealth.

404.—By the Same

DIOPHANTES with the hydrocele, when he wants to cross to the other side, never gets into the ferry-boat, but putting all his packages and his donkey on the hydrocele, sails across hoisting a sheet. So that in vain have the Tritons glory in the waters if a man with a hydrocele can do the same.

405.—By the Same [5]

CROOK-NOSED Nicon has an admirable nose for wine, but he can't tell quickly what it is like, for scarcely

as well as luxuries, but I have no idea what is the "garland" alluded to.

[3] The threshold of the gods in Homer is brazen; brassless here of course means penniless.

[4] The phrase means also "to serve," and the point of l. 3 also seems to depend on the same double meaning.

[5] More probably by Nicarchus.

εν τρισὶν ὥραις γὰρ θεριναῖς μόλις αἰσθάνετ᾽ αὐτός,
ὡς ἂν ἔχων πηχῶν ῥῖνα διακοσίων.
ὦ μεγάλου μυκτῆρος· ὅταν ποταμὸν διαβαίνῃ, 5
θηρεύει τούτῳ πολλάκις ἰχθύδια.

406.—ΝΙΚΑΡΧΟΥ

Τοῦ γρυποῦ Νίκωνος ὁρῶ τὴν ῥῖνα, Μένιππε·
αὐτὸς δ᾽ οὐ μακρὰν φαίνεται εἶναι ἔτι.
πλὴν ἥξει, μείνωμεν ὅμως· εἰ γὰρ πολύ, πέντε
τῆς ῥινὸς σταδίους, οἴομαι, οὐκ ἀπέχει.
ἀλλ᾽ αὐτὴ μέν, ὁρᾷς, προπορεύεται· ἢν δ᾽ ἐπὶ
βουνὸν 5
ὑψηλὸν στῶμεν, καὐτὸν ἐσοψόμεθα.

407.—ΤΟΥ ΑΥΤΟΥ

Τὸν λεπτὸν θακεῦντα Μενέστρατον εἴαρος ὥρῃ
μύρμηξ ἐξελθὼν εἵλκυσεν εἰς ῥαγάδα·
μυῖα δ᾽ ἐπιπτᾶσ᾽ αὐτὸν ἀνήρπασεν, ὡς Γανυμήδη
αἰετὸς εἰς θαλάμους οὐρανίους Κρονίδεω·
πίπτεν δ᾽ ἐκ χειρῶν μυίης, κοὐδ᾽ ὡς θίγε γαίης, 5
ἐκ δ᾽ ἀράχνης ἱστοῦ τῶν βλεφάρων κρέμαται.

408.—ΛΟΥΚΙΑΝΟΥ

Τὴν κεφαλὴν βάπτεις, τὸ δὲ γῆρας οὔποτε βάψεις,
οὐδὲ παρειάων ἐκτανύσεις ῥυτίδας.
μὴ τοίνυν τὸ πρόσωπον ἅπαν ψιμύθῳ κατάπλαττε,
ὥστε προσωπεῖον, κοὐχὶ πρόσωπον ἔχειν.
οὐδὲν γὰρ πλέον ἐστί· τί μαίνεαι; οὔποτε φῦκος 5
καὶ ψίμυθος τεύξει τὴν Ἑκάβην Ἑλένην.

in three summer hours[1] does he smell it himself, since his nose is two hundred cubits long. O what a huge nose! When he crosses a river he often catches little fish with it.

406.—NICARCHUS

I SEE Nicon's hooked nose, Menippus, and it is evident that he himself is not far off. Well, he will come; let us wait all the same, for at most he is not, I suppose, more than half a mile from his nose. But it, as you see, comes on in front of him, and if we stand on a high hill we shall get a view of him too.

407.—BY THE SAME

As lean Menestratus was sitting in spring-time an ant came out and pulled him into a crevice; but a fly flew up and carried him off, just as the eagle carried Ganymede to the heavenly chamber of Zeus. He fell from the fly's hands, but not even so did he light on the earth, but is hanging by his eyelids from a spider's web.

408.—LUCIAN

You dye your hair, but you will never dye your old age, or smooth out the wrinkles of your cheeks. Then don't plaster all your face with white lead, so that you have not a face, but a mask; for it serves no purpose. Why are you out of your wits? Rouge and paste will never turn Hecuba into Helen.

---

[1] As twelve hours were counted from sunrise to sunset, summer hours were longest.

409.—ΓΑΙΤΟΥΛΙΚΟΥ

Τετράκις ἀμφορέως περὶ χείλεσι χείλεα θεῖσα
Σειληνὶς πάσας ἐξερόφησε τρύγας.
εὐχαίτα Διόνυσε, σὲ δ᾽ ὕδασιν οὐκ ἐμίηνεν·
ἀλλ᾽ οἷος πρώτης ἦλθες ἀπ᾽ οἰνοπέδης,
τοῖόν σε προὔπινεν ἀφειδέως, ἄγγος ἔχουσα   5
εἰσότε καὶ νεκύων ἦλθεν ἐπὶ ψάμαθον.

410.—ΛΟΥΚΙΑΝΟΥ

Τοῦ πωγωνοφόρου Κυνικοῦ, τοῦ βακτροπροσαίτου,
εἴδομεν ἐν δείπνῳ τὴν μεγάλην σοφίαν.
θέρμων μὲν γὰρ πρῶτον ἀπέσχετο καὶ ῥαφανίδων,
μὴ δεῖν δουλεύειν γαστρὶ λέγων ἀρετήν.
εὖτε δ᾽ ἐν ὀφθαλμοῖσιν ἴδεν χιονώδεα βόλβαν   5
στρυφνήν, ἢ πινυτὸν ἤδη ἔκλεπτε νόον,
ᾔτησεν παρὰ προσδοκίαν, καὶ ἔτρωγεν ἀληθῶς,
κοὐδὲν ἔφη βόλβαν τὴν ἀρετὴν ἀδικεῖν.

411.—ΑΔΕΣΠΟΤΟΝ

Εἰς βαλανεῖον ἐκπύρωτον

Τοῦτο πυρὰν μᾶλλον κλήζειν δεῖ, κοὐ βαλανεῖον,
ἤν ποθ᾽ ὁ Πηλείδης ἦψε Μενοιτιάδῃ,
ἢ τὸν Μηδείης στέφανον, τὸν †γείτονα Ἐρινὺς
ἐν θαλάμοις Γλαύκης εἵνεκεν Αἰσονίδου.
φεῖσαί μου, βαλανεῦ, πρὸς τοῦ Διός· εἰμὶ γὰρ ἀνὴρ   5
πάντα γράφων τὰ βροτῶν ἔργα καὶ ἀθανάτων,
εἰ δὲ πρόκειταί σοι πολλοὺς ζῶντας κατακαίειν.
ἅπτε πυρὰν ξυλίνην, δήμιε, μὴ λιθίνην.

409.—GAETULICUS

FOUR times putting her lips to the lips of the jar Silenis drank up the last dregs. Fair-haired Dionysus, she defiled thee not with water, but even as thou first didst come from the vineyard she used to quaff thee generously, holding a cup even until she went to the sands of the dead.

410.—LUCIAN

WE saw at supper the great wisdom of the Cynic, that bearded beggar with the staff. To begin with he abstained from pulse and radishes, saying that virtue should not be the belly's slave. But when he saw before his eyes a snow-white sow's womb with sharp sauce, a dish that soon stole away his prudent mind, he asked for some unexpectedly, and really started eating, saying that a sow's womb does no harm to virtue.

411.—ANONYMOUS

On an overheated Bath

YOU should call this not a bath but rather a funeral pyre such as Achilles lit for Patroclus, or Medea's crown that the Fury set afire (?) in the bridal chamber of Glauce because of Jason. Spare me, bathman, for God's sake, for I am a man who write all the deeds of men and gods. But if it is your purpose to burn numbers of us alive, light a wooden pyre, executioner, and not a stone one.

412.—ΑΝΤΙΟΧΟΥ

Ψυχὴν μὲν γράψαι χαλεπόν, μορφὴν δὲ χαράξαι
ῥάδιον· ἀλλ' ἐπὶ σοὶ τοὐμπαλιν ἀμφότερον.
τῆς μὲν γὰρ ψυχῆς τὸ διάστροφον ἔξω ἄγουσα
ἐν τοῖς φαινομένοις ἡ Φύσις εἰργάσατο·
τὸν δ' ἐπὶ τῆς μορφῆς θόρυβον καὶ σώματος ὕβριν   5
πῶς ἄν τις γράψαι, μηδ' ἐσιδεῖν ἐθέλων;

413.—ΑΜΜΙΑΝΟΥ

Ὡς κῆπον τεθυκώς, δεῖπνον παρέθηκεν Ἀπελλῆς,
οἰόμενος βόσκειν ἀντὶ φίλων πρόβατα.
ἦν ῥαφανίς, σέρις ἦν, τῆλις, θρίδακες, πράσα,
βολβοί,
ὤκιμον, ἡδύοσμον, πήγανον, ἀσπάραγος·
δείσας δ' ἐκ τούτων μὴ καὶ χόρτον παραθῇ μοι,   5
δειπνήσας θέρμους ἡμιβρεχεῖς, ἔφυγον.

414.—ΗΔΥΛΟΥ

Λυσιμελοῦς Βάκχου καὶ λυσιμελοῦς Ἀφροδίτης
γεννᾶται θυγάτηρ λυσιμελὴς ποδάγρα.

415.—ΑΝΤΙΠΑΤΡΟΥ ἢ ΝΙΚΑΡΧΟΥ

Τίς σοῦ, Μεντορίδη, προφανῶς οὕτως μετέθηκεν
τὴν πυγήν, οὗπερ τὸ στόμ' ἔκειτο πρὸ τοῦ;
βδεῖς γάρ, κοὐκ ἀναπνεῖς, φθέγγῃ δ' ἐκ τῶν καταγείων.
θαῦμά μ' ἔχει τὰ κάτω πῶς σου ἄνω γέγονεν.

416.—ΑΔΗΛΟΝ

Χρήματα καὶ πόρναις παραγίνεται· οὐκ ἀλεγίζω.
μισείτω με τάλας χρυσὸς ὁ πορνοφίλας.

412.—ANTIOCHUS

To paint the soul is difficult, to sketch the outward shape is easy, but in your case both are just the opposite. For Nature, bringing outside the perversity of your soul, has wrought so that it is a visible object; but as for the tumult of your person and the offensiveness of your body, how could one paint it when one does not even wish to look on it?

413.—AMMIANUS

Apelles gave us a supper as if he had butchered a garden, thinking he was feeding sheep and not friends. There were radishes, chicory, fenugreek, lettuces, leeks, onions, basil, mint, rue, and asparagus. I was afraid that after all these things he would serve me with hay, so when I had eaten some half-soaked lupins I went off.

414.—HEDYLUS

The daughter of limb-relaxing Bacchus and limb-relaxing Aphrodite is limb-relaxing Gout.

415.—ANTIPATER or NICARCHUS

Who, Mentorides, so obviously transferred your anus to the place where your mouth formerly was? For you break wind and do not breathe, and you speak from the lower storey. I wonder how your lower parts came to be your upper!

416.—Anonymous

Money comes into the hands of whores too. I care not. Let wretched gold that loves whores hate me.

417.—ΑΔΗΛΟΝ

Ἐπὶ γυναικὶ πρεσβυτέρᾳ νέῳ ἐνοχλησάσῃ

Ἄλλην δρῦν βαλάνιζε, Μενέσθιον· οὐ γὰρ ἔγωγε
ἔκκαιρον μήλων προσδέχομαι ῥυτίδα·
ἀλλ᾽ αἰεὶ πεπόθηκα συνακμάζουσαν ὀπώρην.
ὥστε τί πειράζεις λευκὸν ἰδεῖν κόρακα;

418.—ΤΡΑΙΑΝΟΥ ΒΑΣΙΛΕΩΣ

Ἀντίον ἠελίου στήσας ῥίνα καὶ στόμα χάσκων,
δείξεις τὰς ὥρας πᾶσι παρερχομένοις.

419.—ΦΙΛΩΝΟΣ

Αἱ πολιαὶ σὺν νῷ γεραρώτεραι· αἱ γὰρ ἄτερ νοῦ
μᾶλλον τῶν πολλῶν εἰσὶν ὄνειδος ἐτῶν.

420.—ΑΛΛΟ

Αἱ τρίχες, ἢν σιγᾷς, εἰσὶ φρένες· ἢν δὲ λαλήσῃς,
ὡς αἱ τῆς ἥβης, οὐ φρένες, ἀλλὰ τρίχες.

421.—ΑΠΟΛΛΙΝΑΡΙΟΥ

Ἂν μὲν ἀπόντα λέγῃς με κακῶς, οὐδὲν ἀδικεῖς με,
ἂν δὲ παρόντα καλῶς, ἴσθι κακῶς με λέγων.

422.—ΑΝΤΙΟΧΟΥ

Εἰς ἀπαίδευτον ἐπιδειξάμενον

Βήσας, εἰ φρένας εἶχεν, ἀπήγχετο· νῦν δ᾽ ὑπ᾽ ἀνοίας
καὶ ζῇ καὶ πλουτεῖ, καὶ μετὰ τὴν πάροδον.

---

[1] i.e. it is as difficult to get hold of me as to meet with a white crow.

417.—ANONYMOUS

On an Elderly Woman annoying a Young Man

SHAKE the acorns off another oak, Menesthion; for I do not accept wrinkled apples past their season, but have ever desired fruit in its prime like myself; so why try to see a white crow?[1]

418.—THE EMPEROR TRAJAN

IF you put your nose pointing to the sun and open your mouth wide, you will show all passers-by the time of day.[2]

419.—PHILO

GREY hairs are more venerable together with good sense, for when they are not accompanied by sense they are rather a reproach to advanced age.

420.—ANONYMOUS

YOUR grey hairs, if you keep silent, are wisdom, but if you speak they are not wisdom but hairs, like those of youth.

421.—APOLLINARIUS

IF you speak ill of me in my absence you do me no injury; but if you speak well of me in my presence, know that you are speaking ill of me.

422.—ANTIOCHUS

On an Illiterate Man speaking in Public

BESAS, if he had any sense, would have hanged himself, but now, being such a fool, he both lives and grows rich even after his appearance in public.

[2] Your nose would act as the index of a sun-dial. In ῥίνα the emperor has been guilty of a false quantity.

423.—ΕΛΛΑΔΙΟΥ

Βάπτων πάντα, βαφεῦ, καὶ χρωματίοις μεταβάλλων,
καὶ πενίην βάψας, πλούσιος ἐξεφάνης.

424.—ΠΙΣΩΝΟΣ

Γαίης ἐκ Γαλατῶν μηδ᾽ ἄνθεα, ἧς ἀπὸ κόλπων
ἀνθρώποις ὀλέτειραι Ἐρινύες ἐβλάστησαν.

425.—ΑΔΗΛΟΝ

Γινώσκειν σε θέλω, Πλακιανέ, σαφῶς, ὅτι πᾶσα
ἔγχαλκος γραῖα πλουσία ἐστὶ σορός.

426.—ΑΛΛΟ

Εἰς Ὀπιανὸν ἡγεμόνα πότην

Γράμμα περισσὸν ἔχεις τὸ προκείμενον· ἢν ἀφέλῃ τις
τοῦτό σοι, οἰκεῖον κτήσῃ ἁπλῶς ὄνομα.

427.—ΛΟΥΚΙΑΝΟΥ

Δαίμονα πολλὰ λαλῶν ὀζόστομος ἐξορκιστὴς
ἐξέβαλ᾽, οὐχ ὅρκων, ἀλλὰ κόπρων δυνάμει.

428.—ΤΟΥ ΑΥΤΟΥ

Εἰς τί μάτην νίπτεις δέμας Ἰνδικόν; ἴσχεο τέχνης·
οὐ δύνασαι δνοφερὴν νύκτα καθηλιάσαι.

423.—HELLADIUS

DYER who dyest all things and changest them with thy colours, thou hast dyed thy poverty too, and turned out a rich man.

424.—PISO

DON'T expect flowers from the land of Galatia, from whose bosom sprang the Furies, destroyers of men.[1]

425.—ANONYMOUS

I WOULD have you know, Placianus, that every old woman with money is a rich coffin.

426.—ANONYMOUS

On Opianus, a hard-drinking Governor

THE first letter of your name is superfluous; if one takes it away you will acquire by simple means a name that suits you.[2]

427.—LUCIAN

THE exorcist with the stinking mouth cast out many devils by speaking, not by the virtue of his exorcisms, but by that of dung.

428.—BY THE SAME

WHY do you wash in vain your Indian body? Give up that device. You cannot shed the sunlight on dark night.

---

[1] There was no legend of the Galatian origin of the Furies; he must mean the natives.   [2] *i.e.* Pianus (*pino*, I drink).

429.—ΤΟΥ ΑΥΤΟΥ

Ἐν πᾶσιν μεθύουσιν Ἀκίνδυνος ἤθελε νήφειν,
τοὔνεκα καὶ μεθύειν αὐτὸς ἔδοξε μόνος.

430.—ΤΟΥ ΑΥΤΟΥ

Εἰ τὸ τρέφειν πώγωνα δοκεῖς σοφίαν περιποιεῖν,
καὶ τράγος εὐπώγων αἶψ' ὅλος[1] ἐστὶ Πλάτων.

431.—ΤΟΥ ΑΥΤΟΥ

Εἰ ταχὺς εἰς τὸ φαγεῖν καὶ πρὸς δρόμον ἀμβλὺς ὑπάρχεις
τοῖς ποσί σου τρῶγε, καὶ τρέχε τῷ στόματι.

432.—ΤΟΥ ΑΥΤΟΥ

Ἔσβεσε τὸν λύχνον μῶρος, ψυλλῶν ὑπὸ πολλῶν
δακνόμενος, λέξας· "Οὐκέτι με βλέπετε."

433.—ΤΟΥ ΑΥΤΟΥ

Ζωγράφε, τὰς μορφὰς κλέπτεις μόνον· οὐ δύνασαι δὲ
φωνὴν συλῆσαι χρώματι πειθόμενος.

434.—ΤΟΥ ΑΥΤΟΥ

Ἢν ἐσίδῃς κεφαλὴν μαδαράν, καὶ στέρνα, καὶ ὤμους,
μηδὲν ἐρωτήσῃς· μῶρον ὁρᾷς φαλακρόν.

435.—ΤΟΥ ΑΥΤΟΥ

Θαυμάζειν μοι ἔπεισιν, ὅπως Βύτος ἐστὶ σοφιστής,
οὔτε λόγον κοινόν, οὔτε λογισμὸν ἔχων.

[1] αἴπολος MS.: corr. Unger.

429.—By the Same

ACINDYNUS wished to keep sober when all the others were drunk; therefore he was the only man who was thought to be drunk.

430.—By the Same

IF you think that to grow a beard is to acquire wisdom, a goat with a fine beard is at once a complete Plato.

431.—By the Same

IF you are quick at eating and tardy in running, eat with your feet and run with your mouth.

432.—By the Same

A FOOL put out the lamp when he was bitten by many fleas, saying: "You can't see me any longer."

433.—By the Same

PAINTER, thou stealest the form only, and canst not, trusting in thy colours, capture the voice.

434.—By the Same

IF you see a hairless head, breast, and shoulders, make no enquiries; it is a bald fool that you see.[1]

435.—By the Same

IT strikes me as wonderful how Bytus is a sophist, since he has neither common speech nor reason.

[1] This possibly refers to a Cynic, as they used to go about with bare breasts and shoulders.

436.—ΤΟΥ ΑΥΤΟΥ

Θᾶττον ἔην λευκοὺς κόρακας πτηνάς τε χελώνας
εὑρεῖν, ἢ δόκιμον ῥήτορα Καππαδόκην.

437.—ΑΡΑΤΟΥ

Αἰάζω Διότιμον, ὃς ἐν πέτραισι κάθηται,
Γαργαρέων παισὶν βῆτα καὶ ἄλφα λέγων.

438.—ΜΕΝΑΝΔΡΟΥ

Κορινθίῳ πίστευε, καὶ μὴ χρῶ φίλῳ.

439.—ΔΙΦΙΛΟΥ

Τὸ μὲν Ἄργος ἵππιον, οἱ δ᾽ ἐνοικοῦντες λύκοι.

440.—ΠΙΤΤΑΚΟΥ

Μεγαρεῖς δὲ φεῦγε πάντας· εἰσὶ γὰρ πικροί.

441.—ΦΙΛΙΣΚΟΥ

Ὁ Πειραιεὺς κάρυον μέγ᾽ ἐστὶ καὶ κενόν.

442.—ΑΔΕΣΠΟΤΟΝ

Τρίς με τυραννήσαντα τοσαυτάκις ἐξεδίωξεν
δῆμος Ἐρεχθῆος, καὶ τρὶς ἐπηγάγετο,
τὸν μέγαν ἐν βουλῇ Πεισίστρατον, ὃς τὸν Ὅμηρον
ἤθροισα, σποράδην τὸ πρὶν ἀειδόμενον·
ἡμέτερος γὰρ κεῖνος ὁ χρύσεος ἦν πολιήτης,   5
εἴπερ Ἀθηναῖοι Σμύρναν ἀπῳκίσαμεν.

436.—By the Same

You will sooner find white crows and winged tortoises than a Cappadocian who is an accomplished orator.

437.—ARATUS

I lament for Diotimus,[1] who sits on stones repeating Alpha and Beta to the children of Gargarus.

438.—MENANDER

Trust in (?) a Corinthian and don't make him a friend.

439.—DIPHILUS

Argos is the land of horses, but the inhabitants are wolves.

440.—PITTACUS (?)[2]

Avoid all Megarians, for they are bitter.

441.—PHILISCUS

The Piraeus is a big nut and empty.

442.—Anonymous

Thrice I reigned as tyrant, and as many times did the people of Erechtheus expel me and thrice recall me, Pisistratus, great in council, who collected the works of Homer formerly sung in fragments.   For that man of gold was our fellow-citizen, if we Athenians colonized Smyrna.

---

[1] The epigram is not meant to be satirical.   Diotimus was a poet obliged to gain his living by teaching in an obscure town.   [2] We expect the name of a comic poet.

BOOK XII

STRATO'S *MUSA PUERILIS*

STRATO, whose name this book bears, lived probably in the reign of Hadrian. It has generally been supposed that the whole book is an anthology of poems on this peculiar subject made by him, but it seems more probable to me that Strato published merely a collection of his own poems, and that it was Cephalas or some other Byzantine who inserted into it all the poems of this nature he found in the older Anthologies. The final epigram (No. 258), which was obviously placed by Strato at the end of his collection, certainly refers only to poems by Strato himself, and the same is true of the words prefixed to the book by Cephalas. He must have derived the statement, unless it is a mere excuse for the immorality of the poems, from some one who had personal knowledge of Strato. Again, among the poems by Meleager included are eight relating to women, six of them being on women whose names end in the diminutive form (Phanion, Callistion, Thermion, Timarion, Dorcion), which has evidently been mistaken for a masculine name. A more ludicrous blunder is the inclusion here of the pretty verses of Asclepiades (No. 50) *addressed to himself.* Strato himself could never have made such blunders, and they can only be attributed to a Byzantine. Of the poems thus inserted only a very few (12, 18, 24–28, 34, 35, 173) are from the *Stephanus* of Philippus, the remainder consisting of a large block of poems from Meleager's *Stephanus* and a few isolated ones from the same source (14, 22, 23, 29–33, 36–172, 230, 256–7). The arrangement under motives is very marked in these. We cannot suppose that Meleager separated the love-poems relating to boys in his *Stephanus* from those relating to women, as the *Stephanus* was not arranged under subjects at all, and we must attribute both the selection and the arrangement under motives to the Byzantines.

These homosexual attachments were a notable feature of Greek and Roman life and were spoken of frankly, since they were not then regarded as disgraceful, being indeed rather fashionable. Readers must take this into consideration, and especially in estimating Meleager, so much of whose personal work is comprised in this book. It is noteworthy that among the most beautiful of his poems are just some of those I have mentioned addressed to girls and included by mistake here. In the rest, if I err not, we miss the distinguishing note of passion, which his other love-poems so often have. The elements of his imagery of love are all here—Love and His mother, burning arrows and stormy seas—but somewhat devoid of soul and at times disfigured by a coarseness foreign to his gentle spirit. These attachments were in his case rather a matter of fashion than of passion.[1]

Strato himself is frankly homosexual. He writes good and at times pretty verse, but he is, as a rule, quite *terre à terre* and sometimes very gross.

---

[1] There was no reason for putting No. 132 (perhaps the most exquisite of all his poems) and No. 133 in this Book.

IB

ΣΤΡΑΤΩΝΟΣ ΜΟΥΣΑ ΠΑΙΔΙΚΗ

Καὶ τίς ἂν εἴην εἰ πάντων σοι τῶν εἰρημένων τὴν γνῶσιν ἐκθέμενος τὴν Στράτωνος τοῦ Σαρδιανοῦ Παιδικὴν Μοῖσαν ἀπεκρυψάμην, ἣν αὐτὸς παίζων πρὸς τοὺς πλησίον ἀπεδείκνυτο, τέρψιν οἰκείαν τὴν ἀπαγγελίαν τῶν ἐπιγραμμάτων, οὐ τὸν νοῦν, ποιούμενος. ἔχου τοίνυν τῶν ἑξῆς· ἐν χορείαις γὰρ ἥ γε σώφρων, κατὰ τὸν τραγικόν, οὐ διαφθαρήσεται.

1.—ΣΤΡΑΤΩΝΟΣ

Ἐκ Διὸς ἀρχώμεσθα, καθὼς εἴρηκεν Ἄρατος·
  ὑμῖν δ', ὦ Μοῦσαι, σήμερον οὐκ ἐνοχλῶ.
εἰ γὰρ ἐγὼ παῖδάς τε φιλῶ καὶ παισὶν ὁμιλῶ,
  τοῦτο τι πρὸς Μούσας τὰς Ἑλικωνιάδας;

2.—ΤΟΥ ΑΥΤΟΥ

Μὴ ζήτει δέλτοισιν ἐμαῖς Πρίαμον παρὰ βωμοῖς,
  μηδὲ τὰ Μηδείης πένθεα καὶ Νιόβης,
μηδ' Ἴτυν ἐν θαλάμοις, καὶ ἀηδόνας ἐν πετάλοισιν·
  ταῦτα γὰρ οἱ πρότεροι πάντα χύδην ἔγραφον·
ἀλλ' ἱλαραῖς Χαρίτεσσι μεμιγμένον ἡδὺν Ἔρωτα,   5
  καὶ Βρόμιον· τούτοις δ' ὀφρύες οὐκ ἔπρεπον.

3.—ΤΟΥ ΑΥΤΟΥ

Τῶν παίδων, Διόδωρε, τὰ προσθέματ' εἰς τρία πίπτει
  σχήματα, καὶ τούτων μάνθαν' ἐπωνυμίας.

BOOK XII

STRATO'S *MUSA PUERILIS*

And what kind of man should I be, reader, if after setting
forth all that precedes for thee to study, I were to
conceal the Puerile Muse of Strato of Sardis, which he
used to recite to those about him in sport, taking
personal delight in the diction of the epigrams, not in
their meaning. Apply thyself then to what follows,
for "in dances," as the tragic poet says, "a chaste
woman will not be corrupted."

1.—STRATO

"Let us begin from Zeus," as Aratus said, and
you, O Muses, I trouble not to-day. For if I love
boys and associate with boys, what is that to the
Muses of Helicon?

2.—By the Same

Look not in my pages for Priam by the altar, nor
for the woes of Medea and Niobe, nor for Itys in his
chamber and the nightingales amid the leaves; for
earlier poets wrote of all these things in profusion.
But look for sweet Love mingled with the jolly
Graces, and for Bacchus. No grave face suits them.

3.—By the Same

My dear Diodorus, the forepokers of boys fall into
three shapes; learn their names. Well, name the

283

τὴν ἔτι μὲν γὰρ ἄθικτον ἀκμὴν λάλου ὀνόμαζε,
κωκὼ τὴν φυσᾶν ἄρτι καταρχομένην·
τὴν δ' ἤδη πρὸς χεῖρα σαλευομένην, λέγε σαύραν·   5
τὴν δὲ τελειοτέρην, οἶδας ἃ χρή σε καλεῖν.

4.—ΤΟΥ ΑΥΤΟΥ

Ἀκμῇ δωδεκέτους ἐπιτέρπομαι· ἔστι δὲ τούτου
χὠ τρισκαιδεκέτης πουλὺ ποθεινότερος·
χὠ τὰ δὶς ἑπτὰ νέμων, γλυκερώτερον ἄνθος Ἐρώτων·
τερπνότερος δ' ὁ τρίτης πεντάδος ἀρχόμενος·
ἐξεπικαιδέκατον δὲ θεῶν ἔτος· ἑβδόματον δὲ   5
καὶ δέκατον ζητεῖν οὐκ ἐμόν, ἀλλὰ Διός.
εἰ δ' ἐπὶ πρεσβυτέρους τις ἔχει πόθον, οὐκέτι παίζει,
ἀλλ' ἤδη ζητεῖ "τὸν δ' ἀπαμειβόμενος."

5.—ΤΟΥ ΑΥΤΟΥ

Τοὺς λευκοὺς ἀγαπῶ, φιλέω δ' ἅμα τοὺς μελιχρώδεις
καὶ ξανθούς, στέργω δ' ἔμπαλι τοὺς μέλανας.
οὐδὲ κόρας ξανθὰς παραπέμπομαι· ἀλλὰ περισσῶς
τοὺς μελανοφθάλμους αἰγλοφανεῖς τε φιλῶ.

6.—ΤΟΥ ΑΥΤΟΥ

Πρωκτὸς καὶ χρυσὸς τὴν αὐτὴν ψῆφον ἔχουσιν·
ψηφίζων δ' ἀφελῶς τοῦτό ποθ' εὗρον ἐγώ.

7.—ΤΟΥ ΑΥΤΟΥ

Σφιγκτὴρ οὐκ ἔστιν παρὰ παρθένῳ, οὐδὲ φίλημα
ἁπλοῦν, οὐ φυσικὴ χρωτὸς ἐϋπνοΐη,

one of still untouched maturity " lalu "; " coco "
the one just beginning to swell out; but the one
already heaving to your hand—speak of it as
" lizard ". As for the more perfect specimen, you
know what you ought to call it.

4.—By the Same

I DELIGHT in the prime of a boy of twelve, but one
of thirteen is much more desirable. He who is four-
teen is a still sweeter flower of the Loves, and one
who is just beginning his fifteenth year is yet more
delightful. The sixteenth year is that of the gods,
and as for the seventeenth it is not for me, but for
Zeus, to seek it. But if one has a desire for those
still older, he no longer plays, but now seeks " And
answering him back." [1]

5.—By the Same

I LIKE them pale, and I also love those with a skin
the colour of honey, and the fair too; and on the
other hand I am taken by the black-haired. Nor do
I dismiss brown eyes; but above all I love sparkling
black eyes.

6.—By the Same

THE numerical value of the letters in πρωκτὸς
(anus) and χρυσὸς (gold) is the same.[2] I once
found this out reckoning up casually.

7.—By the Same

IN a maid there is no question of a real sphincter
nor a simple kiss, no natural nice smell of the skin,
nor of that sweet sexy talk or limpid look. Besides,

---

[1] Common in Homer.   [2] Making in Greek 1570.

οὐ λόγος ἡδὺς ἐκεῖνος ὁ πορνικός, οὐδ᾿ ἀκέραιον
βλέμμα, διδασκομένη δ᾿ ἐστὶ κακιοτέρα.
ψυχροῦνται δ᾿ ὄπιθεν πᾶσαι· τὸ δὲ μεῖζον ἐκεῖνο,   5
οὐκ ἔστιν ποῦ θῇς τὴν χέρα πλαζομένην.

8.—ΤΟΥ ΑΥΤΟΥ

Εἶδον ἐγώ τινα παῖδα †ἐπανθοπλοκοῦντα κόρυμβον,
ἄρτι παρερχόμενος τὰ στεφανηπλόκια·
οὐδ᾿ ἄτρωτα παρῆλθον· ἐπιστὰς δ᾿ ἥσυχος αὐτῷ
φημὶ "Πόσου πωλεῖς τὸν σὸν ἐμοὶ στέφανον;"
μᾶλλον τῶν καλύκων δ᾿ ἐρυθαίνετο, καὶ κατακύψας   5
φησὶ "Μακρὰν χώρει, μή σε πατὴρ ἐσίδῃ."
ὠνοῦμαι προφάσει στεφάνους, καὶ οἴκαδ᾿ ἀπελθὼν
ἐστεφάνωσα θεούς, κεῖνον ἐπευξάμενος.

9.—ΤΟΥ ΑΥΤΟΥ

Ἄρτι καλός, Διόδωρε, σύ, καὶ φιλέουσι πέπειρος·
ἀλλὰ καὶ ἢν γήμῃς, οὐκ ἀπολειψόμεθα.

10.—ΤΟΥ ΑΥΤΟΥ

Εἰ καί σοι τριχόφοιτος ἐπεσκίρτησεν ἴουλος,
καὶ τρυφεραὶ κροτάφων ξανθοφυεῖς ἕλικες,
οὐδ᾿ οὕτω φεύγω τὸν ἐρώμενον· ἀλλὰ τὸ κάλλος
τούτου, κἂν πώγων, κἂν τρίχες, ἡμέτερον.

11.—ΤΟΥ ΑΥΤΟΥ

Ἐχθὲς ἔχων ἀνὰ νύκτα Φιλόστρατον, οὐκ ἐδυνήθην,
κείνου, πῶς εἴπω; πάντα παρασχομένου.
ἀλλ᾿ ἐμὲ μηκέτ᾿ ἔχοιτε φίλοι φίλον, ἀλλ᾿ ἀπὸ
    πύργου
ῥίψατ᾿, ἐπεὶ λίην Ἀστυάναξ γέγονα.

when she's being taught she's worse. And they're all cold behind; but a greater nuisance is this—there's no place where you can put your wandering hand.

8.—By the Same

Just now, as I was passing the place where they make garlands, I saw a boy interweaving flowers with a bunch of berries. Nor did I pass by unwounded, but standing by him I said quietly, "For how much will you sell me your garland?" He grew redder than his roses, and turning down his head said, "Go right away in case my father sees you." I bought some wreaths as a pretence, and when I reached home crowned the gods, beseeching them to grant me him.

9.—By the Same

Now thou art fair, Diodorus, and ripe for lovers, but even if thou dost marry, we shall not abandon thee.

10.—By the Same

Even though the invading down and the delicate auburn curls of thy temples have leapt upon thee, that does not make me shun my beloved, but his beauty is mine, even if there be a beard and hairs.

11.—By the Same

Yesterday I had Philostratus for the night, but was incapable, though he (how shall I say it?) made every possible offer. No longer, my friends, count me your friend, but throw me off a tower as I have become too much of an Astyanax.[1]

---

[1] The son of Hector, thrown from a tower by the Greeks. The pun is on Asty, a privative and στύειν (make erect).

12.—ΦΛΑΚΚΟΥ

Ἄρτι γενειάζων ὁ καλὸς καὶ στερρὸς ἐρασταῖς
παιδὸς ἐρᾷ Λάδων. σύντομος ἡ Νέμεσις.

13.—ΣΤΡΑΤΩΝΟΣ

Ἰητροὺς εὑρόν ποτ' ἐγὼ λείους δυσέρωτας,
τρίβοντας φυσικῆς φάρμακον ἀντιδότου.
οἱ δέ γε φωραθέντες, "Ἔχ' ἡσυχίην" ἐδέοντο·
κἀγὼ ἔφην "Σιγῶ, καὶ θεραπεύσετέ με."

14.—ΔΙΟΣΚΟΡΙΔΟΥ

Δημόφιλος τοιοῖσδε φιλήμασιν εἰ πρὸς ἐραστὰς
χρήσεται ἀκμαίην, Κύπρι, καθ' ἡλικίην,
ὡς ἐμὲ νῦν ἐφίλησεν ὁ νήπιος, οὐκέτι νύκτωρ
ἥσυχα τῇ κείνου μητρὶ μενεῖ πρόθυρα.

15.—ΣΤΡΑΤΩΝΟΣ

Εἰ Γραφικοῦ πυγαῖα σανὶς δέδαχ' ἐν βαλανείῳ,
ἄνθρωπος τί πάθω; καὶ ξύλον αἰσθάνεται.

16.—ΤΟΥ ΑΥΤΟΥ

Μὴ κρύπτῃς τὸν ἔρωτα, Φιλόκρατες· αὐτὸς ὁ δαίμων
λακτίζειν κραδίην ἡμετέρην ἱκανός·
ἀλλ' ἱλαροῦ μετάδος τι φιλήματος. ἔσθ' ὅτε καὶ σὺ
αἰτήσεις τοιάνδ' ἐξ ἑτέρων χάριτα.

17.—ΑΔΗΛΟΝ

Οὔ μοι θῆλυς ἔρως ἐγκάρδιος, ἀλλά με πυρσοὶ
ἄρσενες ἀσβέστῳ θῆκαν ὑπ' ἀνθρακιῇ.
πλειότερον τόδε θάλπος· ὅσον δυνατώτερος ἄρσην
θηλυτέρης, τόσσον χὠ πόθος ὀξύτερος.

12.—FLACCUS

JUST as he is getting his beard, Lado, the fair youth, cruel to lovers, is in love with a boy. Nemesis is swift.

13.—STRATO

I ONCE found some beardless doctors, not prone to love, grinding a natural antidote for it. They, being lovesick, besought me to keep it quiet, and I said, "I am mum, but you must cure me."

14.—DIOSCORIDES

IF Demophilus, when he reaches his prime, gives such kisses to his lovers as he gives me now he is a child, no longer shall his mother's door remain quiet at night.

15.—STRATO

IF a plank pinched Graphicus' behind in the bath, what will become of me, a man? Even wood feels.

16.—BY THE SAME

SEEK not to hide our love, Philocrates; the god himself without that hath sufficient power to trample on my heart. But give me a taste of a blithe kiss. The time shall come when thou shalt beg such favour from others.

17.—ANONYMOUS

THE love of women touches not my heart, but male brands have heaped unquenchable coals of fire on me. Greater is this heat; by as much as a man is stronger than a woman, by so much is this desire sharper.

18.—ΑΛΦΕΙΟΤ ΜΙΤΤΛΗΝΑΙΟΤ

Τλήμονες, οἷς ἀνέραστος ἔφυ βίος· οὔτε γὰρ ἔρξαι
  εὐμαρές, οὔτ᾽ εἰπεῖν ἐστί τι νόσφι πόθων.
καὶ γὰρ ἐγὼ νῦν εἰμὶ λίην βραδύς· εἰ δ᾽ ἐπίδοιμι
  Ξεινόφιλον, στεροπῆς πτήσομαι ὀξύτερος.
τοὔνεκεν οὐ φεύγειν γλυκὺν ἵμερον, ἀλλὰ διώκειν,   5
  πᾶσι λέγω. ψυχῆς ἐστὶν Ἔρως ἀκόνη.

19.—ΑΔΗΛΟΝ

Οὐ δύναμαί σε θέλων θέσθαι φίλον· οὔτε γὰρ αἰτεῖς,
  οὔτ᾽ αἰτοῦντι δίδως, οὔθ᾽ ἃ δίδωμι δέχῃ.

20.—ΙΟΤΛΙΟΤ ΛΕΩΝΙΔΑ

Ὁ Ζεὺς Αἰθιόπων πάλι τέρπεται εἰλαπίναισιν,
  ἢ χρυσὸς Δανάης εἴρπυσεν εἰς θαλάμους·
θαῦμα γὰρ εἰ Περίανδρον ἰδὼν οὐχ ἥρπασε γαίης
  τὸν καλόν· ἢ φιλόπαις οὐκέτι νῦν ὁ θεός.

21.—ΣΤΡΑΤΩΝΟΣ

Κλέψομεν ἄχρι τίνος τὰ φιλήματα, καὶ τὰ λαθραῖα
  νεύσομεν ἀλλήλοις ὄμμασι φειδομένοις;
μέχρι τίνος δ᾽ ἀτέλεστα λαλήσομεν, ἀμβολίαισι
  ζευγνύντες κενεὰς ἔμπαλιν ἀμβολίας;
μέλλοντες τὸ καλὸν δαπανήσομεν· ἀλλὰ πρὶν ἐλθεῖν   5
  τὰς φθονεράς, Φείδων, θῶμεν ἐπ᾽ ἔργα λόγοις.

22.—ΣΚΥΘΙ<Ν>ΟΤ

Ἦλθέν μοι μέγα πῆμα, μέγας πόλεμος, μέγα μοι
  πῦρ,
  Ἥλισσος πλήρης τῶν ἐς ἔρωτ᾽ ἐτέων,

18.—ALPHEIUS OF MYTILENE

UNHAPPY they whose life is loveless; for without love it is not easy to do aught or to say aught. I, for example, am now all too slow, but were I to catch sight of Xenophilus I would fly swifter than lightning. Therefore I bid all men not to shun but to pursue sweet desire; Love is the whetstone of the soul.

19.—ANONYMOUS

THOUGH I would, I cannot make thee my friend · for neither dost thou ask, nor give to me when I ask, nor accept what I give.

20.—JULIUS LEONIDAS

ZEUS is again rejoicing in the banquets of the Ethiopians,[1] or, turned to gold, hath stolen to Danae's chamber; for it is a marvel that, seeing Periander, he did not carry off from Earth the lovely youth or is the god no longer a lover of boys?

21.—STRATO

How long shall we steal kisses and covertly signal to each other with chary eyes? How long shall we talk without coming to a conclusion, linking again and again idle deferment to deferment? If we tarry we shall waste the good; but before the envious ones[2] come, Phidon, let us add deeds to words.

22.—SCYTHINUS

THERE has come to me a great woe, a great war, a great fire. Elissus, full of the years ripe for love,

---

[1] Homer, *Il.* i. 423.   [2] Hairs.

αὐτὰ τὰ καίρι' ἔχων ἑκκαίδεκα, καὶ μετὰ τούτων
πάσας καὶ μικρὰς καὶ μεγάλας χάριτας,
καὶ πρὸς ἀναγνῶναι φωνὴν μέλι, καὶ τὸ φιλῆσαι   5
χείλεα, καὶ τὸ λαβεῖν ἔνδον, ἀμεμπτότατον.
καὶ τί πάθω; φησὶν γὰρ ὁρᾶν μόνον· ἦ ῥ' ἀγρυπνήσω
πολλάκι, τῇ κενεῇ κύπριδι χειρομαχῶν.

23.—ΜΕΛΕΑΓΡΟΥ

Ἠγρεύθην ὁ πρόσθεν ἐγώ ποτε τοῖς δυσέρωσι
κώμοις ἠϊθέων πολλάκις ἐγγελάσας·
καί μ' ἐπὶ σοῖς ὁ πτανὸς Ἔρως προθύροισι, Μυΐσκε,
στῆσεν ἐπιγράψας "Σκῦλ' ἀπὸ Σωφροσύνης."

24.—ΛΑΤΡΕΑ

Εἴ μοι χαρτὸς ἐμὸς Πολέμων καὶ σῶος ἀνέλθοι,
οἷος α< .. Δήλου> κοίρανε, πεμπόμενος,
ῥέξειν οὐκ ἀπόφημι τὸν ὀρθροβόην παρὰ βωμοῖς
ὄρνιν, ὃν εὐχωλαῖς ὡμολόγησα τεαῖς·
εἰ δέ τι τῶν ὄντων τότε οἱ πλέον ἢ καὶ ἔλασσον   5
ἔλθοι ἔχων, λέλυται τοὐμὸν ὑποσχέσιον.
ἦλθε δὲ σὺν πώγωνι.   τόδ' εἰ φίλον αὐτὸς ἑαυτῷ
εὔξατο, τὴν θυσίην πρᾶσσε τὸν εὐξάμενον.

25.—ΣΤΑΤΥΛΛΙΟΥ ΦΛΑΚΚΟΥ

Σῶόν μοι Πολέμωνα μολεῖν, ὅτ' ἔπεμπον, Ἀπόλλω
ᾐτούμην, θυσίην ὄρνιν ὑποσχόμενος.
ἦλθε δέ μοι Πολέμων λάσιος γένυν.   οὐ μὰ σέ,
       Φοῖβε,
ἦλθεν ἐμοί, πικρῷ δ' ἐξέφυγέν με τάχει.
οὐκέτι σοι θύω τὸν ἀλέκτορα.   μή με σοφίζου,   5
κωφὴν μοι σταχύων ἀντιδιδοὺς καλάμην.

just at that fatal age of sixteen, and having withal
every charm, small and great, a voice which is honey
when he reads and lips that are honey to kiss, and a
thing faultless for taking in. What will become of
me? He bids me look only. Verily I shall often lie
awake fighting with my hands against this empty
love.

23.—MELEAGER

I am caught, I who once laughed often at the seren-
ades of young men crossed in love. And at thy gate,
Myiscus, winged Love has fixed me, inscribing on
me "Spoils won from Chastity."

24.—TULLIUS LAUREAS

If my Polemo return welcome and safe, as he was,
Lord of Delos, when we sent him on his way, I do
not refuse to sacrifice by thy altar the bird, herald of
the dawn, that I promised in my prayers to thee.
But if he come possessing either more or less of
anything than he had then, I am released from my
promise.—But he came with a beard. If he himself
prayed for this as a thing dear to him, exact the
sacrifice from him who made the prayer.

25.—STATYLLIUS FLACCUS

When I bade farewell to Polemo I prayed for him
to return safe and sound to me, Apollo, promising a
sacrifice of a fowl. But Polemo came to me with a
hairy chin. No, Phoebus, I swear it by thyself, he
came not to me, but fled from me with cruel fleetness.
I no longer sacrifice the cock to thee. Think not to
cheat me, returning me for full ears empty chaff.

26.—ΤΟΥ ΑΥΤΟΥ

Εἴ μοι σωζόμενος Πολέμων ὃν ἔπεμπον ἀνέλθοι
  <φοινίξειν βωμοὺς ὡμολόγησα τεούς>.
νῦν θ' αὐτῷ Πολέμων ἀνασώζεται· οὐκέτ' ἀφῖκται,
  Φοῖβε, δασὺς δ' ἥκων οὐκέτι σῶος ἐμοί.
αὐτὸς ἴσως σκιάσαι γένυν εὔξατο· θυέτω αὐτός,   5
  ἀντία ταῖσιν ἐμαῖς ἐλπίσιν εὐξάμενος.

27.—ΤΟΥ ΑΥΤΟΥ

Σαῖς ἴκελον προὔπεμπον ἐγὼ Πολέμωνα παρειαῖς,
  ἢν ἔλθῃ, θύσειν ὄρνιν ὑποσχόμενος·
οὐ δέχομαι φθονεροῖς, Παιάν, φρίσσοντα γενείοις,
  τοιούτου τλήμων εἴνεκεν εὐξάμενος.
οὐδὲ μάτην τίλλεσθαι ἀναίτιον ὄρνιν ἔοικεν,   5
  ἢ συντιλλέσθω, Δήλιε, καὶ Πολέμων.

28.—ΝΟΥΜΗΝΙΟΥ ΤΑΡΣΕΩΣ

Κῦρος κύριός ἐστι· τί μοι μέλει, εἰ παρὰ γράμμα;
  οὐκ ἀναγινώσκω τὸν καλόν, ἀλλὰ βλέπω.

29.—ΑΛΚΑΙΟΥ

Πρώταρχος καλός ἐστι, καὶ οὐ θέλει· ἀλλὰ θελήσει
  ὕστερον· ἡ δ' ὥρη λαμπάδ' ἔχουσα τρέχει.

30.—ΤΟΥ ΑΥΤΟΥ

Ἡ κνήμη, Νίκανδρε, δασύνεται· ἀλλὰ φύλαξαι,
  μή σε καὶ ἡ πυγὴ ταὐτὸ παθοῦσα λάθῃ·
καὶ γνώσῃ φιλέοντος ὅση σπάνις. ἀλλ' ἔτι καὶ νῦν
  τῆς ἀμετακλήτου φρόντισον ἡλικίης.

26.—By the Same

If the Polemo I parted from came back to me in safety, I promised to sacrifice to thee. But now Polemo is saved for himself. It is no longer he who has come back to me, Phoebus, and arriving with a beard, he is no longer saved for me. He perhaps prayed himself for his chin to be darkened. Let him then make the sacrifice himself, as he prayed for what was contrary to all my hopes.

27.—By the Same

When I saw Polemo off, his cheeks like thine, Apollo, I promised to sacrifice a fowl if he came back. I do not accept him now his spiteful cheeks are bristly. Luckless wretch that I was to make a vow for the sake of such a man! It is not fair for the innocent fowl to be plucked in vain, or let Polemo be plucked, too, Lord of Delos.

28.—NUMENIUS OF TARSUS

Cyrus is Lord (*cyrius*). What does it matter to me if he lacks a letter? I do not read the fair, I look on him.

29.—ALCAEUS

Protarchus is fair and does not wish it; but later he will, and his youth races on holding a torch.[1]

30.—By the Same

Your leg, Nicander, is getting hairy, but take care lest your back-side also gets the same unnoticed. Then shall you know how rare lovers are. But even now reflect that youth is irrevocable.

---

[1] As in this torch race the torch was handed on by one racer to another, so is it with the light of youthful beauty.

31.—ΦΑΝΙΟΤ

Ναὶ Θέμιν, ἀκρήτου καὶ τὸ σκύφος ᾧ σεσάλευμαι,
  Πάμφιλε, βαιὸς ἔχει τὸν σὸν ἔρωτα χρόνος·
ἤδη γὰρ καὶ μηρὸς ὑπὸ τρίχα, καὶ γένυς ἡβᾷ,
  καὶ Πόθος εἰς ἑτέρην λοιπὸν ἄγει μανίην.
ἀλλ᾽ ὅτε <σοι> σπινθῆρος ἔτ᾽ ἴχνια βαιὰ λέλειπται,   5
  φειδωλὴν ἀπόθου· Καιρὸς Ἔρωτι φίλος.

32.—ΘΥΜΟΚΛΕΟΤΣ

Μέμνῃ που, μέμνῃ, ὅτε τοι ἔπος ἱερὸν εἶπον·
  "Ὥρη κάλλιστον, χ᾽ ὥρη ἐλαφρότατον·
ὥρην οὐδ᾽ ὁ τάχιστος ἐν αἰθέρι παρφθάσει ὄρνις.
  νῦν ἴδε, πάντ᾽ ἐπὶ γῆς ἄνθεα σεῦ κέχυται.

33.—ΜΕΛΕΑΓΡΟΤ

Ἦν καλὸς Ἡράκλειτος, ὅτ᾽ ἦν ποτέ· νῦν δὲ παρ᾽ ἥβην
  κηρύσσει πόλεμον δέρρις ὀπισθοβάταις.
ἀλλά, Πολυξενίδη, τάδ᾽ ὁρῶν, μὴ γαῦρα φρυάσσου·
  ἔστι καὶ ἐν γλουτοῖς φυομένη Νέμεσις.

34.—ΑΤΤΟΜΕΔΟΝΤΟΣ

Πρὸς τὸν παιδοτρίβην Δημήτριον ἐχθὲς ἐδείπνουν,
  πάντων ἀνθρώπων τὸν μακαριστότατον.
εἷς αὐτοῦ κατέκειθ᾽ ὑποκόλπιος, εἷς ὑπὲρ ὦμον,
  εἷς ἔφερεν τὸ φαγεῖν, εἷς δὲ πιεῖν ἐδίδου·
ἡ τετρὰς ἡ περίβλεπτος. ἐγὼ παίζων δὲ πρὸς αὐτὸν   5
  φημὶ "Σὺ καὶ νύκτωρ, φίλτατε, παιδοτριβεῖς;"

31.—PHANIAS

By Themis and the bowl of wine that made me totter, thy love, Pamphilus, has but a little time to last. Already thy thigh has hair on it and thy cheeks are downy, and Desire leads thee henceforth to another kind of passion. But now that some little vestiges of the spark are still left thee, put away thy parsimony. Opportunity is the friend of Love.

32.—THYMOCLES

Thou rememberest, I trust, thou rememberest the time when I spoke to thee the holy verse, "Beauty is fairest and beauty is nimblest." Not the fleetest bird in the sky shall outstrip beauty. Look, now, how all thy blossoms are shed on the earth.

33.—MELEAGER

Heraclitus was fair, when there was a Heraclitus, but now that his prime is past, a screen of hide [1] declares war on those who are behind-mounters. But, son of Polyxenus, seeing this, be not insolently haughty. Even on the buttocks too there is a Nemesis growing.

34.—AUTOMEDON

Yesterday I supped with the boy's trainer, Demetrius, the most blessed of all men. One lay on his lap, one stooped over his shoulder, one brought him the dishes, and another served him with drink —the admirable quartette. I said to him in fun, "Do you, my dear friend, work the boys at night too?"

[1] Such were used in war in defend walls.

35.—ΔΙΟΚΛΕΟΥΣ

Χαῖρέ ποτ᾽ οὐκ εἰπόντα προσεῖπέ τις· "'Αλλ' ὁ
περισσὸς
κάλλεϊ νῦν Δάμων οὐδὲ τὸ χαῖρε λέγει.
ἥξει τις τούτου χρόνος ἔκδικος· εἶτα δασυνθεὶς
ἄρξῃ χαῖρε λέγειν οὐκ ἀποκρινομένοις."

36.—ΑΣΚΛΗΠΙΑΔΟΥ ΑΔΡΑΜΥΤΤΗΝΟΥ

Νῦν αἰτεῖς, ὅτε λεπτὸς ὑπὸ κροτάφοισιν ἴουλος
ἕρπει καὶ μηροῖς ὀξὺς ἔπεστι χνόος·
εἶτα λέγεις "῞Ηδιον ἐμοὶ τόδε." καὶ τίς ἂν εἴποι
κρείσσονας αὐχμηρὰς ἀσταχύων καλάμας;

37.—ΔΙΟΣΚΟΡΙΔΟΥ

Πυγὴν Σωσάρχοιο διέπλασεν 'Αμφιπολίτεω
μυελίνην παίζων ὁ βροτολοιγὸς ῎Ερως,
Ζῆνα θέλων ἐρεθίξαι, ὁθούνεκα τῶν Γανυμήδους
μηρῶν οἱ τούτου πουλὺ μελιχρότεροι.

38.—ΡΙΑΝΟΥ

῾Ωραί σοι Χάριτές τε κατὰ γλυκὺ χεῦαν ἔλαιον,
ὦ πυγά· κνώσσειν δ᾽ οὐδὲ γέροντας ἐᾷς.
λέξον μοι τίνος ἐσσὶ μάκαιρα τύ, καὶ τίνα παίδων
κοσμεῖς; ἁ πυγὰ δ᾽ εἶπε· " Μενεκράτεος."

39.—ΑΔΗΛΟΝ

'Εσβέσθη Νίκανδρος, ἀπέπτατο πᾶν ἀπὸ χροιῆς
ἄνθος, καὶ χαρίτων λοιπὸν ἔτ᾽ οὐδ᾽ ὄνομα,
ὃν πρὶν ἐν ἀθανάτοις ἐνομίζομεν. ἀλλὰ φρονεῖτε
μηδὲν ὑπὲρ θνητούς, ὦ νέοι· εἰσὶ τρίχες.

35.—DIOCLES

ONE thus addressed a boy who did not say good day: "And so Damon, who excels in beauty, does not even say good-day now! A time will come that will take vengeance for this. Then, grown all rough and hairy, you will give good-day first to those who do not give it you back.

36.—ASCLEPIADES OF ADRAMYTTIUM

Now you offer yourself, when the tender bloom is advancing under your temples and there is a prickly down on your thighs. And then you say, "I prefer this." But who would say that the dry stubble is better than the eared corn?

37.—DIOSCORIDES

LOVE, the murderer of men, moulded soft as marrow the back-side of Sosarchus of Amphipolis in fun, wishing to irritate Zeus because his thighs are much more honeyed than those of Ganymede.

38.—RHIANUS

THE Hours and Graces shed sweet oil on thee, and thou lettest not even old men sleep. Tell me whose blest darling thou art and which of the boys thou adornest. And the backside's answer was, "Menecrates' darling."

39.—ANONYMOUS

NICANDER's light is out. All the bloom has left his complexion, and not even the name of charm survives, Nicander whom we once counted among the immortals. But, ye young men, let not your thoughts mount higher than beseems a mortal; there are such things as hairs.

40.—ΑΔΗΛΟΝ

Μὴ 'κδύσῃς, ἄνθρωπε, τὸ χλαίνιον, ἀλλὰ θεώρει
    οὕτως ἀκρολίθου κἀμὲ τρόπον ξοάνου.
γυμνὴν Ἀντιφίλου ζητῶν χάριν, ὡς ἐπ' ἀκάνθαις
    εὑρήσεις ῥοδέαν φυομένην κάλυκα.

41.—ΜΕΛΕΑΓΡΟΥ

Οὐκέτι μοι Θήρων γράφεται καλός, οὐδ' ὁ πυραυγὴς
    πρίν ποτε, νῦν δ' ἤδη δαλός, Ἀπολλόδοτος.
στέργω θῆλυν ἔρωτα· δασυτρώγλων δὲ πίεσμα
    λασταύρων μελέτω ποιμέσιν αἰγοβάταις.

42.—ΔΙΟΣΚΟΡΙΔΟΥ

Βλέψον ἐς Ἑρμογένην πλήρει χερί, καὶ τάχα πρήξεις
    παιδοκόραξ ὧν σοι θυμὸς ὀνειροπολεῖ,
καὶ στυγνὴν ὀφρύων λύσεις τάσιν· ἢν δ' ἁλιεύῃ
    ὀρφανὸν ἀγκίστρου κύματι δοὺς κάλαμον,
ἕλξεις ἐκ λιμένος πολλὴν δρόσον· οὐδὲ γὰρ αἰδὼς   5
    οὐδ' ἔλεος δαπάνῳ κόλλοπι συντρέφεται.

43.—ΚΑΛΛΙΜΑΧΟΥ

Ἐχθαίρω τὸ ποίημα τὸ κυκλικόν, οὐδὲ κελεύθῳ
    χαίρω τις πολλοὺς ὧδε καὶ ὧδε φέρει·
μισῶ καὶ περίφοιτον ἐρώμενον, οὐδ' ἀπὸ κρήνης
    πίνω· σικχαίνω πάντα τὰ δημόσια.
Λυσανίη, σὺ δὲ ναίχι καλὸς καλός· ἀλλὰ πρὶν εἰπεῖν   5
    τοῦτο σαφῶς, ἠχὼ φησί τις "Ἄλλος ἔχει."

40.—ANONYMOUS

TAKE not off my cloak, Sir, but look on me even as if I were a draped statue with the extremities only of marble. If you wish to see the naked beauty of Antiphilus you will find the rose growing as if on thorns.

41.—MELEAGER

I DO not count Thero fair any longer, nor Apollodotus, once gleaming like fire, but now already a burnt-out torch. I care for the love of women. Let it be for goat-mounting herds to press in their arms hairy pansy-boys.

42.—DIOSCORIDES

WHEN you look on Hermogenes, boy-vulture, have your hands full, and perhaps you will succeed in getting that of which your heart dreams, and will relax the melancholy contraction of your brow. But if you fish for him, committing to the waves a line devoid of a hook, you will pull plenty of water out of the harbour; for neither pity nor shame dwells with an expensive screw-boy.

43.—CALLIMACHUS

I DETEST the poem which belongs to the Serial kind, and do not love a road that carries many this way and that. I hate, too, a beloved who is in circulation, and I do not drink from a fountain. All public things disgust me. Lysianias, yes indeed thou art fair, fair. But before I can say this clearly an echo says, " He is another's." [1]

[1] Echo would of course have answered ἔχει ἄλλος το ναίχι καλός.

44.—ΓΛΑΤΚΟΤ

Ἦν ὅτε παῖδας ἔπειθε πάλαι ποτὲ δῶρα φιλεῦντας
ὄρτυξ, καὶ ῥαπτὴ σφαῖρα, καὶ ἀστράγαλοι·
νῦν δὲ λοπὰς καὶ κέρμα· τὰ παίγνια δ᾽ οὐδὲν ἐκεῖνα
ἰσχύει. ζητεῖτ᾽ ἄλλο τι, παιδοφίλαι.

45.—ΠΟΣΕΙΔΙΠΠΟΤ

Ναὶ ναὶ βάλλετ᾽, Ἔρωτες· ἐγὼ σκοπὸς εἷς ἅμα
πολλοῖς
κεῖμαι. μὴ φείσησθ᾽, ἄφρονες· ἢν γὰρ ἐμὲ
νικήσητ᾽, ὀνομαστοὶ ἐν ἀθανάτοισιν ἔσεσθε
τοξόται, ὡς μεγάλης δεσπόται ἰοδόκης.

46.—ΑΣΚΛΗΠΙΑΔΟΤ

Οὐκ εἴμ᾽ οὐδ᾽ ἐτέων δύο κεἴκοσι, καὶ κοπιῶ ζῶν.
Ὤρωτες, τί κακὸν τοῦτο; τί με φλέγετε;
ἢν γὰρ ἐγώ τι πάθω, τί ποιήσετε; δῆλον, Ἔρωτες,
ὡς τὸ πάρος παίξεσθ᾽ ἄφρονες ἀστραγάλοις.

47.—ΜΕΛΕΑΓΡΟΤ

Ματρὸς ἔτ᾽ ἐν κόλποισιν ὁ νήπιος ὀρθρινὰ παίζων
ἀστραγάλοις τοὐμὸν πνεῦμ᾽ ἐκύβευσεν Ἔρως.

48.—ΤΟΥ ΑΥΤΟΥ

Κεῖμαι· λὰξ ἐπίβαινε κατ᾽ αὐχένος, ἄγριε δαῖμον.
οἶδά σε, ναὶ μὰ θεούς, ναὶ[1] βαρὺν ὄντα φέρειν·
οἶδα καὶ ἔμπυρα τόξα. βαλὼν δ᾽ ἐπ᾽ ἐμὴν φρένα
πυρσούς,
οὐ φλέξεις· ἤδη πᾶσα γάρ ἐστι τέφρη.

[1] I write ναὶ βαρὺν : καὶ βαρὺν MS.

44.—GLAUCUS

THERE was a time long, long ago, when boys who like presents were won by a quail, or a sewn ball, or knuckle-bones, but now they want rich dishes or money, and those playthings have no power. Search for something else, ye lovers of boys.

45.—POSIDIPPUS

YEA, yea, ye Loves, shoot. I alone stand here a target for many all at once. Spare me not, silly children; for if ye conquer me ye shall be famous among the immortals for your archery, as masters of a mighty quiver.

46.—ASCLEPIADES

I AM not yet two and twenty, and life is a burden to me. Ye Loves, why thus maltreat me; why set me afire? For if I perish, what will you do? Clearly, Loves, you will play, silly children, at your knuckle-bones as before.

47.—MELEAGER

LOVE, the baby still in his mother's lap, playing at dice in the morning, played my soul away.

48.—BY THE SAME

I AM down; set thy foot on my neck, fierce demon. I know thee, yea by the gods, yea heavy art thou to bear: I know, too, thy fiery arrows. But if thou set thy torch to *my* heart, thou shalt no longer burn it; already it is all ash.

49.—ΤΟΥ ΑΥΤΟΥ

Ζωρι πότει, δύσερως, καὶ σοῦ φλόγα τὰν φιλόπαιδα
κοιμάσει λάθας δωροδότας Βρόμιος·
ζωροπότει, καὶ πλῆρες ἀφυσσάμενος σκύφος οἴνας,
ἔκκρουσον στυγερὰν ἐκ κραδίας ὀδύναν.

50.—ΑΣΚΛΗΠΙΑΔΟΥ

Πῖν', Ἀσκληπιάδη· τί τὰ δάκρυα ταῦτα; τί πάσχεις;
οὐ σὲ μόνον χαλεπὴ Κύπρις ἐληΐσατο,
οὐδ' ἐπὶ σοὶ μούνῳ κατεθήξατο τόξα καὶ ἰοὺς
πικρὸς Ἔρως. τί ζῶν ἐν σποδιῇ τίθεσαι;
πίνωμεν Βάκχου ζωρὸν πόμα· δάκτυλος ἀώς·   5
ἢ πάλι κοιμιστὰν λύχνον ἰδεῖν μένομεν;
πίνωμεν, δύσερως·[1] μετά τοι χρόνον οὐκέτι πουλύν,
σχέτλιε, τὴν μακρὰν νύκτ' ἀναπαυσόμεθα.

51.—ΚΑΛΛΙΜΑΧΟΥ

Ἔγχει, καὶ πάλιν εἰπέ, Διοκλέος· οὐδ' Ἀχελῷος
κείνου τῶν ἱερῶν αἰσθάνεται κυάθων.
καλὸς ὁ παῖς, Ἀχελῷε, λίην καλός· εἰ δέ τις οὐχὶ
φησὶν—ἐπισταίμην μοῦνος ἐγὼ τὰ καλά.

52.—ΜΕΛΕΑΓΡΟΥ

Οὔριος ἐμπνεύσας ναύταις Νότος, ὦ δυσέρωτες,
ἥμισύ μευ ψυχᾶς ἅρπασεν Ἀνδράγαθον.

---

[1] πίνωμεν δύσερως Kaibel : πίνωμεν οὐ γὰρ ἔρως MS.

---

[1] cp. Bk. V. 136, imitated from this.

49.—By the Same

DRINK strong wine, thou unhappy lover, and Bacchus, the giver of forgetfulness, shall send to sleep the flame of thy love for the lad. Drink, and draining the cup full of the vine-juice drive out abhorred pain from thy heart.

50.—ASCLEPIADES

DRINK, Asclepiades. Why these tears? What aileth thee? Not thee alone hath cruel Cypris taken captive; not for thee alone hath bitter Love sharpened his arrows. Why whilst yet alive dost thou lie in the dust? Let us quaff the unmixed drink of Bacchus. The day is but a finger's breadth. Shall we wait to see again the lamp that bids us to bed? Let us drink, woeful lover. It is not far away now, poor wretch, the time when we shall rest through the long night.

51.—CALLIMACHUS

To the Cup-bearer [1]

POUR in the wine and again say "To Diocles," nor does Achelous [2] touch the ladlefuls hallowed to him. Beautiful is the boy, Achelous, passing beautiful; and if any say "Nay"—let me alone know what beauty is.

52.—MELEAGER

THE South Wind, blowing fair for sailors, O ye who are sick for love, has carried off Andragathus, my

---

[2] The river, used for water in general; but I confess to not understanding the reference to Achelous in l. 3. Perhaps it means "Ye water-drinkers."

τρὶς μάκαρες νᾶες, τρὶς δ' ὄλβια κύματα πόντου,
τετράκι δ' εὐδαίμων παιδοφορῶν ἄνεμος.
εἴθ' εἴην δελφίς, ἵν' ἐμοῖς βαστακτὸς ἐπ' ὤμοις   5
πορθμευθεὶς ἐσίδῃ τὰν γλυκόπαιδα Ῥόδον.

53.—ΤΟΥ ΑΥΤΟΥ

Εὔφορτοι νᾶες πελαγίτιδες, αἳ πόρον Ἕλλης
πλεῖτε, καλὸν κόλποις δεξάμεναι Βορέην,
ἤν που ἐπ' ἠϊόνων Κῴαν κατὰ νᾶσον ἴδητε
Φανίον εἰς χαροπὸν δερκομέναν πέλαγος,
τοῦτ' ἔπος ἀγγείλαιτε, καλαὶ νέες, ὥς με κομίζει   5
ἵμερος οὐ ναύταν, ποσσὶ δὲ πεζοπόρον.
εἰ γὰρ τοῦτ' εἴποιτ', εὐάγγελοι,[1] αὐτίκα καὶ Ζεὺς
οὔριος ὑμετέρας πνεύσεται εἰς ὀθόνας.

54.—ΤΟΥ ΑΥΤΟΥ

Ἀρνεῖται τὸν Ἔρωτα τεκεῖν ἡ Κύπρις, ἰδοῦσα
ἄλλον ἐν ἠιθέοις Ἵμερον Ἀντίοχον.
ἀλλά, νέοι, στέργοιτε νέον Πόθον· ἦ γὰρ ὁ κοῦρος
εὕρηται κρείσσων οὗτος Ἔρωτος Ἔρως.

55.—ΑΔΗΛΟΝ, οἱ δὲ ΑΡΤΕΜΩΝΟΣ

Λητοΐδη, σὺ μὲν ἔσχες ἁλίρρυτον αὐχένα Δήλου,
κοῦρε Διὸς μεγάλου, θέσφατα πᾶσι λέγων·
Κεκροπίαν δ' Ἐχέδημος, ὁ δεύτερος Ἀτθίδι Φοῖβος,
ᾧ καλὸν ἁβροκόμης ἄνθος ἔλαμψεν Ἔρως.
ἡ δ' ἀνὰ κῦμ' ἄρξασα καὶ ἐν χθονὶ πατρὶς Ἀθήνη   5
νῦν κάλλει δούλην Ἑλλάδ' ὑπηγάγετο.

---

[1] εὐάγγελοι Piccolos : εὐ τέλοι MS. with a space after εὐ.

soul's half.   Thrice happy the ships, thrice fortunate
the waves of the sea, and four times blessed the
wind that bears the boy.   Would I were a dolphin
that, carried on my shoulders, he could cross the
seas to look on Rhodes, the home of sweet lads.

53.—By the Same

Richly loaded ocean ships that sail down the
Hellespont, taking to your bosoms the good North
Wind, if haply ye see on the beach of Cos Phanion
gazing at the blue sea, give her this message, good
ships, that Desire carries me there not on shipboard,
but faring on my feet.[1]   For if you tell her this, ye
bearers of good tidings, straight shall Zeus also
breathe the gale of his favour into your sails.

54.—By the Same

Cypris denies that she gave birth to Love now
that she sees Antiochus among the young men, a
second Love.   But, ye young men, love this new
Love; for of a truth this boy has proved to be a
Love better than Love.

55.—Anonymous, or some say by ARTEMON

Child of Leto, son of Zeus the great, who utterest
oracles to all men, thou art lord of the sea-girt height
of Delos; but the lord of the land of Cecrops is
Echedemus, a second Attic Phoebus whom soft-haired
Love lit with lovely bloom.   And his city Athens,
once mistress of the sea and land, now has made all
Greece her slave by beauty.

[1] I think we must understand that he actually contem-
plated coming to Cos (or rather to the coast opposite) by
land.

56.—ΜΕΛΕΑΓΡΟΤ

Εἰκόνα μὲν Παρίην ζωογλύφος ἄννσ' Ἔρωτος
  Πραξιτέλης, Κύπριδος παῖδα τυπωσάμενος,
νῦν δ' ὁ θεῶν κάλλιστος Ἔρως ἔμψυχον ἄγαλμα,
  αὑτὸν ἀπεικονίσας, ἔπλασε Πραξιτέλην·
ὄφρ' ὁ μὲν ἐν θνατοῖς, ὁ δ' ἐν αἰθέρι φίλτρα βραβεύῃ, 5
  γῆς θ' ἅμα καὶ μακάρων σκηπτροφορῶσι πόθοι.
ὀλβίστη Μερόπων ἱερὰ πόλις, ἃ θεόπαιδα
  καινὸν Ἔρωτα νέων θρέψεν ὑφαγεμόνα.

57.—ΤΟΥ ΑΥΤΟΥ

Πραξιτέλης ὁ πάλαι ζωογλύφος ἁβρὸν ἄγαλμα
  ἄψυχον, μορφᾶς κωφὸν ἔτευξε τύπον,
πέτρον ἐνειδοφορῶν· ὁ δὲ νῦν, ἔμψυχα μαγεύων,
  τὸν τριπανοῦργον Ἔρωτ' ἔπλασεν ἐν κραδίᾳ.
ἦ τάχα τοὔνομ' ἔχει ταὐτὸν μόνον, ἔργα δὲ κρέσσω, 5
  οὐ λίθον, ἀλλὰ φρενῶν πνεῦμα μεταρρυθμίσας.
ἵλαος πλάσσοι τὸν ἐμὸν τρόπον, ὄφρα τυπώσας
  ἐντὸς ἐμὴν ψυχὴν ναὸν Ἔρωτος ἔχῃ.

58.—ΡΙΑΝΟΤ

Ἡ Τροιζὴν ἀγαθὴ κουροτρόφος· οὐκ ἂν ἁμάρτοις
  αἰνήσας παίδων οὐδὲ τὸν ὑστάτιον.
τόσσον δ' Ἐμπεδοκλῆς φανερώτερος, ὅσσον ἐν ἄλλοις
  ἄνθεσιν εἰαρινοῖς καλὸν ἔλαμψε ῥόδον.

56.—MELEAGER

PRAXITELES the sculptor wrought a statue of Love in Parian marble, fashioning the son of Cypris. But now Love, the fairest of the gods, making his own image, hath moulded Praxiteles, a living statue, so that the one amid mortals and the other in heaven may be the dispenser of love-charms, and a Love may wield the sceptre on earth as among the immortals. Most blessed the holy city of the Meropes,[1] which nurtured a new Love, son of a god, to be the prince of the young men.

57.—BY THE SAME

PRAXITELES the sculptor of old time wrought a delicate image, but lifeless, the dumb counterfeit of beauty, endowing the stone with form; but this Praxiteles of to-day, creator of living beings by his magic, hath moulded in my heart Love, the rogue of rogues. Perchance, indeed, his name only is the same, but his works are better, since he hath transformed no stone, but the spirit of the mind. Graciously may he mould my character, that when he has formed it he may have within me a temple of Love, even my soul.

58.—RHIANUS

TROEZEN is a good nurse; thou shalt not err if thou praisest even the last of her boys. But Empedocles excels all in brilliance as much as the lovely rose outshines the other flowers of spring.

---

[1] Cos.

59.—ΜΕΛΕΑΓΡΟΥ

Ἁβρούς, ναὶ τὸν Ἔρωτα, τρέφει Τύρος· ἀλλὰ
    Μυΐσκος
ἔσβεσεν ἐκλάμψας ἀστέρας ἠέλιος.

60.—ΤΟΥ ΑΥΤΟΥ

Ἢν ἐνίδω Θήρωνα, τὰ πάνθ᾿ ὁρῶ· ἢν δὲ τὰ πάντα
βλέψω, τόνδε δὲ μή, τἄμπαλιν οὐδὲν ὁρῶ.

61.—ΑΔΗΛΟΝ

Ἄθρει· μὴ διὰ παντὸς ὅλαν κατάτηι:᾿, Ἀρίβαζε,
τὰν Κνίδον· ἁ πέτρα θρυπτομένα φέρεται.

62.—ΑΛΛΟ

Ματέρες αἱ Περσῶν, καλὰ μὲν καλὰ τέκνα τεκεσθε·
ἀλλ᾿ Ἀρίβαζος ἐμοὶ κάλλιον ἢ τὸ καλόν.

63.—ΜΕΛΕΑΓΡΟΥ

Σιγῶν Ἡράκλειτος ἐν ὄμμασι τοῦτ᾿ ἔπος αὐδᾶ·
    " Καὶ Ζηνὸς φλέξω πῦρ τὸ κεραυνοβόλον."
ναὶ μὴν καὶ Διόδωρος ἐνὶ στέρνοις τόδε φωνεῖ·
    " Καὶ πέτρον τήκω χρωτὶ χλιαινόμενος."
δύστανος, παίδων ὃς ἐδέξατο τοῦ μὲν ἀπ᾿ ὄσσων   5
    λαμπάδα, τοῦ δὲ πόθοις τυφόμενον γλυκὺ πῦρ.

64.—ΑΛΚΑΙΟΥ

Ζεὺς Πίσης μεδέων, Πειθήνορα, δεύτερον υἷα
    Κύπριδος, αἰπεινῷ στέψον ὑπὸ Κρονίῳ·

59.—MELEAGER

DELICATE children, so help me Love, doth Tyre nurture, but Myiscus is the sun that, when his light bursts forth, quenches the stars.

60.—BY THE SAME

IF I see Thero, I see everything, but if I see everything and no Thero, I again see nothing.

61.—ANONYMOUS

LOOK! consume not all Cnidus utterly, Aribazus; the very stone is softened and is vanishing.

62.—ANONYMOUS

YE Persian mothers, beautiful, yea beautiful are the children ye bear, but Aribazus is to me a thing more beautiful than beauty.

63.—MELEAGER

HERACLITUS in silence speaks thus from his eyes: "I shall set aflame even the fire of the bolts of Zeus." Yea, verily, and from the bosom of Diodorus comes this voice: "I melt even stone warmed by my body's touch." Unhappy he who has received a torch from the eyes of the one, and from the other a sweet fire smouldering with desire.

64.—ALCAEUS

ZEUS, Lord of Pisa, crown under the steep hill of Cronos [1] Peithenor, the second son of Cypris. And,

[1] At Olympia.

μηδέ μοι οἰνοχόον κυλίκων σέθεν αἰετὸς ἀρθεὶς
μάρψαις ἀντὶ καλοῦ, κοίρανε, Δαρδανίδου.
εἰ δέ τι Μουσάων τοι ἐγὼ φίλον ὤπασα δῶρον,　　5
νεύσαις μοι θείου παιδὸς ὁμοφροσύνην.

65.—ΜΕΛΕΑΓΡΟΥ

Εἰ Ζεὺς κεῖνος ἔτ' ἐστίν, ὁ καὶ Γανυμήδεος ἀκμὴν
ἁρπάξας, ἵν' ἔχῃ νέκταρος οἰνοχόον,
κἠμοὶ τὸν καλὸν ἐστὶν <ἐνὶ> σπλάγχνοισι Μυΐσκον
κρύπτειν, μή με λάθῃ παιδὶ βαλὼν πτέρυγας.

66.—ΑΔΗΛΟΝ

Κρίνατ', Ἔρωτες, ὁ παῖς τίνος ἄξιος. εἰ μὲν ἀληθῶς
ἀθανάτων, ἐχέτω· Ζανὶ γὰρ οὐ μάχομαι.
εἰ δέ τι καὶ θνατοῖς ὑπολείπεται, εἴπατ', Ἔρωτες,
Δωρόθεος τίνος ἦν, καὶ τίνι νῦν δέδοται.
ἐν φανερῷ φωνεῦσιν· ἐμὴ χάρις.—ἀλλ' ἀποχωρεῖ.　　5
μὴ †μετι πρὸς τὸ καλὸν καὶ σὺ μάταια φέρῃ.

67.—ΑΔΗΛΟΝ

Τὸν καλὸν οὐχ ὁρόω Διονύσιον. ἆρά γ' ἀναρθείς,
Ζεῦ πάτερ, <ἀθανάτοις> δεύτερος οἰνοχοεῖ;
αἰετέ, τὸν χαρίεντα, ποτὶ πτερὰ πυκνὰ τινάξας,
πῶς ἔφερες; μή που κνίσματ' ὄνυξιν ἔχει;

68.—ΜΕΛΕΑΓΡΟΥ

Οὐκ ἐθέλω Χαρίδαμον· ὁ γὰρ καλὸς εἰς Δία λεύσσει,
ὡς ἤδη νέκταρ τῷ θεῷ οἰνοχοῶν·

---

[1] I take the last line to be addressed to the boy, Dorotheus,
who would not abide by the verdict of the Loves, but this

Lord, I pray thee become no eagle on high to seize him for thy cup-bearer in place of the fair Trojan boy. If ever I have brought thee a gift from the Muses that was dear to thee, grant that the god-like boy may be of one mind with me.

65.—MELEAGER

If Zeus still be he who stole Ganymede in his prime that he might have a cup-bearer of the nectar, I, too, may hide lovely Myiscus in my heart, lest before I know it he swoop on the boy with his wings.

66.—ANONYMOUS

Judge, ye Loves, of whom the boy is worthy. If truly of the god, let him have him, for I do not contend with Zeus. But if there is something left for mortals too, say, Loves, whose was Dorotheus and to whom is he now given. Openly they call out that they are in my favour; but he departs. I trust that thou, too, mayst not be attracted to beauty in vain.[1]

67.—ANONYMOUS

I see not lovely Dionysius. Has he been taken up to heaven, Father Zeus, to be the second cup-bearer of the immortals ? Tell me, eagle, when thy wings beat rapidly over him, how didst thou carry the pretty boy ? has he marks from thy claws?

68.—MELEAGER

I wish not Charidemus to be mine; for the fair boy looks to Zeus, as if already serving the god with

line is corrupt, and the whole is rather obscure. There was evidently a terrestrial rival in addition to Zeus.

οὐκ ἐθέλω· τί δέ μοι τὸν ἐπουρανίων βασιλῆα
　ἄνταθλον νίκης τῆς ἐν ἔρωτι λαβεῖν;
ἀρκοῦμαι δ', ἢν μοῦνον ὁ παῖς ἀνιὼν ἐς Ὄλυμπον,　5
　ἐκ γῆς νίπτρα ποδῶν δάκρυα τἀμὰ λάβῃ,
μναμόσυνον στοργῆς· γλυκὺ δ' ὄμμασι νεῦμα δίυγρον
　δοίη, καί τι φίλημ' ἁρπάσαι ἀκροθιγές.
τἆλλα δὲ πάντ' ἐχέτω Ζεύς, ὡς θέμις· εἰ δ' ἐθελήσοι,
　ἦ τάχα που κἠγὼ γεύσομαι ἀμβροσίας.　10

69.—ΑΔΗΛΟΝ

Ζεῦ, προτέρῳ τέρπου Γανυμήδεϊ· τὸν δ' ἐμόν, ὦναξ,
　Δέξανδρον δέρκευ τηλόθεν· οὐ φθονέω.
εἰ δὲ βίῃ τὸν καλὸν ἀποίσεαι, οὐκέτ' ἀνεκτῶς
　δεσπόζεις· ἀπίτω καὶ τὸ βιοῦν ἐπὶ σοῦ.

70.—ΜΕΛΕΑΓΡΟΥ

Στήσομ' ἐγὼ καὶ Ζηνὸς ἐναντίον, εἴ σε, Μυΐσκε,
　ἁρπάζειν ἐθέλοι νέκταρος οἰνοχόον.
καίτοι πολλάκις αὐτὸς ἐμοὶ τάδ' ἔλεξε· "Τί ταρβεῖς;
　" οὔ σε βαλῶ ζήλοις· οἶδα παθὼν ἐλεεῖν."
χὠ μὲν δὴ τάδε φησίν· ἐγὼ δ', ἢν μυῖα παραπτῇ,　5
　ταρβῶ μὴ ψεύστης Ζεὺς ἐπ' ἐμοὶ γέγονεν.

71.—ΚΑΛΛΙΜΑΧΟΥ

Θεσσαλικὲ Κλεόνικε τάλαν, τάλαν· οὐ μὰ τὸν ὀξὺν
　ἥλιον, οὐκ ἔγνων· σχέτλιε, ποῦ γέγονας;
ὀστέα σοι καὶ μοῦνον ἔτι τρίχες. ἦ ῥά σε δαίμων
　οὑμὸς ἔχει, χαλεπῇ δ' ἤντεο θευμορίῃ;

nectar. I wish it not. What profits it me to have the king of heaven as a competitor for victory in love? I am content if only the boy, as he mounts to Olympus, take from earth my tears to wash his feet in memory of my love; and could he but give me one sweet, melting glance and let our lips just meet as I snatch one kiss! Let Zeus have all the rest, as is right; but yet, if he were willing, perchance I, too, should taste ambrosia.

69.—Anonymous

Take thy delight, Zeus, with thy former Ganymede, and look from afar, O King, on my Dexandrus. I grudge it not. But if thou carriest away the fair boy by force, no longer is thy tyranny supportable. Let even life go if I must live under thy rule.

70.—MELEAGER

I will stand up even against Zeus if he would snatch thee from me, Myiscus, to pour out the nectar for him. And yet Zeus often told me himself, "What dost thou dread? I will not smite thee with jealousy; I have learnt to pity, for myself I have suffered." That is what he says, but I, if even a fly [1] buzz past, am in dread lest Zeus prove a liar in my case.

71.—CALLIMACHUS

Thessalian Cleonicus, poor wretch, poor wretch! By the piercing sun I did not know you, man. Where have you been? You are nothing but hair and bone. Can it be that my evil spirit besets you, and you have met with a cruel stroke from heaven? I see it;

---

[1] *i.e.* no eagle, but a fly.

ἔγνων· Εὐξίθεός σε συνήρπασε· καὶ σὺ γὰρ ἐλθὼν   5
τὸν καλόν, ὦ μοχθήρ', ἔβλεπες ἀμφοτέροις.

72.—ΜΕΛΕΑΓΡΟΥ

Ἤδη μὲν γλυκὺς ὄρθρος· ὁ δ' ἐν προθύροισιν ἄυπνος
Δᾶμις ἀποψύχει πνεῦμα τὸ λειφθὲν ἔτι,
σχέτλιος, Ἡράκλειτον ἰδών· ἔστη γὰρ ὑπ' αὐγὰς
ὀφθαλμῶν, βληθεὶς κηρὸς ἐς ἀνθρακιήν.
ἀλλά μοι ἔγρεο, Δᾶμι δυσάμμορε· καὐτὸς Ἔρωτος   5
ἕλκος ἔχων ἐπὶ σοῖς δάκρυσι δακρυχέω.

73.—ΚΑΛΛΙΜΑΧΟΥ

Ἥμισύ μευ ψυχῆς ἔτι τὸ πνέον, ἥμισυ δ' οὐκ οἶδ'
εἴτ' Ἔρος εἴτ' Ἀΐδης ἥρπασε· πλὴν ἀφανές.
ἦ ῥά τιν' ἐς παίδων πάλιν ᾤχετο; καὶ μὲν ἀπεῖπον
πολλάκι· "Τὴν δρῆστιν μὴ ὑποδέχεσθε, νέοι."
†ουκισυ δίφησον·[1] ἐκεῖσε γὰρ ἡ λιθόλευστος   5
κείνη καὶ δύσερως οἶδ' ὅτι που στρέφεται.

74.—ΜΕΛΕΑΓΡΟΥ

Ἤν τι πάθω, Κλεόβουλε, (τὸ γὰρ πλέον ἐν πυρὶ
παίδων
βαλλόμενος κεῖμαι λείψανον ἐν σποδιῇ·)
λίσσομαι, ἀκρήτῳ μέθυσον, πρὶν ὑπὸ χθόνα θέσθαι,
κάλπιν, ἐπιγράψας "Δῶρον Ἔρως Ἀΐδῃ."

75.—ΑΣΚΛΗΠΙΑΔΟΥ

Εἰ πτερά σοι προσέκειτο, καὶ ἐν χερὶ τόξα καὶ ἰοί,
οὐκ ἂν Ἔρως ἐγράφη Κύπριδος, ἀλλὰ σύ, παῖς.

---

[1] δίφησον Schneider : νιφησον MS. The remainder cannot
be restored. A proper name must have stood here.

Euxitheus has run away with you. Yes, when you came here, you rascal, you were looking at the beauty with **both** eyes.

72.—MELEAGER

Sweet dawn has come, and lying sleepless in the porch Damis is breathing out the little breath he has left, poor wretch, all for having looked on Heraclitus; for he stood under the rays of his eyes like wax thrown on burning coals. But come, awake, all luckless Damis! I myself bear Love's wound, and shed tears for thy tears.

73.—CALLIMACHUS

It is but the half of my soul that still breathes, and for the other half I know not if it be Love or Death that hath seized on it, only it is gone. Is it off again to one of the lads? And yet I told them often, "Receive not, ye young men, the runaway." Seek for it at * * , for I know it is somewhere there that the gallows-bird,[1] the love-lorn, is loitering.

74.—MELEAGER

If I perish, Cleobulus (for cast, nigh all of me, into the flame of lads' love, I lie, a burnt remnant, in the ashes), I pray thee make the urn drunk with wine ere thou lay it in earth, writing thereon, "Love's gift to Death."

75.—ASCLEPIADES

If thou hadst wings on thy back, and a bow and arrows in thy hand, not Love but thou wouldst be described as the son of Cypris.

---

[1] Literally, " who deserves to be stoned to death."

76.—ΜΕΛΕΑΓΡΟΥ

Εἰ μὴ τόξον Ἔρως, μηδὲ πτερά, μηδὲ φαρέτραν,
  μηδὲ πυριβλήτους εἶχε πόθων ἀκίδας,
οὐκ, αὐτὸν τὸν πτανὸν ἐπόμνυμαι, οὔποτ᾽ ἂν ἔγνως
  ἐκ μορφᾶς τίς ἔφυ Ζωΐλος ἢ τίς Ἔρως.

77.—ΑΣΚΛΗΠΙΑΔΟΥ ἢ ΠΟΣΕΙΔΙΠΠΟΥ

Εἰ καθύπερθε λάβοις χρύσεα πτερά, καί σευ ἀπ᾽
  ὤμων
τείνοιτ᾽ ἀργυρέων ἰοδόκος φαρέτρη,
καὶ σταίης παρ᾽ Ἔρωτα, φίλ᾽, ἀγλαόν, οὐ μὰ τὸν
  Ἑρμῆν,
  οὐδ᾽ αὐτὴ Κύπρις γνώσεται ὃν τέτοκεν.

78.—ΜΕΛΕΑΓΡΟΥ

Εἰ χλαμύδ᾽ εἶχεν Ἔρως, καὶ μὴ πτερά, μηδ᾽ ἐπὶ νώτων
  τόξα τε καὶ φαρέτραν, ἀλλ᾽ ἐφόρει πέτασον,
ναί, τὸν γαῦρον ἔφηβον ἐπόμνυμαι, Ἀντίοχος μὲν
  ἦν ἂν Ἔρως, ὁ δ᾽ Ἔρως τἄμπαλιν Ἀντίοχος.

79.—ΑΔΗΛΟΝ

Ἀντίπατρός μ᾽ ἐφίλησ᾽ ἤδη λήγοντος ἔρωτος,
  καὶ πάλιν ἐκ ψυχρῆς πῦρ ἀνέκαυσε τέφρης·
δὶς δὲ μιῆς ἄκων ἔτυχον φλογός. ὦ δυσέρωτες,
  φεύγετε, μὴ πρήσω τοὺς πέλας ἀψάμενος.

80.—ΜΕΛΕΑΓΡΟΥ

Ψυχὴ δυσδάκρυτε, τί σοι τὸ πεπανθὲν Ἔρωτος
  τραῦμα διὰ σπλάγχνων αὖθις ἀναφλέγεται;

76.—MELEAGER

IF Love had neither bow, nor wings, nor quiver, nor the barbed arrows of desire dipped in fire, never, I swear it by the winged boy himself, couldst thou tell from their form which is Zoilus and which is Love.

77.—ASCLEPIADES or POSIDIPPUS

IF thou wert to grow golden wings above, and on thy silvery shoulders were slung a quiver full of arrows, and thou wert to stand, dear, beside Love in his splendour, never, by Hermes I swear it, would Cypris herself know which is her son.

78.—MELEAGER

IF Love had a chlamys and no wings, and wore no bow and quiver on his back, but a petasus,[1] yea, I swear it by the splendid youth himself, Antiochus would be Love, and Love, on the other hand, Antiochus.

79.—ANONYMOUS

ANTIPATER kissed me when my love was on the wane, and set ablaze again the fire from the cold ash. So against my will I twice encountered one flame. Away, ye who are like to be love-sick, lest touching those near me I burn them.

80.—MELEAGER

SORE weeping soul, why is Love's wound that was assuaged inflamed again in thy vitals? No, No! for

---

[1] The *chlamys* and *petasus* (a broad-brimmed hat) were the costume of the *ephebi* (youths of seventeen to twenty).

μή, μή, πρὸς σὲ Διός, μή, πρὸς Διός, ὦ φιλάβουλε,
  κινήσῃς τέφρῃ πῦρ ὑπολαμπόμενον.
αὐτίκα γάρ, λήθαργε κακῶν, πάλιν εἴ σε φυγοῦσαν   5
  λήψετ᾽ Ἔρως, εὑρὼν δραπέτιν αἰκίσεται.

81.—ΤΟΥ ΑΥΤΟΥ

Ψυχαπάται δυσέρωτες, ὅσοι φλόγα τὰν φιλόπαιδα
  οἴδατε, τοῦ πικροῦ γευσάμενοι μέλιτος,
ψυχρὸν ὕδωρ †νίψαι,[1] ψυχρόν, τάχος, ἄρτι τακείσης
  ἐκ χιόνος τῇ ᾽μῇ χεῖτε περὶ κραδίῃ·
ἦ γὰρ ἰδεῖν ἔτλην Διονύσιον. ἀλλ᾽, ὁμόδουλοι,   5
  πρὶν ψαῦσαι σπλάγχνων, πῦρ ἀπ᾽ ἐμεῦ σβέσατε.

82.—ΤΟΥ ΑΥΤΟΥ

Ἔσπευδον τὸν Ἔρωτα φυγεῖν· ὁ δὲ βαιὸν ἀνάψας
  φανίον ἐκ τέφρης, εὗρέ με κρυπτόμενον·
κυκλώσας δ᾽ οὐ τόξα, χερὸς δ᾽ ἀκρώνυχα δισσόν,
  κνίσμα πυρὸς θραύσας, εἰς μὲ λαθὼν ἔβαλεν·
ἐκ δὲ φλόγες πάντη μοι ἐπέδραμον. ὦ βραχὺ
  φέγγος   5
λάμψαν ἐμοὶ μέγα πῦρ, Φανίον, ἐν κραδίᾳ.

83.—ΤΟΥ ΑΥΤΟΥ

Οὔ μ᾽ ἔτρωσεν Ἔρως τόξοις, οὐ λαμπάδ᾽ ἀνάψας,
  ὡς πάρος, αἰθομέναν θῆκεν ὑπὸ κραδίᾳ·
σύγκωμον δὲ Πόθοισι φέρων Κύπριδος μυροφεγγὲς
  φανίον, ἄκρον ἐμοῖς ὄμμασι πῦρ ἔβαλεν·
ἐκ δέ με φέγγος ἔτηξε. τὸ δὲ βραχὺ φανίον ὤφθη   5
  πῦρ ψυχῆς τῇ ᾽μῇ καιόμενον κραδίᾳ.

---

[1] Possibly νιφάδα, snow.

320

God's sake, No! For God's sake, O thou lover of unwisdom, stir not the fire that yet glows under the ashes! For straightway, O unmindful of past woe, if Love catch thee again, he shall vilely use the truant he has found.

81.—By the Same

Love-sick deceivers of your souls, ye who know the flame of lads' love, having tasted the bitter honey, pour about my heart cold water, cold, and quickly, water from new-melted snow. For I have dared to look on Dionysius. But, fellow-slaves, ere it reach my vitals, put the fire in me out.

82.—By the Same

I made haste to escape from Love; but he, lighting a little torch from the ashes, found me in hiding. He bent not his bow, but the tips of his thumb and finger, and breaking off a pinch of fire secretly threw it at me. And from thence the flames rose about me on all sides. O Phanion,[1] little light that set ablaze in my heart a great fire.

83.—By the Same

Eros wounded me not with his arrows, nor as erst lighting his torch did he hold it blazing under my heart; but bringing the little torch of Cypris with scented flame, the companion of the Loves in their revels, he struck my eyes with the tip of its flame. The flame has utterly consumed me, and that little torch proved to be a fire of the soul burning in my heart.

[1] In this and the following epigram he plays on her name, which means a little torch.

84.—ΤΟΥ ΑΥΤΟΥ

Ὤνθρωποι, βωθεῖτε· τὸν ἐκ πελάγευς ἐπὶ γαῖαν
ἄρτι με πρωτόπλουν ἴχνος ἐρειδόμενον
ἕλκει τῇδ᾽ ὁ βίαιος Ἔρως· φλόγα δ᾽ οἷα προφαίνων
παιδὸς †ἀπεστρέπτει[1] κάλλος ἐραστὸν ἰδεῖν.
βαίνω δ᾽ ἴχνος ἐπ᾽ ἴχνος, ἐν ἀέρι δ᾽ ἡδὺ τυπωθὲν   5
εἶδος ἀφαρπάζων χείλεσιν ἡδὺ φιλῶ.
ἀρά γε τὴν πικρὰν προφυγὼν ἅλα, πουλύ τι κείνης
πικρότερον χέρσῳ κῦμα περῶ Κύπριδος;

85.—ΤΟΥ ΑΥΤΟΥ

Οἰνοπόται δέξασθε τὸν ἐκ πελάγευς, ἅμα πόντον
καὶ κλῶπας προφυγόντ᾽, ἐν χθονὶ δ᾽ ὀλλύμενον.
ἄρτι γὰρ ἐκ νηός με μόνον πόδα θέντ᾽ ἐπὶ γαῖαν
ἀγρεύσας ἕλκει τῇδ᾽ ὁ βίαιος Ἔρως,
ἐνθάδ᾽ ὅπου τὸν παῖδα διαστείχοντ᾽ ἐνόησα·   5
αὐτομάτοις δ᾽ ἄκων ποσσὶ ταχὺς φέρομαι.
κωμάζω δ᾽ οὐκ οἶνον ὑπὸ φρένα, πῦρ δὲ γεμισθείς.
ἀλλὰ φίλοι, ξεῖνοι, βαιὸν ἐπαρκέσατε,
ἀρκέσατ᾽, ὦ ξεῖνοι, κἀμὲ Ξενίου πρὸς Ἔρωτος
δέξασθ᾽ ὀλλύμενον τὸν φιλίας ἱκέτην.   10

86.—ΤΟΥ ΑΥΤΟΥ

Ἁ Κύπρις θήλεια γυναικομανῆ φλόγα βάλλει·
ἄρσενα δ᾽ αὐτὸς Ἔρως ἵμερον ἀνιοχεῖ.
ποῖ ῥέψω; ποτὶ παῖδ᾽ ἢ ματέρα; φαμὶ δὲ καὐτὰν
Κύπριν ἐρεῖν· "Νικᾷ τὸ θρασὺ παιδάριον."

---

[1] I conjecture ἐπέστρεψεν and render so.

84.—By the Same

SAVE me, good sirs! No sooner, saved from the sea, have I set foot on land, fresh from my first voyage, than Love drags me here by force, and as if bearing a torch in front of me, turns me to look on the loveliness of a boy. I tread in his footing, and seizing on his sweet image, formed in air, I kiss it sweetly with my lips. Have I then escaped the briny sea but to cross on land the flood of Cypris that is far more bitter?

85.—By the Same

RECEIVE me, ye carousers, the newly landed, escaped from the sea and from robbers, but perishing on land. For now just as, leaving the ship, I had but set my foot on the earth, violent Love caught me and drags me here, here where I saw the boy go through the gate; and albeit I would not I am borne hither swiftly by my feet moving of their own will. I come thus as a reveller filled with fire about my spirit, not with wine. But, dear strangers, help me a little, help me, strangers, and for the sake of Love the Hospitable[1] receive me who, nigh to death, supplicate for friendship.

86.—By the Same

IT is Cypris, a woman, who casts at us the fire of passion for women, but Love himself rules over desire for males. Whither shall I incline, to the boy or to his mother? I tell you for sure that even Cypris herself will say, "The bold brat wins."

---

[1] The title *Xenius* (Protector of strangers) was proper to Zeus. Meleager transfers it to Love.

87.—ΑΔΗΛΟΝ

Τλῆμον Ἔρως, οὐ θῆλυν ἐμοὶ πόθον, ἀλλά τιν' αἰεὶ
 δινεύεις στεροπὴν καύματος ἀρσενικοῦ.
ἄλλοτε γὰρ Δήμωνι πυρούμενος, ἄλλοτε λεύσσων
 Ἰσμηνόν, δολιχοὺς αἰὲν ἔχω καμάτους.
οὐ μούνοις δ' ἐπὶ τοῖσι δεδόρκαμεν· ἀλλ' ἐπιπάντων   5
 ἄρκυσι πουλυμανῆ κανθὸν ἐφελκόμεθα.

88.—ΑΔΗΛΟΝ

Δισσοί με τρύχουσι καταιγίζοντες ἔρωτες,
 Εὔμαχε, καὶ δισσαῖς ἐνδέδεμαι μανίαις·
ἦ μὲν ἐπ' Ἀσάνδρου κλίνω δέμας, ἦ δὲ πάλιν μοι
 ὀφθαλμὸς νεύει Τηλέφου ὀξύτερος.
τμήξατ', ἐμοὶ τοῦθ' ἡδύ, καὶ εἰς πλάστιγγα δικαίην   5
 νειμάμενοι, κλήρῳ τἀμὰ φέρεσθε μέλη.

89.—ΑΔΗΛΟΝ

Κύπρι, τί μοι τρισσοὺς ἐφ' ἕνα σκοπὸν ἤλασας ἰούς,
 ἐν δὲ μιῇ ψυχῇ τρισσὰ πέπηγε βέλη;
καὶ τῇ μὲν φλέγομαι, τῇ δ' ἕλκομαι· ἦ δ' ἀπονεύσω,
 διστάζω, λάβρῳ δ' ἐν πυρὶ πᾶς φλέγομαι.

90.—ΑΔΗΛΟΝ

Οὐκέτ' ἐρῶ.   πεπάλαικα πόθοις τρισίν· εἰς μὲν
  ἑταίρης,
εἰς δέ με παρθενικῆς, εἰς δέ μ' ἔκαυσε νέου·
καὶ κατὰ πᾶν ἤλγηκα. γεγύμνασμαι μέν, ἑταίρης
 πείθων τὰς ἐχθρὰς οὐδὲν ἔχοντι θύρας·

87.—Anonymous

Persistent Love, thou ever whirlest at me no desire for woman, but the lightning of burning longing for males. Now burnt by Damon, now looking on Ismenus, I ever suffer long pain. And not only on these have I looked, but my eye, ever madly roving, is dragged into the nets of all alike.

88.—Anonymous

Two loves, descending on me like the tempest, consume me, Eumachus, and I am caught in the toils of two furious passions. On this side I bend towards Asander, and on that again my eye, waxing keener, turns to Telephus. Cut me in two, I should love that, and dividing the halves in a just balance, carry off my limbs, each of you, as the lot decides.

89.—Anonymous

Cypris, why at one target hast thou shot three arrows, why are three barbs buried in one soul? On this side I am burning, on the other I am being dragged; I am all at a loss which way to turn, and in the furious fire I burn away utterly.

90.—Anonymous

No longer do I love. I have wrestled with three passions that burn: one for a courtesan, one for a maiden, and one for a lad. And in every way I suffer pain. For I have been sore exercised, seeking to persuade the courtesan's doors to open, the foes of

ἔστρωμαι δὲ κόρης ἐπὶ παστάδος αἰὲν ἄϋπνος,   5
  ἐν τὸ ποθεινότατον παιδὶ φίλημα διδούς.
οἴμοι· πῶς εἴπω πῦρ τὸ τρίτον; ἐκ γὰρ ἐκείνου
  βλέμματα καὶ κενεὰς ἐλπίδας οἶδα μόνον.

91.—ΠΟΛΥΣΤΡΑΤΟΥ

Δισσὸς Ἔρως αἴθει ψυχὴν μίαν. ὦ τὰ περισσὰ
  ὀφθαλμοὶ πάντη πάντα κατοσσόμενοι,
εἴδετε τὸν χρυσέαισι περίσκεπτον χαρίτεσσιν
  Ἀντίοχον, λιπαρῶν ἄνθεμον ἠϊθέων.
ἀρκείτω· τί τὸν ἡδὺν ἐπηυγάσσασθε καὶ ἁβρὸν   5
  Στασικράτη, Παφίης ἔρνος ἰοστεφάνου;
καίεσθε, τρύχεσθε, καταφλέχθητέ ποτ' ἤδη·
  οἱ δύο γὰρ ψυχὴν οὐκ ἂν ἕλοιτε μίαν.

92.—ΜΕΛΕΑΓΡΟΥ

Ὦ προδόται ψυχῆς, παίδων κύνες, αἰὲν ἐν ἰξῷ
  Κύπριδος ὀφθαλμοὶ βλέμματα χριόμενοι,
ἡρπάσατ' ἄλλον Ἔρωτ', ἄρνες λύκον, οἷα κορώνη
  σκορπίον, ὡς τέφρη πῦρ ὑποθαλπόμενον.
δρᾶθ' ὅ τι καὶ βούλεσθε. τί μοι νενοτισμένα χεῖτε   5
  δάκρυα, πρὸς δ' Ἱκέτην αὐτομολεῖτε τάχος;
ὀπτᾶσθ' ἐν κάλλει, τύφεσθ' ὑποκαόμενοι νῦν,
  ἄκρος ἐπεὶ ψυχῆς ἐστὶ μάγειρος Ἔρως.

93.—ΡΙΑΝΟΥ

Οἱ παῖδες λαβύρινθος ἀνέξοδος· ᾖ γὰρ ἂν ὄμμα
  ῥίψῃς, ὡς ἰξῷ τοῦτο προσαμπέχεται.

---

[1] This seems to be the meaning ; had he wished to say he
had kissed her once only he must have used the aorist.

him who has nothing, and again ever sleepless I make
my bed on the girl's couch, giving the child but one
thing and that most desirable, kisses.[1] Alack! how
shall I tell of the third flame? For from that I have
gained naught but glances and empty hopes.

91 —POLYSTRATUS

A DOUBLE love burns one heart. O eyes that cast
yourselves in every direction on everything that ye
need not, ye looked on Antiochus, conspicuous by his
golden charm, the flower of our brilliant youth. It
should be enough. Why did ye gaze on sweet and
tender Stasicrates, the sapling of violet-crowned
Aphrodite? Take fire, consume, be burnt up once
for all; for the two of you could never win one
heart.[2]

92.—MELEAGER

O EYES, betrayers of the soul, boy-hunting hounds,
your glances ever smeared with Cypris' bird-lime, ye
have seized on another Love, like sheep catching a
wolf, or a crow a scorpion, or the ash the fire that
smoulders beneath it. Do even what ye will. Why
do you shed showers of tears and straight run off
again to Hiketas? Roast yourselves in beauty, con-
sume away now over the fire, for Love is an admirable
cook of the soul.

93.—RHIANUS

Boys are a labyrinth from which there is no way
out; for wherever thou castest thine eye it is fast

---

[2] This last line seems to me obscure, as the heart, to judge
from line 1, must be his own, not that of the beloved.

τῇ μὲν γὰρ Θεόδωρος ἄγει ποτὶ πίονα σαρκὸς
　ἀκμὴν καὶ γυίων ἄνθος ἀκηράσιον·
τῇ δὲ Φιλοκλῆος χρύσεον ῥέθος, ὃς τὸ καθ' ὕψος　　5
　οὐ μέγας, οὐρανίῃ δ' ἀμφιτέθηλε χάρις.
ἢν δ' ἐπὶ Λεπτίνεω στρέψῃς δέμας, οὐκέτι γυῖα
　κινήσεις, ἀλύτῳ δ' ὡς ἀδάμαντι μενεῖς
ἴχνια κολληθείς· τοῖον σέλας ὄμμασιν αἴθει
　κοῦρος καὶ νεάτους ἐκ κορυφῆς ὄνυχας.　　　　　10
χαίρετε καλοὶ παῖδες, ἐς ἀκμαίην δὲ μόλοιτε
　ἥβην, καὶ λευκὴν ἀμφιέσαισθε κόμην.

94.—ΜΕΛΕΑΓΡΟΥ

Τερπνὸς μὲν Διόδωρος, ἐν ὄμμασι δ' Ἡράκλειτος,
　ἡδυεπὴς δὲ Δίων, ὀσφύϊ δ' Οὐλιάδης.
ἀλλὰ σὺ μὲν ψαύοις ἁπαλόχροος, ᾧ δέ, Φιλόκλεις,
　ἔμβλεπε, τῷ δὲ λάλει, τὸν δὲ . . . τὸ λειπόμενον·
ὡς γνῷς οἷος ἐμὸς νόος ἄφθονος· ἢν δὲ Μυΐσκῳ　5
　λίχνος ἐπιβλέψῃς, μηκέτ' ἴδοις τὸ καλόν.

95.—ΤΟΥ ΑΥΤΟΥ

Εἴ σε Πόθοι στέργουσι, Φιλόκλεες, ἥ τε μυρόπνους
　Πειθώ, καὶ κάλλευς ἀνθολόγοι Χάριτες,
ἀγκὰς ἔχοις Διόδωρον, ὁ δὲ γλυκὺς ἀντίος ᾄδοι
　Δωρόθεος, κείσθω δ' εἰς γόνυ Καλλικράτης,
ἰαίνοι δὲ Δίων τόδ' εὔστοχον ἐν χερὶ τείνων　　　5
　σὸν κέρας, Οὐλιάδης δ' αὐτὸ περισκυθίσαι,
δοίη δ' ἡδὺ φίλημα Φίλων, Θήρων δὲ λαλῆσαι,
　θλίβοις δ' Εὐδήμου τιτθὸν ὑπὸ χλαμύδι.

entangled as if by bird-lime. Here Theodorus attracts
thee to the plump ripeness of his flesh and the un-
adulterate bloom of his limbs, and there it is the
golden face of Philocles, who is not great in stature,
but heavenly grace environs him. But if thou turnest
to look on Leptines thou shalt no more move thy
limbs, but shalt remain, thy steps glued as if by in-
dissoluble adamant; such a flame hath the boy in his
eyes to set thee afire from thy head to thy toe and
finger tips. All hail, beautiful boys! May ye come
to the prime of youth and live till grey hair clothe
your heads.

94.—MELEAGER

DELIGHTFUL is Diodorus and the eyes of all are on
Heraclitus, Dion is sweet-spoken, and Uliades has
lovely loins. But, Philocles, touch the delicate-skinned
one, and look on the next and speak to the third,
and for the fourth—etcetera; so that thou mayst see
how free from envy my mind is. But if thou cast
greedy eyes on Myiscus, mayst thou never see beauty
again.

95.—BY THE SAME

PHILOCLES, if thou art beloved by the Loves and
sweet-breathed Peitho, and the Graces that gather
a nosegay of beauty, mayst thou have thy arm round
Diodorus, may sweet Dorotheus stand before thee
and sing, may Callicrates lie on thy knee. May Dio
warm this your horn (that hits its target well),
stretching it out in his hand, may Uliades peel it, may
Philo give you a sweet kiss, may Theron chatter
away, and may you press Eudemus' breast under his

329

εἰ γάρ σοι τάδε τερπνὰ πόροι θεός, ὦ μάκαρ, οἵαν
ἀρτύσεις παίδων Ῥωμαϊκὴν λοπάδα.　　　　　　10

96.—ΑΔΗΛΟΝ

Οὔτι μάταν θνατοῖσι φάτις τοιάδε βοᾶται,
ὡς " οὐ πάντα θεοὶ πᾶσιν ἔδωκαν ἔχειν."
εἶδος μὲν γὰρ ἄμωμον, ἐπ᾽ ὄμμασι δ᾽ ἁ περίσαμος
αἰδώς, καὶ στέρνοις ἀμφιτέθαλε χάρις,
οἷσι καὶ ἠϊθέους ἐπιδάμνασαι· ἀλλ᾽ ἐπὶ ποσσὶν　　5
οὐκέτι τὰν αὐτὰν δῶκαν ἔχειν σε χάριν.
πλὴν κρηπὶς κρύψει ποδὸς ἴχνιον, ὠγαθὲ Πύρρε,
κάλλεϊ δὲ σφετέρῳ τέρψει ἀγαλλόμενον.

97.—ΑΝΤΙΠΑΤΡΟΥ

Εὐπάλαμος ξανθὸν μὲν ἐρεύθεται, ἶσον Ἔρωτι,
μέσφα ποτὶ Κρητῶν ποιμένα Μηριόνην·
ἐκ δέ νυ Μηριόνεω Ποδαλείριος οὐκέτ᾽ ἐς Ἠὼ
νεῖται· ἴδ᾽ ὡς φθονερὰ παγγενέτειρα φύσις.
εἰ γὰρ τῷ τά τ᾽ ἔνερθε τά θ᾽ ὑψόθεν ἶσα πέλοιτο,　　5
ἦν ἂν Ἀχιλλῆος φέρτερος Αἰακίδεω.

98.—ΠΟΣΕΙΔΙΠΠΟΥ

Τὸν Μουσῶν τέττιγα Πόθος δήσας ἐπ᾽ ἀκάνθαις
κοιμίζειν ἐθέλει, πῦρ ὑπὸ πλευρὰ βαλών·
ἡ δὲ πρὶν ἐν βίβλοις πεπονημένη ἄλλ᾽ ἀθερίζει
ψυχή, ἀνιηρῷ δαίμονι μεμφομένη.

---

[1] I gather that a " Roman platter " was a large dish containing various *hors-d'œuvres*, and not an elaborate made dish, but I find no information in dictionaries. One might render "frittura Romana," a mixed dish familiar to those who know Roman cookery.

cloak. For if God were to grant thee all these delights, blessed man, what a Roman salad[1] of boys wouldst thou dress.

96.—ANONYMOUS

NOT in vain is this saying bruited among mortals, "The gods have not granted everything to every-one." Faultless is thy form, in thy eyes is illustrious modesty, and the bloom of grace is on thy bosom. And with all these gifts thou vanquishest the young men; but the gods did not grant to thee to have the same grace in thy feet. But, good Pyrrhus, this boot shall hide thy foot[2] and give joy to thee, proud of its beauty.[3]

97.—ANTIPATER

EUPALAMUS is ruddy red like Love, as far as Meriones,[4] the captain of the Cretans; but from Meriones onwards Podaleirius no longer goes back to the Dawn: see how envious Nature, the universal mother, is. For if his lower parts were equal to his upper he would excel Achilles, the grandson of Aeacus.

98.—POSIDIPPUS

LOVE, tying down the Muses' cicada[5] on a bed of thorns, would lull it there, holding fire[6] under its sides. But the Soul, sore tried of old amid books, makes light of other pain, yet upbraids the ruthless god.

[2] Literally, "the step of thy foot," indicating that the malformation was in the actual foot, not, e.g. in the ankle.

[3] The verses seem to have been sent with a present of a pair of ornamental boots.

[4] He means his thighs (*meros*). In line 5 there is a play on Podaleirius, "lily-footed," and so pale and unlike the rosy dawn, but the joke is obscure.

[5] The poet's soul.   [6] i.e. a torch.

99.—ΑΔΗΛΟΝ

Ἠγρεύθην ὑπ' Ἔρωτος ὁ μηδ' ὄναρ, οὐδ' ἔμαθον πῦρ
  ἄρσεν[1] ποιμαίνειν θερμὸν ὑπὸ κραδίας,
ἠγρεύθην. ἀλλ' οὔ με κακῶν πόθος, ἀλλ' ἀκέραιον
  σύντροφον αἰσχύνῃ βλέμμα κατηνθράκισεν.
τηκέσθω Μουσέων ὁ πολὺς πόνος· ἐν πυρὶ γὰρ νοῦς 5
  βέβληται, γλυκερῆς ἄχθος ἔχων ὀδύνης.

100.—ΑΔΗΛΟΝ

Εἰς οἵων με πόθων λιμένα ξένον, ὦ Κύπρι, θεῖσα
  οὐκ ἐλεεῖς, καὐτὴ πεῖραν ἔχουσα πόνων;
ἢ μ' ἐθέλεις ἄτλητα παθεῖν καὶ τοῦτ' ἔπος εἰπεῖν,
  "Τὸν σοφὸν ἐν Μούσαις Κύπρις ἔτρωσε μόνη";

101.—ΜΕΛΕΑΓΡΟΥ

Τόν με Πόθοις ἄτρωτον ὑπὸ στέρνοισι Μυΐσκος
  ὄμμασι τοξεύσας, τοῦτ' ἐβόησεν ἔπος·
"Τὸν θρασὺν εἷλον ἐγώ· τὸ δ' ἐπ' ὀφρύσι κεῖνο
  φρύαγμα
σκηπτροφόρου σοφίας ἠνίδε ποσσὶ πατῶ."
τῷ δ', ὅσον ἀμπνεύσας, τόδ' ἔφην· "Φίλε κοῦρε,
  τί θαμβεῖς; 5
καὐτὸν ἀπ' Οὐλύμπου Ζῆνα καθεῖλεν Ἔρως."

102.—ΚΑΛΛΙΜΑΧΟΥ

Ὡγρευτής, Ἐπίκυδες, ἐν οὔρεσι πάντα λαγωὸν
  διφᾷ, καὶ πάσης ἴχνια δορκαλίδος,

[1] I write πῦρ ἄρσεν : περ ἄρσενα MS.

99.—Anonymous

I am caught by Love, I who had never dreamt it,
and never had I learnt to feed a male flame hot
beneath my heart. I am caught. Yet it was no
longing for evil, but a pure glance, foster-brother of
modesty, that burnt me to ashes. Let it consume
away, the long labour of the Muses; for my mind is
cast in the fire, bearing the burden of a sweet pain.

100.—Anonymous

To what strange haven of desire hast thou brought
me, Cypris, and pitiest me not, although thou thyself
hast experience of the pain? Is it thy will that I
should suffer the unbearable and speak this word,
"Cypris alone has wounded the man wise in the
Muses' lore"?

101.—MELEAGER

Myiscus, shooting me, whom the Loves could not
wound, under the breast with his eyes, shouted out
thus: "It is I who have struck him down, the over-
bold, and see how I tread underfoot the arrogance
of sceptred wisdom that sat on his brow." But I,
just gathering breath enough, said to him, "Dear
boy, why art thou astonished? Love brought down
Zeus himself from Olympus."

102.—CALLIMACHUS

The huntsman on the hills, Epicydes, tracks every
hare and the slot of every hind through the frost

στίβη καὶ νιφετῷ κεχρημένος.   ἦν δέ τις εἴπῃ,
" Τῆ, τόδε βέβληται θηρίον," οὐκ ἔλαβεν.
χοὐμὸς ἔρως τοιόσδε· τὰ μὲν φεύγοντα διώκειν   5
οἶδε, τὰ δ' ἐν μέσσῳ κείμενα παρπέταται.

103.—ΑΔΗΛΟΝ

Οἶδα φιλεῖν φιλέοντας· ἐπίσταμαι, ἤν μ' ἀδικῇ τις,
μισεῖν· ἀμφοτέρων εἰμὶ γὰρ οὐκ ἀδαής.

104.—ΑΔΗΛΟΝ

Οὑμὸς ἔρως παρ' ἐμοὶ μενέτω μόνον· ἢν δὲ πρὸς ἄλλου
φοιτήσῃ, μισῶ κοινὸν ἔρωτα, Κύπρι.

105.—ΑΣΚΛΗΠΙΑΔΟΥ

Μικρὸς Ἔρως ἐκ μητρὸς ἔτ' εὐθήρατος ἀποπτάς,
ἐξ οἴκων ὑψοῦ Δάμιδος οὐ πέτομαι·
ἀλλ' αὐτοῦ, φιλέων τε καὶ ἀζήλωτα φιληθείς,
οὐ πολλοῖς, εὐκρὰς δ' εἷς ἑνὶ συμφέρομαι.

106.—ΜΕΛΕΑΓΡΟΥ

Ἓν καλὸν οἶδα τὸ πᾶν, ἕν μοι μόνον οἶδε τὸ λίχνον
ὄμμα, Μυΐσκον ὁρᾶν· τἆλλα δὲ τυφλὸς ἐγώ.
πάντα δ' ἐκεῖνος ἐμοὶ φαντάζεται· ἆρ' ἐσορῶσιν
ὀφθαλμοὶ ψυχῇ πρὸς χάριν, οἱ κόλακες;

107.—ΑΔΗΛΟΝ

Τὸν καλόν, ὦ Χάριτες, Διονύσιον, εἰ μὲν ἕλοιτο
τἀμά, καὶ εἰς ὥρας αὖθις ἄγοιτε καλόν·

and snow. But if one say to him, "Look, here is a beast lying wounded," he will not take it. And even so is my love; it is wont to pursue the fleeing game,[1] but flies past what lies in its path.

103.—ANONYMOUS

I KNOW well to love them who love me, and I know to hate him who wrongs me, for I am not unversed in both.

104.—ANONYMOUS

LET my love abide with me alone; but if it visit others, I hate, Cypris, a love that is shared.

105.—ASCLEPIADES

I AM a little love that flew away, still easy to catch, from my mother's nest, but from the house of Damis I fly not away on high; but here, loving and beloved without a rival, I keep company not with many, but with one in happy union.

106.—MELEAGER

I KNOW but one beauty in the world; my greedy eye knows but one thing, to look on Myiscus, and for all else I am blind. He represents everything to me. Is it just on what will please the soul that the eyes look, the flatterers?

107.—ANONYMOUS

YE Graces, if lovely Dionysius' choice be for me, lead him on as now from season to season in ever-

---

[1] Horace, *Sat.* i. 2, 105 *seq.*

εἰ δ᾽ ἕτερον στέρξειε παρεὶς ἐμέ, μύρτον ἕωλον
ἐρρίφθω ξηροῖς φυρόμενον σκυβάλοις.

108.—ΔΙΟΝΥΣΙΟΥ

Εἰ μὲν ἐμὲ στέρξεις, εἴης ἰσόμοιρος, Ἄκρατε,
Χίῳ, καὶ Χίου πουλὺ μελιχρότερος·
εἰ δ᾽ ἕτερον κρίναις ἐμέθεν πλέον, ἀμφὶ σὲ βαίη
κώνωψ ὀξηρῷ τυφόμενος κεράμῳ.

109.—ΜΕΛΕΑΓΡΟΥ

Ὁ τρυφερὸς Διόδωρος ἐς ἠϊθέους φλόγα βάλλων
ἤγρευται λαμυροῖς ὄμμασι Τιμαρίου,
τὸ γλυκύπικρον Ἔρωτος ἔχων βέλος. ἦ τόδε καινὸν
θάμβος ὁρῶ· φλέγεται πῦρ πυρὶ καιόμενον.

110.—ΤΟΥ ΑΥΤΟΥ

Ἤστραψε γλυκὺ κάλλος· ἰδοὺ φλόγας ὄμμασι βάλλει.
ἆρα κεραυνομάχαν παῖδ᾽ ἀνέδειξεν Ἔρως;
χαῖρε Πόθων ἀκτῖνα φέρων θνατοῖσι, Μυΐσκε,
καὶ λάμποις ἐπὶ γᾷ πυρσὸς ἐμοὶ φίλιος.

111.—ΑΔΗΛΟΝ

Πτανὸς Ἔρως, σὺ δὲ ποσσὶ ταχύς· τὸ δὲ κάλλος ὁμοῖο
ἀμφοτέρων. τόξοις, Εὔβιε, λειπόμεθα.

112.—ΑΔΗΛΟΝ

Εὐφαμεῖτε νέοι· τὸν Ἔρωτ᾽ ἄγει Ἀρκεσίλαος,
πορφυρέῃ δήσας Κύπριδος ἁρπεδόνῃ.

renewed beauty, but if, passing me over, he love another, let him be cast out like a stale myrtle-berry mixed with the dry sweepings.

108.—DIONYSIUS

IF thou lovest me, Acratus,[1] mayest thou be ranked with Chian wine, yea and even more honey-sweet; but if thou preferest another to me, let the gnats buzz about thee as in the fume of a jar of vinegar.

109.—MELEAGER

DELICATE Diodorus, casting fire at the young men, has been caught by Timarion's wanton eyes, and bears, fixed in him, the bitter-sweet dart of Love. Verily this is a new miracle I see; fire is ablaze, burnt by fire.

110.—BY THE SAME

IT lightened sweet beauty; see how he flasheth flame from his eyes. Hath Love produced a boy armed with the bolt of heaven? Hail! Myiscus, who bringest to mortals the fire of the Loves, and mayest thou shine on earth, a torch befriending me.

111.—ANONYMOUS

WINGED is Love and thou art swift of foot, and the beauty of both is equal. We are only second to him, Eubius, because we have no bow and arrows.

112.—ANONYMOUS

SILENCE, ye young men; Arcesilaus is leading Love hither, having bound him with the purple cord of Cypris.

---

[1] The name means " unwatered wine."

113.—ΜΕΛΕΑΓΡΟΤ

Καὐτὸς Ἔρως ὁ πτανὸς ἐν αἰθέρι δέσμιος ἧλω,
ἀγρευθεὶς τοῖς σοῖς ὄμμασι, Τιμάριον.

114.—ΤΟΥ ΑΥΤΟΥ

Ἠοῦς ἄγγελε, χαῖρε, Φαεσφόρε, καὶ ταχὺς ἔλθοις
Ἔσπερος, ἣν ἀπάγεις, λάθριος αὖθις ἄγων.

115.—ΑΔΗΛΟΝ

Ἄκρητον μανίην ἔπιον· μεθύων μέγα μύθοις
ὥπλισμαι πολλὴν εἰς ὁδὸν ἀφροσύναν.
κωμάσομαι· τί δέ μοι βροντέων μέλει, ἢ τί κεραυνῶν;
ἢν βάλλῃ, τὸν ἔρωθ᾽ ὅπλον ἄτρωτον ἔχων.

116.—ΑΔΗΛΟΝ

Κωμάσομαι· μεθύω γὰρ ὅλος μέγα. παῖ, λάβε τοῦτον
τὸν στέφανον, τὸν ἐμοῖς δάκρυσι λουόμενον·
μακρὴν δ᾽ οὐχὶ μάτην ὁδὸν ἵξομαι· ἔστι δ᾽ ἀωρὶ
καὶ σκότος· ἀλλὰ μέγας φανὸς ἐμοὶ Θεμίσων.

117.—ΜΕΛΕΑΓΡΟΤ

Βεβλήσθω κύβος· ἅπτε· πορεύσομαι. Ἠνίδε, τόλμα,
οἰνοβαρές. Τίν᾽ ἔχεις φροντίδα; κωμάσομαι.[1]
κωμάσομαι; Ποῖ, θυμέ, τρέπῃ; Τί δ᾽ ἔρωτι λογισμός;
ἅπτε τάχος. Ποῦ δ᾽ ἡ πρόσθε λόγων μελέτη;

[1] I slightly alter the received punctuation in this line.

113.—MELEAGER

EVEN Love himself, the winged, hath been made captive in the air, taken by thy eyes, Timarion.

114.—BY THE SAME

STAR of the Morning, hail, thou herald of dawn! and mayest thou quickly come again, as the Star of Eve, bringing again in secret her whom thou takest away.

115.—ANONYMOUS

I HAVE quaffed untempered madness, and all drunk with words I have armed myself with much frenzy for the way. I will march with music to her door, and what care I for God's thunder and what for his bolts, I who, if he cast them, carry love as an impenetrable shield?

116.—ANONYMOUS

I WILL go to serenade him, for I am, all of me, mighty drunk. Boy, take this wreath that my tears bathe. The way is long, but I shall not go in vain; it is the dead of night and dark, but for me Themison is a great torch.

117.—MELEAGER

" LET the die be cast; light the torch; I will go." " Just look! What daring, heavy with wine as thou art!" " What care besets thee? I will go revelling to her, I will go." " Whither dost thou stray, my mind?" " Doth love take thought? Light up at once." " And where is all thy old study of logic?"

Ἐρρίφθω σοφίας ὁ πολὺς πόνος· ἐν μόνον οἶδα   5
τοῦθ᾽, ὅτι καὶ Ζηνὸς λῆμα καθεῖλεν Ἔρως.

118.—ΚΑΛΛΙΜΑΧΟΥ

Εἰ μὲν ἑκών, Ἀρχῖν᾽, ἐπεκώμασα, μυρία μεμφου·
εἰ δ᾽ ἀέκων ἥκω, τὴν προπέτειαν ὅρα·
ἄκρητος καὶ ἔρως μ᾽ ἠνάγκασαν· ὧν ὁ μὲν αὐτῶν
εἷλκεν, ὁ δ᾽ οὐκ εἴα σώφρονα θυμὸν ἔχειν.
ἐλθὼν δ᾽ οὐκ ἐβόησα, τίς ἢ τίνος, ἀλλ᾽ ἐφίλησα   5
τὴν φλιήν· εἰ τοῦτ᾽ ἔστ᾽ ἀδίκημ᾽, ἀδικῶ.

119.—ΜΕΛΕΑΓΡΟΥ

Οἶσω, ναὶ μὰ σέ, Βάκχε, τὸ σὸν θράσος· ἀγέο, κώμων
ἄρχε· θεὸς θνατὰν ἀνιόχει[1] κραδίαν·
ἐν πυρὶ γενναθεὶς στέργεις φλόγα τὰν ἐν ἔρωτι,
καί με πάλιν δήσας τὸν σὸν ἄγεις ἱκέτην.
ἦ προδότας κἄπιστος ἔφυς· τεὰ δ᾽ ὄργια κρύπτειν   5
αὐδῶν, ἐκφαίνειν τἀμὰ σὺ νῦν ἐθέλεις.

120.—ΠΟΣΕΙΔΙΠΠΟΥ

Εὐοπλῶ, καὶ πρὸς σὲ μαχήσομαι, οὐδ᾽ ἀπερoῦμαι
θνητὸς ἐών· σὺ δ᾽, Ἔρως, μηκέτι μοι πρόσαγε.
ἢν με λάβῃς μεθύοντ᾽, ἄπαγ᾽ ἔκδοτον· ἄχρι δὲ νήφω,
τὸν παραταξάμενον πρὸς σὲ λογισμὸν ἔχω.

[1] I write ἀνιόχει : ἀνιοχεῖ MS.

"**Away** with the long labour of wisdom; this one thing alone I know, that Love brought to naught the high mind of Zeus himself."[1]

118.—CALLIMACHUS

If I came to thee in revel, Archinus, willingly, load me with ten thousand reproaches; but if I am here against my will, consider the vehemence of the cause. Strong wine and love compelled me; one of them pulled me and the other would not let me be sober-minded.   But when I came I did not cry who I was or whose, but I kissed the door-post: if that be a sin, I sinned.

119.—MELEAGER

I shall bear, Bacchus, thy boldness, I swear it by thyself; lead on, begin the revel; thou art a god; govern a mortal heart. Born in the flame, thou lovest the flame love hath, and again leadest me, thy suppliant, in bonds.   Of a truth thou art a traitor and faithless, and while thou biddest us hide thy mysteries, thou wouldst now bring mine to light.

120.—POSIDIPPUS

I am well armed, and will fight with thee and not give in, though I am a mortal.   And thou, Love, come no more against me. If thou findest me drunk, carry me off a prisoner, but as long as I keep sober I have Reason standing in battle array to meet thee.

- The poem is in the form of a dialogue with himself.

121.—ΡΙΑΝΟΥ

Ἦ ῥά νύ τοι, Κλεόνικε, δι᾽ ἀτραπιτοῖο κιόντι
στεινῆς ἤντησαν ταὶ λιπαραὶ Χάριτες·
καί σε ποτὶ ῥοδέαισιν ἐπηχύναντο χέρεσσιν,
κοῦρε; πεποίησαι δ᾽ ἡλίκος ἐσσὶ χάρις.
τηλόθι μοι μάλα χαῖρε· πυρὸς δ᾽ οὐκ ἀσφαλὲς ἆσσον 5
ἕρπειν αὐηρήν, ἃ φίλος, ἀνθέρικα.

122.—ΜΕΛΕΑΓΡΟΥ

Ὦ Χάριτες, τὸν καλὸν Ἀρισταγόρην ἐσιδοῦσαι
ἀντίον, εἰς τρυφερὰς ἠγκαλίσασθε χέρας·
οὕνεκα καὶ μορφᾷ βάλλει φλόγα, καὶ γλυκυμυθεῖ
καίρια, καὶ σιγῶν ὄμμασι τερπνὰ λαλεῖ.
τηλόθι μοι πλάζοιτο. τί δὲ πλέον; ὡς γὰρ Ὀλύμπου 5
Ζεὺς νέον οἶδεν ὁ παῖς μακρὰ κεραυνοβολεῖν.

123.—ΑΔΗΛΟΝ

Πυγμῇ νικήσαντα τὸν Ἀντικλέους Μενέχαρμον
λημνίσκοις μαλακοῖς ἐστεφάνωσα δέκα,
καὶ τρισσῶς ἐφίλησα πεφυρμένον αἵματι πολλῷ·
ἀλλ᾽ ἐμοὶ ἦν σμύρνης κεῖνο μελιχρότερον.

124.—ΑΔΗΛΟΝ, οἱ δὲ ΑΡΤΕΜΩΝΟΣ

Λάθρη παπταίνοντα παρὰ φλιὴν Ἐχέδημον
λάθριος ἀκρήβην τὸν χαρίεντ᾽ ἔκυσα.
δειμαίνω·[1] καὶ γάρ μοι ἐνύπνιος ἦλθε φαρέτρην
αἰωρῶν,[2] καὶ δοὺς ὤχετ᾽ ἀλεκτρυόνας,

---

[1] I write δειμαίνω : δειμαίνων MS.
[2] I write αἰωρῶν : αἰταίων MS.

121.—RHIANUS

TELL me, Cleonicus, did the bright Graces meet thee walking in a narrow lane and take thee in their rosy arms, dear boy, that thou hast become such a Grace as thou art? From afar I bid thee all hail, but ah! dear, it is not safe for a dry corn-stalk to draw nearer to the fire.

122.—MELEAGER

YE Graces, looking straight on lovely Aristagoras, you took him to the embrace of your soft arms; and therefore he shoots forth flame by his beauty, and discourses sweetly when it is meet, and if he keep silence, his eyes prattle delightfully. Let him stray far away, I pray; but what does that help? For the boy, like Zeus from Olympus, has learnt of late to throw the lightning far.

123.—ANONYMOUS

WHEN Menecharmus, Anticles' son, won the boxing match, I crowned him with ten soft fillets, and thrice I kissed him all dabbled with blood as he was, but the blood was sweeter to me than myrrh.

124.—ARTEMON (?)

As Echedemus was peeping out of his door on the sly, I slyly kissed that charming boy who is just in his prime. Now I am in dread, for he came to me in a dream, bearing a quiver, and departed after giving

ἄλλοτε μειδιόων, ὁτὲ δ᾽ οὐ φίλος.   ἀλλὰ μελισσέων 5
ἑσμοῦ καὶ κνίδης καὶ πυρὸς ἠψάμεθα;

125.—ΜΕΛΕΑΓΡΟΥ

Ἡδύ τί μοι διὰ νυκτὸς ἐνύπνιον ἁβρὰ γελῶντος
ὀκτωκαιδεκέτους παιδὸς ἔτ᾽ ἐν χλαμύδι
ἤγαγ᾽ Ἔρως ὑπὸ χλαῖναν· ἐγὼ δ᾽ ἁπαλῷ περὶ χρωτὶ
στέρνα βαλὼν κενεὰς ἐλπίδας ἐδρεπόμαν.
καί μ᾽ ἔτι νῦν θάλπει μνήμης πόθος· ὄμμασι δ᾽ ὕπνον 5
ἀγρευτὴν πτηνοῦ φάσματος αἰὲν ἔχω.
ὦ δύσερως ψυχή, παῦσαί ποτε καὶ δι᾽ ὀνείρων
εἰδώλοις κάλλευς κωφὰ χλιαινομένη.

126.—ΤΟΥ ΑΥΤΟΥ

Ἦρκταί μευ κραδίας ψαύειν πόνος· ἦ γὰρ ἀλύων
ἀκρονυχεὶ ταύταν ἔκνισ᾽ ὁ θερμὸς Ἔρως·
εἶπε δὲ μειδήσας· "Ἕξεις πάλι τὸ γλυκὺ τραῦμα,[1]
ὦ δύσερως, λάβρῳ καιόμενος μέλιτι."
ἐξ οὗ δὴ νέον ἔρνος ἐν ἠϊθέοις Διόφαντον   5
λεύσσων οὔτε φυγεῖν οὔτε μένειν δύναμαι.

127.—ΤΟΥ ΑΥΤΟΥ

Εἰνόδιον στείχοντα μεσαμβρινὸν εἶδον Ἄλεξιν,
ἄρτι κόμαν καρπῶν κειρομένου θέρεος.
διπλαῖ δ᾽ ἀκτῖνές με κατέφλεγον· αἱ μὲν Ἔρωτος,
παιδὸς ἀπ᾽ ὀφθαλμῶν, αἱ δὲ παρ᾽ ἠελίου.
ἀλλ᾽ ἂς μὲν νὺξ αὖθις ἐκοίμισεν· ἃς δ᾽ ἐν ὀνείροις 5
εἴδωλον μορφῆς μᾶλλον ἀνεφλόγισεν.

[1] γράμμα MS.: corr. Graef.

me fighting cocks,[1] but at one time smiling, at another
with no friendly look.   But have I touched a swarm
of bees, and a nettle, and fire?

125.—MELEAGER

Love in the night brought me under my mantle
the sweet dream of a softly-laughing boy of eighteen,
still wearing the chlamys;[2] and I, pressing his tender
flesh to my breast, culled empty hopes. Still does the
desire of the memory heat me, and in my eyes still
abideth sleep that caught for me in the chase that
winged phantom.   O soul, ill-starred in love, cease
at last even in dreams to be warmed all in vain by
beauty's images.

126.—By the Same

Pain has begun to touch my heart, for hot Love,
as he strayed, scratched it with the tip of his nails,
and, smiling, said, " Again, O unhappy lover, thou
shalt have the sweet wound, burnt by biting honey.''
Since when, seeing among the youths the fresh sap-
ling Diophantus, I can neither fly nor abide.

127.—By the Same

I saw Alexis walking in the road at noon-tide, at
the season when the summer was just being shorn of
the tresses of her fruits ; and double rays burnt me,
the rays of love from the boy's eyes and others from
the sun. The sun's night laid to rest again, but
love's were kindled more in my dreams by the

---

[1] Of doubtful import.   These birds were common presents
of lovers, but to see them in a dream betided quarrels.

[2] See note on No. 78.

λυσίπονος δ' ἑτέροις ἐπ' ἐμοὶ πόνον ὕπνος ἔτευξεν
ἔμπνουν πῦρ ψυχῇ κάλλος ἀπεικονίσας.

128.—ΤΟΥ ΑΥΤΟΥ

Αἰπολικαὶ σύριγγες, ἐν οὔρεσι μηκέτι Δάφνιν
φωνεῖτ', αἰγιβάτῃ Πανὶ χαριζόμεναι·
μηδὲ σὺ τὸν στεφθέντα, λύρη, Φοίβοιο προφῆτι,
δάφνῃ παρθενίῃ μέλψ' Ὑάκινθον ἔτι.
ἦν γὰρ ὅτ' ἦν Δάφνις μὲν Ὀρειάσι,[1] σοὶ δ' Ὑάκινθος   5
τερπνός· νῦν δὲ Πόθων σκῆπτρα Δίων ἐχέτω.

129.—ΑΡΑΤΟΥ

Ἀργεῖος Φιλοκλῆς "Ἄργει " καλός·" αἱ δὲ Κορίνθου
στῆλαι, καὶ Μεγαρέων ταὐτὸ[2] βοῶσι τάφοι·
γέγραπται καὶ μέχρι λοετρῶν Ἀμφιαράου,
ὡς καλός.   ἀλλ' ὀλίγον·[3] γράμμασι λειπόμεθα·
τῷδ' οὐ γὰρ πέτραι ἐπιμάρτυρες, ἀλλὰ 'Ριηνὸς[4]   5
αὐτὸς ἰδών· ἑτέρου δ' ἐστὶ περισσότερος.

130.—ΑΔΗΛΟΝ

Εἶπα, καὶ αὖ πάλιν εἶπα· "Καλός, καλός·" ἀλλ'
    ἔτι φήσω,
ὡς καλός, ὡς χαρίεις ὄμμασι Δωσίθεος.

---

[1] Ὀρειάσι Dilthey : ἐν οὔρεσι MS.
[2] I write ταὐτὸ (I think the correction has been previously made) : ταῦτα MS.
[3] I write ὀλίγον : ὀλίγοι MS.
[4] 'Ριηνός Maas : Πριηνεύς MS. *cp.* No. 93.

phantom of beauty. So sleep, who releases others from toil, brought pain to me, imaging in my soul a loveliness which is living fire.

128.—BY THE SAME

YE pastoral pipes, no longer call on Daphnis in the mountains to please Pan the goat-mounter; and thou, lyre, spokesman of Phoebus, sing no longer of Hyacinthus crowned with maiden laurel. For Daphnis, when there was a Daphnis, was the delight of the Mountain Nymphs, and Hyacinthus was thine; but now let Dion wield the sceptre of the Loves.

129.—ARATUS

PHILOCLES of Argos is "fair"[1] at Argos, and the columns of Corinth and tombstones of Megara announce the same. It is written that he is fair as far as Amphiaraus' Baths.[2] But that is little; they are only letters that beat us.[3] For they are not stones that testify to this Philocles' beauty, but Rhianus, who saw him with his own eyes, and he is superior to the other one.

130.—ANONYMOUS

I SAID and said it again, "He is fair, he is fair," but I will still say it, that Dositheus is fair and has

---

[1] It was the habit to write or cut the name of the beloved, adding the word καλὸs (fair), on stones or trees. See the following epigram.

[2] Near Oropus on the confines of Attica and Boeotia.

[3] *i.e.* it is only the evidence of these inscriptions that is in favour of Philocles of Argos. The evidence of our eyes is in favour of the other

οὐ δρυός, οὐδ' ἐλάτης ἐχαράξαμεν, οὐδ' ἐπὶ τοίχου
τοῦτ' ἔπος· ἀλλ' ἐν ἐμῇ καῦσεν [1] Ἔρως κραδίᾳ.
εἰ δέ τις οὐ φήσει, μὴ πείθεο. ναὶ μὰ σέ, δαῖμον, 5
ψεύδετ'· ἐγὼ δ' ὁ λέγων τἀτρεκὲς οἶδα μόνος.

131.—ΠΟΣΕΙΔΙΠΠΟΥ

Ἁ Κύπρον, ἅ τε Κύθηρα, καὶ ἃ Μίλητον ἐποιχνεῖς
καὶ καλὸν Συρίης ἱπποκρότου δάπεδον,
ἔλθοις ἵλαος Καλλιστίῳ, ἣ τὸν ἐραστὴν
οὐδέ ποτ' οἰκείων ὦσεν ἀπὸ προθύρων.

132.—ΜΕΛΕΑΓΡΟΥ

Οὔ σοι ταῦτ' ἐβόων, ψυχή; "Ναὶ Κύπριν, ἀλώσει,
ὦ δύσερως, ἰξῷ πυκνὰ προσιπταμένη·"
οὐκ ἐβόων; εἷλέν σε πάγη. τί μάτην ἐνὶ δεσμοῖς
σπαίρεις; αὐτὸς Ἔρως τὰ πτερά σου δέδεκεν,
καὶ σ' ἐπὶ πῦρ ἔστησε, μύροις δ' ἔρρανε λιπόπνουν, 5
δῶκε δὲ διψώσῃ δάκρυα θερμὰ πιεῖν.

132ᴀ.—ΤΟΥ ΑΥΤΟΥ

Ἁ ψυχὴ βαρύμοχθε, σὺ δ' ἄρτι μὲν ἐκ πυρὸς αἴθῃ,
ἄρτι δ' ἀναψύχεις, πνεῦμ' ἀναλεξαμένη.
τί κλαίεις; τὸν ἄτεγκτον ὅτ' ἐν κόλποισιν Ἔρωτα
ἔτρεφες, οὐκ ᾔδεις ὡς ἐπὶ σοὶ τρέφετο;
οὐκ ᾔδεις; νῦν γνῶθι καλῶν ἄλλαγμα τροφείων, 5
πῦρ ἅμα καὶ ψυχρὰν δεξαμένη χιόνα.
αὐτὴ ταῦθ' εἵλου· φέρε τὸν πόνον. ἄξια πάσχεις
ὧν ἔδρας, ὀπτῷ καιομένη μέλιτι.

[1] I write καῦσεν : ἴσχετ' MS.

348

lovely eyes. These words we engraved on no oak
or pine, no, nor on a wall, but Love burnt them into
my heart. But if any man deny it, believe him not.
Yea, by thyself, O God, I swear he lies, and I who
say it alone know the truth.

131.—POSIDIPPUS

GODDESS who hauntest Cyprus and Cythera and
Miletus and the fair plain of Syria that echoes to
the tread of horses, come in gracious mood to Cal-
listion, who never repulsed a lover from her door.[1]

132.—MELEAGER

DID I not cry it to thee, my soul, "By Cypris, thou
wilt be taken, O thou love-lorn, that fliest again and
again to the limed bough"? Did I not cry it? And
the snare has caught thee. Why dost thou struggle
vainly in thy bonds? Love himself hath bound thy
wings and set thee on the fire, and sprays thee with
scents when thou faintest, and gives thee when thou
art athirst hot tears to drink.

132A.—BY THE SAME

O SORE-AFFLICTED soul, now thou burnest in the
fire and now thou revivest, recovering thy breath.
Why dost thou weep? When thou didst nurse merci-
less Love in thy bosom knewest thou not that he
was being nursed for thy bane? Didst thou not
know it? Now learn to know the pay of thy good
nursing, receiving from him fire and cold snow there-
with. Thyself thou hast chosen this; bear the pain.
Thou sufferest the due guerdon of what thou hast
done, burnt by his boiling honey.

---

[1] The epigram is a prayer by the courtesan Callistion.

133.—ΤΟΥ ΑΥΤΟΥ

Διψῶν ὡς ἐφίλησα θέρευς ἀπαλόχροα παῖδα,
  εἶπα τότ' αὐχμηρὰν δίψαν ἀποπροφυγών·
" Ζεῦ πάτερ, ἆρα φίλημα τὸ νεκτάρεον Γανυμήδευς
  πίνεις, καὶ τόδε σοι χείλεσιν οἰνοχοεῖ;
καὶ γὰρ ἐγὼ τὸν καλὸν ἐν ἠιθέοισι φιλήσας   5
  Ἀντίοχον, ψυχῆς ἡδὺ πέπωκα μέλι."

134.—ΚΑΛΛΙΜΑΧΟΥ

Ἕλκος ἔχων ὁ ξεῖνος ἐλάνθανεν· ὡς ἀνιηρὸν
  πνεῦμα διὰ στηθέων, εἶδες, ἀνηγάγετο,
τὸ τρίτον ἡνίκ' ἔπινε· τὰ δὲ ῥόδα φυλλοβολεῦντα
  τὢνδρὸς ἀπὸ στεφάνων πάντ' ἐγένοντο χαμαί.
ὤπτηται μέγα δή τι· μὰ δαίμονας, οὐκ ἀπὸ ῥυσμοῦ 5
  εἰκάζω· φωρὸς δ' ἴχνια φὼρ ἔμαθον.

135.—ΑΣΚΛΗΠΙΑΔΟΥ

Οἶνος ἔρωτος ἔλεγχος· ἐρᾶν ἀρνεύμενον ἡμῖν
  ἤτασαν αἱ πολλαὶ Νικαγόρην προπόσεις.
καὶ γὰρ ἐδάκρυσεν καὶ ἐνύστασε, καί τι κατηφὲς
  ἔβλεπε, χὠ σφιγχθεὶς οὐκ ἔμενε στέφανος.

136.—ΑΔΗΛΟΝ

Ὄρνιθες ψίθυροι, τί κεκράγατε; μή μ' ἀνιᾶτε,
  τὸν τρυφερῇ παιδὸς σαρκὶ χλιαινόμενον,
ἑζόμεναι πετάλοισιν ἀηδόνες· εὕδε λάληθρον
  θῆλυ γένος, δέομαι, μείνατ' ἐφ' ἡσυχίης.

133.—By the Same

In summer, when I was athirst, I kissed the tender-fleshed boy and said, when I was free of my parching thirst, "Father Zeus, dost thou drink the nectareous kiss of Ganymede, and is this the wine he tenders to thy lips?" For now that I have kissed Antiochus, fairest of our youth, I have drunk the sweet honey of the soul.

134.—CALLIMACHUS

Our guest has a wound and we knew it not. Sawest thou not with what pain he heaved his breath up from his chest when he drank the third cup? And all the roses, casting their petals, fell on the ground from the man's wreaths. There is something burns him fiercely; by the gods I guess not at random, but a thief myself, I know a thief's footprints.

135.—ASCLEPIADES

Wine is the proof of love. Nicagoras denied to us that he was in love, but those many toasts convicted him. Yes! he shed tears and bent his head, and had a certain downcast look, and the wreath bound tight round his head kept not its place.

136.—Anonymous

Ye chattering birds, why do you clamour? Vex me not, as I lie warmed by the lad's delicate flesh, ye nightingales that sit among the leaves. Sleep, I implore you, ye talkative women-folk;[1] hold your peace.

---

[1] The nightingale was Philomela.

137.—ΜΕΛΕΑΓΡΟΥ

Ὀρθροβόας, δυσέρωτι κακάγγελε, νῦν, τρισάλαστε,
ἐννύχιος κράζεις πλευροτυπῆ κέλαδον,
γαῦρος ὑπὲρ κοίτας, ὅτε μοι βραχὺ τοῦτ' ἔτι νυκτὸς
ζῇ τὸ[1] φιλεῖν, ἐπ' ἐμαῖς δ' ἁδὺ γελᾷς ὀδύναις.
ἅδε φίλα θρεπτῆρι χάρις; ναὶ τὸν βαθὺν ὄρθρον,   5
ἔσχατα γηρύσῃ ταῦτα τὰ πικρὰ μέλη.

138.—ΜΝΑΣΑΛΚΟΥ

Ἄμπελε, μήποτε φύλλα χαμαὶ σπεύδουσα βαλέσθαι
δείδιας ἑσπέριον Πλειάδα δυομέναν;
μεῖνον ἐπ' Ἀντιλέοντι πεσεῖν ὑπὸ τὶν γλυκὺν ὕπνον,
ἐς τότε, τοῖς καλοῖς πάντα χαριζομένα.

139.—ΚΑΛΛΙΜΑΧΟΥ

Ἔστι τι, ναὶ τὸν Πᾶνα, κεκρυμμένον, ἔστι τι ταύτῃ,
ναὶ μὰ Διώνυσον, πῦρ ὑπὸ τῇ σποδιῇ·
οὐ θαρσέω. μὴ δή με περίπλεκε· πολλάκι λήθει
τοῖχον ὑποτρώγων ἡσύχιος ποταμός.
τῷ καὶ νῦν δείδοικα, Μενέξενε, μή με παρεισδὺς   5
οὗτος ὁ †σειγαρνης[2] εἰς τὸν ἔρωτα βάλῃ.

140.—ΑΔΗΛΟΝ

Τὸν καλὸν ὡς ἰδόμαν Ἀρχέστρατον, οὐ μὰ τὸν Ἑρμᾶν,
οὐ καλὸν αὐτὸν ἔφαν· οὐ γὰρ ἄγαν ἐδόκει.

---

[1] I write ζῇ τὸ : καὶ τὸ MS.
[2] σιγέρπης Bentley, and I render so.

137.—MELEAGER

CRIER of the dawn, caller of evil tidings to a love-sick wight, now, thrice accursed, just when love has only this brief portion of the night left to live, thou crowest in the dark, beating thy sides with thy wings all exultant above thy bed, and makest sweet mockery over my pains. Is this the loving thanks thou hast for him who reared thee? I swear it by this dim dawn, it is the last time thou shalt chant this bitter song.

138.—MNASALCAS

VINE, dost thou fear the setting of the Pleiads in the west,[1] that thou hastenest to shed thy leaves on the ground? Tarry till sweet sleep fall on Antileon beneath thee; tarry till then, bestower of all favours on the fair.

139.—CALLIMACHUS

THERE is, I swear it by Pan, yea, by Dionysus, there is some fire hidden here under the embers. I mistrust me. Embrace me not, I entreat thee. Often a tranquil stream secretly eats away a wall at its base. Therefore now too I fear, Menexenus, lest this silent crawler find his way into me and cast me into love.

140.—ANONYMOUS

WHEN I saw Archestratus the fair I said, so help me Hermes I did, that he was not fair; for he seemed not passing fair to me. I had but spoken the

[1] The season in Autumn at which the vines begin to lose their leaves.

εἶπα, καὶ ἁ Νέμεσίς με συνάρπασε, κεὐθὺς ἐκείμαν
ἐν πυρί, παῖς[1] δ᾽ ἐπ᾽ ἐμοὶ Ζεὺς ἐκεραυνοβόλει.
τὸν παῖδ᾽ ἱλασόμεσθ᾽, ἢ τὰν θεόν; ἀλλὰ θεοῦ μοι   5
ἔστιν ὁ παῖς κρέσσων· χαιρέτω ἁ Νέμεσις.

141.—ΜΕΛΕΑΓΡΟΥ

Ἐφθέγξω, ναὶ Κύπριν, ἃ μὴ θεός, ὦ μέγα τολμᾶν
    θυμὲ μαθών· Θήρων σοὶ καλὸς οὐκ ἐφάνη·
σοὶ καλὸς οὐκ ἐφάνη Θήρων· ἀλλ᾽ αὐτὸς ὑπέστης,
    οὐδὲ Διὸς πτήξας πῦρ τὸ κεραυνοβόλον.
τοιγάρ, ἰδού, τὸν πρόσθε λάλον προΰθηκεν ἰδέσθαι   5
    δεῖγμα θρασυστομίης ἡ βαρύφρων Νέμεσις.

142.—ΡΙΑΝΟΥ

Ἰξῷ Δεξιόνικος ὑπὸ χλωρῇ πλατανίστῳ
    κόσσυφον ἀγρεύσας, εἷλε κατὰ πτερύγων·
χὡ μὲν ἀναστενάχων ἀπεκώκυεν ἱερὸς ὄρνις.
    ἀλλ᾽ ἐγώ, ὦ φίλ᾽ Ἔρως, καὶ θαλεραὶ Χάριτες,
εἴην καὶ κίχλη καὶ κόσσυφος, ὡς ἂν ἐκείνου   5
    ἐν χερὶ καὶ φθογγὴν καὶ γλυκὺ δάκρυ βάλω.

143.—ΑΔΗΛΟΝ

Ἑρμῆ, τοξευθεὶς ἐξέσπασε πικρὸν <ὀϊστὸν>
. . . .
. . . . ἐφήβῳ.[2]
Κἠγὼ τὴν αὐτήν, ξεῖνε, λέλογχα τύχην.
Ἀλλά μ᾽ Ἀπολλοφάνους τρύχει πόθος. Ὦ φιλάεθλε,   5
    ἔφθασας· εἰς ἓν πῦρ οἱ δύ᾽ ἐνηλάμεθα.

---

[1] παῖς Pierson : πᾶς MS.
[2] It seems certain that owing to an error by the copyist, a couplet has been lost, ἐφήβῳ being the last word of the missing line 3. I supply ὀϊστὸν at the end of line 1.

word and Nemesis seized me, and at once I lay in the flames and Zeus, in the guise of a boy, rained his lightning on me. Shall I beseech the boy or the goddess for mercy? But to me the boy is greater than the goddess. Let Nemesis go her way.

141.—MELEAGER

By Cypris, thou hast spoken what not even a god might, O spirit, who hast learnt to be too daring. Theron seemed not fair to thee. He seemed not fair to thee, Theron. But thou thyself hast brought it on thee, not dreading even the fiery bolts of Zeus. Wherefore, lo! indignant Nemesis hath exposed thee, once so voluble, to be gazed at, as an example of an unguarded tongue.

142.—RHIANUS

Dexionicus, having caught a blackbird with lime under a green plane-tree, held it by the wings, and it, the holy bird,[1] screamed complaining. But I, dear Love, and ye blooming Graces, would fain be even a thrush or a blackbird, so that in his hand I might pour forth my voice and sweet tears.

143.—Anonymous

"O Hermes, when shot he extracted the bitter arrow . . ." "And I, O stranger, met with the same fate." "But desire for Apollophanes wears me away." "O lover of sports, thou hast outstripped me; we both have leapt into the same fire."[2]

[1] Holy because it is a singing bird.

[2] The verses seem to have been a dialogue between a statue of Hermes in the gymnasium and a stranger, but owing to their mutilation it is difficult to make sense of them. It is evident from the context of No. 144 (the poems here being arranged under motives) that the god was represented as being in love.

144.—ΜΕΛΕΑΓΡΟΥ

Τί κλαίεις, φρενολῃστά; τί δ' ἄγρια τόξα καὶ ἰοὺς
ἔρριψας, διφυῆ ταρσὸν ἀνεὶς πτερύγων;
ἦ ῥά γε καὶ σὲ Μυΐσκος ὁ δύσμαχος ὄμμασιν αἴθει;
ὡς μόλις οἳ' ἔδρας πρόσθε παθὼν ἔμαθες.

145.—ΑΔΗΛΟΝ

Παύετε, παιδοφίλαι, κενεὸν πόνον· ἴσχετε μόχθων,
δύσφρονες· ἀπρήκτοις ἐλπίσι μαινόμεθα.
ἶσον ἐπὶ ψαφαρὴν ἀντλεῖν ἅλα, κἀπὸ Λιβύσσης
ψάμμου ἀριθμητὴν ἀρτιάσαι ψεκάδα,
ἶσον καὶ παίδων στέργειν πόθον, οἷς τὸ κεναυχὲς   5
κάλλος ἐνὶ χθονίοις ἡδύ τ' ἐν ἀθανάτοις.
δέρκεσθ' εἰς ἐμὲ πάντες· ὁ γὰρ πάρος εἰς κενὸν ἡμῶν
μόχθος ἐπὶ ξηροῖς ἐκκέχυτ' αἰγιαλοῖς.

146.—ΡΙΑΝΟΥ

Ἀγρεύσας τὸν νεβρὸν ἀπώλεσα, χὠ μὲν ἀνατλὰς
μυρία, καὶ στήσας δίκτυα καὶ στάλικας,
σὺν κενεαῖς χείρεσσιν ἀπέρχομαι· οἱ δ' ἀμόγητοι
τἀμὰ φέρουσιν, Ἔρως· οἷς σὺ γένοιο βαρύς.

147.—ΜΕΛΕΑΓΡΟΥ

Ἅρπασται· τίς τόσσον ἐναιχμάσαι ἄγριος εἴη;
τίς τόσος ἀντᾶραι καὶ πρὸς Ἔρωτα μάχην;
ἅπτε τάχος πεύκας. καίτοι κτύπος· Ἡλιοδώρας.
βαῖνε πάλιν στέρνων ἐντὸς ἐμῶν, κραδίη.

144.—MELEAGER
To Love

Why weepest thou, O stealer of the wits? Why hast thou cast away thy savage bow and arrows, folding thy pair of outstretched wings? Doth Myiscus, ill to combat, burn thee, too, with his eyes? How hard it has been for thee to learn by suffering what evil thou wast wont to do of old!

145.—Anonymous

Rest, ye lovers of lads, from your empty labour; cease from your troubles, ye perverse men; we are maddened by never fulfilled hopes. It is like to baling the sea on to the dry land and reckoning the number of grains in the Libyan sand to court the love of boys, whose vainglorious beauty is sweet to men and gods alike. Look on me, all of you; for all my futile toil of the past is as water shed on the dry beach.

146.—RHIANUS

I caught the fawn and lost him; I, who had taken countless pains and set up the nets and stakes, go away empty-handed, but they who toiled not carry off my quarry, O Love. May thy wrath be heavy upon them.

147.—MELEAGER

They have carried her off! Who so savage as to do such armed violence? Who so strong as to raise war against Love himself? Quick, light the torches! But a footfall; Heliodora's! Get thee back into my bosom, O my heart.[1]

[1] Not finding her he fears she has been carried off, but is reassured by hearing her step.

148.—ΚΑΛΛΙΜΑΧΟΥ

Οἶδ' ὅτι μου πλούτου κενεαὶ χέρες· ἀλλά, Μένιππε,
μὴ λέγε, πρὸς Χαρίτων, τοὐμὸν ὄνειρον ἐμοί.
ἀλγέω τὴν διὰ παντὸς ἔπος τόδε πικρὸν ἀκούωι·
ναί, φίλε, τῶν παρὰ σοῦ τοῦτ' ἀνεραστότατον.

149.—ΤΟΥ ΑΥΤΟΥ

"Ληφθήσῃ, περίφευγε, Μενέκρατες·" εἶπα Πανήμου
εἰκάδι, καὶ Λώου τῇ—τίνι; τῇ δεκάτῃ
ἦλθεν ὁ βοῦς ὑπ' ἄροτρον ἑκούσιος. εὖγ' ἐμὸς Ἑρμᾶς,
εὖγ' ἐμός· οὐ παρὰ τὰς εἴκοσι μεμφόμεθα.

150.—ΤΟΥ ΑΥΤΟΥ

Ὡς ἀγαθὰν Πολύφαμος ἀνεύρατο τὰν ἐπαοιδὰν
τὠραμένῳ· ναὶ Γᾶν, οὐκ ἀμαθὴς ὁ Κύκλωψ.
αἱ Μοῖσαι τὸν ἔρωτα κατισχναίνοντι, Φίλιππε·
ἦ πανακὲς πάντων φάρμακον ἁ σοφία.
τοῦτο, δοκέω, χἀ λιμὸς ἔχει μόνον ἐς τὰ πονηρὰ   5
τὠγαθόν, ἐκκόπτει τὰν φιλόπαιδα νόσον.
ἔσθ' ἁμὶν †χἀκαστὰς ἀφειδέα πρὸς τὸν Ἔρωτα.
τοῦτ' εἶπαι " Κείρευ τὰ πτερά, παιδάριον·
οὐδ' ὅσον ἀτταραγόν σε δεδοίκαμες"· αἱ γὰρ ἐπῳδαὶ
οἴκοι τῶ χαλεπῶ τραύματος ἀμφότεραι.   10

151.—ΑΔΗΛΟΝ

Εἴ τινά που παίδων ἐρατώτατον ἄνθος ἔχοντα
εἶδες, ἀδιστάκτως εἶδες Ἀπολλόδοτον.

---

[1] i.e. what I know too well ; cp. Bk. VI. 310.

148.—CALLIMACHUS

I KNOW my hands are empty of wealth, but, by the Graces I beseech thee, Menippus, tell me not my own dream.[1] It hurts me to hear continually these bitter words. Yes, my dear, this is the most unloving thing in all thy bearing to me.

149.—BY THE SAME

"You will be caught, Menecrates, do all you can to escape," I said on the twentieth of Panemus; and in Loius[2] on what day?—the tenth—the ox came of his own accord under the yoke of the plough. Well done, my Hermes![3] well done, my own! I don't complain of the twenty days' delay.

150.—BY THE SAME

How capital the charm for one in love that Polyphemus discovered! Yea, by the Earth, he was not unschooled, the Cyclops. The Muses make Love thin, Philippus; of a truth learning is a medicine that cures every ill. This, I think, is the only good that hunger, too, has to set against its evils, that it extirpates the disease of love for boys. I have plenty of cause for saying to Love " Thy wings are being clipped, my little man. I fear thee not a tiny bit." For at home I have both the charms for the severe wound.

151.—ANONYMOUS

STRANGER, if thou sawest somewhere among the boys one whose bloom was most lovely, undoubtedly

---

[2] The month following Panemus.
[3] Hermes was the giver of good luck.

εἰ δ' ἐσιδών, ὦ ξεῖνε, πυριφλέκτοισι πόθοισιν
οὐκ ἐδάμης, πάντως ἢ θεὸς ἢ λίθος εἶ.

152.—ΑΔΗΛΟΝ

Μάγνης Ἡράκλειτος, ἐμοὶ πόθος, οὔτι σίδηρον
πέτρῳ, πνεῦμα δ' ἐμὸν κάλλει ἐφελκόμενος.

153.—ΑΣΚΛΗΠΙΑΔΟΤ

Πρόσθε μοι Ἀρχεάδης ἐθλίβετο· νῦν δὲ τάλαιναν
οὐδ' ὅσσον παίζων εἰς ἔμ' ἐπιστρέφεται.
οὐδ' ὁ μελιχρὸς Ἔρως ἀεὶ γλυκύς· ἀλλ' ἀνιήσας
πολλάκις ἡδίων γίνετ' ἐρῶσι θεός.

154.—ΜΕΛΕΑΓΡΟΤ

Ἡδὺς ὁ παῖς, καὶ τοὔνομ' ἐμοὶ γλυκύς ἐστι Μυΐσκος
καὶ χαρίεις· τίν' ἔχω μὴ οὐχὶ φιλεῖν πρόφασιν;
καλὸς γάρ, ναὶ Κύπριν, ὅλος καλός· εἰ δ' ἀνιηρός,
οἶδε τὸ πικρὸν Ἔρως συγκεράσαι μέλιτι.

155.—ΑΔΗΛΟΝ

α. Μή μ' εἴπῃς πάλιν ὧδε. β. Τί δ' αἴτιος; αὐτὸς
ἔπεμψε.
α. Δεύτερον οὖν φήσεις; β. Δεύτερον. εἶπεν· Ἴθι.
ἀλλ' ἔρχευ, μὴ μέλλε. μένουσί σε. α. Πρῶτον ἐκείνους
εὑρήσω, χἤξω· τὸ τρίτον οἶδα πάλαι.

¹ I write ἐκείνους : ἐκείνου MS.

---

¹ Meaning either a native of Magnesia (as the boy was) or
the Magnesian stone, the magnet.
² A dialogue between a slave and a boy he is sent to invite.

thou sawest Apollodotus. And if, having seen him,
thou wast not overcome by burning fiery desire. of a
surety thou art either a god or a stone.

152.—Anonymous

HERACLITUS, my beloved, is a Magnet,[1] not attract-
ing iron by stone, but my spirit by his beauty.

153.—ASCLEPIADES
(*The Complaint of a Girl*)

TIME was when Archeades loved to sit close to me,
but now not even in play does he turn to look at me,
unhappy that I am. Not even Love the honeyed is
ever sweet, but often he becomes a sweeter god to
lovers when he torments them.

154.—MELEAGER

SWEET is the boy, and even the name of Myiscus
is sweet to me and full of charm. What excuse have
I for not loving? For he is beautiful, by Cypris,
entirely beautiful; and if he gives me pain, why, it
is the way of Love to mix bitterness with honey.

155.—Anonymous

A. DON'T speak to me again like that. *B.* How
am I to blame? He sent me himself. *A.* What!
will you say it a second time? *B.* A second time.
He said "Go." But come, don't delay, they are
waiting for you. *A.* First of all I will find *them* and
then I will come. I know from experience what the
third story will be.[2]

I take the point of it to be that the man pretends that there
will be other guests to "chaperon" the boy. The boy
refuses to believe this, and declines a *tête-à-tête*. The point
of the last words, however, is obscure.

156.—ΑΔΗΛΟΝ

Εἰαρινῷ χειμῶνι πανείκελος, ὦ Διόδωρε,
  οὑμὸς ἔρως, ἀσαφεῖ κρινόμενος πελάγει·
καὶ ποτὲ μὲν φαίνεις πολὺν ὑετόν, ἄλλοτε δ' αὖτε
  εὔδιος, ἁβρὰ γελῶν δ' ὄμμασιν ἐκκέχυσαι.
τυφλὰ δ', ὅπως ναυηγὸς ἐν οἴδματι, κύματα μετρῶν   5
  δινεῦμαι, μεγάλῳ χείματι πλαζόμενος.
ἀλλά μοι ἢ φιλίης ἔκθες σκοπὸν ἢ πάλι μίσους,
  ὡς εἰδῶ ποτέρῳ κύματι νηχόμεθα.

157.—ΜΕΛΕΑΓΡΟΥ

Κύπρις ἐμοὶ ναύκληρος, Ἔρως δ' οἴακα φυλάσσει
  ἄκρον ἔχων ψυχῆς ἐν χερὶ πηδάλιον·
χειμαίνει δ' ὁ βαρὺς πνεύσας Πόθος, οὕνεκα δὴ νῦν
  παμφύλῳ παίδων νήχομαι ἐν πελάγει.[1]

158.—ΤΟΥ ΑΥΤΟΥ

Σοί με Πόθων δέσποινα θεὴ πόρε, σοί με, Θεόκλεις,
  ἁβροπέδιλος Ἔρως γυμνὸν ὑπεστόρεσεν,
ξεῖνον ἐπὶ ξείνης, δαμάσας ἀλύτοισι χαλινοῖς·
  ἱμείρω δὲ τυχεῖν ἀκλινέος φιλίας.
ἀλλὰ σὺ τὸν στέργοντ' ἀπαναίνεαι, οὐδέ σε θέλγει   5
  οὐ χρόνος, οὐ ξυνῆς σύμβολα σωφροσύνης.
ἵλαθ', ἄναξ, ἵληθι· σὲ γὰρ θεὸν ὥρισε Δαίμων·
  ἐν σοί μοι ζωῆς πείρατα καὶ θανάτου.

---

[1] Or " a sea of boys of *every tribe*," this being the original
meaning of *pamphylus.*

156.—Anonymous

EVEN like unto a storm in springtime, Diodorus, is my love, determined by the moods of an uncertain sea. At one time thou displayest heavy rain-clouds, at another again the sky is clear and thy eyes melt in a soft smile. And I, like a shipwrecked man in the surge, count the blind waves as I am whirled hither and thither at the mercy of the mighty storm. But show me a landmark either of love or of hate, that I may know in which sea I swim.

157.—MELEAGER

CYPRIS is my skipper and Love keeps the tiller, holding in his hand the end of my soul's rudder, and the heavy gale of Desire drives me storm-tossed; for now I swim verily in a Pamphylian[1] sea of boys.

158.—By the Same

THE goddess, queen of the Desires, gave me to thee, Theocles; Love, the soft-sandalled, laid me low for thee to tread on, all unarmed, a stranger in a strange land, having tamed me by his bit that grippeth fast. But now I long to win a friendship in which I need not stoop.[2] But thou refusest him who loves thee, and neither time softens thee nor the tokens we have of our mutual continence. Have mercy on me, Lord, have mercy! for Destiny ordained thee a god; with thee rest for me the issues of life and death.

[2] *i.e.* as I did when my passion made me abject.

159.—ΤΟΥ ΑΥΤΟΥ

Ἐν σοὶ τἀμά, Μυΐσκε, βίου πρυμνήσι' ἀνῆπται·
  ἐν σοὶ καὶ ψυχῆς πνεῦμα τὸ λειφθὲν ἔτι.
ναὶ γὰρ δὴ τὰ σά, κοῦρε, τὰ καὶ κωφοῖσι λαλεῦντα
  ὄμματα, καὶ μὰ τὸ σὸν φαιδρὸν ἐπισκύνιον,
ἤν μοι συννεφὲς ὄμμα βάλῃς ποτέ, χεῖμα δέδορκα·   5
  ἢν δ' ἱλαρὸν βλέψῃς, ἡδὺ τέθηλεν ἔαρ.

160.—ΑΔΗΛΟΝ

Θαρσαλέως τρηχεῖαν ὑπὸ σπλάγχνοισιν ἀνίην
  οἴσω, καὶ χαλεπῆς δεσμὸν ἀλυκτοπέδης.
οὐ γάρ πω, Νίκανδρε, βολὰς ἐδάημεν Ἔρωτος
  νῦν μόνον, ἀλλὰ πόθων πολλάκις ἡψάμεθα.
καὶ σὺ μέν, Ἀδρήστεια, κακῆς ἀντάξια βουλῆς   5
  τῖσαι, καὶ μακάρων πικροτάτη Νέμεσις.

161.—ΑΣΚΛΗΠΙΑΔΟΤ

Δόρκιον ἡ φιλέφηβος ἐπίσταται, ὡς ἁπαλὸς παῖς,
  ἔσθαι πανδήμου Κύπριδος ὠκὺ βέλος,
ἵμερον ἀστράπτουσα κατ' ὄμματος, ἠδ' ὑπὲρ ὤμων
  . . . .
  . . . . .¹   5
σὺν πετάσῳ γυμνὸν μηρὸν ἔφαινε χλαμύς.

162.—ΤΟΥ ΑΥΤΟΥ

Οὔπω τοξοφορῶν οὐδ' ἄγριος,² ἀλλὰ νεογνὸς
  οὑμὸς Ἔρως παρὰ τὴν Κύπριν ὑποστρέφεται,
δέλτον ἔχων χρυσέην· τὰ Φιλοκράτεος δὲ Διαύλου
  τραυλίζει ψυχῆς φίλτρα κατ' Ἀντιγένους.

¹ Two lines lost.   ² I write οὐδ' ἄγριος : οὐδάριος MS.

¹ The *chlamys* and *petasus* (hat) were the proper costume of the *ephebi*.

364

159.—By the Same

My life's cable, Myiscus, is made fast to thee; in thee is all the breath that is left to my soul. For by thy eyes, dear boy, that speak even to the deaf, and by thy bright brow I swear it, if ever thou lookest at me with a clouded eye I see the winter, but if thy glance be blithe, the sweet spring bursts into bloom.

160.—Anonymous

Bravely shall I bear the sharp pain in my vitals and the bond of the cruel fetters. For it is not now only, Nicander, that I learn to know the wounds of love, but often have I tasted desire. Do both thou, Adrasteia, and thou, Nemesis, bitterest of the immortals, exact due vengeance for his evil resolve.

161.—ASCLEPIADES

Dorcion, who loves to sport with the young men, knows how to cast, like a tender boy, the swift dart of Cypris the Popular, flashing desire from her eye, and over her shoulders . . . with her boy's hat, her chlamys[1] showed her naked thigh.

162.—By the Same

My Love, not yet carrying a bow, or savage, but a tiny child, returns to Cypris, holding a golden writing tablet, and reading from it he lisps the love-charms that Diaulus' boy, Philocrates, used to conquer the soul of Antigenes.[2]

[2] As the following poems show, this epigram relates to the loves of two young boys, both of whom seem to have been beloved by the poet.

163.—ΤΟΥ ΑΥΤΟΥ

Εὗρεν Ἔρως τί καλῷ μίξει καλόν, οὐχὶ μάραγδον
  χρυσῷ, ὃ μήτ' ἀνθεῖ, μήτε γένοιτ' ἐν ἴσῳ,
οὐδ' ἐλέφαντ' ἐβένῳ, λευκῷ μέλαν, ἀλλὰ Κλέανδρον
  Εὐβιότῳ, Πειθοῦς ἄνθεα καὶ Φιλίης.

164.—ΜΕΛΕΑΓΡΟΥ

Ἡδὺ μὲν ἀκρήτῳ κεράσαι γλυκὺ νᾶμα μελισσῶν·
  ἡδὺ δὲ παιδοφιλεῖ· καὐτὸν ἐόντα καλόν,
οἷα τὸν ἀβροκόμην στέργει Κλεόβουλον Ἄλεξις·
  ἀθάνατον τούτῳ[1] Κύπριδος οἰνόμελι.

165.—ΤΟΥ ΑΥΤΟΥ

Λευκανθὴς Κλεόβουλος· ὁ δ' ἀντία τοῦδε μελίχρους
  Σώπολις, οἱ δισσοὶ Κύπριδος ἀνθοφόροι.
τοὔνεκά μοι παίδων ἕπεται πόθος· οἱ γὰρ Ἔρωτες
  ἐκ λευκοῦ πλέξαι[2] φασί με καὶ μέλανος.

166.—ΑΣΚΛΗΠΙΑΔΟΥ

Τοῦθ' ὅ τί μοι λοιπὸν ψυχῆς, ὅ τι δή ποτ', Ἔρωτες,
  τοῦτό γ' ἔχειν πρὸς θεῶν ἡσυχίην ἄφετε·
ἢ μὴ δὴ τόξοις ἔτι βάλλετέ μ', ἀλλὰ κεραυνοῖς·
  ναὶ πάντως τέφρην θέσθε με κἀνθρακιήν.
ναί, ναί, βάλλετ', Ἔρωτες· ἐνεσκληκὼς γὰρ ἀνίαις,   5
  ἐξ ὑμέων τοῦτ' οὖν, εἴ γέ τι, βούλομ' ἔχειν.

[1] I write ἀθ. τούτῳ : θνατὸν ὄντως τὸ MS.
[2] So Salmasius : πλέξειν ἐκ λευκοῦ MS.

---

[1] There were priestesses of Aphrodite so entitled.

163.—By the Same

Love has discovered what beauty to mix with beauty ; not emerald with gold, which neither sparkles nor could ever be its equal, nor ivory with ebony, black with white, but Cleander with Eubiotus, two flowers of Persuasion and Friendship.

164.—MELEAGER

Sweet it is to mix with wine the bees' sugary liquor, and sweet to love a boy when oneself is lovely too, even as Alexis now loves soft-haired Cleobulus. These two are the immortal metheglin of Cypris.

165.—By the Same

Cleobulus is a white blossom, and Sopolis, who stands opposite him, is of honey tint—the two flower-bearers of Cypris [1] . . . Therefrom comes my longing for the lads ; for the Loves say they wove me of black and white. [2]

166.—ASCLEPIADES

Let this that is left of my soul, whatever it be, let this at least, ye Loves, have rest for heaven's sake. Or else no longer shoot me with arrows but with thunderbolts, and make me utterly into ashes and cinders. Yea ! yea ! strike me, ye Loves ; for withered away as I am by distress, I would have from you, if I may have aught, this little gift.

[2] He puns on his name (*melas* = black, *argos* = white). There certainly would seem to be a couplet missing in the middle, for " therefrom " can only mean " in consequence of my name."

167.—ΜΕΛΕΑΓΡΟΥ

Χειμέριον μὲν πνεῦμα· φέρει δ' ἐπὶ σοί με, Μυΐσκε,
ἁρπαστὸν κώμοις ὁ γλυκύδακρυς Ἔρως.
χειμαίνει δὲ βαρὺς πνεύσας Πόθος, ἀλλά μ' ἐς ὅρμον
δέξαι, τὸν ναύτην Κύπριδος ἐν πελάγει.

168.—ΠΟΣΕΙΔΙΠΠΟΥ

Ναννοῦς καὶ Λύδης ἐπίχει δύο, καὶ φιλεράστου
Μιμνέρμου, καὶ τοῦ σώφρονος Ἀντιμάχου·
συγκέρασον τὸν πέμπτον ἐμοῦ· τὸν δ' ἕκτον ἑκάστου,
Ἡλιόδωρ', εἶπας, ὅστις ἐρῶν ἔτυχεν·
ἕβδομον Ἡσιόδου, τὸν δ' ὄγδοον εἶπον Ὁμήρου,   5
τὸν δ' ἔνατον Μουσῶν, Μνημοσύνης δέκατον.
μεστὸν ὑπὲρ χείλους πίομαι, Κύπρι· τἆλλα δ'
Ἔρωτες
νήφοντ' οἰνωθέντ' οὐχὶ λίην ἄχαριν.

169.—ΔΙΟΣΚΟΡΙΔΟΥ

Ἐξέφυγον, Θεόδωρε, τὸ σὸν βάρος. ἀλλ' ὅσον εἶπας
" Ἐξέφυγον τὸν ἐμὸν δαίμονα πικρότατον,"
πικρότερός με κατέσχεν. Ἀριστοκράτει δὲ λατρεύωι
μυρία, δεσπόσυνον καὶ τρίτον ἐκδέχομαι.

170.—ΤΟΥ ΑΥΤΟΥ

Σπονδὴ καὶ λιβανωτέ, καὶ οἱ κρητῆρι μιγέντες
δαίμονες, οἳ φιλίης τέρματ' ἐμῆς ἔχετε,
ὑμέας, ὦ σεμνοί, μαρτύρομαι, οὓς ὁ μελίχρως
κοῦρος Ἀθήναιος πάντας ἐπωμόσατο.

---

[1] The lady-loves of whom Mimnermus and Antimachus
sung.

368

167.—MELEAGER

WINTRY is the wind, but Love the sweet-teared bears me, swept away by the revel, towards thee, Myiscus. And Desire's heavy gale tosses me. But receive me, who sail on the sea of Cypris, into thy harbour.

168.—POSIDIPPUS

POUR in two ladles of Nanno and Lyde[1] and one of the lovers' friend, Mimnermus, and one of wise Antimachus, and with the fifth mix in myself, Heliodorus, and with the sixth say, "Of everyone who ever chanced to love." Say the seventh is of Hesiod, and the eighth of Homer, and the ninth of the Muses, and the tenth of Mnemosyne. I drink the bowl full above the brim, Cypris, and for the rest the Loves . . . not very displeasing when either sober or drunk.[2]

169.—DIOSCORIDES

I ESCAPED from your weight, Theodorus, but no sooner had I said "I have escaped from my most cruel tormenting spirit" than a crueller one seized on me, and slaving for Aristocrates in countless ways, I am awaiting even a third master.

170.—BY THE SAME

LIBATION and Frankincense, and ye Powers mixed in the bowl, who hold the issues of my friendship, I call you to witness, solemn Powers, by all of whom the honey-complexioned boy Athenaeus swore.

---

[2] Jacobs is right, I think, in his opinion that this verse, which does not seem to be corrupt, is out of its place here.

171.—ΤΟΥ ΑΥΤΟΥ

Τὸν καλόν, ὡς ἔλαβες, κομίσαις πάλι πρός με θεωρὸν
Εὐφραγόρην, ἀνέμων πρηΰτατε Ζέφυρε,
εἰς ὀλίγων τείνας μηνῶν μέτρον· ὡς καὶ ὁ μικρὸς
μυριετὴς κέκριται τῷ φιλέοντι χρόνος.

172.—ΕΥΗΝΟΥ

Εἰ μισεῖν πόνος ἐστί, φιλεῖν πόνος, ἐκ δύο λυγρῶν
αἱροῦμαι χρηστῆς ἕλκος ἔχειν ὀδύνης.

173.—ΦΙΛΟΔΗΜΟΥ

Δημώ με κτείνει καὶ Θέρμιον· ἡ μὲν ἑταίρη,
Δημονόη [1] δ᾽ οὔπω Κύπριν ἐπισταμένη.
καὶ τῆς μὲν ψαύω· τῆς δ᾽ οὐ θέμις. οὐ μὰ σέ, Κύπρι,
οὐκ οἶδ᾽ ἢν εἰπεῖν δεῖ με ποθεινοτέρην.
Δημάριον λέξω τὴν παρθένον· οὐ γὰρ ἕτοιμα   5
βούλομαι, ἀλλὰ ποθῶ πᾶν τὸ φυλασσόμενον.

174.—ΦΡΟΝΤΩΝΟΣ

Μέχρι τίνος πολεμεῖς μ᾽, ὦ φίλτατε Κῦρε; τί ποιεῖς;
τὸν σὸν Καμβύσην οὐκ ἐλεεῖς; λέγε μοι.
μὴ γίνου Μῆδος· Σάκας γὰρ ἔσῃ μετὰ μικρόν,
καί σε ποιήσουσιν ταὶ τρίχες Ἀστυάγην.

175.—ΣΤΡΑΤΩΝΟΣ

Ἢ μὴ ζηλοτύπει δούλοις ἐπὶ παισὶν ἑταίρους,
ἢ μὴ θηλυπρεπεῖς οἰνοχόους πάρεχε.

---

[1] So Kaibel : δημώ· ἡ MS.

---

[1] Me dos, "give not"; cp. Bk. V. 63.

171.—By the Same

Zephyr, gentlest of the winds, bring back to me the lovely pilgrim Euphragoras, even as thou didst receive him, not extending his absence beyond a few months' space; for to a lover's mind a short time is as a thousand years.

172.—EVENUS

If to hate is pain and to love is pain, of the two evils I choose the smart of kind pain.

173.—PHILODEMUS

Demo and Thermion are killing me.   Thermion is a courtesan and Demo a girl who knows not Cypris yet.   The one I touch, but the other I may not. By thyself, Cypris, I swear, I know not which I should call the more desirable.   I will say it is the virgin Demo; for I desire not what is ready to hand, but long for whatever is kept under lock and key.

174.—FRONTO

How long wilt thou resist me, dearest Cyrus? What art thou doing?   Dost thou not pity thy Cambyses? tell me.   Become not a Mede,[1] for soon thou shalt be a Scythian[2] and the hairs will make thee Astyages.[3]

175.—STRATO

Either be not jealous with your friends about your slave boys, or do not provide girlish-looking cup-

[2] "Bearded"; for *sakos* means a beard.   The names are all taken from the *Cyropaedia* of Xenophon.
[3] See No. 11.

τίς γὰρ ἀνὴρ ἐς ἐρωτ' ἀδαμάντινος; ἢ τίς ἀτειρὴς
    οἴνῳ; τίς δὲ καλοὺς οὐ περίεργα βλέπει;
ζώντων ἔργα τάδ' ἐστίν· ὅπου δ' οὐκ εἰσὶν ἔρωτες   5
    οὐδὲ μέθαι, Διοφῶν, ἢν ἐθέλῃς, ἄπιθι·
κἀκεῖ Τειρεσίην ἢ Τάνταλον ἐς πότον ἕλκε,
    τὸν μὲν ἐπ' οὐδὲν ἰδεῖν, τὸν δ' ἐπὶ μοῦνον ἰδεῖν.

176.—ΤΟΥ ΑΥΤΟΥ

Στυγνὸς δὴ τί, Μένιππε, κατεσκέπασαι μέχρι πέζης,
    ὁ πρὶν ἐπ' ἰγνύης λῶπος ἀνελκόμενος;
ἢ τί κάτω κύψας με παρέδραμες, οὐδὲ προσειπών;
    οἶδα τί με κρύπτεις· ἤλυθον ἃς ἔλεγον.

177.—ΤΟΥ ΑΥΤΟΥ

Ἑσπερίην Μοῖρίς με, καθ' ἢν ὑγιαίνομεν ὥρην,
    οὐκ οἶδ' εἴτε σαφῶς, εἴτ' ὄναρ, ἠσπάσατο.
ἤδη γὰρ τὰ μὲν ἄλλα μάλ' ἀτρεκέως ἐνόησα,
    χὠκόσα μοι προσέφη, χὠκόσ' ἐπυνθάνετο·
εἰ δέ με καὶ πεφίληκε τεκμαίρομαι· εἰ γὰρ ἀληθές,   5
    πῶς ἀποθειωθεὶς πλάζομ' ἐπιχθόνιος;

178.—ΤΟΥ ΑΥΤΟΥ

Ἐξεφλέγην, ὅτε Θεῦδις ἐλάμπετο παισὶν ἐν ἄλλοις,
    οἷος ἐπαντέλλων ἀστράσιν ἠέλιος.
τοὔνεκ' ἔτι φλέγομαι καὶ νῦν, ὅτε νυκτὶ λαχνοῦται·
    δυόμενος γάρ, ὅμως ἥλιός ἐστιν ἔτι.

bearers. For who is of adamant against love, or who succumbs not to wine, and who does not look curiously at pretty boys? This is the way of living men, but if you like, Diophon, go away to some place where there is no love and no drunkenness, and there induce Tiresias or Tantalus to drink with you, the one to see nothing and the other only to see.

176.—By the Same

Why are you draped down to your ankles in that melancholy fashion, Menippus, you who used to tuck up your dress to your thighs? Or why do you pass me by with downcast eyes and without a word? I know what you are hiding from me. They have come, those things I told you would come.

177.—By the Same

Last evening Moeris, at the hour when we bid good night, embraced me, I know not whether in reality or in a dream. I remember now quite accurately everything else, what he said to me and the questions he asked, but whether he kissed me too or not I am at a loss to know; for if it be true, how is it that I, who then became a god, am walking about on earth?

178.—By the Same

I caught fire when Theudis shone among the other boys, like the sun that rises on the stars. Therefore I am still burning now, when the down of night overtakes him, for though he be setting, yet he is still the sun.

179.—ΤΟΥ ΑΥΤΟΥ

'Ωμοσά σοι, Κρονίδη, μηπώποτε, μηδ' ἐμοὶ αὐτῷ
  ἐξειπεῖν ὅ τι μοι Θεῦδις ἔειπε λαβεῖν.
ψυχὴ δ' ἡ δυσάπιστος ἀγαλλομένη πεπότηται
  ἠέρι, καὶ στέξαι τἀγαθὸν οὐ δύναται·
ἀλλ' ἐρέω, σύγγνωθι σύ μοι, κεῖνος δὲ πέπεισται. 5
  Ζεῦ πάτερ, ἀγνώστου τίς χάρις εὐτυχίης;

180.—ΤΟΥ ΑΥΤΟΥ

Καῦμά μ' ἔχει μέγα δή τι· σὺ δ', ὦ παῖ, παύεο
    λεπτὸν
  ἠέρι δινεύων ἐγγὺς ἐμεῖο λίνον.
ἄλλο τι πῦρ ἐμοῦ ἔνδον ἔχω κυάθοισιν ἀναφθέν,
  καὶ περὶ σῇ ῥιπῇ μᾶλλον ἐγειρόμενον.

181.—ΤΟΥ ΑΥΤΟΥ

Ψευδέα μυθίζουσι, Θεόκλεες, ὡς ἀγαθαὶ μὲν
  αἱ Χάριτες, τρισσαὶ δ' εἰσὶ κατ' 'Ορχομενόν·
πεντάκι γὰρ δέκα σεῖο περισκιρτῶσι πρόσωπα,
  τοξοβόλοι, ψυχέων ἅρπαγες ἀλλοτρίων.

182.—ΤΟΥ ΑΥΤΟΥ

Ταῦτά με νῦν τὰ περισσὰ φιλεῖς, ὅτ' ἔρωτος ἀπέσβη
  πυρσός, ὅτ' οὐδ' ἄλλως ἡδὺν ἔχω σε φίλον.
μέμνημαι γὰρ ἐκεῖνα τὰ δύσμαχα· πλὴν ἔτι, Δάφνι,
  ὀψὲ μέν, ἀλλ' ἐχέτω καὶ μετάνοια τόπον.

183.—ΤΟΥ ΑΥΤΟΥ

Τίς χάρις, 'Ηλιόδωρε, φιλήμασιν, εἴ με λάβροισιν
  χείλεσι μὴ φιλέεις ἀντιβιαζόμενος,

179.—By the Same

I swore to thee, son of Cronos, that never, not even to myself, would I utter what Theudis told me I might have. But my froward soul flies high in exultation and cannot contain the good. But I will out with it: pardon me, Zeus, "He yielded." Father Zeus, what delight is there in good fortune that is known to none?

180.—By the Same

I feel some burning heat; but cease, boy, from waving in the air near me the napkin of fine linen. I have another fire within me lit by the wine thou didst serve, and aroused more with thy fanning.

181.—By the Same

It is a lying fable, Theocles, that the Graces are good and that there are three of them in Orchomenus; for five times ten dance round thy face, all archeresses, ravishers of other men's souls.

182.—By the Same

Now thou givest me these futile kisses, when the fire of love is quenched, when not even apart from it do I regard thee as a sweet friend. For I remember those days of thy stubborn resistance. Yet even now, Daphnis, though it be late, let repentance find its place.

183.—By the Same

What delight, Heliodorus, is there in kisses, if thou dost not kiss me, pressing against me with

ἀλλ' ἐπ' ἄκροις ἀσάλευτα μεμυκόσιν, οἷα κατ' οἴκους
καὶ δίχα σοῦ με φιλεῖ πλάσμα τὸ κηρόχυτον;

184.—ΤΟΥ ΑΥΤΟΥ

Μὴ σπεύσῃς Μενέδημον ἑλεῖν δόλῳ, ἀλλ' ἐπίνευσον
ὀφρύσι, καὶ φανερῶς αὐτὸς ἐρεῖ· " Πρόαγε."
οὐ γὰρ ἀνάβλησις· φθάνει δέ τε καὶ τὸν ἄγοντα·
οὐδ' ἀμάρης, ποταμοῦ δ' ἐστὶν ἑτοιμότερος.

185.—ΤΟΥ ΑΥΤΟΥ

Τοὺς σοβαροὺς τούτους καὶ τοὺς περιπορφυροσήμους
παῖδας, ὅσους ἡμεῖς οὐ προσεφιέμεθα,
ὥσπερ σῦκα πέτραισιν ἐπ' ἀκρολόφοισι πέπειρα
ἔσθουσιν γῦπες, Δίφιλε, καὶ κόρακες.

186.—ΤΟΥ ΑΥΤΟΥ

Ἄχρι τίνος ταύτην τὴν ὀφρύα τὴν ὑπέροπτον,
Μέντορ, τηρήσεις, μηδὲ τὸ χαῖρε λέγων,
ὡς μέλλων αἰῶνα μένειν νέος, ἢ διὰ παντὸς
ὀρχεῖσθαι πυρίχην; καὶ τὸ τέλος πρόβλεπε.
ἥξει σοι πώγων, κακὸν ἔσχατον, ἀλλὰ μέγιστον   5
καὶ τότ' ἐπιγνώσῃ τί σπάνις ἐστὶ φίλων.

187.—ΤΟΥ ΑΥΤΟΥ

Πῶς ἀναγινώσκειν, Διονύσιε, παῖδα διδάξεις,
μηδὲ μετεκβῆναι φθόγγον ἐπιστάμενος;

greedy lips, but on the tips of mine with thine closed and motionless, as a wax image at home kisses me even without thee?

184.—By the Same

Study not to capture Menedemus by craft, but sign to him with your eyebrows and he will say openly, "Go on, I follow." For there is no delay, and he even "outrunneth him who guides him," [1] and is more expeditious not than a water-channel [2] but than a river.

185.—By the Same

These airified boys, with their purple-edged robes, whom we cannot get at, Diphilus, are like ripe figs on high crags, which the vultures and ravens eat.

186.—By the Same

How long, Mentor, shalt thou maintain this arrogant brow, not even bidding "good day," as if thou shouldst keep young for all time or tread for ever the pyrrhic dance? Look forward and consider thy end too. Thy beard will come, the last of evils but the greatest, and then thou shalt know what scarcity of friends is.

187.—By the Same

How, Dionysius, shall you teach a boy to read when you do not even know how to make the transition from one note to another? You have passed so

---

[1] Hom. *Il.* xxi. 262.   [2] *Ib.* 259.

ἐκ νήτης μετέβης οὕτως ταχὺς εἰς βαρύχορδον
φθόγγον, ἀπ᾽ ἰσχνοτάτης εἰς τάσιν ὀγκοτάτην.
πλὴν οὐ βασκαίνω· μελέτα μόνον· ἀμφοτέρους δὲ   5
κρούων, τοῖς φθονεροῖς Λάμβδα καὶ Ἄλφα λέγε.

188.—ΤΟΥ ΑΥΤΟΥ

Εἴ σε φιλῶν ἀδικῶ καὶ τοῦτο δοκεῖς ὕβριν εἶναι,
τὴν αὐτὴν κόλασιν καὶ σὺ φίλει με λαβών.

189.—ΤΟΥ ΑΥΤΟΥ

Τίς σε κατεστεφάνωσε ρόδοις ὅλον; εἰ μὲν ἐραστής,
ἆ μάκαρ· εἰ δ᾽ ὁ πατήρ, ὄμματα καὐτὸς ἔχει.

190.—ΤΟΥ ΑΥΤΟΥ

Ὄλβιος ὁ γράψας σε, καὶ ὄλβιος οὗτος ὁ κάλλει
τῷ σῷ νικᾶσθαι κηρὸς ἐπιστάμενος.
θριπὸς ἐγὼ καὶ σύρμα τερηδόνος εἴθε γενοίμην,
ὡς ἀναπηδήσας τὰ ξύλα ταῦτα φάγω.

191.—ΤΟΥ ΑΥΤΟΥ

Οὐκ ἐχθὲς παῖς ἦσθα; καὶ οὐδ᾽ ὄναρ οὗτος ὁ πώγων
ἤλυθε· πῶς ἀνέβη τοῦτο τὸ δαιμόνιον,
καὶ τριχὶ πάντ᾽ ἐκάλυψε τὰ πρὶν καλά; φεῦ, τί
τὸ θαῦμα;
ἐχθὲς Τρωίλος ὤν, πῶς ἐγένου Πρίαμος;

---

[1] Probably, as the commentators explain, having some
sort of sexual meaning. There is double meaning in all the
rest of the epigram, but it is somewhat obscure and had best
remain so.

quickly from the highest note to a deep one, from the slightest rise to the most voluminous. Yet I bear you no grudge; only study, and striking both notes say Lambda and Alpha[1] to the envious.

188.—By the Same

IF I do you a wrong by kissing you, and you think this an injury, kiss me too, inflicting the same on me as a punishment.

189.—By the Same

WHO crowned all thy head with roses? If it was a lover, blessed is he, but if it was thy father he too has eyes.

190.—By the Same

BLEST is he who painted thee, and blest is this wax that knew how to be conquered by thy beauty. Would I could become a creeping wood-worm[2] that I might leap up and devour this wood.

191.—By the Same

WAST thou not yesterday a boy, and we had never even dreamt of this beard coming? How did this accursed thing spring up, covering with hair all that was so pretty before? Heavens! what a marvel! Yesterday you were Troilus[3] and to-day how have you become Priam?

[2] He mentions two kinds, but we cannot distinguish them.
[3] Priam's youngest son.

192.—ΤΟΥ ΑΥΤΟΥ

Οὐ τέρπουσι κόμαι με, περισσότεροί τε κίκιννοι,
  τέχνης, οὐ φύσεως ἔργα διδασκόμενοι·
ἀλλὰ παλαιστρίτου παιδὸς ῥύπος ὁ ψαφαρίτης,
  καὶ χροιὴ μελέων σαρκὶ λιπαινομένη.
ἡδὺς ἀκαλλώπιστος ἐμὸς πόθος· ἡ δὲ γοῆτις   5
  μορφὴ θηλυτέρης ἔργον ἔχει Παφίης.

193.—ΤΟΥ ΑΥΤΟΥ

Οὐδὲ Σμυρναῖαι Νεμέσεις ὅ τι σοὶ 'πιλέγουσιν,
  'Αρτεμίδωρε, νοεῖς· " Μηδὲν ὑπὲρ τὸ μέτρον."
ἀλλ' οὕτως ὑπέροπτα καὶ ἄγρια κοὐδὲ πρέποντα
  κωμῳδῷ φθέγγῃ, πάνθ' ὑποκρινόμενος.
μνησθήσῃ τούτων, ὑπερήφανε· καὶ σὺ φιλήσεις,   5
  καὶ κωμῳδήσεις τὴν 'Αποκλειομένην.

194.—ΤΟΥ ΑΥΤΟΥ

Εἰ Ζεὺς ἐκ γαίης θνητοὺς ἔτι παῖδας ἐς αἴθρην
  ἥρπαζεν, γλυκεροῦ νέκταρος οἰνοχόους,
αἰετὸς ἂν πτερύγεσσιν 'Αγρίππαν τὸν καλὸν ἡμῶν
  ἤδη πρὸς μακάρων ἦγε διηκονίας.
ναὶ μὰ σὲ γάρ, Κρονίδη, κόσμου πάτερ, ἢν ἐσα-
    θρήσῃς,   5
  τὸν Φρύγιον ψέξεις αὐτίκα Δαρδανίδην.

195.—ΤΟΥ ΑΥΤΟΥ

Ἄνθεσιν οὐ τόσσοισι φιλοζέφυροι χλοάουσι
  λειμῶνες, πυκιναῖς εἴαρος ἀγλαΐαις,

---

[1] Two Nemeses were worshipped at Smyrna and are often
represented on the coins of that city.

192.—By the Same

I am not charmed by long hair and needless ring-
lets taught in the school of Art, not of Nature, but
by the dusty grime of a boy fresh from the play-
ground and the colour given to the limbs by the
gloss of oil.   My love is sweet when unadorned, but
a fraudulent beauty has in it the work of female
Cypris.

193.—By the Same

Thou dost not even take to heart, Artemidorus,
what the Avenging Goddesses of Smyrna[1] say to
thee, "Nothing beyond due measure," but thou art
always acting, talking loud in a tone so arrogant
and savage, not even becoming in an actor.   Thou
shalt remember all this, haughty boy; thou, too,
shalt love and play the part of "The barred-out
lady."[2]

194.—By the Same

If Zeus still carried off mortal boys from earth to
the sky to be ministrants of the sweet nectar, an
eagle would ere this have borne my lovely Agrippa
on his wings to the service of the immortals.   For
yea, by thyself I swear it, Son of Cronos, Father of
the world, if thou lookest on him thou wilt at once
find fault with the Phrygian boy of the house of
Dardanus.[3]

195.—By the Same

The meads that love the Zephyr are not abloom
with so many flowers, the crowded splendour of the

[2] The title of a play by Posidippus the comic poet.
[3] Ganymede.

ὅσσους εὐγενέτας, Διονύσιε, παῖδας ἀθρήσεις,
  χειρῶν Κυπρογενοῦς πλάσματα καὶ Χαρίτων.
ἔξοχα δ' ἐν τούτοις Μιλήσιος ἠνίδε θάλλει,   5
  ὡς ῥόδον εὐόδμοις λαμπόμενον πετάλοις.
ἀλλ' οὐκ οἶδεν ἴσως, ἐκ καύματος ὡς καλὸν ἄνθος,
  οὕτω τὴν ὥρην ἐκ τριχὸς ὀλλυμένην.

196.—ΤΟΥ ΑΥΤΟΥ

Ὀφθαλμοὺς σπινθῆρας ἔχεις, θεόμορφε Λυκῖνε,
  μᾶλλον δ' ἀκτῖνας, δέσποτα, πυρσοβόλους.
ἀντωπὸς βλέψαι βαιὸν χρόνον οὐ δύναμαί σοι·
  οὕτως ἀστράπτεις ὄμμασιν ἀμφοτέροις.

197.—ΤΟΥ ΑΥΤΟΥ

" Καιρὸν γνῶθι " σοφῶν τῶν ἑπτά τις, εἶπε, Φίλιππε·
  πάντα γὰρ ἀκμάζοντ' ἐστὶν ἐραστότερα·
καὶ σίκυος πρῶτός που ἐπ' ἀνδήροισιν ὀραθεὶς
  τίμιος, εἶτα συῶν βρῶμα πεπαινόμενος.

198.—ΤΟΥ ΑΥΤΟΥ

Ἡλικίης φίλος εἰμὶ καὶ οὐδένα παῖδα προτάσσω,
  πρὸς τὸ καλὸν κρίνων· ἄλλο γὰρ ἄλλος ἔχει.

199.—ΤΟΥ ΑΥΤΟΥ

Ἄρκιον ἤδη μοι πόσιος μέτρον· εὐσταθίη γὰρ
  λύεται ἤ τε φρενῶν ἤ τε διὰ στόματος.
χὠ λύχνος ἔσχισται διδύμην φλόγα, καὶ δὶς ἀριθμέω,
  πολλάκι πειράζων, τοὺς ἀνακεκλιμένους.

spring-tide, as are the high-born boys thou shalt see,
Dionysius, all moulded by Cypris and the Graces.
And chief among them, look, flowers Milesius, like a
rose shining with its sweet-scented petals. But per-
chance he knows not, that as a lovely flower is killed
by the heat, so is beauty by a hair.

196.—By the Same

Thy eyes are sparks, Lycinus, divinely fair; or
rather, master mine, they are rays that shoot forth
flame. Even for a little season I cannot look at thee
face to face, so bright is the lightning from both.

197.—By the Same

" Know the time " said one of the seven sages;
for all things, Philippus, are more loveable when in
their prime. A cucumber, too, is a fruit we honour
at first when we see it in its garden bed, but after,
when it ripens, it is food for swine.

198.—By the Same

I am a friend of youth and prefer not one boy to
another, judging them by their beauty; for one has
one charm, another another.

199.—By the Same

I have drunk already in sufficient measure, for
both my mind's and my tongue's steadiness is re-
laxed. The flame of the lamp is torn into two, and
I count the guests double, though I try over and

383

ἤδη δ' οὐκέτι μοῦνον ἐπ' οἰνοχόον σεσόβημαι,   5
  ἀλλὰ πάρωρα βλέπω κἠπὶ τὸν ὑδροχόον.

200.—ΤΟΥ ΑΥΤΟΥ

Μισῶ δυσπερίληπτα φιλήματα, καὶ μαχιμώδεις
  φωνάς, καὶ σθεναρὴν ἐκ χερὸς ἀντίθεσιν·
καὶ μὴν καὶ τόν, ὅτ' ἐστὶν ἐν ἀγκάσιν, εὐθὺ θέλοντα
  καὶ παρέχοντα χύδην, οὐ πάνυ δή τι θέλω·
ἀλλὰ τὸν ἐκ τούτων ἀμφοῖν μέσον, οἷον ἐκεῖνον   5
  τὸν καὶ μὴ παρέχειν εἰδότα καὶ παρέχειν.

201.—ΤΟΥ ΑΥΤΟΥ

Εἰ μὴ νῦν Κλεόνικος ἐλεύσεται, οὐκέτ' ἐκεῖνον
  δέξομ' ἐγὼ μελάθροις, οὐ μὰ τὸν—οὐκ ὀμόσω.
εἰ γὰρ ὄνειρον ἰδὼν οὐκ ἤλυθεν, εἶτα παρείη
  αὔριον, οὐ παρὰ τὴν σήμερον ὀλλύμεθα.

202.—ΤΟΥ ΑΥΤΟΥ

Πτηνὸς Ἔρως ἄγαγέν με δι' ἠέρος, ἡνίκα, Δᾶμι,
  γράμμα σὸν εἶδον, ὅ μοι δεῦρο μολεῖν σ' ἔλεγεν·
ῥίμφα δ' ἀπὸ Σμύρνης ἐπὶ Σάρδιας· ἔδραμεν ἄν μοι
  ὕστερον εἰ Ζήτης ἔτρεχεν, ἢ Κάλαϊς.

203.—ΤΟΥ ΑΥΤΟΥ

Οὐκ ἐθέλοντα φιλεῖς με, φιλῶ δ' ἐγὼ οὐκ ἐθέλοντα·
  εὔκολος ἢν φεύγω, δύσκολος ἢν ἐπάγω.

---

[1] He means the constellation Aquarius, into which Ganymede was said to have been transformed.

over again. And now not only am I in a flutter for the wine-pourer, but I look, out of season, at the Water-pourer [1] too.

200.—By the Same

I HATE resistance to my embrace when I kiss, and pugnacious cries, and violent opposition with the hands, but at the same time I have no great desire for him who, when he is in my arms, is at once ready and abandons himself effusively. I wish for one half-way between the two, such as is he who knows both how to give himself and how not to give himself.

201.—By the Same

IF Cleonicus does not come now I will never receive him in my house, by —. I will not swear; for if he did not come owing to a dream he had, and then does appear to-morrow, it is not all over with me because of the loss of this one day.

202.—By the Same

WINGED Love bore me through the air, Damis, when I saw your letter which told me you had arrived here; and swiftly I flew from Smyrna to Sardis; if Zetes or Calais [2] had been racing me they would have been left behind.

203.—By the Same

You kiss me when I don't wish it, and you don't wish it when I kiss you; when I fly you are facile, when I attack you are difficult.

[1] The winged sons of Boreas.

204.—ΤΟΥ ΑΥΤΟΥ

" Χρύσεα χαλκείων " νῦν εἴπατε· "δὸς λάβε" παίζει
Σωσιάδας ὁ καλός, καὶ Διοκλῆς ὁ δασύς.
τίς κάλυκας συνέκρινε βάτῳ, τίς σῦκα μύκησιν;
ἄρνα γαλακτοπαγῆ τίς συνέκρινε βοΐ;
οἷα δίδως, ἀλόγιστε, καὶ ἔμπαλιν οἷα κομίζῃ·
οὕτω Τυδείδης Γλαῦκον ἐδωροδόκει.

205.—ΤΟΥ ΑΥΤΟΥ

Παῖς τις ὅλως ἁπαλὸς τοῦ γείτονος οὐκ ὀλίγως με
κνίζει· πρὸς τὸ θέλειν δ' οὐκ ἀμύητα γελᾷ·
οὐ πλεῦν δ' ἐστὶν ἐτῶν δύο καὶ δέκα. νῦν ἀφύλακτοι
ὄμφακες· ἢν δ' ἀκμάσῃ, φρούρια καὶ σκόλοπες.

206.—ΤΟΥ ΑΥΤΟΥ

α. Ἦν τούτῳ †φωνῆς, τὸ μέσον λάβε, καὶ κατακλίνας
ζεύγνυε, καὶ πρώσας πρόσπεσε, καὶ κάτεχε.
β. Οὐ φρονέεις, Διόφαντε· μόλις δύναμαι γὰρ ἔγωγε
ταῦτα ποιεῖν· παίδων δ' ἡ πάλη ἔσθ' ἑτέρα.
μοχλοῦ καὶ μένε, Κῦρι, καὶ ἐμβάλλοντος ἀνάσχου·
πρῶτον συμμελετᾶν ἢ μελετᾶν μαθέτω.

207.—ΤΟΥ ΑΥΤΟΥ

Ἐχθὲς λουόμενος Διοκλῆς ἀνενήνοχε σαύραν
ἐκ τῆς ἐμβάσεως τὴν Ἀναδυομένην.

---

[1] Hom. *Il.* vi. 236.
[2] The terms are all technical ones of the wrestling school,
many of them, of course, bearing a double meaning.

204.—By the Same

Now you may say, "Golden gifts tor brazen." [1]
Sosiades the fair and Diocles the bushy are playing
at "Give and take." Who compares roses with
brambles, or figs with toadstools? Who compares
a lamb like curdled milk with an ox? What dost
thou give, thoughtless boy, and what dost thou re-
ceive in return? Such gifts did Diomede give to
Glaucus.

205.—By the Same

My neighbour's quite tender young boy provokes
me not a little, and laughs in no novice manner to
show me that he is willing. But he is not more than
twelve years old. Now the unripe grapes are un-
guarded; when he ripens there will be watchmen
and stakes.

206.—By the Same

A. "If you are minded to do thus, take your ad-
versary by the middle, and laying him down get
astride of him, and shoving forward, fall on him and
hold him tight." *B.* "You are not in your right
senses, Diophantus. I am only just capable of doing
this, but boys' wrestling is different. Fix yourself
fast and stand firm, Cyris, and support it when I close
with you. He should learn to practise with a fellow
before learning to practise himself." [2]

207.—By the Same

Yesterday Diocles in the bath brought up a lizard [3]
from the tub, "Aphrodite rising from the waves." [4]

There are, it seems to me, two speakers, the boy's (Cyris)
wrestling-master, Diophantus, and the author himself.
[3] *cp.* No. 3.   [4] Apelles' celebrated picture.

ταύτην εἰ τις ἔδειξεν ᾿Αλεξάνδρῳ τότ᾿ ἐν ῎Ιδῃ,
τὰς τρεῖς ἂν ταύτης προκατέκρινε θεάς.

208.—ΤΟΥ ΑΥΤΟΥ

Εὐτυχές, οὐ φθονέω, βιβλίδιον· ἦ ῥά σ᾿ ἀναγνοὺς
παῖς τις ἀναθλίψει, πρὸς τὰ γένεια τιθείς·
ἢ τρυφεροῖς σφίγξει περὶ χείλεσιν, ἢ κατὰ μηρῶν
εἰλήσει δροσερῶν, ὦ μακαριστότατον·
πολλάκι φοιτήσεις ὑποκόλπιον, ἢ παρὰ δίφρους   5
βληθὲν τολμήσεις κεῖνα θιγεῖν ἀφόβως.
πολλὰ δ᾿ ἐν ἠρεμίῃ προλαλήσεις· ἀλλ᾿ ὑπὲρ ἡμῶν,
χαρτάριον, δέομαι, πυκνότερόν τι λάλει.

209.—ΤΟΥ ΑΥΤΟΥ

Μήτε λίην στυγνὸς παρακέκλισο, μήτε κατηφής,
Δίφιλε, μηδ᾿ εἴης παιδίον ἐξ ἀγέλης.
ἔστω που προύνικα φιλήματα, καὶ τὰ πρὸ ἔργων
παίγνια, πληκτισμοί, κνίσμα, φίλημα,[1] λόγος.

210.—ΤΟΥ ΑΥΤΟΥ

Τρεῖς ἀρίθμει τοὺς πάντας ὑπὲρ λέχος, ὧν δύο δρῶσιν,
καὶ δύο πάσχουσιν.   θαῦμα δοκῶ τι λέγειν.
καὶ μὴν οὐ ψεῦδος· δυσὶν εἷς μέσσος γὰρ ὑπουργεῖ
τέρπων ἐξόπιθεν, πρόσθε δὲ τερπόμενος.

211.—ΤΟΥ ΑΥΤΟΥ

Εἰ μὲν ἔφυς ἀμύητος ἀκμὴν ὑπὲρ οὗ σ᾿ ἔτι πείθω,
ὀρθῶς ἂν δείσαις, δεινὸν ἴσως δοκέων.

---

[1] I conjecture κνίσματα βλέμμα and render so.

If someone had shown it to Paris then in Ida, he would have pronounced the three goddesses to be less fair than it.

208.—By the Same

Happy little book,[1] I grudge it thee not; some boy reading thee will rub thee, holding thee under his chin, or press thee against his delicate lips, or will roll thee up resting on his tender thighs, O most blessed of books.   Often shalt thou betake thee into his bosom, or, tossed down on his chair, shalt dare to touch those parts without fear, and thou shalt talk much before him all alone with him; but I pray thee, little book, speak something not unoften on my behalf.

209.—By the Same

Lie not by me with so sour a face and so dejected, Diphilus, and be not a boy of the common herd. Put a little wantonness into your kisses and the preliminaries to the works, toying, touching, scratching, your look and your words.

210.—By the Same

Count all who are on a bed as three, of whom two are in action, two submissive.   It looks as if I'm telling some miracle.   Still, it's no lie.   For one in the middle serves two, giving joy behind, getting joy in front.

211.—By the Same

If you were still uninitiated in the matter about which I go on trying to persuade you, you would be right in being afraid, thinking it is perhaps some-

[1] In the form of a roll, of course; this explains several of the phrases.

εἰ δέ σε δεσποτικὴ κοίτη πεποίηκε τεχνίτην,
τί φθονέεις δοῦναι, ταὐτὸ λαβών, ἑτέρῳ;
ὃς μὲν γὰρ καλέσας ἐπὶ τὸ χρέος, εἶτ᾽ ἀπολύσας,   5
εὕδει κύριος ὤν, μηδὲ λόγου μεταδούς·
ἄλλη δ᾽ ἔνθα τρυφή· παίξεις ἴσα, κοινὰ λαλήσεις,
τἄλλα δ᾽ ἐρωτηθεὶς κοὐκ ἐπιτασσόμενος.

212.—ΤΟΥ ΑΥΤΟΥ

Αἰαῖ μοι· τί πάλιν δεδακρυμενον, ἢ τι κατηφές,
παιδίον; εἶπον ἁπλῶς· μηδ᾽ ὀδύνα· τί θέλεις:
τὴν χέρα μοι κοίλην προσενήνοχας· ὡς ἀπόλωλα·
μισθὸν ἴσως αἰτεῖς· τοῦτ᾽ ἔμαθες δὲ πόθεν;
οὐκέτι σοι κοπτῆς φίλιαι πλάκες οὐδὲ μελιχρὰ   5
σήσαμα, καὶ καρύων παίγνιος εὐστοχίη·
ἀλλ᾽ ἤδη πρὸς κέρδος ἔχεις φρένας. ὡς ὁ διδάξας
τεθνάτω· οἷόν μου παιδίον ἠφάνικεν.

213.—ΤΟΥ ΑΥΤΟΥ

Τῷ τοίχῳ κέκλικας τὴν ὀσφύα τὴν περίβλεπτον,
Κῦρι· τί πειράζεις τὸν λίθον; οὐ δύναται.

214.—ΤΟΥ ΑΥΤΟΥ

Δός μοι, καὶ λάβε χαλκόν. ἐρεῖς ὅτι " Πλούσιός εἰμι."
δώρησαι τοίνυν τὴν χάριν, ὡς βασιλεύς.

215.—ΤΟΥ ΑΥΤΟΥ

Νῦν ἔαρ εἶ, μετέπειτα θέρος· κἄπειτα τί μέλλεις
Κῦρις; βούλευσαι, καὶ καλάμη γὰρ ἔσῃ.

thing formidable. But if your master's bed has made
you proficient in it, why do you grudge granting the
favour to another, receiving the same? For he, after
summoning you to the business, dismisses you, and
being your lord and master, goes to sleep without
even addressing a word to you. But here you will
have other enjoyments, playing on equal terms, talk-
ing together, and all else by invitation and not by
order.

212.—By the Same

Woe is me! Why in tears again and so woe-
begone, my lad? Tell me plainly; don't give me
pain; what do you want? You hold out the hollow
of your hand to me. I am done for! You are begging
perhaps for payment; and where did you learn that?
You no longer love slices of seed-cake and sweet
sesame, and nuts to play at shots with, but already
your mind is set on gain. May he who taught you
perish! What a boy of mine he has spoilt!

213.—By the Same

You rest your splendid loins against the wall,
Cyris. Why do you tempt the stone? It is incapable.

214.—By the Same

Grant it me and take the coin. You will say " I
am rich." Then, like a king, make me a present of
the favour.

215.—By the Same

Now thou art spring, and afterward summer, and
next what shalt thou be, Cyris? Consider, for thou
shalt be dry stubble too.

216.—ΤΟΥ ΑΥΤΟΥ

Νῦν ὀρθή, κατάρατε, καὶ εὔτονος, ἡνίκα μηδέν·
ἡνίκα δ᾽ ἦν ἐχθές, οὐδὲν ὅλως ἀνέπνεις.

217.—ΤΟΥ ΑΥΤΟΥ

Ἤδη ἐπὶ στρατιῆς ὁρμᾷς, ἔτι παῖς ἀδαὴς ὢν
καὶ τρυφερός. τί ποιεῖς, οὗτος, ὅρα· μετάθου.
οἴμοι· τίς σ᾽ ἀνέπεισε λαβεῖν δόρυ· τίς χερὶ πέλτην;
τίς κρύψαι ταύτην τὴν κεφαλὴν κόρυθι;
ὦ μακαριστὸς ἐκεῖνος, ὅτις ποτέ, καινὸς Ἀχιλλεύς   5
τοίῳ ἐνὶ κλισίῃ τερπόμενος Πατρόκλῳ.

218.—ΤΟΥ ΑΥΤΟΥ

Μέχρι τίνος σε γελῶντα μόνον, μηδὲν δὲ λαλοῦντα
οἴσομεν; εἶπον ἁπλῶς ταῦτα σύ, Πασίφιλε.
αἰτῶ, καὶ σὺ γελᾷς· πάλιν αἰτῶ, κοὐκ ἀποκρίνῃ·
δακρύω, σὺ γελᾷς. βάρβαρε, τοῦτο γέλως;

219.—ΤΟΥ ΑΥΤΟΥ

Καὶ μισθοὺς αἰτεῖτε, διδάσκαλοι; ὡς ἀχάριστοι
ἐστέ· τί γάρ; τὸ βλέπειν παιδία μικρὸν ἴσως;
καὶ τούτοισι λαλεῖν, ἀσπαζομένους τε φιλῆσαι;
τοῦτο μόνον χρυσῶν ἄξιον οὐχ ἑκατόν;
πεμπέτω, εἴ τις ἔχει καλὰ παιδία· κἀμὲ φιλείτω,   5
μισθὸν καὶ παρ᾽ ἐμοῦ λαμβανέτω τί θέλει.

220.—ΤΟΥ ΑΥΤΟΥ

Οὐχὶ τὸ πῦρ κλέψας δέδεσαι, κακόβουλε Προμηθεῦ,
ἀλλ᾽ ὅτι τὸν πηλὸν τοῦ Διὸς ἠφάνισας.

216.—By the Same

Now you're upright, damn you, and stiff, when nothing is there. But when there *was* something yesterday, you heaved no breath at all.

217.—By the Same

So soon thou rushest to the wars, still an ignorant boy and delicate. What art thou doing? Ho! look to it, change thy resolve. Alas! who persuaded thee to grasp the spear? Who bad thee take the shield in thy hand or hide that head in a helmet? Most blessed he, whoe'er he be, who, some new Achilles, shall take his pleasure in the tent with such a Patroclus!

218.—By the Same

How long shall I bear with thee, thus laughing only and never uttering a word? Tell me this plainly, Pasiphilus. I entreat and thou laughest; I entreat again and no answer; I weep and thou laughest. Cruel boy, is this a laughing matter?

219.—By the Same

You want payment too, you schoolmasters! How ungrateful you are! For why? Is it a small thing to look on boys and speak to them, and kiss them when you greet them? Is not this alone worth a hundred pounds? If anyone has good-looking boys, let him send them to me and let them kiss me, and receive whatever payment they wish from me.

220.—By the Same

Thou art not in fetters for stealing the fire, ill-advised Prometheus, but because thou didst spoil

πλάττων ἀνθρώπους, ἔβαλες τρίχας· ἔνθεν ὁ δεινὸς
πώγων, καὶ κνήμη παισὶ δασυνομένη.
εἶτά σε δαρδάπτει Διὸς αἰετός, ὃς Γανυμήδην   5
ἥρπασ'· ὁ γὰρ πώγων καὶ Διός ἐστ' ὀδύνη.

221.—ΤΟΥ ΑΥΤΟΥ

Στεῖχε πρὸς αἰθέρα δῖον, ἀπέρχεο παῖδα κομίζων,
αἰετέ, τὰς διφυεῖς ἐκπετάσας πτέρυγας,
στεῖχε τὸν ἁβρὸν ἔχων Γανυμήδεα, μηδὲ μεθείης
τὸν Διὸς ἡδίστων οἰνοχόον κυλίκων·
φείδεο δ' αἱμάξαι κοῦρον γαμψώνυχι ταρσῷ,   5
μὴ Ζεὺς ἀλγήσῃ, τοῦτο βαρυνόμενος.

222.—ΤΟΥ ΑΥΤΟΥ

Εὐκαίρως ποτὲ παιδοτρίβης, λεῖον προδιδάσκων,
εἰς τὸ γόνυ γνάμψας, μέσσον ἐπαιδοτρίβει,
τῇ χερὶ τοὺς κόκκους ἐπαφώμενος. ἀλλὰ τυχαίως
τοῦ παιδὸς χρήζων, ἦλθεν ὁ δεσπόσυνος·
ὃς δὲ τάχος τοῖς ποσσὶν ὑποζώσας ἀνέκλινεν   5
ὕπτιον, ἐμπλέξας τῇ χερὶ τὴν φάρυγα.
ἀλλ' οὐκ ὢν ἀπάλαιστος ὁ δεσπόσυνος προσέειπεν·
" Παῦσαι· πνιγίζεις," φησί, "τὸ παιδάριον."

223.—ΤΟΥ ΑΥΤΟΥ

Τερπνὸν ὅλως τὸ πρόσωπον ἐμοὶ προσιόντος ἀπαρκεῖ·
οὐκέτι δ' ἐξόπιθεν καὶ παριόντα βλέπω.
οὕτω γὰρ καὶ ἄγαλμα θεοῦ καὶ νηὸν ὁρῶμεν
ἀντίον, οὐ πάντως καὶ τὸν ὀπισθόδομον.

the clay of Zeus. In moulding men thou didst add hairs, and hence comes the horrible beard, and hence boys' legs grow rough. For this thou art devoured by Zeus' eagle, which carried off Ganymede; for the beard is a torment to Zeus, too.

221.—By the Same

Hie thee to holy Heaven, eagle; away, bearing the boy, thy twin wings outspread. Go, holding tender Ganymede, and let him not drop, the ministrant of Zeus' sweetest cups. And take heed not to make the boy bleed with the crooked claws of thy feet, lest Zeus, sore aggrieved thereby, suffer pain.

222.—By the Same

Once a wrestling-master, taking advantage of the occasion, when he was giving a lesson to a smooth boy, forced him to kneel down, and set about working on his middle stroking the berries with one hand. But by chance the master of the house came, wanting the boy. The teacher threw him quickly on his back, getting astride of him and grasping him by the throat. But the master of the house, who was not unversed in wrestling, said to him, " Stop, you are smuggering[1] the boy."

223.—By the Same

His face as he approaches seems altogether delightful to me, and that suffices, and I turn not my head to look at him again as he passes. For thus do we look at the statue of a god and a temple, in front, but need not look at the back chamber too.

---

[1] There is word-play on πνίγω and πυγίζω.

224.—ΤΟΥ ΑΥΤΟΥ

Εἰς ἀγαθὴν συνέβημεν ἀταρπιτόν, ἦν ἀπὸ πρώτης
φράζευ ὅπως ἔσται, Δίφιλε, καὶ μονίμη.
ἄμφω γὰρ πτηνόν τι λελόγχαμεν· ἔστι μὲν ἐν σοὶ
κάλλος, ἔρως δ' ἐν ἐμοί· καίρια δ' ἀμφότερα.
ἄρτι μὲν ἁρμοσθέντα μένει χρόνον· εἰ δ' ἀφύλακτα 5
μίμνετον ἀλλήλων, ᾤχετ' ἀποπτάμενα.

225.—ΤΟΥ ΑΥΤΟΥ

Οὐδέποτ' ἠελίου φάος ὄρθριον ἀντέλλοντος
μίσγεσθαι ταύρῳ χρὴ φλογόεντα κύνα,
μή ποτε καρπολόχου Δημήτερος ὑγρανθείσης,
βρέξῃς τὴν λασίην Ἡρακλέους ἄλοχον.

226.—ΤΟΥ ΑΥΤΟΥ

Πάννυχα μυδαλόεντα πεφυρμένος ὄμματα κλαυθμῷ
ἄγρυπνον ἀμπαύω θυμὸν ἀδημονίῃ,
ἥ με κατ' οὖν ἐδάμασσεν ἀποζευχθέντος ἑταίρου,
μοῦνον ἐπεί με λιπὼν εἰς ἰδίην Ἔφεσον
χθιζὸς ἔβη Θεόδωρος· ὃς εἰ πάλι μὴ ταχὺς ἔλθοι, 5
οὐκέτι μουνολεχεῖς κοίτας ἀνεξόμεθα.

227.—ΤΟΥ ΑΥΤΟΥ

Ἤν τινα καὶ παριδεῖν ἐθέλω καλὸν ἀντισυναντῶν,
βαιὸν ὅσον παραβὰς εὐθὺ μεταστρέφομαι.

228.—ΤΟΥ ΑΥΤΟΥ

Παῖδα μὲν ἠλιτόμηνον ἐς ἄφρονα καιρὸν ἁμαρτεῖν,
τῷ πείθοντι φέρει πλεῖον ὕβρισμα φίλῳ.

224.—By the Same

WE walk together in a good path, Diphilus, and take thou thought how it shall continue to be even as it was from the beginning. To the lot of each has fallen a winged thing; for in thee is beauty and in me love; but both are fugitive. Now they remain in unison for a season, but if they do not guard one another they take wing and are gone.

225.—By the Same

WHEN the sunlight is rising at dawn, never should you join the blazing Dog with the Bull lest one day, when Demeter, Mother of Grain, has been given a soaking, you wet Heracles' hairy wife.[1]

226.—By the Same

ALL night long, my dripping eyes tear-stained, I strive to rest my spirit that grief keeps awake— grief for this separation from my friend since yesterday, when Theodorus, leaving me here alone, went to his own Ephesus. If he come not back soon I shall be no longer able to bear the solitude of my bed.

227.—By the Same

EVEN if I desire to avoid looking at a pretty boy when I meet him, I have scarcely passed him when I at once turn round.

228.—By the Same

THAT an immature boy should do despite to his insensible age carries more disgrace to the friend who tempts him than to himself, and for a grown-up

---

[1] Hebe, the word ἥβη meaning also the pubes.

ἤδη δ᾽ ἐν νεότητι παρήλικα παιδικὰ πάσχειν,
τῷ παρέχοντι πάλιν τοῦτο δὶς αἰσχρότερον.
ἔστι δ᾽ ὅτ᾽ ἀμφοτέροις τὸ μὲν οὐκέτι, Μοῖρι, τὸ δ᾽
    οὔπω   5
ἀπρεπές, οἷον ἐγὼ καὶ σὺ τὸ νῦν ἔχομεν.

229.—ΤΟΥ ΑΥΤΟΥ

Ὡς ἀγαθὴ θεός ἐστι, δι᾽ ἣν ὑπὸ κόλπον, Ἄλεξι,
πτύομεν, ὑστερόπουν ἁζόμενοι Νέμεσιν.
ἣν σὺ μετερχομένην οὐκ ἔβλεπες, ἀλλ᾽ ἐνόμιζες
ἕξειν τὸ φθονερὸν κάλλος ἀειχρόνιον.
νῦν δὲ τὸ μὲν διόλωλεν· ἐλήλυθε δ᾽ ἡ τριχάλεπτος   5
δαίμων· χοὶ θέραπες νῦν σε παρερχόμεθα.

230.—ΚΑΛΛΙΜΑΧΟΥ

Τὸν τὸ καλὸν μελανεῦντα Θεόκριτον, εἰ μὲν ἔμ᾽ ἔχθει,
τετράκι μισοίης· εἰ δὲ φιλεῖ, φιλέοις·
ναίχι πρὸς εὐχαίτεω Γανυμήδεος, οὐράνιε Ζεῦ,
καὶ σύ ποτ᾽ ἠράσθης. οὐκέτι μακρὰ λέγω.

231.—ΣΤΡΑΤΩΝΟΣ

Εὐκλείδῃ φιλέοντι πατὴρ θάνεν· ἂ μάκαρ αἰεί,
καὶ πρὶν ἐς ὅττι θέλοι χρηστὸν ἔχων πατέρα
καὶ νῦν εὔφρονα νεκρόν. ἐγὼ δ᾽ ἔτι λάθρια παίζω·
φεῦ μοίρης τε κακῆς καὶ πατρὸς ἀθανάτου.

232.—ΣΚΥΘΙΝΟΥ

Ὀρθὸν νῦν ἕστηκας ἀνώνυμον οὐδὲ μαραίνῃ,
ἐντέτασαι δ᾽ ὡς ἂν μή ποτε παυσόμενον·

398

youth to submit to sodomy, his season for which is past, is twice as disgraceful to him who consents as it is to his tempter. But there is a time, Moeris, when it is no longer unseemly in the one, and not yet so in the other, as is the case with you and me at present.

229.—BY THE SAME

WHAT a good goddess is that Nemesis, to avert whom, dreading her as she treadeth behind us, we spit in our bosom! Thou didst not see her at thy heels, but didst think that for ever thou shouldst possess thy grudging beauty. Now it has perished utterly; the very wrathful [1] goddess has come, and we, thy servants, now pass thee by.

230.—CALLIMACHUS

IF Theocritus, the beautifully brown, hate me, hate thou him, Zeus, four times as much, but if he love me, love him. Yea, by fair-haired Ganymede, celestial Zeus, thou too wert once in love. I say nothing further.

231.—STRATO

EUCLIDES, who is in love, has lost his father. Ah, the ever lucky fellow! His father used ever to be good-natured to him about anything he wished, and now is a benevolent corpse. But I must still play in secret. Alas for my evil fate and my father's immortality!

232.—SCYTHINUS

YOU unnamed thing, now you stand erect and do not wilt in the least, but are on the stretch like one

---

[1] There is a pun on τρίχα, hair.

ἀλλ' ὅτε μοι Νεμεσηνὸς ὅλον παρέκλινεν ἑαυτόν,
πάντα διδοὺς ἃ θέλω, νεκρὸν ἀπεκρέμασο.
τείνεο, καὶ ῥήσσου, καὶ δάκρυε· πάντα ματαίως,   5
οὐχ ἕξεις ἔλεον χειρὸς ἀφ' ἡμετέρης.

233.—ΦΡΟΝΤΩΝΟΣ

Τὴν ἀκμὴν Θησαυρὸν ἔχειν, κωμῳδέ, νομίζεις,
οὐκ εἰδὼς αὐτὴν Φάσματος ὀξυτέρην.
ποιήσει σ' ὁ χρόνος Μισούμενον, εἶτα Γεωργόν,
καὶ τότε μαστεύσεις τὴν Περικειρομένην.

234.—ΣΤΡΑΤΩΝΟΣ

Εἰ κάλλει καυχᾷ, γίνωσχ' ὅτι καὶ ῥόδον ἀνθεῖ·
ἀλλὰ μαρανθὲν ἄφνω σὺν κοπρίοις ἐρίφη.
ἄνθος γὰρ καὶ κάλλος ἴσον χρόνον ἐστὶ λαχόντα·
ταῦτα δ' ὁμῇ φθονέων ἐξεμάρανε χρόνος.

235.—ΤΟΥ ΑΥΤΟΥ

Εἰ μὲν γηράσκει τὸ καλόν, μετάδος, πρὶν ἀπέλθῃ·
εἰ δὲ μένει, τί φοβῇ τοῦθ' ὃ μενεῖ διδόναι;

236.—ΤΟΥ ΑΥΤΟΥ

Εὐνοῦχός τις ἔχει καλὰ παιδία· πρὸς τίνα χρῆσιν;
καὶ τούτοισι βλάβην οὐχ ὁσίην παρέχει.
ὄντως ὡς ὁ κύων φάτνῃ ῥόδα, μωρὰ δ' ὑλακτῶν
οὔθ' αὑτῷ παρέχει τἀγαθόν, οὔθ' ἑτέρῳ.

---

[1] All these are titles of pieces by Menander. "The
Countryman" seems to have dealt with marital jealousy, as

that will never stop. But when Nemesenus curved
his whole self to me, granting all I want, you hung
as a dead thing. Be stretched, burst apart and
weep—all in vain. You'll get no pity from my hand.

233.—FRONTO

COMEDIAN, thou deemest that thy prime is "The
Treasure," knowing not that it is swifter to depart
than "The Phantom." Time will make thee "The
Hated Man" and then "The Countryman," and then
thou shalt seek "The Clipped Lady." [1]

234.—STRATO

IF thou gloriest in thy beauty, know that the rose
too blooms, but withers of a sudden and is cast away
on the dunghill. To blossom and to beauty the same
time is allotted, and envious time withers both
together.

235.—BY THE SAME

IF beauty grows old, give me of it ere it depart;
but if it remains with thee, why fear to give what
shall remain thine?

236.—BY THE SAME

A CERTAIN eunuch has good-looking servant-boys—
for what use?—and he does them abominable injury.
Truly, like the dog in the manger with the roses,
and stupidly barking, he neither gives the good thing
to himself nor to anyone else.

did "The Clipped Lady," but I fail to see the exact point.
cp. Agathias' imitation of this, Bk. V. 218.

237.—ΤΟΥ ΑΥΤΟΥ

Χαῖρε σύ, μισοπόνηρε πεπλασμένε, χαῖρε, βάναυσε
  ὁ πρῴην ὀμόσας μηκέτι μὴ διδόναι.
μηκέτι νῦν ὀμόσῃς. ἔγνωκα γάρ, οὐδέ με λήθεις·
  οἶδα τὸ ποῦ, καὶ πῶς, καὶ τίνι, καὶ τὸ πόσου.

238.—ΤΟΥ ΑΥΤΟΥ

Ἀλλήλοις παρέχουσιν ἀμοιβαδίην ἀπόλαυσιν
  οἱ κύνεοι πῶλοι μειρακιενόμενοι·
ἀμφαλλὰξ δὲ οἱ αὐτοὶ ἀπόστροφα νωτοβατοῦνται,
  τὸ δρᾷν καὶ τὸ παθεῖν ἀντιπεραινόμενοι.
οὐ πλεονεκτεῖται δ' οὐδ' ἅτερος· ἄλλοτε μὲν γὰρ   5
  ἵσταται ὁ προδιδοὺς ἄλλοτ' ὄπισθε πάλιν.
τοῦτ' ἐστὶν πάντως τὸ προοίμιον· εἰς γὰρ ἀμοιβήν,
  ὡς λέγεται, κνήθειν οἶδεν ὄνος τὸν ὄνον.

239.—ΤΟΥ ΑΥΤΟΥ

Πέντ' αἰτεῖς, δέκα δώσω· ἐείκοσι δ' †ἀντία ἕξεις.
  ἀρκεῖ σοι χρυσοῦς; ἤρκεσε καὶ Δανάῃ.

240.—ΤΟΥ ΑΥΤΟΥ

Ἤδη μοι πολιαὶ μὲν ἐπὶ κροτάφοισιν ἔθειραι,
  καὶ πέος ἐν μηροῖς ἀργὸν ἀποκρέμαται·
ὄρχεις δ' ἄπρηκτοι, χαλεπὸν δέ με γῆρας ἱκάνει.
  οἴμοι· πυγίζειν οἶδα, καὶ οὐ δύναμαι.

241.—ΤΟΥ ΑΥΤΟΥ

Ἄγκιστρον πεπόηκας, ἔχεις ἰχθὺν ἐμέ, τέκνον·
  ἕλκε μ' ὅπου βούλει· μὴ τρέχε, μή σε φύγω.

237.—By the Same

Off with thee, pretended hater of evil; off with thee, low-minded boy, who didst swear so lately that never again wouldst thou grant me it. Swear no longer now; for I know, and thou canst not conceal it from me, where it was, and how, and with whom, and for how much.

238.—By the Same

Puppy-dogs in youthful zest provide for each others pleasure in mutual exchange, and by turns switch round and are also mounted behind, completing action and submission in succession. But neither of two gains over the other; for the one which gave earlier now stands in the rear instead. This is simply the prelude. For by fair exchange, as the saying goes, donkey knows how to tickle donkey.

239.—By the Same

You ask for five drachmas: I will give ten and you will . . . have twenty. Is a gold sovereign enough for you? Sovereign gold was enough for Danae.[1]

240.—By the Same

By now the hairs on my temples are hoary and my poker hangs slack between my thighs. My testicles are inactive and old age hard to bear comes on me. Oh dear! I know how to commit sodomy, but can't do it.

241.—By the Same

You have made a hook, my child, and I am the fish you have caught. Pull me where you will, but don't run or you might lose me.

[1] We have the same pun in Bk. V. 31. The point of the epigram is obscure.

242.—ΤΟΥ ΑΥΤΟΥ

Πρῴην τὴν σαύραν ῥοδοδάκτυλον, Ἄλκιμ', ἔδειξας·
νῦν αὐτὴν ἤδη καὶ ῥοδόπηχυν ἔχεις.

243.—ΤΟΥ ΑΥΤΟΥ

Εἴ με τὸ πυγίζειν ἀπολώλεκε, καὶ διὰ τοῦτο
†ἐκτρέφομαι ποδαγρῶν, Ζεῦ, κρεάγραν με πόει.

244.—ΤΟΥ ΑΥΤΟΥ

Ἢν ἐσίδω τινὰ λευκόν, ἀπόλλυμαι· ἢν δὲ μελίχρουν,
καίομαι· ἢν ξανθὸν δ', εὐθὺς ὅλος λέλυμαι.

245.—ΤΟΥ ΑΥΤΟΥ

Πᾶν ἄλογον ζῷον βινεῖ μόνον· οἱ λογικοὶ δὲ
τῶν ἄλλων ζῴων τοῦτ' ἔχομεν τὸ πλέον,
πυγίζειν εὑρόντες. ὅσοι δὲ γυναιξὶ κρατοῦνται,
τῶν ἀλόγων ζῴων οὐδὲν ἔχουσι πλέον.

246.—ΤΟΥ ΑΥΤΟΥ

Ζεῦγος ἀδελφειῶν με φιλεῖ. οὐκ οἶδα τίν' αὐτῶν
δεσπόσυνον κρίνω· τοὺς δύο γὰρ φιλέω.
χὠ μὲν ἀποστείχει, ὁ δ' ἐπέρχεται· ἔστι δὲ τοῦ μὲν
κάλλιστον τὸ παρόν, τοῦ δὲ τὸ λειπόμενον.

247.—ΤΟΥ ΑΥΤΟΥ

Οἷον ἐπὶ Τροίῃ ποτ' ἀπὸ Κρήτης, Θεόδωρε,
Ἰδομενεὺς θεράποντ' ἤγαγε Μηριόνην,

242.—By the Same

[See Bk. XI. No. 21.]

243.—By the Same

If sodomy has left me a ruin, and because of it I am footsnared by gout, make me, O Zeus, into a fleshhook.[1]

244.—By the Same

If I see a white boy it is the death of me, and if it be a honey-complexioned one I am on fire; but if it be a flaxen-haired one I am utterly melted.

245.—By the Same

Every unreasoning animal pokes the female only, but we creatures of reason have the advantage over animals in this—we invented sodomy. But all who are in the power of women have no advantage over unreasoning animals.

246.—By the Same

A pair of brothers love me. I know not which of them I should decide to take for my master, for I love them both. One goes away from me and the other approaches. The best of the one is his presence, the best of the other my desire for him in his absence.

247.—By the Same

Theodorus, as once Idomeneus brought from Crete to Troy Meriones to be his squire, such a dexterous

---

[1] The reading and the joke are obscure.

τοῖον ἔχω σε φίλον περιδέξιον. ἢ γὰρ ἐκεῖνος
ἄλλα μὲν ἦν θεράπων, ἄλλα δ᾽ ἑταιρόσυνος·
καὶ σὺ τὰ μὲν βιότοιο πανήμερος ἔργα τέλει μοι·   5
νύκτα δὲ[1] πειρῶμεν, ναὶ Δία, Μηριόνην.

248.—ΤΟΥ ΑΥΤΟΥ

Τίς δύναται γνῶναι τὸν ἐρώμενον εἰ παρακμάζει,
πάντα συνὼν αὐτῷ μηδ᾽ ἀπολειπόμενος;
τίς δύνατ᾽ οὐκ ἀρέσαι τὴν σήμερον, ἐχθὲς ἀρέσκων;
εἰ δ᾽ ἀρέσει, τί παθὼν αὔριον οὐκ ἀρέσει;

249.—ΤΟΥ ΑΥΤΟΥ

Βουποίητε μέλισσα, πόθεν μέλι τοὐμὸν ἰδοῦσα
παιδὸς ἐφ᾽ ὑαλέην ὄψιν ὑπερπέτασαι;
οὐ παύσῃ βομβεῦσα, καὶ ἀνθολόγοισι θέλουσα
ποσσὶν ἐφάψασθαι χρωτὸς ἀκηροτάτου;
ἔρρ᾽ ἐπὶ σοὺς μελίπαιδας ὅποι ποτέ, δραπέτι, σίμ-
βλους,   5
μή σε δάκω· κἠγὼ κέντρον ἔρωτος ἔχω.

250.—ΤΟΥ ΑΥΤΟΥ

Νυκτερινὴν ἐπίκωμος ἰὼν μεταδόρπιον ὥρην
ἄρνα λύκος θυρέτροις εὖρον ἐφεστάοτα,
υἱὸν Ἀριστοδίκου τοῦ γείτονος· ὃν περιπλεχθεὶς
ἐξεφίλουν ὅρκοις πολλὰ χαριζόμενος.
νῦν δ᾽ αὐτῷ τί φέρων δωρήσομαι; οὔτ᾽ ἀπάτης γὰρ   5
ἄξιος, Ἑσπερίης οὔτ᾽ ἐπιορκοσύνης.

[1] I write νύκτα δὲ: νῦν δέ γε MS.

friend have I in thee; for Meriones was in some things his servant, in others his minion.   And do thou, too, all day go about the business of my life, but at night, by Heaven, let us essay Meriones.[1]

248.—By the Same

Who can tell if his beloved begins to pass his prime, if he is ever with him and never separated? Who that pleased yesterday can fail to please to-day, and if he please now, what can befall him to make him displease to-morrow?

249.—By the Same

Ox-born bee, why, catching sight of my honey, dost thou fly across to the boy's face, smooth as glass? Wilt thou not cease thy humming and thy effort to touch his most pure skin with thy flower-gathering feet?   Off to thy honey-bearing hive, where'er it be, thou truant, lest I bite thee!   I, too, have a sting, even love's.

250.—By the Same

Going out in revel at night after supper, I, the wolf, found a lamb standing at the door, the son of my neighbour Aristodicus, and throwing my arms round him I kissed him to my heart's content, promising on my oath many gifts.   And now what present shall I bring to him?   He does not deserve cheating or Italian perfidy.

---

[1] For the pun on this name see No. 97.

251.—ΤΟΥ ΑΥΤΟΥ

Πρόσθε μὲν ἀντιπρόσωπα φιλήματα καὶ τὰ πρὸ
  πείρας
εἴχομεν· ἧς γὰρ ἀκμήν, Δίφιλε, παιδάριον.
νῦν δέ σε τῶν ὄπιθεν γουνάζομαι, οὐ παρεόντων
ὕστερον· ἔστω γὰρ πάντα καθ' ἡλικίην.

252.—ΤΟΥ ΑΥΤΟΥ

Ἐμπρήσω σε, θύρη, τῇ λαμπάδι, καὶ τὸν ἔνοικον
συμφλέξας μεθύων, εὐθὺς ἄπειμι φυγάς,
καὶ πλώσας Ἀδριανὸν ἐπ' οἴνοπα πόντον, ἀλήτης
φωλήσω γε θύραις νυκτὸς ἀνοιγομέναις.

253.—ΤΟΥ ΑΥΤΟΥ

Δεξιτερὴν ὀλίγον δὸς ἐπὶ χρόνον, οὐχ ἵνα παύσῃς
(κεῖ μ' ὁ καλὸς χλεύην ἔσχε) χοροιτυπίης.
ἀλλ', εἰ μὴ πλευρῇ παρεκέκλιτο πατρὸς ἀκαίρως,
οὐκ ἂν δή με μάτην εἶδε μεθυσκόμενον.

254.—ΤΟΥ ΑΥΤΟΥ

Ἐκ ποίου ναοῦ, πόθεν ὁ στόλος οὗτος Ἐρώτων,
πάντα καταστίλβων; ἄνδρες, ἀμαυρὰ βλέπω.
τίς τούτων δοῦλος, τίς ἐλεύθερος; οὐ δύναμ' εἰπεῖν.
ἄνθρωπος τούτων κύριος; οὐ δύναται.
εἰ δ' ἐστίν, μείζων πολλῷ Διός, ὃς Γανυμήδην   5
ἔσχε μόνως, θεὸς ὢν πηλίκος· ὃς δὲ πόσους;

251.—By the Same

HITHERTO we had kisses face to face, and all that precedes the trial; for you were still a little boy, Diphilus. "But now I supplicate for them behind, that will be no longer with thee"[1] afterwards; for let all things be as befits our age.

252.—By the Same

I WILL burn thee, door, with the torch; and burning him who is within, too, in my drunken fury, I will straight depart a fugitive, and sailing over the purple Adriatic, shall, in my wanderings, at least lie in ambush at doors that open at night.

253.—By the Same

GIVE me thy right hand for a time, not to stop me from the dance, even though the fair boy made mockery of me. But if he had not been lying at the wrong time next his father, he would not, I swear, have seen me drunk to no purpose.

254.—By the Same

FROM what temple, whence comes this band of Loves shedding radiance on all? Sirs, my eyes are dazed. Which of them are slaves, which freemen? I cannot tell. Is their master a man? It is impossible; or if he be, he is much greater than Zeus, who only had Ganymede, though such a mighty god. While how many has this man!

[1] Hom. *Od.* xi. 66. The author misapplies Homer's words.

255.—ΤΟΥ ΑΥΤΟΥ

Οὐδ' αὐτη σ' ἡ λέξις, ἀκοινώνητε, διδάσκει,
ἐξ ἐτύμου φωνῆς ῥήμασιν ἑλκομένη;
πᾶς φιλόπαις λέγεται, Διονύσιε, κοὐ φιλοβούπαις.
πρὸς τοῦτ' ἀντειπεῖν μή τι πάλιν δύνασαι;
Πύθι' ἀγωνοθετῶ, σὺ δ' Ὀλύμπια· χοὺς ἀποβάλλων 5
ἐκκρίνω, τούτους εἰς τὸν ἀγῶνα δέχῃ.

256.—ΜΕΛΕΑΓΡΟΥ

Παγκαρπόν σοι, Κύπρι, καθήρμοσε, χειρὶ τρυγήσας
παίδων ἄνθος, Ἔρως ψυχαπάτην στέφανον.
ἐν μὲν γὰρ κρίνον ἡδὺ κατέπλεξεν Διόδωρον,
ἐν δ' Ἀσκληπιάδην, τὸ γλυκὺ λευκόϊον.
ναὶ μὴν Ἡράκλειτον ἐπέπλεκεν, ὡς ἀπ' ἀκάνθης   5
†εἰς ῥόδον,[1] οἰνάνθη δ' ὥς τις ἔθαλλε Δίων·
χρυσάνθη δὲ κόμαισι κρόκον Θήρωνα συνῆψεν·
ἐν δ' ἔβαλ' ἑρπύλλου κλωνίον Οὐλιάδην,
ἁβροκόμην δὲ Μυΐσκον, ἀειθαλὲς ἔρνος ἐλαίης·
ἱμερτοὺς δ' Ἀρέτου κλῶνας ἀπεδρέπετο.   10
ὀλβίστη νήσων ἱερὰ Τύρος, ἣ τὸ μυρόπνουν
ἄλσος ἔχει παίδων Κύπριδος ἀνθοφόρον.

257.—ΤΟΥ ΑΥΤΟΥ

Ἁ πύματον καμπτῆρα καταγγέλλουσα κορωνίς,
ἑρκοῦρος γραπταῖς πιστοτάτα σελίσιν,
φαμὶ τὸν ἐκ πάντων ἠθροισμένον εἰς ἕνα μόχθον
ὑμνοθετᾶν βύβλῳ τᾷδ' ἐνελιξάμενον

---

[1] I conjecture φῦ ῥόδον and render so, taking the first ὡς
as = ὅτε. The bloom of Heraclitus and Dion was con-
temporary.

---

[1] Which were held later in the year.

255.—By the Same

Unsociable man! does not the word itself teach you by the words from which it is truly derived? Everyone is called a lover of boys, not a lover of big boys. Have you any retort to that? I preside over the Pythian games, you over the Olympian,[1] and those whom I reject and remove from the list you receive as competitors.

256.—MELEAGER

Love hath wrought for thee, Cypris, gathering with his own hands the boy-flowers, a wreath of every blossom to cozen the heart. Into it he wove Diodorus the sweet lily and Asclepiades the scented white violet. Yea, and thereupon he pleated Heraclitus when, like a rose, he grew from the thorns, and Dion when he bloomed like the blossom of the vine. He tied on Theron, too, the golden-tressed saffron, and put in Uliades, a sprig of thyme, and soft-haired Myiscus the ever-green olive shoot, and despoiled for it the lovely boughs of Aretas. Most blessed of islands art thou, holy Tyre, which hast the perfumed grove where the boy-blossoms of Cypris grow.[2]

257.—By the Same

I, the flourish that announce the last lap's finish, most trusty keeper of the bounds of written pages, say that he who hath completed his task, including in this roll the work of all poets gathered into one,

[2] This, being a list of the boys Meleager himself knew at Tyre, cannot, as has been supposed, be the proem to a section of his *Stephanus*. The following epigram, on the other hand (if by Meleager), certainly stood at the end of the whole *Stephanus*.

ἐκτελέσαι Μελέαγρον, ἀείμνηστον δὲ Διοκλεῖ   5
ἄνθεσι συμπλέξαι μουσοπόλον στέφανον.
οὖλα δ᾽ ἐγὼ καμφθεῖσα δρακοντείοις ἴσα νώτοις,
σύνθρονος ἵδρυμαι τέρμασιν εὐμαθίας.

258.—ΣΤΡΑΤΩΝΟΣ

Ἤ τάχα τις μετόπισθε κλύων ἐμὰ παίγνια ταῦτα.
πάντας ἐμοὺς δόξει τοὺς ἐν ἔρωτι πόνους·
ἄλλα δ᾽ ἐγὼν ἄλλοισιν ἀεὶ φιλόπαισι χαράσσω
γράμματ᾽, ἐπεί τις ἐμοὶ τοῦτ᾽ ἐνέδωκε θεός.

is Meleager, and that it was for Diocles he wove
from flowers this wreath of verse, whose memory
shall be evergreen. Curled in coils like the back
of a snake, I am set here enthroned beside the last
lines of his learned work.

258.—STRATO

Perchance someone in future years, listening to
these trifles of mine, will think these pains of love
were all my own. No! I ever scribble this and that
for this and that boy-lover, since some god gave me
this gift.

INDEXES

GENERAL INDEX

Actors, *see* Singers

Adonis, *see* Aphrodite

Adrasteia, XII. 160

Alexandria, XI. 262, 306

Anastasius I., emperor (491–518 A.D.), XI. 270, 271

Antimachus, elegiac poet (5th cent. B.C.), XII. 168

Anubis, dog-headed god, XI. 212, 360

Aphrodite, prayers to, X. 21, XII. 131 ; Pandemos, XII. 161 ; Aphrodite, Adonis, and Eros, statues of, XI. 174

Apollo, sacrifice to, XI. 324 ; prayers to, X. 25, XII. 24–27; statue of, XI. 177

Apostles, twelve (?), X. 56

Aratus, XI. 318

Archilochus, lyric and iambic poet (7th cent. B.C.), birthday of, XI. 20

Argos, XII. 129 ; bad name of the Argives, XI. 439

Aristarchus, the grammarian, XI. 140, 347

Aristoxenus, philosopher and writer on music (4th cent. B.C.), XI. 352

Asta in Italy, clay of, XI. 27

Astrologers, *see* Prophets

Athens, degradation of citizenship at, XI. 319

Athletes, epigrams on, XI. 82–86, 258, 316

Augustus, XI. 75

Barbers, epigrams on, XI. 190, 191, 288

Baths, epigrams on, XI. 243, 411

Callias, tragic poet (3rd cent. B.C.), XI. 12

Callimachus, XI. 130, 275, 321, 347

Canastra in Thrace, home of Giants, XI. 63

Cappadocians, bad name of, XI. 237, 238

Castalia, fountain of at Delphi, XI. 24

Centaurs, XI. 1, 12

Cephallenia, X. 25

Chians, bad name of, XI. 235

Choerilus of Samos, epic poet (5th cent. B.C.), XI. 218

Cilicians, bad name of, XI. 236

Cinaedi, epigram on, XI. 272

Cleanthes, Stoic philosopher (3rd cent. B.C.), XI. 296

Cnidus, XII. 61

Commodus, the emperor, XI. 269

Cos, XII. 53

Cowards, epigrams on, XI. 210, 211

Cronos, statue of, XI. 183

Cynaegirus (*see* Indexes to Vols. II. and III.), XI. 335

Cynic philosophers, epigrams on, XI. 153–158, 410, 434

Cyprus, bad Greek spoken in, XI. 146

Danae, XII. 239

Dancers, epigrams on, XI. 195, 253–255

Daphnis, mythical shepherd, XII. 128

Diogenes, XI. 158

Dionysius, tyrant of Heraclea (4th cent. B.C.), X. 54

Dionysius, Stoic philosopher (4th cent. B.C.), X. 38

Dionysus, X. 18 ; feast of, X. 40

Diotimus, poet and grammarian (3rd cent. B.C.), XI. 437

Ephesus, XII. 226

Epicrates, comic poet (3rd cent. B.C.), XI. 12

417

GENERAL INDEX

GENERAL INDEX

INDEX OF AUTHORS INCLUDED IN THIS VOLUME

M = Wreath of Meleager
Ph = Wreath of Philippus
Ag = Cycle of Agathias

(For explanation of these terms, v. Introduction to vol. i. page v.)

INDEX OF AUTHORS

INDEX OF AUTHORS